MARKET, STATE, AND
COMMUNITY

MARKET, STATE, AND COMMUNITY

*Theoretical Foundations of
Market Socialism*

DAVID MILLER

CLARENDON PRESS · OXFORD

1989

Oxford University Press, Walton Street, Oxford OX2 6DP

Oxford New York Toronto
Delhi Bombay Calcutta Madras Karachi
Petaling Jaya Singapore Hong Kong Tokyo
Nairobi Dar es Salaam Cape Town
Melbourne Auckland

and associated companies in
Berlin Ibadan

Oxford is a trade mark of Oxford University Press

Published in the United States
by Oxford University Press (USA)

British Library Cataloguing in Publication Data
Miller, David
Market, state, and community: theoretical foundations
of market socialism.
1. Socialism. Economic aspects
I. Title
335
ISBN 0–19–827340–1

Library of Congress Cataloging in Publication Data
Miller, David (David Leslie)
Market, state, and community: theoretical foundations of market
socialism/David Miller.
Bibliography: p. Includes index.
1. Mixed economy. 2. Socialism. 3. Libertarianism. I. Title.
HB90.M54 1989 330.12'6—dc20 89–3365
ISBN 0–19–827340–1

Typeset by Wyvern Typesetting, Bristol
Printed in Great Britain by
Bookcraft Ltd.
Midsomer Norton, Bath

To
Sue, Sarah, and James

Preface

THIS book contains the fruits of a dozen years' reflection on the question whether it is possible to envisage a market economy that fulfils the core ideals of socialism. Its plan may become clearer if I explain how my thinking has evolved over that period. I began in the early 1970s with fairly ill-defined socialist beliefs that seemed naturally to entail an antipathy to markets as a means of economic co-ordination, a point of view which I suppose is still fairly common. I was shaken out of it by encountering, in the middle part of that decade, various libertarian writings that set out polemically, but still powerfully, the arguments in favour of markets. These encounters left me with two basic convictions. One was that the libertarian position itself—the belief in a minimal state and economic *laissez-faire*—was ill founded and untenable. The other was that the pro-market arguments found in libertarian writings were none the less strong in themselves, and deserved to convince socialists. To render these two convictions coherent required a two-pronged strategy. The first line of attack was to expose, as clearly as possible, the fallacies of the libertarian position in its various guises, without rejecting its basic insight into the virtue of markets. The second line was to work out a theory of socialism that included a full-blooded, unapologetic commitment to a market economy.

I pursued these two tasks more or less side by side for several years. The results can be found in the first and second parts of the book respectively. As these investigations neared their end, a third issue took on increasing significance. What kind of political system would be needed if a socialist market economy was to function in an ethically acceptable way? Answering this question required as radical a break with traditional socialist ideas as did the defence of market socialism as an economic system. The results are presented in the third part of the book, which proposes an account of the politics of democratic socialism.

Preliminary versions of some parts of this work have already appeared in print, as acknowledged below. Preparing the book itself has involved more or less extensive rewriting of this material, and readers are asked to treat the present text as superseding these earlier attempts. The lengthy period of maturation has enabled me to benefit to an almost indecent extent from the critical reaction of the many audiences who have had parts of the book's argument thrust upon them. Although it is primarily a work of political theory, these audiences have included philosophers, lawyers, economists, and sociologists as well as political scientists, and I believe the book would be immeasurably poorer without the input it has received from all these quarters. It is invidious to single out individuals, but I would like to express my particular gratitude to the following, who read and commented on one or more sections of the book: Jerry Cohen, Jon Elster, Iain Hampsher-Monk, Anthony Heath, Brian Hindley, Martin Hollis, Kurt Klappholz, Robert Lane, Andrew Mason, Bhikhu Parekh, Joseph Raz, John Roemer, Alan Ryan, Hillel Steiner, David Tucker, Robert Van der Veen, and Albert Weale. Bob Goodin has been an unfailing source of advice, support, and criticism throughout, and he and Desmond King both kindly agreed to read and assess the final manuscript. I have learnt much from them and should have learnt more. John Gray has done more than he may realize, through public and private debate over many years, and through giving me the opportunity to defend my ideas against libertarian critics on several occasions, to encourage a book whose conclusions he strongly contests. Equally valuable criticism, from the opposite quarter, was provided by the membership of the Fabian Society's Socialist Philosophy Group. I should like in particular to thank Saul Estrin, Julian Le Grand, and Raymond Plant for their sympathetic encouragement of the project.

It is widely believed not without justification, that Official Fellows at Nuffield College enjoy conditions of service so favourable that sabbatical leave should be unnecessary. I found none the less that my period as a Visiting Fellow at the University of Melbourne in 1986 was crucial to the planning and writing of the book, and I should like to record my warmest thanks to the members of the Department of Political Science, and of Ormond College, for their hospitality, and for providing the ideal setting in which to carry out research of this kind.

Ann Bowes, with help from Elaine Herman, has been in charge of word-processing operations throughout the book's gestation.

This is now the fifth book she has helped me produce, and each delivery seems to have gone more smoothly than the last. I am led by such metaphors to my last and greatest debt, acknowledged in the dedication: to Sue, for moral support at all times, and practical help and encouragement when most needed; to Sarah, for dispelling the grey gloom of theory for two delightful years; and to James, for delaying his arrival just long enough to allow the last words to be written.

Oxford
September 1988   David Miller

Acknowledgements

I AM grateful to the respective publishers for permission to incorporate material drawn from the following sources:

'Justice and Property', *Ratio*, 22 (1980), 1–14.

'Market Neutrality and the Failure of Co-operatives', *British Journal of Political Science*, 11 (1981), 301–29.

'Constraints on Freedom', *Ethics*, 94 (1983–4), 66–86.

'Reply to Oppenheim', *Ethics*, 95 (1984–5), 310–14.

'Exploitation in the Market', in A. Reeve (ed.), *Modern Theories of Exploitation* (London: Sage, 1987).

'Marx, Communism and Markets', *Political Theory*, 15 (1987), 182–204.

'Socialism and Toleration', in S. Mendus (ed.), *Justifying Toleration* (Cambridge: Cambridge University Press, 1988).

'Altruism and the Welfare State', in J. D. Moon (ed.), *Rights, Responsibilities and Welfare* (Boulder and London: Westview Press, 1988).

'The Ethical Significance of Nationality', *Ethics*, 98 (1987–8), 647–62.

Contents

INTRODUCTION

I

My aim in this book is to work out a political theory for democratic socialism, and in particular to defend a certain view of socialism, which I call market socialism, against the challenge posed by the neo-liberal thinkers of the New Right. The practical relevance of such a project should hardly need stressing. Socialist ideas have, over the last decade or so at least, been pushed on to the defensive by the resurgence of neo-liberal—that is, market-oriented, anti-state—thinking, to the extent that many have thought to write the obituary of socialism itself. Alongside this movement of ideas, there has been a general shift of public policy away from long-established forms of economic intervention by the state towards greater reliance on market mechanisms. This has been true not only in Western countries, where markets have always been relied upon to provide most goods and services, but also in Eastern Europe and China, where the recent past has seen a variety of reform movements, all to a greater or lesser extent involving a turn away from central planning towards co-ordination through markets.

So much is familiar ground. We do not need to decide how far the shift in policy was a result of a shift in ideas, and how far the popularity of certain ideas stemmed from the fact that they chimed in with developments that were occurring for independent reasons. Granted only that ideas have *some* influence on the course of events, the need for a radical review of the socialist idea itself, as a political project in the late twentieth century, has become a matter of some urgency. There is a widespread perception that traditional socialist policies have become outmoded; socialist and labour parties that have held on to them have fared poorly at the hands of their electorates, whereas those that have succeeded in winning power, such as the French and the Australian, have done so by studiously distancing themselves from the old ideas. The result has been an intellectual vacuum which can only be filled by a radical redefinition of the meaning of socialism.

Such a rethinking ought ideally to be carried on at two levels. At one level there are issues of policy: how best can the basic aims of socialism be put into practice, given a modern industrial society in which most citizens enjoy what is by historical standards an extraordinarily high level of personal freedom and welfare? At another level there are questions about the basic aims themselves: what *are* the fundamental aims of socialism, and how are they to be justified? Most of my argument here takes place at this second and more abstract level, although always with at least half an eye on the policy questions. Towards the end of the book I come back more directly to the practical meaning of socialism and the question whether it has a political future at all.

Although an ideal treatment would run smoothly from basic premisses to practical conclusions, I do not make much apology for this focus on matters of principle. In the political context outlined above, there has inevitably been a good deal of 'revisionist' writing on the Left, roughly on the model (in Britain) of Anthony Crosland's *The Future of Socialism*, first published some thirty years ago.[1] Much of this literature is worthy and sensible, but it tends to be flabby when dealing with conceptual and ethical issues. The cause of the libertarian Right, on the other hand, has been aided by such works of undoubted intellectual power as Nozick's *Anarchy, State and Utopia*, Hayek's *Law, Legislation and Liberty*, and Oakeshott's, *On Human Conduct*, all published within a short space of time in the middle 1970s.[2] Even if one is critical of the positions taken in these books, there is no escaping the fact that they do advance arguments of a suitably basic kind for a libertarian position in politics. They need to be taken seriously as political theory which starts with conceptual and moral argument and derives conclusions from this about the proper role and constitution of the state that turn out to be radically at variance with prevailing practice. Anyone who believes that the conclusions are wrong is obliged to show with some care where the premisses are at fault, or where the intervening chain of argument is defective.

I attempt to do this in the first part of the book, where the

---

[1] C. A. R. Crosland, *The Future of Socialism* (London: Cape, 1956).

[2] R. Nozick, *Anarchy, State and Utopia* (Oxford: Blackwell, 1974); F. A. Hayek, *Law, Legislation and Liberty*, 3 vols. (London: Routledge and Kegan Paul, 1973–9); M. Oakeshott, *On Human Conduct* (Oxford: Clarendon Press, 1975).

central tenets of libertarianism are scrutinized and (I hope) rebutted. I use 'libertarianism' here as a blanket term for political philosophies which hold that the state should be more or less confined to the minimal role of safeguarding persons and their property, including unlimited rights of private ownership. In the society envisioned by libertarians, everything would be handed over to market mechanisms, supplemented where appropriate by charitable schemes to help those unable to fend for themselves. Some libertarians would be prepared to relax this to the extent of permitting the state to provide a limited range of public goods (such as a public road system) and perhaps a safety net in the form of income supplements for the very poor. Others would diverge in the opposite direction, arguing that even personal protection can be provided on a market basis without any call upon the state.[3] These internal differences will not be my concern. My focus is the broad claim that a good society can be built entirely around private property and market mechanisms. I want to examine the arguments used to support this broad claim and to show where they are deficient.

One of libertarianism's great sources of strength is what might be called its theoretical monism. Everything appears to stem from one central and fundamental insight. On closer inspection this appearance turns out to be largely illusory. For one thing, different libertarians centre their thought in different places— Nozick and Hayek, for instance, take up contrasting positions in moral philosophy.[4] For another, even a thinker as purportedly monistic as Nozick turns out in practice to rely in different places on different sorts of argument—sometimes defending freedom of exchange, for instance, in terms of people's absolute rights to do what they wish with their possessions, sometimes in terms of its efficiency as a means of satisfying preferences. Nonetheless the appearance of simplicity and coherence persists, and it invites us to ask whether a political theory that aims to compete with libertarianism ought not to aim for a similar monism. This largely explains, I believe, the attractiveness of John Rawls's book *A*

---

[3] At this point libertarianism changes from being an extreme form of liberalism to being a kind of anarchism. I have discussed anarchist libertarianism in *Anarchism* (London: Dent, 1984), ch. 3.

[4] There is a helpful examination of this diversity in N. P. Barry, *On Classical Liberalism and Libertarianism* (London: Macmillan, 1986).

Theory of Justice[5] both to social-democrats and to non-Marxist socialists. Here, it seems, is a book whose conclusions are non-libertarian (they are liberal in the American sense, social-democratic in the European sense) based on a single, persuasive central idea.

Despite the allure of monism, it must be rejected. When we think seriously about a political matter, it is rarely the case that we light on some single guiding principle that alone will resolve the issue. Instead we find that we have to arbitrate between several competing values, none of which we feel inclined, on reflection, to abandon. The solution we choose will be the one that on balance gives us the most of what we value—or to put the point in a quasi-technical way, that puts us on the highest feasible indifference curve, representing our preferences as between various combinations of the values at stake.[6] Nor can the slope of these indifference curves be deduced from some general theory. We must rely simply on our judgements about where the balance should be struck between considerations such as freedom, justice, and aggregate utility in particular cases, and try to fit these judgements into a consistent pattern.

My strategy in the present book is to take these considerations one at a time and see what they imply about the shape of our social institutions. The overall aim is to show that market socialism represents an attractive mix of values that are widely shared among our contemporaries. It matches the aspirations of our age. I do not try to single out one crucial or decisive argument for that system. Nor do I try to show that the values I call into play are timeless or transcendent. My view of the political theorist's role in relation to the society he is examining is close to Michael Walzer's: the theorist's job is to offer a critical interpretation of the understandings and commitments that he shares with his fellow citizens.[7] He cannot reasonably aspire to stand apart from his society and ground his case on abstract principles of universal validity.

[5] J. Rawls, *A Theory of Justice* (Cambridge, Mass: Harvard University Press, 1971).

[6] This way of thinking about political choice goes back to B. Barry *Political Argument* (London: Routledge and Kegan Paul, 1965), ch. 1.

[7] This view is presented briefly in the preface to M. Walzer, *Spheres of Justice* (Oxford: Martin Robertson, 1983) and at greater length in his 'Interpretation and Social Criticism' in *The Tanner Lectures on Human Values*, vol. viii, ed. S. M. McMurrin (Salt Lake City: University of Utah Press; Cambridge: Cambridge University Press, 1988).

There is a further respect in which the argument advanced here runs parallel to Walzer's. Walzer has the interesting idea that a just society must be made up of a number of distinct institutional spheres in which goods are allocated according to radically different principles. Detailed examination of this idea must await another occasion, but meanwhile the basic point, that value pluralism implies institutional pluralism, can be taken on board. The implication here cannot be strict, since it is not intrinsically incoherent to suggest that one and the same institution might serve several different values. As an empirical matter, however, it turns out that to obtain the best combination of the values we share, we need a range of institutions that counter-balance one another—one institution making good the deficit of others in promoting a particular goal. I shall illustrate this shortly in the case of market socialism. The insight that to do justice to the plurality of basic values we need to create an institutional balance has found its clearest expression in the liberal tradition, but it is an idea that democratic socialists must now embrace. In contemporary debate, it is the libertarian Right who most often present themselves as the champions of a simple-minded monism. We should not try to respond to this challenge by being equally simple-minded in turn. An adequate political theory of socialism must acknowledge complexity, both in its ethical foundations and in the institutional framework it recommends.

II

I have presented market socialism as an alternative both to libertarianism and to older forms of socialism which I have claimed to be outdated. My next task is to explain in greater detail what is meant by this idea, and how it stands in relation to the socialist tradition as a whole. But before presenting a brief sketch of market socialism as an economic system, one procedural objection must be set aside. It is sometimes disputed whether a socialist should be in the business of discussing possible versions of socialism at all. There is a tradition, stemming from Marx, which holds that the job of the socialist intellectual is simply to hasten the downfall of capitalism by a remorseless exposure of its deficiencies. The shape of future socialism is determined by historical forces outside the conscious control of anyone in the present age. Many socialists do indeed work to this job description. They attack this or that feature of capitalism, and 'socialism' becomes simply a compilation of negatives (no exploitation, no war, no environmental destruction, no subordination of women, etc., etc.). No attempt is made to integrate these undoubtedly desirable aims into some coherent account of the economics and politics of an alternative system. But whatever the justification for such a stance on the part of Marx himself, faced as he was with some of the wilder fantasies of the utopian socialists,[8] it is no longer either intellectually defensible or politically advantageous to maintain it. Socialism is no longer an unsullied ideal; *faute de mieux*, people will identify it with the unattractive form of statism that has emerged over the last half-century in Eastern Europe. Moreover the potential recipients of the socialist message are no longer the proletariat of Marx's conception (real or imaginary) with nothing to lose but their chains. The working class has a substantial stake in contemporary capitalism, which has provided it both with relative economic prosperity and with highly valued personal and political freedoms (we know too that the manual working class constitutes a steadily shrinking fraction of the total population). A viable socialist programme must convince a broad constituency that these benefits can be preserved and others added to them in a socialist society — and this requires something more than airy anti-capitalist oratory.

The case for market socialism can best be introduced by considering briefly the defects of the main existing versions of socialism—namely state socialism as practised in the Soviet Union and elsewhere, and social democracy as implemented to a greater or lesser degree in Western European countries in the post-war period.

State socialism attempts as far as possible to substitute central planning for the working of economic markets. Its strength is that it allows the enormous resources commanded by the state to be concentrated on specific projects—hence the considerable achievements of the Soviet Union in heavy industry, armaments, space exploration and so forth. Its corresponding economic defect is that planned production is unable to respond as quickly

---

[8] This was the derogatory term applied by Marx and Engels to early socialists such as Owen, Cabet, and Fourier who drew up detailed blueprints for the socialist communities of the future.

and flexibly to consumers' preferences as a market — hence the well-documented failures of the state socialist systems in the day-to-day production of consumer goods.[9] There are, however, other and perhaps more important criticisms to be made. One is that central planning in practice negates democracy. Given the enormous task involved in comprehensively planning a complex modern economy, there is no way to avoid the creation of a large bureaucratic machine. Even if the formalities of electoral democracy can be preserved (an issue on which the arguments seem to me inconclusive), power will inevitably gravitate to those with the specialist knowledge to oversee the planning apparatus. Thus planning of this kind is of its nature élitist. If we see socialism as involving among other things a more democratic political system, we cannot embrace the statist model.[10]

At a much lower level, central planning severely restricts the scope for workers' self-management. If the latter idea is to have any serious meaning, it must include a substantial degree of control over decisions about which goods and services are to be produced, the technique of production to be used, the scale of the enterprise, and so forth. But a planned economy cannot function unless such decisions are transferred to the central authority, which must set production targets, pricing policy, employment policy, etc. for each unit of production. Thus the scope for workers' control will be confined to relatively minor matters, such as the number of tea-breaks in a day, which have no noticeable impact on the planners' targets. Equally serious, workers' freedom to change employment will be circumscribed. Although labour can be allocated through a market, using wage incentives, each person's choice is confined to the set of jobs that the planners decide to make available. Someone wishing to exercise a skill or try out a new idea not catered for in the plan will be frustrated.[11]

Together with the economic defects referred to earlier, these democratic defects are fatal for state socialism, and in my view justify its poor reputation among ordinary people in the west—a

---

[9] There is a convenient summary in A. Nove, *The Economics of Feasible Socialism* (London: Allen and Unwin, 1983).

[10] This case is well made in R. A. Dahl, *Dilemmas of Pluralist Democracy* (New Haven and London: Yale University Press, 1982), ch. 6.

[11] I have expanded slightly on these claims in 'Why Markets?' in J. Le Grand and S. Estrin, *Market Socialism* (Oxford: Oxford University Press, 1989).

reputation no doubt further sullied by capitalist propaganda, but by no means merely its creature.

The social-democratic alternative is much less obviously flawed. Social democracy can be seen essentially as an attempt to use the power of the state to humanize capitalism. The productive advantages of capitalism are to be retained, but some of its human costs eliminated. First, economic management techniques are to be used to smooth out business cycles and maintain full employment, which in turn will increase the bargaining power of workers *vis-à-vis* their employers. Second, the tax system is to be used to correct the excessive inequalities of income and wealth that an unreformed capitalist economy throws up. Third, a politically funded welfare state is to serve to eliminate poverty, provide for those with special needs, and contribute further to the reduction of inequality.[12]

There is no reason to doubt either the practical success or the continuing political appeal of this programme, if compared with a full-blown policy of capitalist *laissez-faire* which not even the most libertarian of present-day governments would dare to follow. But the social-democratic strategy has increasingly evident limitations as an embodiment of socialist ideals. First, it is no longer clear that Keynesian methods can be used in the desired manner to secure full employment, particularly in a heavily unionized economy. The effect may be inflationary, in which case income redistribution is likely to occur less between employers and workers as such than between weakly organized workers and strongly organized workers occupying strategic positions in the economy. Second, there is substantial evidence that the impact of fiscal measures on the overall distribution of income and wealth has so far been quite limited;[13] and the effectiveness of more

[12] A classic statement of the social-democratic case is Crosland, *The Future of Socialism*.

[13] In saying this I am of course entering a minefield. There is enormous dispute about which elements should be included in estimates of income and wealth-holding, about the appropriate measure of inequality, and so forth. Even more important, it is almost impossible to isolate the impact of government redistribution from spontaneous changes in patterns of income and wealth distribution caused by demographic, economic, and social factors. There has, for instance, been a slow but steady decline in this century in the proportion of wealth held (in Britain) by the very rich, but it is not clear how much of this change can be explained by government tax policy. If one looks simply at the final outcome, a relevant figure is that the top 10% of households enjoy post-tax incomes (including both cash and benefits in kind) some ten times greater than those of the bottom 10%. For this figure, calculated for 1985, see T. Stark, *A new A-Z of Income and Wealth* (London: Fabian

INTRODUCTION 9

stringent measures (a more steeply progressive income tax, say, or a wealth tax) must remain open to doubt. Such measures are liable either to be circumvented on a large scale, or else to have damaging repercussions on the economy itself—leading to under-investment, capital flight, and so forth. Finally, although the welfare state has been fairly successful as a means of tackling poverty (in an absolute sense) and of channelling resources to people with special needs, it has been far less successful as a vehicle for overall equality. The reason, in brief, is that freely provided services such as education and medical care may be used more effectively by those who are already better off to an extent which eliminates (and occasionally even reverses) the progressive element in their funding through income tax.[14]

The danger, therefore, with the social-democratic programme is that it may lead merely to an expanded state sector, with a corresponding increase in the tax burden carried by nearly all social groups but without any very appreciable increase in social equality. The perception of this possibility may account for the recent defection of some groups — skilled workers especially—to parties with more libertarian aims.

Market socialism represents an attempt to come to terms with these defects in state socialism and social democracy while still holding on to certain core socialist ideals.[15] By implication it has the following four aims (at least): (a) to obtain the efficiency advantages of markets in the production of most goods and services; (b) to confine the economic role of the state in a way that makes democratic government feasible; (c) to protect the autonomy of workers, both as individuals and as members of self-managed enterprises; (d) to bring about a much more equal

Society, 1988); for a general discussion see A. B. Atkinson, *The Economics of Inequality*, 2nd edn. (Oxford: Clarendon Press, 1983), esp. chs. 4, 6, and 7).

[14] See J. Le Grand, *The Strategy of Equality: Redistribution and the Social Services* (London: Allen and Unwin, 1982); R. Goodin and J. Le Grand, *Not only the Poor: the Middle Classes and the Welfare State* (London: Allen and Unwin, 1987).

[15] In earlier economic discussion, 'market socialism' came to be used as a term for the system devised principally by Oskar Lange in the 1930s, in response to critics who claimed that rational economic calculation was impossible under socialism. The Lange model is best regarded as an adaptation of a planned economy in which enterprise managers are given the freedom to adjust their inputs and outputs according to pre-set criteria, but prices are still determined by a central planning board. As will be seen, market socialism in the sense used in this book involves a more extensive use of markets. For the earlier model, see O. Lange and F. Taylor, *On the Economic Theory of Socialism* (Minneapolis: University of Minnesota Press, 1938).

distribution of primary income (rather than relying entirely on secondary redistribution). Assuming for the moment that these are desirable ends, how may they be achieved?

The key idea is that the market mechanism is retained as a means of providing most goods and services, while the ownership of capital is socialized. Consider the following arrangements: all productive enterprises are constituted as workers' co-operatives, leasing their operating capital from an outside investment agency. Each enterprise makes its own decisions about products, methods of production, prices, etc., and competes for custom in the market. Net profits form a pool out of which incomes are paid. Each enterprise is democratically controlled by those who work for it, and among the issues they must decide is how to distribute income within the co-operative.

I shall refer to this as the pure model of market socialism. Let us consider in a little more detail what its ground rules might be. Enterprises hire capital from the investment agency at a fixed rate of interest and subject to certain conditions. They have rights of use in the capital that they hire, but not full rights of ownership. This means that the value of their fixed assets must be maintained: capital cannot be treated as income, nor loaned to other enterprises. There must also be bankruptcy rules: enterprises that cannot provide their members with a subsistence income must, after a certain period of time, be wound up, with the workers transferring to other co-operatives. Each enterprise must maintain its democratic form. It is entitled to expand, but only by taking on additional workers as full members with equal voting rights. This is equivalent to a ban on the hiring of wage labour. Subject to this constraint, however, co-operatives may adopt whatever internal management structure they prefer. They will no doubt wish to have executive committees, committees for specialist tasks, etc., depending on their size and the nature of their business.

Workers have a free choice of which enterprise to apply to join; equally, enterprises can choose whether to take on new members or not. On the exit side, there are to be no compulsory redundancies, but workers can choose to leave if they wish, probably after an agreed-upon period of notice. The effect of these provisions is to create a labour market in which pay differentials within each co-operative can be expected to reflect the return to different skills and responsibilities across the economy as a whole—although a co-operative which opted to depart from this pattern (say, in the extreme case, paying all members equally) would be at liberty to do so.

The investment agencies are given a somewhat complex task to perform. As the custodians of social capital, they have to strike a balance between potentially conflicting demands. On the one hand, they must allocate it efficiently, investing extra money where the marginal returns are likely to be greatest. On the other hand, they must take account of wider social factors, for instance the employment needs of particular regions. Their relationship with individual co-operatives is also a delicate one. In order to reach intelligent investment decisions, they need to know a good deal about the future production plans of each co-operative. At the same time, it is essential that the autonomy of the co-operatives is preserved, and that the investment agencies do not acquire surrogate management functions. This makes the question of how the investment agencies should be constituted (whether as public bodies, private banks, etc.) a key one for market socialists. There is as yet no consensus about the answer; I shall return to the issue briefly in Chapter 12.

III

The book's overall purpose is to take the system just described and examine it in the light of some fundamental ideals of social and political theory. The aim of Part I is to demonstrate that the main arguments advanced to support libertarianism do not in fact support such a system, and may indeed count in favour of market socialism; whereas in Part II I take up some aspects of the traditional socialist critique of capitalism and show that an economy of the kind outlined above is not vulnerable to these criticisms. (Part I, then, aims to convert neo-liberals to market socialism, while Part II tries to rally socialists; the purpose of Part III is explained shortly.) Before launching into this detailed examination, however, there are some immediate questions about market socialism that deserve a brief reply in order to convince the reader that the system envisioned is a serious candidate for scrutiny.

One issue is whether workers' co-operatives are an appropriate form for running the whole of industry. Many existing co-operatives operate on a very small scale, and this has led some people to conclude that they are only appropriate in cottage industries. But the co-operative form can in fact work success-fully in units of up to about 500 people; obviously as the size of the unit increases, there has to be more formal structure (specialist committees, for example), but there can still be effective democratic control overall. It is interesting to note that, even with the giant corporations that currently exist, the numbers employed in each *plant* are less than this on average (in a study of the hundred largest enterprises in Britain the figure was 430); moreover, plant sizes have been diminishing quite rapidly, presumably as a result of labour-saving technology. What typi-cally makes the big corporation big is the number of plants it incorporates, not the size of each unit. So, with the very different system of ownership I am envisaging, it would be possible to contemplate the break-up of corporations into autonomous units, which would no doubt in some cases continue to collaborate closely in their production schedules, etc.

Advanced technology as such poses no problem for co-operat-ive production, and indeed this arrangement may come most naturally to a work-force most of whom have specialist skills to contribute. What may be more problematic is technical change, in so far as this requires a high rate of membership turnover. A co-operative relies on solidarity building up among its members, and as we have noted will incorporate into its constitution a rule guaranteeing each person job security. Major restructuring would clearly cause difficulties. An established co-operative might well take precautions against this outcome, by for instance instituting a retraining scheme. However, it is better to remain open-minded here, and to concede that there may be industries which, at a particular time, are ill suited to co-operative produc-tion.[16] There may, for instance, be room for capital–labour partnerships, enterprises where rights of control are divided between a capital board and a board representing the work-force. In the real world, therefore, we may need to contemplate an

[16] For fuller discussion, see D. Miller and S. Estrin, 'Market Socialism: A Policy for Socialists', in I. Forbes (ed.), *Market Socialism: Whose Choice?*, Fabian Pamphlet No. 516 (London: Fabian Society, 1986); S. Estrin, 'Workers' Co-operatives: Their Merits and Their Limitations', in Le Grand and Estrin, *Market Socialism*.

impure model of market socialism in which different enterprise forms co-exist, reflecting the special conditions prevailing in different branches of industry. For the purposes of the more abstract discussion in the following chapters, however, I shall continue to work with the pure model.

A second issue is whether an economy in which the productive units are co-operatives will display macroeconomic efficiency properties analogous to those of a capitalist economy. If we make the standard (and admittedly unrealistic) assumptions of neo-classical economics, it can be shown that a capitalist economy will gravitate towards a competitive equilibrium that is Pareto-optimal (no-one can be made better off without at least one other person being made worse off). Pareto-optimality is only a weak form of efficiency; none the less, since the appeal of market socialism lies partly in its promise of better economic performance than centrally planned economies, it is important that it should be efficient in at least this sense. It can be shown that a co-operative economy tends towards a competitive equilibrium, and indeed that the equilibrium allocation (what is produced, and in what quantities, etc., etc.) is structurally identical to the capitalist equilibrium.[17] The two systems do, however, rely on different equilibriating mechanisms. For reasons that we shall explore in Chapter 3 below, co-operatives will not in general respond to changes in the market in the same way as capitalist firms, since the incentives facing their members are different from those facing the owners of such firms. In certain rather idealized conditions, a co-operative might behave 'perversely', for instance by reducing its output of goods in response to a price rise.[18] For the economy to move towards an equilibrium, the crucial condition is that workers can freely establish new co-operatives and liquidate those that are no longer profitable.[19] In practical terms, this means that the efficiency of the system will depend on the success of the investment agencies in stimulating enterprise creation and allo-

[17] See J. H. Drèze, 'Some Theory of Labour Management and Participation', *Econometrica*, 44 (1976), 1125–39; J. Vanek, *The General Theory of Labor-Managed Market Economics* (Ithaca: Cornell University Press, 1970), ch. 7.

[18] This was first shown in B. Ward, 'The Firm in Illyria: Market Syndicalism', *American Economic Review*, 48(1958), 566–89. For reasons why such perverse behaviour is unlikely to occur in practice, see Vanek, *General Theory*, chs. 2–3.

[19] See Vanek, *General Theory*, esp. chs. 5, 7, and 14.

cating capital in sectors of the economy where demand outstrips supply.

All of this so far remains at the level of economic theory. If we try to estimate the performance of a co-operative economy in the real world, the difficulty is that we have no full-scale examples to consult. (Yugoslavia, which is sometimes cited in this connection, is a very poor example: even during the period when the Yugoslav economy approximated most closely to market socialism as understood here, prices were subject to political control, co-operatives were not obliged to pay market-clearing prices for their capital, and so forth.)[20] It is hard to tell, therefore, whether market socialism would be more or less efficient in practice than capitalism. On the negative side, the absence of private ownership in industry might be expected to deter speculative ventures—enterprises established to produce radically new products, where demand is unknown and returns therefore highly uncertain. On the positive side, the co-operative form, in which each member of the enterprise has a direct stake in the profitability of his firm, should promote efficient working practices, and draw upon the creative skills of the whole membership. On this question of overall efficiency I shall remain agnostic.[21] It is enough to say that there are no strong reasons to expect a market socialist economy to be less efficient than competitive capitalism. The crucial arguments to be deployed in *favour* of market socialism rely upon other values: freedom, justice, democracy at work.

A final preliminary issue is whether market socialism will be sufficiently egalitarian to satisfy socialists. A system of this kind will inevitably generate income inequalities of two kinds: inequalities within co-operatives, stemming from differences of skill and responsibility among the members, and inequalities between co-operatives, stemming from variations in market

[20] For discussion of Yugoslavia in the light of economic models of market socialism, see S. Estrin, *Self-Management: Economic Theory and Yugoslav Practice* (Cambridge: Cambridge University Press, 1983); H. Lydall, *Yugoslav Socialism: Theory and Practice* (Oxford: Clarendon Press, 1984); J. Vanek, 'The Yugoslav Economy Viewed through the Theory of Labor Management', in id., *The Labor-Managed Economy* (Ithaca: Cornell University Press, 1977); D. D. Milenkovitch, *Plan and Market in Yugoslav Economic Thought* (New Haven and London: Yale University Press, 1971).

[21] There is a thoughtful and balanced discussion of this question in D. D. Milenkovitch, 'Is Market Socialism Efficient?' in A. Zimbalist (ed.), *Comparative Economic Systems* (Boston: Kluwer-Nijhoff, 1984).

conditions and economic performance.[22] Inequalities of the first
kind are likely to be substantially smaller than those obtaining
(even between employees) in capitalist firms, or indeed in state
socialist bureaucracies. Co-operatives build up solidarity
between their members, allowing them to offset to some extent
the scarcity prices that different kinds of labour would otherwise
command, given freedom of entry into and exit from firms.
Moreover it seems unlikely that the income differences we
currently find in capitalist firms can be attributed solely to labour
market factors; rather, the commanding role of the top managers
of such firms allows them to extract a proportion of profit in the
form of income. Where co-operatives have been established,
their internal income ratios do not usually exceed three or four to
one.[23] As for inequalities between co-operatives, the crucial
question is whether such inequalities will tend to persist and
accumulate over time, or whether the market can be expected to
operate so as to cancel them out in the long term. I give reasons
for taking the latter view in Chapters 6 and 7 below.

Primary income will not, then, be distributed equally under
market socialism, but there is good reason to expect that its
distribution will be substantially more equal than under capitalism.[24] This primary equalization should not, however, be seen as
entirely superseding secondary redistribution by agencies of the
state. There will still be a strong case for tax-funded welfare
programmes to help those with special needs. There will also be
various groups who require a system of income maintenance: the
handicapped, those who opt out of the labour market (for instance
to raise children), workers in enterprises that temporarily fail to
make a profit, and others. Although the most distinctive element
in market socialism is the idea of workers' co-operatives using
socially owned capital competing in a market, this is not meant to
be an exhaustive specification. Market socialism is thus less a
straightforward rejection of social-democratic ideas than a more
radical and egalitarian development of those ideas.

---

[22] At the beginning of ch. 6, I briefly discuss the question whether a fully egalitarian
market economy is a feasible possibility and conclude that it is not.

[23] See, for instance, the analysis of the Mondragon co-ops in H. Thomas and C.
Logan, *Mondragon: An Economic Analysis* (London: Allen and Unwin, 1982), ch. 6.

[24] A further issue is whether the anticipated inequalities can be shown to be just by
some criterion of social justice. I address this in ch. 6.

IV

An immediate implication of the points made in the previous section is that a full account of market socialism must involve a theory of the nature and role of the state. Although initially defined in economic terms, market socialism requires political management, not only to ensure that the market works effectively but, at a deeper level, to ensure that the system as a whole conforms to our ethical criteria (for instance in matters of income distribution). But political regulation of the desired kind cannot be conjured up with the wave of a wand. We need an analysis of how the state as an institution may be expected to operate, and how it stands in relation to its citizens.

In developing such an analysis, we shall need to draw on the resources of both the liberal and the socialist traditions, since neither tradition provides us with a ready-made answer. The liberal tradition has been preoccupied with the problem of limiting the state's activities: it is a fertile source of ideas about constitutional mechanisms for controlling the power of individuals and groups. But in liberalism there is little understanding of the state as a vehicle of collective identity, as an institution which allows us as citizens to mould the world in accordance with our ethical beliefs. The socialist tradition does, on occasion, recognize this more elevated role for the state, but its view of the workings of that institution tends to be simplistic. There are two main variants. On the one hand we have a picture of the state as a benevolent machine staffed by public-spirited bureaucrats—the picture of the French positivists and the Fabians. On the other hand we have a picture of the state as an assembly of radical democracies, with the collective will emerging spontaneously from citizens gathering all over the country—the view of radicals in the Marxist and anarchist traditions. Neither of these variants, one might say, has an adequate understanding of politics as an activity persisting under socialism: both regard the state as a form of public authority that transcends the cut and thrust of political disagreement.

In Part III, I attempt to develop a more adequate theory of the state, one whose central notion is that of citizenship. I argue first that citizenship represents the only viable form of society-wide community under modern conditions, and that nostalgic visions of unitary community, still cherished by some socialists, must be abandoned. I go on to maintain that authentic citizenship requires a certain way of practising politics, namely politics as a form of dialogue whose aim is consensus about matters of common concern. This in turn, however, obliges us to think about the issue of how to create a common political culture out of a diversity of private cultures, which has repercussions for our practice of toleration. Finally, I provide a brief sketch of the kind of state that is appropriate to market socialism. The main thesis is that, in order both for citizenship to be practical and for the market to operate effectively, the socialist state must be formally constituted, internally differentiated, and limited in scope.

The second and third parts of the book are related in a way which may be familiar to devotees of Hegel but which may otherwise seem puzzling. In Part II much stress is laid on the importance of the market economy in allowing people to flourish as individuals: markets respond to the fact that we are each of us unique persons with distinct tastes and preferences. In Part III the emphasis is laid on community, on bringing about conditions under which we are able to order the world in accordance with our common will. Some may believe that these two horses cannot both be run at once. I disagree. We are complex creatures, needing both to differentiate ourselves from others and live a private life, and to align ourselves with shared traditions and engage with our fellows in the public realm. These impulses—towards differentiation and privacy and towards community and publicity—are differently weighted in different people, but it is rare to find someone in whom either impulse has been completely extinguished. Our present political culture encourages the first impulse at the expense of the second, but it is worth recalling that the conditions for differentiation and privacy are never secure unless at least some people are willing to assume public responsibility. A society without public life cannot be one in which individuality can flourish in safety. Once this point is appreciated, the juxtaposition in this book of arguments for market freedom and for unity in political culture may seem less paradoxical.

The book's title is intended to capture the apexes within which its argument moves. 'Market', 'state', and 'community' may be thought of as describing three ways in which people may relate to one another; by extension, they refer to three ways in which people may be provided with goods and services.[25] As participants in a market, people's relationships are those of voluntary exchange. Each obtains what he wants by offering some equivalent benefit in return. As citizens of a state, people's relationships are constituted by formal rules specifying what each is entitled and obliged to do. Goods are allocated by requiring some to provide them and empowering others to receive them. As members of a community, people are related by ties of identity which give rise to informal obligations of mutual aid. Within certain limits, people can obtain benefits simply by calling on the goodwill of fellow-members.

We can use this simple matrix to characterize the various positions discussed in the book. Take libertarianism first. Here markets are given a central role to play, with the state's function being merely to enforce the basic rights that the working of markets presupposes. Community is regarded as an optional extra: people may choose to associate in communities and take on special responsibilities if they wish, but there is no reason to build this into the social framework itself.

Traditional socialism simply reverses this picture. Markets have no part to play in the good society. They are entirely superseded by state and community in some combination. For the more idealistic socialists, the state was a transitional institution, destined eventually to be replaced entirely by the voluntary ties of community, conceived as extending to whole societies (and even beyond). Those who took a more realistic view saw the state's role as a permanent one. Community was to be applauded, but it could not be relied upon to get the work of society done.

Market socialism, in the broader sense now introduced in which it refers to both an economic and a political system, combines these elements in a new way. The market is recognized as the centrepiece of economic life, both for its efficiency as a means of providing goods and services and for its more general liberating qualities. But the market economy cannot function in an acceptable way unless complemented by a democratic state that sets appropriate ground rules, monitors the evolution of

[25] There is a parallel here with the organizing idea of C. Lindblom, *Politics and Markets* (New York: Basic Books, 1977), which offers a general assessment of the relative merits of markets and political processes (especially) as means for achieving social goals.

particular markets over time, rectifies the distribution of income, and directly supplies a range of public goods. Thus market and state operate alongside one another, and the justification of the whole arrangement depends on this counterbalancing. Community is not relied upon in the same direct way to provide goods and services. Nevertheless, the form of community which I call citizenship is an indispensible element in the socialist state. It is because they share a common identity that citizens are able to reach a genuine consensus on matters of policy; without this underlying identity the other components of the system would fall apart.

My task, then, is to show that market socialism is the system that most adequately captures our underlying value-commitments. I begin this task by examining the defects of its main contemporary rival, libertarianism.

PART I

A Critique of Libertarianism

I

FREEDOM

I

As their name implies, libertarians are centrally committed to the value of freedom. Sometimes they speak as though their entire social philosophy flowed from this one single commitment. In fact the matter is more complicated, and other values—justice and efficiency, for instance—play their part in the overall defence of institutions such as private property which libertarians favour. Some of these other strands of argument are unravelled in the chapters that follow. It is appropriate, none the less, to begin with freedom, the idea which gives the libertarian position its greatest rhetorical strength. Who but the most benighted of opponents could fail to see virtue in a social order which extends the greatest possible freedom to all?

Analysis of the idea of freedom assumes particular importance in the debate between libertarians and market socialists, for it is central to the case for market socialism that such a system provides individuals with the greatest possible freedom in economic and political life. The claim for *market* socialism is that it provides people with a wider range of choices—in work, consumption, and so forth—than statist forms of socialism; and the claim for market *socialism* is that it provides these choices for everyone, not merely the privileged few, as does capitalism. To justify these claims, however, it is essential to spell out clearly what freedom means, and how its extent is to be measured. I shall argue here that the libertarian equation of the free society with a capitalist society in which the state plays a minimal economic role rests on a particular interpretation of freedom, and moreover one that collapses on close analysis. What, then, do libertarians mean when they talk about individual freedom?

A common interpretive move is to distinguish between negative and positive senses of freedom: libertarians are said to adopt a negative conception of freedom, their socialist critics a positive conception. Unfortunately this distinction, which has a long and tangled history in political thought, is far from clear, and often leads in practice to conflation of several distinct issues. There is no authoritative rendering to which appeal can be made,[1] but the following represents in my view the most useful account of where the distinction lies.

Negative freedom refers to the absence of external constraints on a person's actions. A person is negatively free to the extent that, if he chose to embark on various courses of action, he would not find himself obstructed by external obstacles; the degree of his freedom depends on the proportion of potential actions that are obstructed, the size of the obstructions, and so forth.[2] What counts as an obstacle is potentially a matter of dispute, and this as we shall see is crucial to the debate between libertarians and their opponents. In general, however, we can say that it is a feature of the agent's environment which makes the action in question less eligible, i.e. tends to deter the agent from performing it. The strongest form of constraint is a physical constraint which makes a proposed action literally impossible to perform—a brick wall standing between me and my potential goal. Other forms of constraint approximate more or less closely to this paradigm case, and the argument is about where the boundaries of the notion should be drawn.

Positive freedom refers to the origins of action in the personal choice of the agent. A person is positively free to the extent that he is himself the source of the decisions that are embodied in his actions; unfree to the extent that these can be traced back to another agency, whether an individual or a collectivity such as a class or state. Freedom in this sense is a matter not of whether the environment obstructs or facilitates an agent's decisions, but of where these decisions themselves originate; it is equivalent to

[1] The starting point for most discussions remains I. Berlin, 'Two Concepts of Liberty', in *Four Essays on Liberty* (Oxford: Oxford University Press, 1969). There are, however, several problems with Berlin's account of the distinction. See esp. J. Gray, 'On Negative and Positive Liberty', *Political Studies*, 28 (1980), 507–26, repr. in Z. Pelczynski and J. Gray (eds.), *Conceptions of Liberty in Political Philosophy* (London: Athlone Press, 1984).

[2] How, if at all, these factors should be aggregated is an issue of great difficulty. It is touched on briefly by Berlin in 'Two Concepts', 130. For fuller discussion, see C. Taylor, 'What's Wrong with Negative Liberty', in A. Ryan (ed.), *The Idea of Freedom* (Oxford: Oxford University Press, 1979), and H. Steiner, 'How Free? Computing Personal Liberty', in A. Phillips Griffiths (ed.), *Of Liberty* (Cambridge: Cambridge University Press, 1983).

self-determination. The person who is unfree is the person who, in Mill's words 'lets the world, or his portion of it, choose his plan of life for him'.[3] A free agent, in contrast, chooses how to act on the basis of his own fundamental beliefs and desires. Once again there can be dispute as to how this idea of free choice is to be interpreted—for instance, over the extent to which *free* choice is to be identified with *rational* choice. So there may be variant conceptions of positive freedom, as of negative freedom.

If the distinction is put in these terms, it becomes clear that the value relationship between the two senses of freedom is not competitive but complementary. Being negatively free means having a large number of possible courses of action to choose between; being positively free means deciding for yourself which course to follow. Without positive freedom, negative liberty would be pointless, because if you are caused to perform a certain action, all that matters is that you are able to carry out that action in particular, and the value of having a range of actions to choose between disappears. On the other hand, in the absence of negative liberty being positively free would be merely frustrating, because you would be unable to act on many of the choices that you might make. Each kind of freedom gives point to the other. Both appeal to the underlying image of a choosing subject who is able to execute his choices in the external world.

In practice, of course, there are a number of possible ways in which negative and positive freedom may collide, depending on the precise conception of each that is being employed. Policies aimed at promoting positive freedom may involve restricting the negative freedom of other agents in certain ways, as when we protect people from exposure to insidious forms of persuasion. A theory of freedom will set out the optimum balance of freedoms, both negative and positive, and specify the legal and social framework best calculated to secure that balance.

Once the distinction between negative and positive freedom is properly understood, we can see that the dispute between libertarians and their critics cannot usefully be analysed as a confrontation between the two senses of freedom. A more accurate diagnosis is the following. First, libertarians stress negative rather than positive freedom not because they attach no

---

[3] J. S. Mill, *On Liberty*, in *Utilitarianism; On Liberty; Representative Government*, ed. A. D. Lindsay (London: Dent, 1964), 117.

value to the latter but because they take it for granted that people will be positively free when they are negatively free. People are, as it were, naturally self-determining. Free them from external constraints and they will spontaneously begin making their own authentic choices. Libertarians, in other words, attach little or no weight to threats to positive freedom that do not take the form of external constraints; they do not respond to Mill's concern that people might not choose to live as authentic individuals even though having the (negative) freedom to do so. Second, libertarians draw the bounds of negative liberty narrowly—how narrowly we shall investigate shortly. In particular they do not see economic arrangements, social conventions and the like as potential obstacles to freedom. Their opponents count in a much wider range of phenomena as relevant to determining how much (negative) freedom a person will typically enjoy in a given society.

The argument, in other words, occurs as much *within* the two senses of freedom as *between* them. For that reason it has a degree of complexity; one might accept the libertarians' attitude to positive freedom but find their notion of negative freedom untenable, or vice versa. I choose to concentrate here on the dispute over negative freedom without supposing that this exhausts the argument. I shall argue that the restrictive libertarian notion of constraint cannot be sustained and, in particular, that the ordinary person's freedom may be increased by economic changes giving him increased command over resources.

II

The libertarian view is that freedom is restricted only by the commands and prohibitions of the state, and by such occurrences of private force and fraud as the state fails to prevent. This view has two major variants. One, which I shall call the extreme thesis, holds that freedom is limited only by the coercive intervention of others in the life of the individual, so that the law, when functioning properly, does not restrict freedom in any respect. The second variant, the moderate thesis, accepts that laws restrict freedom, but argues that a (minimal) legal order provides on balance the maximum personal freedom, since the loss of freedom involved in compliance with law is more than compensated for by the protection provided against invasions by other individuals.

The extreme thesis is to be found in Hayek's *The Constitution of Liberty*, though Hayek's thought on the matter is not altogether consistent. Freedom is defined as the absence of coercion, and coercion as a state of affairs in which the coerced person is made into an instrument of the coercer's will. The state is said to use coercion, but (properly) only in order to prevent worse coercion by private individuals. However, Hayek goes on to argue that in so far as the state exercises its power through the promulgation of general rules, its actions need not be coercive in the first place:

Provided that I know beforehand that if I place myself in a particular position, I shall be coerced and provided that I can avoid putting myself in such a position, I need never be coerced. At least insofar as the rules providing for coercion are not aimed at me personally but are so framed as to apply equally to all people in similar circumstances, they are no different from any of the natural obstacles that affect my plans.[4]

As a consequence:

The conception of freedom under the law that is the chief concern of this book rests on the contention that when we obey laws, in the sense of general abstract rules laid down irrespective of their application to us, we are not subject to another man's will and are therefore free.[5]

This is the extreme thesis.

To assess it, we must first be clear as to the meaning of 'coercion'. A fully adequate definition is not easily given,[6] but as an approximate account I suggest the following: coercion occurs when A, the coercer, attempts to induce B, the coerced, to perform some action that he would not otherwise perform (and that he would prefer not to perform) by threatening to harm B in some manner in the event of non-performance. Successful coercion occurs when the threat works and B performs the action in question; unsuccessful coercion when the threat fails. It is important to underline that the coercion itself consists in the

---

[4] F. A. Hayek, *The Constitution of Liberty* (London: Routledge and Kegan Paul, 1960), 142.

[5] Ibid. 153.

[6] For some of the complications, see R. Nozick, 'Coercion', in P. Laslett, W. G. Runciman, and Q. Skinner (eds.), *Philosophy, Politics and Society*, 4th ser. (Oxford: Blackwell, 1972).

issuing of the threat. If B doesn't perform and the threat is carried out (say, in order to protect the future credibility of the coercer), this act is not normally itself an act of coercion but, for instance, an act of physical harm. If I threaten to smash Jones's windows if he doesn't pay me protection money, the smashing of the windows in case of default is not itself an act of coercion.

We can now detect the first error in Hayek's formulation of the extreme thesis. In his characterization of rules of law, he confuses coercion with the imposition of sanctions for non-compliance. A rule of law, considered in its coercive aspect, typically takes the form: 'Don't do X; if you do, Y will happen to you.' ('Don't exceed 70 mph; if you do, you will be fined at least £100.') If I know about this rule, I can of course avoid having the sanction applied to me, either by observing it directly or by excluding myself from any situation to which it is relevant (for instance, by never driving a motor vehicle). But this does not mean that I have not been coerced; I *have* been coerced, for which the most straightforward evidence is that my behaviour has been altered by the threat of sanctions.

Once this confusion is cleared up, we are left with the claim that the coercion implicit in rules of law is general and predictable and in *this* respect 'no different from any of the natural obstacles that affect my plans'. But although predictable coercion may normally be less unwelcome to the coerced person than unpredictable coercion, this is surely only one of the relevant dimensions of coercion, and we would have no trouble at all finding cases in which, say, a greater amount of predictable coercion was felt to be worse than a lesser amount of unpredictable coercion. Indeed, Hayek has been taken to task by his libertarian colleagues on precisely this point.[7]

There is, however, another strand to Hayek's thinking, examination of which will throw further light on the relationship between freedom and coercion. It is characteristic of coercion that I am not merely forced to change my plans in an unwelcome way by the coercer, but forced to change them in line with his

---

[7] See R. Hamowy, 'Freedom and the Rule of Law in F. A. Hayek', *Il Politico*, 36 (1971),349–77; J. W. N. Watkins, 'Philosophy', in A. Seldon (ed.) *Agenda for a Free Society: Essays on Hayek's The Constitution of Liberty*, (London: Institute of Economic Affairs, 1961); M. Rothbard, *The Ethics of Liberty* (Atlantic Highlands, N.J.: Humanities Press, 1982), ch. 28.

intentions. This is the thought behind Hayek's observation that coercion makes me into an instrument of another's will. In pursuing this thought, we might hope to find another reason why laws are not coercive. For in complying with a law I am not characteristically fulfilling the plans of another agent. Laws, typically, are negative in character: they constrain behaviour rather than directing it. Although in a broad sense we might be said to be fulfilling the intentions of the legislators in complying with them, these intentions do not normally consist in any concrete view about how you or I should lead our lives.

If this is Hayek's thought, there are at least two observations we might make about it. The first is that the thesis that laws are less directive than private forms of coercion can only be a weak empirical generalization. A law may intend to produce a very specific piece of behaviour—say, a law which requires me to maintain my car in a roadworthy condition (specified as a checklist of detailed requirements). Conversely, private coercion may be minimally constraining—the Mafia may leave me free to run my business as I wish, provided only that I hand over a fixed sum to them every week. The second is that Hayek's argument takes us in the direction of a positive theory of freedom. By linking freedom to coercion, and coercion to subjection to the arbitrary will of another, he seems to imply that subjection to general and non-arbitrary rules would not be a limitation of freedom at all.[8] It is the *quality* of the constraint, not the extent of the constraint, that here determines the agent's freedom.

This brings us to the major point. Why, from the point of view of negative freedom, should it matter whether I am obstructed in order to serve another's will, or for some other reason? The negative view takes the agent with his plans and desires and looks at the extent to which his environment obstructs his (actual and potential) aims. Coercion is one form of obstruction—perhaps a particularly unwelcome form—but in principle no different from other kinds. Consider the following example. A rancher each year drives his cattle across open country to sell them at market. One year he finds that his route has been blocked by a settler who has purchased a tract of land and fenced it in. The rancher's freedom

---

[8] See J. Gray, 'Hayek on Liberty, Rights and Justice', *Ethics*, 92 (1981–2), 73–84. For a fuller exploration of the inconsistencies in Hayek's notion of coercion, see C. Kukathas, *Hayek and Modern Liberalism* (Oxford: Clarendon Press, 1989), ch. 5.

has been reduced in a manner that appears not to depend at all on the intentions of the settler. The settler may have intended the rancher to give up his trade, in which case the fencing could be seen as an act of coercion. Alternatively the settler may have had no thought other than the desirability of fencing in his own territory. The rancher may feel more resentment in the first case than in the second—though even this is not necessarily true, since one may bitterly resent the carelessness of other people who, in complete ignorance, do things that seriously impinge on one's life—but such feelings are irrelevant to the issue of freedom. The extent of a person's freedom depends on the number of potential actions of his that are obstructed, not on the reason for which they are obstructed.

It is, therefore, a major error to identify freedom with the absence of coercion. Coercion, when it occurs, may be a serious threat to freedom, since often it involves the narrowing down of the agent's alternatives to a single action, or a small range of actions. But, as we have seen, there are other forms of impediment not helpfully described as coercive which may equally infringe a person's freedom of action. The extreme thesis rests on two conceptual mistakes, one concerning the idea of coercion itself, the other the relation between coercion and freedom. Once these mistakes are brought to light, Hayek's claim that in obeying the general and abstract rules of the state we suffer no loss of freedom loses any plausibility it might have had.

III

Hayek himself switches to the moderate thesis when he concedes that 'even general, abstract rules, equally applicable to all, may possibly constitute severe restrictions on liberty'.[9] The moderate thesis, to recall, allows that laws restrict freedom, but argues that a libertarian order, in which the purpose of law is simply to restrict private infringements of freedom, offers the greatest possible freedom on balance. It presupposes a narrow definition of constraint, according to which legal impediments and private coercion would count as constraints but not, say, the absence of

---

[9] Hayek, *Constitution*, 154.

economic opportunities. We must examine the adequacy of such a definition.

Advocates of this position lay stress on the contrast between freedom and ability, between being free to do something and being able to do it. Such a distinction is clearly necessary. I am free to play the sonatas of Beethoven but, never having learned to play the piano and being anyway naturally inept, I am quite unable to. I am able, but not free, to stroll in the grounds of Buckingham Palace. What is the point of the distinction? Ability is a matter of natural facts, facts about agents and their physical environment. My inability to climb Everest reflects the physical properties of the mountain and my own limited capacities. Freedom, on the other hand, depends on what other agents have done; if an obstacle can be attributed to the action of another human being or beings, we call it a constraint on freedom.

This question about the origins of an obstacle is closely linked to a question about justification. Our language embodies a presumption that people should not obstruct one another's activity. When we say of an obstacle that it renders a person unfree to act, we make a charge that stands in need of rebuttal.[10] Reasons have to be given for the continued presence of the obstacle. Of course such reasons may not be far to seek. Many restrictions of freedom are justified, whether to protect the freedom of other agents, to promote competing values such as welfare and equality, or to protect the agent himself. It is a mistake to think that to describe a state of affairs as involving unfreedom is to settle a political argument; it is, however, to make a move in a political argument. There is no such presumption in cases of simple inability. Someone's inability to act in a certain way is morally or politically relevant only where the inability serves to bring other values into play. The fact that a speleologist is unable to escape from a cave moves us to act because we are independently concerned for his welfare; but the fact that millions of human beings are unable to fly to the moon does not move us at all.

The distinction between freedom and ability is not itself in question between libertarians and their critics; what is at issue is where the line between them should be drawn, or in other words

[10] See S. I. Benn and W. L. Weinstein, 'Being Free to Act and Being a Free Man', *Mind*, 80 (1971), 194–211.

what must be true of an obstacle for it to count as a constraint on freedom. The libertarian construes constraints narrowly. Implied in his claim that freedom is restricted only by laws and private coercion is the view that constraints are obstacles intentionally imposed by human agents. I am unfree when and only when the obstacle that prevents or deters me from doing X was placed there deliberately by some other person or persons. This analysis covers both the law that aims to eliminate certain behaviour and coercive threats of various kinds. On the other hand, economic circumstances, which in a market society are the unintended results of earlier human activity, cannot on this view be seen as constraining, even if they leave some people with very few options indeed.

How adequate is this view of constraint? We have already seen, in the course of discussing freedom and coercion, that the distinction between deliberate and accidental obstruction seems not to have any significance from the point of view of freedom. That is, if Jones acts in such a way that I am prevented or deterred from doing X, it does not matter whether Jones's intention is to discourage me from doing X, or whether he has some other purpose and the obstruction is merely a by-product. *My* freedom is at stake, and what matters is that Jones has acted so as to obstruct me. It may possibly be true that I should resent deliberate obstruction more strongly—though, as I suggested earlier, this is by no means self-evident—but this would only show that I shall *feel* less free in the case where Jones acts deliberately to restrict my freedom. No libertarian will want to confuse feeling free with being free.

If the analysis of constraint in terms of deliberate obstruction breaks down, how might the libertarian try to salvage his position? He might argue that the relevant dividing line lay between obstacles that human beings had *imposed* (intentionally or otherwise) and those that they had merely *failed to remove*. Laws, for instance, require positive enactment; but if economic conditions are such that some people are unable to obtain paid work (say), this at most reflects the failure of other agents generally to provide sufficient employment opportunities. This position rests on a distinction between acts and omissions: obstacles that result from acts are constraints on freedom, whereas obstacles that result from omissions only reduce the ability of the people affected to achieve their ends.

To assess this claim, we need to examine the acts/omissions distinction itself. It may at first sight seem relatively simple to distinguish between acting and failing to act; our language is replete with idioms that embody such a distinction (killing and letting die; hindering and failing to help; preventing and failing to enable; etc.). But this apparent simplicity vanishes as soon as we begin to lengthen and complicate the causal chain between agent and outcome. Consider a rudimentary case. Jones owns a piece of land on which stands a large tree overhanging a neighbouring highway. If Jones saws the tree down, it seems uncontroversial to say that he has blocked the highway and (using the criterion we are considering) constrained potential travellers. If, on the other hand, the tree blows down (but would not have done so if Jones had erected props to hold it up), we should say that Jones has merely failed to stop the tree falling and (by extension) failed to enable the travellers to pass by. But now consider two more difficult cases. In the first, the tree will blow down if (and only if) Jones tills the soil around it, weakening the roots. In the second, the tree will blow down if (and only if) Jones does not till the soil, depriving the tree of nutrients. In each of these cases, would the tree's falling and the blocking of the highway result from an act or an omission? Would the first result from an act and the second from an omission because we would naturally describe the human cause in the active voice in the first case ('tilling the soil') but in the passive voice in the second ('leaving the soil untilled')? But we could easily describe the relevant acts in such a way that the voices were reversed—'failing to keep the ground firm' in the first case and 'keeping the ground firm' in the second. If we describe the cases in this way, there will be constraint in the second case if the tree falls but not in the first.

If the acts/omissions distinction is not to fall prey to linguistic arbitrariness, we must supply it with an objective basis. The only explication known to me that meets this condition is Jonathan Bennett's distinction between positive and negative instrumentality.[11] Bennett's idea is that an agent A is positively instrumental at T in bringing about a result R if, of all the things he might have done at T, only a small proportion lead to R, whereas a large

<hr/>

[11] Jonathan Bennett, 'Morality and Consequences' in *The Tanner Lectures on Human Values*, vol. ii, ed. Sterling M. McMurrin (Salt Lake City: University of Utah Press, 1981).

proportion lead to -R.[12] Thus if Jones saws the tree down, he is positively instrumental in bringing it about that the tree blocks the road because, of all the actions he might have performed at that time, only a tiny percentage would have the result that the tree lies across the road. Negative instrumentality is the converse of this. If the tree falls because Jones fails to prop it up, he is negatively instrumental in bringing about this outcome because nearly all of the actions that he might have performed at the relevant time would have the result that the tree would fall. In theory we should be able to apply this criterion to our two more difficult cases and so decide whether to count Jones's behaviour as an act or an omission in each instance.

As Bennett observes, the resulting distinction between acts and omissions is morally neutral. It neither rests on moral considerations nor, by itself, has any moral implications (that is, if two pieces of behaviour are relevantly similar in every respect except that one is an act and the other an omission, they are morally equivalent).[13] Since, as I have already argued, the distinction between freedom and ability is morally loaded (to say that someone is unfree in a certain respect is to make a charge that stands in need of rebuttal, whereas to say that someone is unable to do something carries no such implication), it cannot rest on the contrast between positive and negative instrumentality. To bring this out, we need to look at cases of accidental acts and at cases of deliberate omissions. These can be made as fantastic as one pleases. Suppose I am picnicking on a cliff top and casually toss aside an apple. A pip takes root, grows into a small tree, and at some later time precipitates a cliff fall that traps Smith in a recess below. Assuming that I am positively instrumental in bringing about this result (which means, roughly, that the fall wouldn't have occurred unless the apple had landed more or less where it did, etc.), Smith has been constrained and his freedom impaired

---

[12] Because of worries about the idea of negative actions, Bennett expresses the criterion in terms of propositions referring to A at T; for simplicity of exposition, I have put it back into the material mode.

[13] The distinction might be *correlated* to some extent with features of behaviour that are morally significant, even though the bare contrast between an act and an omission is not. It may, for instance, turn out that agents are morally responsible for the results of a larger proportion of those pieces of behaviour we should call acts than of those pieces of behaviour we should call omissions; but it does not, of course, follow from this that to describe a piece of behaviour as an act (or an omission) is to say anything morally relevant about it.

(on the acts/omissions criterion). Suppose, on the other hand, that a cliff fall will trap Smith (and I know this) unless I pick up and set aside a small stone on the top. Disliking Smith intensely, I hold back and allow the fall to occur. Since (on reasonable assumptions) I am negatively instrumental in bringing about this result, Smith's freedom remains untouched, and I have merely not enabled him to leave the cliff face.

These two judgements are paradoxical because they fail to capture the sense of our underlying intuition that constraints are obstacles attributable to human agency. In both cases the result depends on a combination of natural factors and human behaviour. But human agency means both more and less than positive instrumentality in the technical sense analysed above. It rests in particular on a view about what the agents in question could reasonably have foreseen. In the first case there is positive instrumentality, but there is no possible way in which I could have anticipated the results of my action, and therefore no relevant sense in which the outcome could be attributed to my agency. In the second case there is not only foresight but intention, even though the instrumentality is negative. On this basis we would normally judge that Smith's freedom has been impaired in the second case but not in the first, in contrast to the verdict that the acts/omissions criterion yields.

How, then, shall we capture the relevant sense of 'human agency'? I believe that we need to employ the notion of moral responsibility. Constraints on freedom are those obstacles for which one or more agents can be held to be morally responsible. The plausibility of this view increases as we look more closely at what the notion of moral responsibility entails.

First, moral responsibility is a narrower notion than causal responsibility. Being causally responsible for something means simply that there is a chain of cause and effect leading from the agent to the outcome; unless we employ something like the acts/omissions distinction to narrow the idea, there will be very little for which human beings cannot in some way be held causally responsible. Moral responsibility, on the other hand, depends on taking a view about what people can reasonably demand of one another. Consider these two cases. In the first, I am driving through a desert and come across a man by the roadside dying of thirst. If I decline to offer him a ride into town (or help him in some other way), I am morally responsible for his subsequent death. In the second, I am driving past the bus stop when someone tries to hitch a lift with me. If I decline to pick him up, I am not morally responsible for his failure to keep an appointment in town. Wherein lies the difference between the two cases? In the first set of circumstances, I have an obligation to help the dying man; if I default, I am morally responsible for the outcome. In the second set of circumstances there is no equivalent obligation to help, even though it would be a nice gesture on my part to do so.

Moral responsibility is not the same as moral culpability, although it is a precondition for the latter. To be morally responsible for something is to be answerable for it, but it may be possible to give a wholly satisfactory answer. Suppose someone tries to blame me for some harm that has befallen Brown. There are three possible responses that I might make. First, I can deny any moral responsibility for the harm—either empirically (I wasn't the person who performed the harmful action) or morally (I had no obligation to protect Brown from harm of that kind). Second, I can accept moral responsibility but deny that the apparent harm really is harm—I might argue that it was good for Brown to be treated in that way. Third, I can accept moral responsibility but argue that the harm to Brown was offset by greater good elsewhere. We are responsible for our moral successes as well as our moral failures. So if we say that constraints on freedom are obstacles for which human agents are morally responsible, we do not imply that all constraints are evil. On the contrary, constraints may be justified in the agent's own interest (as in cases of paternalistic legislation) or in the interests of others who might be harmed if freedom was not restricted. We *do* imply that all constraints stand potentially in need of justification—i.e. that it is always appropriate to ask why a particular constraint is necessary. But this, surely, is implicit in our notion of freedom itself. Freedom, as I have argued already, is a morally loaded term. To describe something as a constraint *is* to raise the question of justification. An analysis in terms of moral responsibility captures this value-loading precisely.

We are now better able to understand what separates libertarians who hold the moderate thesis from their critics. The dispute between them is essentially a dispute over the extent of our moral responsibilities itself. Libertarians construe moral responsibilities narrowly and negatively: we are responsible only for *imposing* costs on others. Their critics take a wider view, according to which we are responsible also for failing to provide in various ways for our fellow human beings. This is a substantive difference, and ultimately it depends on taking a view about what human beings can reasonably demand of one another. We cannot hope to supply a proof that the libertarian position on this issue is mistaken. What we *can* do is bring out as clearly as possible the manner in which the libertarian view of freedom rests on a particular doctrine of moral responsibility, a doctrine which, when its implications are fully spelt out, will not (I believe) seem very attractive. This is as far as argument alone can take us on this issue.

Let us return, then, to the question whether economic conditions might count as constraints on freedom. To focus our enquiry, consider the following possibility: an economy managed on *laissez-faire* lines generates high levels of involuntary unemployment, with far fewer job vacancies of any sort than applicants seeking work. Might the unemployed justifiably complain that their freedom has been diminished by the absence of jobs? We have established that the correct way to answer this question is to decide whether moral responsibility for the absence of work can be attributed to any human agents. How might the libertarian attempt to show that no one is morally responsible for the state of affairs in which levels of unemployment are high?

One possible claim is that the level of unemployment is *inevitable* and no one can be held responsible for what cannot be altered. The form of this answer is correct, but its substance very implausible. We know that government policies affect levels of employment—for instance, that programmes of public expenditure may reduce unemployment in the appropriate circumstances. It may not be easy to forecast the effects of particular policies, but this is not enough to show that the status quo is unalterable. At most, it shows that it may be difficult to select the best means of increasing the freedom of the unemployed.

An alternative claim is that unemployment can be reduced only by imposing (by implication unacceptable) costs elsewhere. If true, this does not show that the freedom of the unemployed has not been diminished; it shows that increasing their freedom would, on balance, be undesirable. This claim involves a judgement about the optimum balance of liberties in a society, or perhaps about the balance between liberty and other ends. Whether we agree or disagree with the judgement, the point at issue—that unemployment reduces the freedom of the unemployed—has been conceded.

Yet another version of the libertarian view is that unemployment is the unintended result of the activities of millions of employers, workers, and so forth, who in the rightful pursuit of their own individual ends create a state of affairs in which there are not enough jobs to go round. This formulation amalgamates three separate claims. The first is that unemployment is an unintended outcome. Even if this is true (and it is easy to overlook the possibility that unemployment may be created deliberately as an economic instrument), we have already seen that restrictions on freedom need not be intentionally imposed. Using our later vocabulary, intention is not necessary to moral responsibility. The second claim is that unemployment is the joint outcome of the activity of many individuals. But the effect of this is to diffuse responsibility rather than destroy it. If I add my straw to the camel's load in circumstances where it can be foreseen that others will do likewise, I bear my share of responsibility for the resulting injury to the camel. In the economic case, we are likely to attribute primary responsibility to the government, as the agency appointed to deal with the macro-effects of individual behaviour—the agency to which we have transferred our basic responsibilities. This of course does not affect the issue at stake, namely whether *anyone* can be held responsible for the plight of the unemployed. The third claim is that agents pursuing their own ends within a market are acting within their rights, and by implication have no responsibility for the ensuing state of affairs. But this is simply to beg the question. We cannot make assumptions about the rights of individuals until we have settled the more basic conceptual issue about where the boundaries of freedom are to be drawn. Until we know whether unemployment impairs the freedom of the unemployed, we cannot vindicate the set of rights enjoyed by participants in a *laissez-faire* economy.[14]

[14] A libertarian might, of course, lay the foundations of rights elsewhere, and use the resulting doctrine to construct his theory of freedom. This would yield what G. A. Cohen has labelled a 'moralized definition of freedom'; see G. A. Cohen, 'Capitalism, Freedom

We see that all the libertarian responses here lead back more or less directly to the issue of whether we are morally responsible for states of affairs which we have not deliberately created but which we have the power to alter. The libertarian view is that we have no such responsibility, even if the states of affairs in question are very hard for some people. I do not think that many of us will share this view, and I shall try to show later that libertarians themselves do not hold to it consistently. Before doing so, however, I want to explore briefly a second possible way of defending the thesis that only laws and private coercion stand as constraints on freedom.

IV

This second approach begins with the observation that it is usually possible to escape from economic obstacles such as unemployment. Some unemployed people go on to get jobs, and a few eventually become wealthy. This seems to imply that those who remain unemployed are not unfree to find work, but simply haven't the ability to do so. Since we all agree that a line must be drawn somewhere between freedom and ability, this line of argument appears to offer a promising defence of the libertarian view. The question is no longer 'Is anyone morally responsible for the existence of this obstacle?' but 'Can the obstacle be surmounted by persons of sufficient ability?' And this in turn raises a general question about the character which an obstacle must have if we are to count it as a constraint on freedom. We surely do not want to say that any feature of a proposed course of action that makes it less attractive to us thereby also makes us less free to undertake it.

It may be helpful here to begin by looking at the most extreme view, namely that we are only unfree to perform those actions that it is impossible for us to perform. This view, which can be traced back to Hobbes, has more recently been defended by Hillel Steiner.[15] Steiner's claim is that 'an individual is unfree if, and

and the Proletariat', in A. Ryan (ed.), *The Idea of Freedom* (Oxford: Oxford University Press, 1979.) I am assuming in the text that the libertarian takes rights *to freedom* as fundamental, so he cannot establish what rights we have without first establishing what our freedom consists in.

[15] H. Steiner, 'Individual Liberty', *Proceedings of the Aristotelian Society*, 65 (1974–5), 33–50.

only if, his doing of any action is rendered impossible by the action of another individual'.[16] He defends this view by pointing out that any other mode of intervention merely alters the desirability of the action in question, and he claims that once any such intervention is allowed to count as a constraint on freedom, all such interventions must be. In particular, there is no coherent basis for distinguishing between threats (which are normally taken to reduce freedom) and offers (which are not). By broadening the class of constraints, we undermine the essential distinction between A being free to do X and A wanting to do X.

We must concede to Steiner that any account of freedom which extends constraint beyond impossibility makes some assumptions about human desires. For if a constraint fails to make an action impossible, it must reduce freedom by making that action less eligible for the agent in question, and 'eligibility' depends on the desires and aversions of the agent himself. If these desires and aversions were to change radically enough, what was formerly a constraint might no longer be so. Against this theoretical disadvantage we must set the extreme narrowness of Steiner's view. Compare the following cases: in the first, a man is imprisoned in a ten-foot-square cage; in the second, a square of the same size is marked out on the ground, the man is placed inside, and told that moments after he steps out of the square he will be shot (there is ample evidence that the threat is not idle). On Steiner's view, the man is free to leave the square in the second case, but not the cage in the first. But is the difference between the cases really relevant for our judgements of freedom? If we examine the relationship between the man and his gaolers, we can say that in each case the man is effectively confined in a ten-foot square by his captors. It is true that in the second case the mechanism of confinement depends on the captive's aversion to being shot; yet this is not some idiosyncratic taste of his, but rather a well-entrenched feature of any normal person's psychology. When applying the notion of freedom we are looking for morally relevant similarities and dissimilarities in relationships between persons, and it is perfectly appropriate if in doing so we rely on psychological facts for which there is such overwhelming evidence.

Steiner's view is not, of course, that of the libertarian, who

---

[16] Steiner, 'Individual Liberty', 33.

regards laws and coercive threats as constraints on freedom even though they do not render the actions concerned impossible to perform. The libertarian must accept the argument advanced in the last paragraph, namely that we become unfree to perform actions when penalties are attached to those actions that would deter the average person from undertaking them. But now let us consider the implications of this position more fully. Note first that the extent of constraint depends upon the size of the threatened sanction considered in the light of assumptions about 'normal' psychology. If we do not standardize the impact of penalties in this way, we should be forced to conclude, for instance, that masochists are left more free by threats of corporal punishment than other people, that poor people are made less free by threatened fines than rich people, and so forth. Nor do we want to have to conclude that clever criminals, who stand a better chance of evading detection, are more free than stupid criminals.[17] These complications are unwelcome in discussions of freedom—and, as I have suggested, we avoid them by considering standard cases.

But if we do this in the case of laws and coercive threats, we must be prepared to follow suit when considering whether economic obstacles may limit freedom. We cannot, merely by pointing to a few exceptional individuals who manage to surmount such obstacles, deny that they exist, any more than we could prove that no laws limit freedom by finding a super-criminal whose activities were entirely unaffected by legal restraints. To return to the example of unemployment, the absence of job vacancies may be a constraint on the freedom of the unemployed despite the fact that some previously unemployed persons have managed to find satisfactory work.

What if escaping unemployment is less a matter of having special abilities than of conscientiously striving to find work? It may then be true that anyone who is currently unemployed could, with sufficient effort, find a job. But if at the same time the total number of job vacancies is far less than the number of unemployed, it must also be true that all the unemployed could not simultaneously find work. We would then have a case of the kind,

---

[17] In case the relevance of this example is not clear, I am assuming that the deterrent effect of a punishment is a product of its size and the chances of its being imposed.

analysed acutely by G. A. Cohen,[18] in which the unemployed taken as individuals would not be constrained, but the unemployed taken collectively would be. Cohen concludes, correctly in my view, that collective unfreedom is often a significant kind of unfreedom. Although the fact that, taken as individuals, we are in a position to avoid constraint may *mitigate* the fact that, taken in the aggregate, we cannot, it does not obliterate the significance of the latter fact. Nor are such examples necessarily confined to economic constraints. We can easily envisage legal cases—say, minor motoring offences—in which it is police policy only to begin arresting and fining offenders when the level of offence passes a certain point.[19] Here, then, each of us is individually free to do the illegal thing provided that most others keep to the law. But this does not mean that, taken collectively, motorists are free to break the law. The case is structurally identical to that of unemployment with a few job vacancies, and our judgements about both cases must run parallel.

The libertarian might argue in reply that, once we allow economic conditions of various kinds to count as constraints on freedom, there will be no way of setting reasonable bounds to the concept. Since people generally dislike paying out money to receive goods, we would have to allow that any pricing system was a form of constraint. But it seems absurd to say that my freedom to acquire goods is impaired whenever a price tag is placed upon them. And indeed it is absurd. However, we already have the means at our disposal to meet this libertarian challenge. An obstacle is a constraint on freedom only when other agents can be held morally responsible for it. Our moral responsibilities are bounded. We are responsible for ensuring that, as far as lies within our power, others enjoy a decent standard of living, but not for ensuring that they enjoy any particular items (unless these items turn out to be indispensable). No one has a moral responsibility to provide others with champagne or caviar. The fact, then, that these items are priced beyond the purses of many does not show that the prices are constraints (a high price placed on bread

[18] G. A. Cohen, 'The Structure of Proletarian Unfreedom', *Philosophy and Public Affairs*, 12 (1983), 3–33.

[19] For instance, through traffic may be banned from a certain street in the interests of the residents; the police may decide to enforce this rule only when the volume of traffic begins to exceed a certain level.

might be a constraint in conditions of scarcity where rationing was
feasible).

V

We return, then, to the underlying libertarian assumption that
our moral responsibilities are entirely negative in character. I
have already conceded that there is no way of dislodging someone
who holds stubbornly to this view. But even committed
libertarians may find it difficult to adhere to in all cases. In
particular, most would concede that there are extreme situations
in which we do have obligations to aid others.[20] Hayek, for
example, considers the case of the owner of a spring in an oasis
who turns out to have a monopoly of the water supply. He
concedes that such a person might exercise coercion by threatening to withhold his vital resource from the other inhabitants of the
oasis. He wants to distinguish such a case from that of a famous
artist who refuses to paint a subject unless he is paid a very high
fee. 'So long as the services of a particular person are not crucial
to my existence or the preservation of what I most value, the
conditions he exacts for rendering these services cannot properly
be called "coercion".'[21] Critics of Hayek have pointed out that
this way of stating the point introduces an unwanted subjective
element into the definition of freedom: whether someone's
refusal to supply me with a good except on his own terms
constitutes a constraint will depend on whether the good is
'crucial to my existence or the preservation of what I most value',
so the scope of freedom will change as my values change.[22] Of
more significance to the present discussion is the fact that
Hayek's analysis of the water-hole case tacitly concedes a positive
obligation to render aid. It is only because the owner of the spring
shares in a common obligation to make the essential means of life

[20] For the hard-line position, see Rothbard, *Ethics of Liberty*. Rothbard's view is that our
only *obligation* is not to aggress against others' persons or property. How we should use our
own assets is a matter of personal morality, having nothing to do with 'political ethics' (see
e.g. p. 152).

[21] Hayek, *Constitution*, 136.

[22] This point has been made forcefully to me by John Gray in private conversation, and
is implicit in Gray, 'Hayek on Liberty, Rights and Justice', 82. See also N. Barry, 'Hayek
on Liberty', in Z. Pelczynski and J Gray (eds.), *Conceptions of Liberty in Political Philosophy*
(London: Athlone Press, 1984), 273.

available to others that the threat to withhold water can be described as coercive. In this respect he is not alone. Nozick, in general a defender of inviolable rights of property,[23] also concedes that 'catastrophes' may trigger what he calls the Lockean proviso on property rights, namely that appropriation is justified only when it does not worsen the position of other people. A situation of severe deprivation, such as that exemplified in the water-hole case, limits the rights of the owner and obliges him to make the scarce resource available on reasonable terms to the deprived.[24]

The intention of libertarians is, of course, to confine these arguments to very extreme cases. Both Hayek and Nozick imply that, in the normal operations of a market economy, no infringements of freedom will occur. But clearly this is a matter of judging the extent of the obligation to provide aid. As we have seen, Hayek's own formulation of the criterion is wide open to objection. The socialist critic will advance a theory of needs, and claim that economic arrangements deprive people of freedom whenever they fail to satisfy the needs so defined. Such a theory will naturally be challengeable. But the libertarian view appears simply arbitrary. Positive obligations are recognized, and their relevance to debates about freedom conceded, but then the extent of these obligations is limited more or less by fiat to life-and-death situations. No argument is given for confining the obligation to render aid so narrowly.

My aim in this chapter has been to expose certain defects in the libertarian view of freedom, and in the accompanying claim that a capitalist society with a minimal state maximizes individual freedom. I first considered and rejected the extreme thesis that only arbitrary coercion infringes freedom. I then considered the more moderate view that freedom is limited by general laws as well as by coercion—but not by economic impediments—with the corollary that a libertarian order limits freedom only for the sake of freedom, and does so with maximum effectiveness. Against this, I have defended the claim that economic impedi-

---

[23] See R. Nozick, *Anarchy, State and Utopia* (Oxford: Blackwell, 1974), esp. ch. 7.

[24] Strictly speaking, the obligation Nozick recognizes is not a general obligation to render aid in catastrophic situations but a conditional obligation on property-owners to release some of their property. You can avoid the obligation by not holding any property. Nozick comes closer than Hayek to taking the view that our moral responsibilities to others are wholly negative.

ments such as unemployment may indeed restrict freedom, so that a freedom-maximizing order must remove such obstacles. It is not an objection that no one has erected these obstacles deliberately, since constraints need not be intentionally imposed. Nor is it an objection that they arise from the activities of many individuals, since this does not prevent the attribution of moral responsibility for their existence. Nor again is it an objection that such obstacles do not literally prevent people from acting as they wish, because the realm of unfreedom stretches beyond simple prevention. All in all, financial and other such obstacles may count as constraints. To show that they do, however, something more than conceptual argument is needed. Moral responsibility for their existence has to be established, which requires in turn a theory of moral obligation. The socialist case rests at this point on a view of obligation that is in principle contestable. Yet it derives persuasive force from the fact that the obligations it invokes must be invoked even by libertarians to handle cases of natural monopoly satisfactorily. The libertarian may, in other words, be faced with an unpleasant choice: either he sticks firmly to a negative theory of obligations and accepts the consequence that monopolistic exchanges can never infringe freedom, or he allows positive obligations of the kind referred to and has to concede at least the possibility that economic transactions are constraining. So although the socialist view of freedom under capitalism invokes a theory of obligation (whose direct justification has not been attempted here), the latter may be much less controversial than the view it supports.

I have not tried to catalogue the various respects in which a market socialist economy may be expected to extend freedom more widely than a capitalist economy. The essential point about a system of the kind described in the Introduction is that both power and economic resources are distributed much more equally than under capitalism, through the co-operative organization of work and public regulation of capital investment. My task has been the fairly specific one of showing that the extent of access to these resources is relevant in establishing how much freedom a person enjoys. A full comparison of capitalism and market socialism would need to show that the greater extent of liberty made available under the latter system more than offsets the particular freedoms—such as the freedom to hire others as salaried employees—that are forgone.[25] I have not attempted such a comparison, though I am fairly confident as to its outcome. This, I believe, explains why libertarians concentrate their efforts on showing that access to resources is normally irrelevant to freedom, and also why a rebuttal of that thesis is so damaging to their position.

Nor have I considered the relevance of markets to positive freedom, freedom as self-determination. I return to this question in chapter 8, where I argue, invoking support from an unlikely quarter, that markets are a practically indispensable means of ensuring that people make autonomous choices about matters such as work and consumption. The upshot of the present discussion is that the extent of market freedom, in its negative aspect, is dependent on the distribution of power and resources, and there is no good reason to believe that a libertarian order will maximize this freedom for the ordinary person.

---

[25] It would also have to consider the extent of political freedom possible under either system. I consider the question of freedom in the socialist state at some length in Part III, esp. chs. 11 and 12.

2

PROCEDURAL JUSTICE

I

Libertarians are not merely concerned to draw out the practical implications of their view of freedom. They also want to show that other values—values like justice and welfare—point in the same direction, towards a free market and a minimal state. The debate about justice is of crucial importance, since many would share Rawls's view that 'justice is the first virtue of social institutions as truth is of systems of thought'.[1] For most participants in the debate, justice means social justice: institutions are just in so far as they tend to generate social outcomes which meet one or more criteria—for instance, criteria of desert or need. Libertarians reject this identification. They see the very notion of social justice as intellectually misguided and as disastrous in its consequences. Justice, properly understood, is a characteristic of the procedures that people follow to reach outcomes, not of the outcomes themselves. Provided that the correct procedures have been observed in people's transactions with one another, the outcome will be just whatever its overall shape or quality.

For such an account to be coherent, it must be possible to explain what distinguishes just from unjust procedures without making any reference to their likely outcomes. I shall examine two attempts to do this, both libertarian in inspiration but markedly different in structure. Nozick offers us a proprietary theory of justice, according to which justice is to be understood in terms of universal principles governing entitlements to property. Hayek analyses justice as conformity to the evolving rules of a spontaneous social order. Nozick's view is narrow and rigid, Hayek's broader and more flexible. After pointing out difficulties in both accounts, I shall offer a brief defence of the idea of social justice. I do not at this point try to connect this idea to the institutional

---

[1] J. Rawls, *A Theory of Justice* (Cambridge, Mass.: Harvard University Press, 1971), 3.

framework of market socialism—this task is deferred until Chapter 6.

II

Nozick proposes the following general analysis of justice: an assignment of goods is just if and only if each person owns the goods he holds, according to the rules of property. Such a theory requires that rules should be provided stating the conditions under which items come to be the property of particular persons. In Nozick's case this is done by setting out three fundamental principles, as follows:

(a) The principle of acquisition, which specifies how objects may originally come to be held as property;

(b) The principle of transfer, which specifies how property titles may be transferred from person to person;

(c) The principle of rectification, which specifies how violations of property rights legitimately acquired under (a) or (b) are to be corrected.[2]

Using these principles Nozick maintains that an allocation of goods is just when everyone included in it has a title to what he holds according to (a), (b) or (c); that is, everyone must own what he holds *either* by original acquisition *or* by transfer *or* as a result of rectification. Such an analysis makes the justice of a property distribution dependent on the history of that distribution (stretching back as far as necessary), not upon its present structural features (e.g. the degree of inequality that it manifests) or upon a correspondence between personal qualities (e.g. merit or need) and holdings. Whatever else may be said about the proprietary theory, Nozick is clearly right to present it as radically different from other, more familiar, accounts of justice.

One condition must obviously be met if such a theory is to be successful. The terms in which justice is analysed must be independent of, and more basic than, the notion of justice itself. If the principle of acquisition, say, can only be defended by recourse to a notion of justice, the analysis falls into a circle whereby justice is explained in terms of legitimate property rights, and legitimate property rights in their turn are explained by reference to justice.

[2] R. Nozick, *Anarchy, State and Utopia* (Oxford: Blackwell, 1974), ch. 7.

Nozick himself recognizes the possibility of sabotaging the proprietary theory by writing in unorthodox principles under (*a*), (*b*) or (*c*): for instance, having as one's principle of transfer the rule 'if one has more than the mean income one must transfer everything one holds above the mean to persons below the mean so as to bring them up to (but not over) the mean',[3] which if followed universally would of course lead towards a structured distribution, namely, perfect equality. To avoid such possibilities, the proprietary theory must rest on independently justifiable axioms. The line of enquiry I shall follow is to see whether this condition can be met.

Nozick makes our task of assessment harder here by failing to specify the *content* of any of the three principles which are necessary to his account of justice. While asserting that there must be a principle of acquisition, for instance, he declines to spell out the principle itself. He does, however, refer to Locke's theory of property acquisition, and I think we may assume that a Lockean account, with some necessary amendments, is what Nozick has in mind. Another proprietary theorist, Murray Rothbard, cites Locke directly on this issue.[4] I shall assume that a plausible proprietary theory of justice will be Lockean in inspiration and proceed to search for the most persuasive way of unpacking Locke's argument concerning the origin and extent of property rights.[5]

III

We may begin by focusing on the notion of property or ownership itself. Although this may appear a relatively clear and uncontroversial idea (at least when compared to our potential *analysandum*, justice), such an appearance is soon dispelled.[6] When, in conventional usage, we speak of an item as someone's

---

[3] Ibid, 157.

[4] M. Rothbard, 'Justice and Property Rights', in S. Blumenfeld (ed.), *Property in a Humane Economy* (LaSalle, Ill.: Open Court, 1976); id. *The Ethics of Liberty* (Atlantic Highlands, N.J.: Humanities Press, 1982).

[5] I do not intend to saddle Locke himself with the proprietary theory. Important contrasts between Locke and Nozick have been noted in V. Held, 'John Locke on Robert Nozick', *Social Research*, 43 (1976), 169–95 and S. B. Drury, 'Locke and Nozick on Property', *Political Studies*, 30 (1982), 28–41. Locke is referred to simply in an attempt to fill the gaps in Nozick's argument.

[6] See the helpful discussion in A. Reeve, *Property* (London: Macmillan, 1986), esp. ch. 2.

property, we are making a claim that is internally complex. According to Honoré's well-known analysis,[7] the 'full liberal' notion of ownership comprises no less than eleven distinct legal relations, most of them separable rights—such as the right to possess, the right to use, the right to manage, and so on. When we say of someone that he owns an object, therefore, we typically assert that he enjoys these rights and others over that thing against the world at large. As indicated, these rights are separable. There is no logical reason why someone who has the right to use an object should also have, say, the right to alienate it (part of Honoré's 'right to the capital'). Nor is there any empirical absurdity in separating the two rights, as there is in separating Shylock's right to a pound of flesh from his right to the blood that necessarily accompanies it. Indeed, we are familiar enough with cases in which the rights normally combined under the heading of property are disassociated—for instance in leases, where the hirer has the rights to possess, use, manage, etc., the object hired, but not the rights to the capital, security, etc.

As Honoré has made clear, there is nothing sacrosanct about the full, liberal notion of ownership.[8] It may be analytically convenient as a starting point when discussing modern systems of law. Historically, however, and from the point of view of social and political theory, there is something to be said for the reverse approach, taking limited rights over things as the norm and full ownership as the exception, conceded only in special cases. All societies may indeed recognize full ownership of at least some items; but, generalizing broadly, we may say that in pre-modern societies full ownership is only recognized in relatively unimportant personal goods, such as apparel and ornaments, whereas in goods that are important to the economic maintenance of the society, only limited rights are permitted.[9] The best example here

---

[7] A. M. Honoré, 'Ownership', in A. G. Guest (ed.), *Oxford Essays in Jurisprudence*, 1st ser. (Oxford: Oxford University Press, 1961).

[8] A. M. Honoré, 'Property, Title and Redistribution', *Archiv fur Rechts-und Sozialphilosophie*, 10 (1977), 107–15. As Honoré puts it, Nozick's rules 'reproduce in outline western systems of property law based on the liberal conception of ownership. According to these notions, ownership is a permanent, exclusive and transmissible interest in property. But this type of property system is neither the only conceivable system, nor the easiest to justify from a moral point of view, nor does it predominate in those societies which are closest to a "state of nature"' (p. 109).

[9] For a fuller account see A. S. Diamond, *Primitive Law, Past and Present* (London: Methuen, 1971), esp. 164–6, 187–90, 211–3, 251–3, 368–72.

is the land, which is of course the primary means of production for nearly all pre-industrial societies. Looking back only as far as English feudalism we see that nothing corresponding to ownership of land is recognized. Instead we find pairs of people—lords and tenants, for example—bound together by particular sets of rights and obligations. The feudal tenant differed from the modern owner (*a*) by the more limited set of rights which he enjoyed over his plot of land; (*b*) by the obligations which necessarily accompanied those rights, for instance the services owed to the lord; (*c*) by the fact that the rights were held against one specific individual rather than against the world at large. One authority comments:

As between the parties, proprietary language is out of place ... The appropriate language is that of obligation, and the terms used all involve two persons. A tenement is not a lawyer's long word for a parcel of land, but what the tenant holds of a lord for service. A tenant is not just one physically in possession but one who has been seised by a lord.[10]

For a more primitive example, we may refer to Gluckman's detailed analysis of Barotse legal ideas.[11] Gluckman found that the Barotse had terms designating the relationship between a person and a material thing which in some sense corresponded to our terms 'owner' and 'ownership'. However, the correspondence was far from exact, for, to begin with, several persons occupying different roles might be spoken of as the 'owner (*mung'a*) of a thing. Thus a plot of land might be said to be 'owned' simultaneously by the king, the village headman, the actual user of the land, and his dependants. Each of these people held specific rights over the land, and to call any of them *mung'a* was a way of vindicating their exercise of those rights in a contest with another role-incumbent. Moreover each set of rights was accompanied by obligations, and the rights were forfeit if the obligations were not discharged. The user of the land had obligations both to those above him in the system of authority—the headman and ultimately the king—and to his wife or wives, and he would lose

[10] S. F. C. Milsom, *The Legal Framework of English Feudalism* (Cambridge: Cambridge University Press, 1976), 39.
[11] M. Gluckman, *The Ideas in Barotse Jurisprudence* (Manchester: Manchester University Press, 1972).

his rights over the land if he defaulted seriously. Gluckman summarizes:

> The relation of *bung'a* [ownership] is not a simple definition of an individual's claim to land; rather, it defines the rights and duties of a person occupying a specific social position of status as part of a complex of rights and duties held in the same land by other persons occupying related social positions. These rights are relative and specific to persons and disputes, but they are all defined by a single term. Thus *bung'a* defines all stabilized relations between persons and land, from which people cannot be expropriated without altering their social positions.[12]

These examples are meant to remind us that the liberal concept of ownership should not be treated as an indispensible category for thinking about socially sanctioned relationships between persons and things. Why should we conceive those relationships in terms of the liberal notion rather than in terms of the feudal notion of dominion, or for that matter in terms of the Barotse notion of *bung'a*? That we find it difficult to avoid using the liberal notion is testimony above all to its familiarity and its congruence with other aspects of our social thinking; it reflects the assumptions of liberal individualism, where a person is seen as a self-determining agent controlling his material environment and recognizing no obligations to others around him, except the negative obligation to respect their spheres of free action. These assumptions are expressed in a concept of property conveying unrestricted control of the thing owned and the absence of accompanying obligations, bar the 'prohibition of harmful use', which entails no more than respect for others' personal and property rights.

We have seen already, in the previous chapter, how similar assumptions lay behind the libertarian interpretation of freedom. But we also saw how hard it was even for libertarians themselves to hold to these assumptions consistently. If the assumptions are challengeable, it follows that the liberal notion of ownership stands in need of defence. We cannot take it for granted that, for any given category of objects, the best arrangement is to grant full rights of ownership in Honoré's sense. Rather, we should expect

---

[12] Gluckman, *The ideas in Barotse Jurisprudence*, 148.

the forms of property we recognize to reflect the underlying values we want to see manifested in social relations, justice among them.

So the first difficulty with a proprietary theory of Nozick's type is that it relies upon an unexamined notion of ownership, which enters the theory as a primitive term. It is assumed that people will have full rights of ownership and questions are then raised about how titles to particular pieces of property are allocated. But this gets the relationship between the concepts of property and justice back to front. Different ideas of justice, in the sense of views about what each person can rightly claim from his fellows, can be seen at work beneath each of the alternative notions of property or quasi-property considered above. We therefore need first to work out our theory of justice, and then consider how best to implement it through a regime of ownership.

Before turning to a second source of difficulty with the proprietary theory, it is worth noting one further way in which the analysis of ownership offered above bears on the debate between libertarians and market socialists. Because they unthinkingly adopt the liberal notion of ownership, libertarians are apt to assume that the relevant question to be asked about any proposed economic system is how ownership titles (by implication, comprehensive titles) are held and transmitted. Thus, faced with arrangements such as those sketched in the Introduction, it is natural for libertarians to ask, for instance, whether co-operatives own their assets, or whether the system is one of state ownership. The correct answer is that it is neither, since the rights that are combined in the liberal notion of ownership are here distributed between different bodies—the co-operatives themselves having the rights to use, draw income from, etc. their assets, while the investment agencies retain the right to the capital and the right to manage, in the sense of deciding how productive assets shall be allocated and under what broad conditions. Other incidents of ownership, such as transmissibility, disappear under these circumstances. It is possible to describe the system in a shorthand way as one of social ownership, but it would be quite wrong to read this as postulating some entity called 'society' which holds the rights held together in liberal property regimes by individuals. Rather, the incidents of ownership are parcelled out in the manner indicated, in accordance with the justifying theory of market socialism.

The point, to conclude, is that uncritical adoption of the liberal notion of ownership not only weakens the credibility of the proprietary theory of justice, but also obscures what is really at stake in the debate between libertarians and their socialist critics over property systems.

IV

Let us now turn to the second aspect of the proprietary theory of justice, the account given of original acquisition. Assuming for the sake of argument that people are to have full property rights in things, how should these titles be distributed? The proprietary theorist's answer is that this depends on the original appropriation of objects and their subsequent passage from hand to hand via the rules of transfer. Much therefore depends on establishing that the original appropriations were legitimate. The principle of acquisition must have a strong independent justification.

Locke argued that a man had property rights in his own body, therefore in his labour as an activity, therefore in those material things that he had 'mixed his labour with'. His title was subject only to the provisos that he should not appropriate more than he could make use of, and that there should be 'enough, and as good left in common for others'.[13] The 'mixing' metaphor is usually interpreted to mean that whatever has been deliberately transformed by labour becomes the property of the labourer. This of course opens up the question of the extent of the material which should be considered to have been transformed by a particular piece of activity, but I leave this aside to concentrate on the principle underlying Locke's position.

It does not seem self-evident that if I own X, and mix X with Y, which is previously unowned, I thereby come to own Y. As Nozick points out himself, if I pour a tin of tomato juice that I own into the sea, so mixing my juice with the sea, we may conclude that I have lost the juice, rather than acquired a title to the ocean. Because my rights to X are alienable, it seems as plausible that I should lose these rights as that I should acquire new ones. In other cases, where the mixing of X and Y is reversible, I shall be thought to have a right to recover my X, but not to possess any Y.

---

[13] J. Locke, *Two Treatises of Government*, ed. P. Laslett (New York: Mentor, 1965), second treatise, ch. 5.

There is also a more fundamental difficulty with the mixing metaphor. As Waldron has pointed out, for the analogy with ordinary cases of mixing X with Y to go through, labour would have to appear in two separate guises, both as the activity of mixing and as the thing that is mixed. But this is impossible. 'We have ingredient and mixture but no mixing, or mixing and mixture but no ingredient. Either way, the ordinary notion of mixing seems quite inappropriate to the case that Locke is describing.'[14]

We must, therefore, regard the mixing metaphor as just that: a metaphor. Taken literally, it gives us no argument at all to show why the labourer should have a property right in the material on which he has laboured. We need instead to investigate what argument Locke might have been advancing under the guise of his metaphor. There are several possibilities, but the most plausible reconstruction, one for which there is some support in the text itself, is to make the justification of property rights one of desert.[15] Locke claims that God gave the world to the 'industrious and rational' and refers to the 'pains' which characteristically accompany labour. He also points out repeatedly that it is labour that adds almost all the value to produced items. The justification of appropriation is then that a person deserves to have those items which his toil and industry have produced, the products being a fitting reward for the effort expended and a compensation for the costs incurred. If this interpretation is followed, the original assertion that a man owns his body can be seen as a way of denying any prior obligations of justice which might interfere with the claim of desert.

This reconstruction strengthens Locke's argument in so far as it allows the theory to handle otherwise paradoxical cases, such as that in which two people independently and without prior agreement 'mix their labour' with some object. Thus suppose one man fells a tree and a second, coming across the fallen tree, fashions a

[14] J. Waldron, 'Two Worries about Mixing One's Labour', *Philosophical Quarterly*, 33(1983), 41.

[15] Olivecrona suggests an alternative view, according to which part of the labourer's personality is infused in the transformed object, so interference with the latter constitutes an assault on the person; see K. Olivecrona, 'Locke's Theory of Appropriation', *Philosophical Quarterly*, 24 (1974), 220–34. This looks to me like a somewhat Hegelian Locke, but note that the implications would be similar to those drawn below—viz. that transformers of *already owned* material would have an equally strong claim as first appropriators.

canoe out of it. The original formulation implies that both have absolute property rights in the transformed object, which is of course absurd. The reconstruction allows us to propose that in such a case the object should be shared between them in proportion to their respective deserts, or if that is not physically possible that one should compensate the other for the estimated value of his labour. On the other hand, the reconstructed version of the argument does not justify such extensive property rights as Locke intended. For performing useful labour one deserves a reward that accurately reflects the value of that labour, and this will not necessarily mean having the object that is actually produced. The value of the latter may be affected by extraneous factors having nothing to do with the producer's deserts. There is also a particular difficulty with property in land, which it was clearly Locke's main intention to justify. It is hard to see how full rights of ownership in land can be vindicated by reference to the deserts of the person who cultivates it—he would seem, at most, to deserve the right of use and the right to the product, as Mill among others saw.[16] So although acceptance of the desert principle creates a presumption that what a man has laboured on he should retain as his property, this presumption is fairly weak and may in many cases be overridden.[17]

However, the main upshot of our reconstruction of Locke's argument is that the proprietary theory of justice is radically undermined. For, first of all, in order to justify the principle of acquisition which the theory requires, we have had to introduce a more primitive notion of justice, namely justice as distribution according to desert. To explain the justice of an allocation of goods by saying that each party to it has rights of ownership which have been legitimately acquired cuts little ice if the principle of acquisition relies in turn on a conception of justice. Second, the proprietary theorist has to explain why the principle of desert applies only to the original acquisition of goods, and not to the distributions which subsequently arise through transfers. Once desert is admitted as a criterion of justice, there is no reason to refrain from using it to assess overall patterns of distribution.

[16] J. S. Mill, *Principles of Political Economy*, Book II, ch. II. 5–6 in *Collected Works of John Stuart Mill*, ed. J. M. Robson, vol. 11 (Toronto: University of Toronto Press, 1965).

[17] For a much fuller discussion, see L. Becker, *Property Rights: Philosophic Foundations* (London: Routledge and Kegan Paul, 1977), ch. 4.

Take a simple example. One year, A decides to work a previously uncultivated patch of ground and (granting for the moment Locke's conclusion in defiance of the difficulties raised above) thereby gains full rights of ownership in the land and its products. The following year A employs B to cultivate the same patch of land in the same manner, paying him a wage to do so. Provided this is voluntarily agreed between the parties, the proprietary theory rules that the transaction and the resulting distribution of property are both just.[18] However, from the point of view of desert, A and B have performed identical activities, and it seems that if ownership rights were the appropriate reward for A in the first year, they must also be for B in the second year. Assuming that B's wage is less valuable than A's rights of ownership, there is clearly an injustice.

Now the proprietary theorist might reply here that although the desert principle does imply a claim on B's part to the same rights of ownership as A, this claim is overridden by the greater good of stable and well-established property rights. He might, in other words, claim that both parties benefit in the long term from a system of property rights which allows A to retain ownership of the land notwithstanding B's claim of desert. This defence treats the stability of property rights as the primary good, and desert as a subsidiary principle used to justify the original allocation of rights but ignored thereafter.

The defence crumbles, however, once we recognize that many different systems of property rights are possible. There is no reason to think that any one of these systems is inherently more stable than the rest. Consider, for instance, a principle of acquisition which, instead of vesting full and perpetual rights in the first cultivator of land, gave the current cultivator at any moment rights of possession and usufruct and nothing more. Land that fell into disuse would then be available to the next cultivator wishing to use it. The merits of this alternative system

---

[18] It may be asked how B could come to accept such an arrangement unless someone (not necessarily A) had violated the second of Locke's limitations on appropriation and so left no land for B to cultivate himself. One may imagine, however, that B is simply misinformed about the availability of land, or else finds it too costly to go where land is available. There is furthermore the difficulty that if Locke's second condition is interpreted too strongly, it may exclude any permanent appropriation whatsoever—so leading, by a different route, to the conclusion I wish to draw. See on this Nozick, *Anarchy, State and Utopia*, 175–7.

are open to discussion (might it give insufficient incentive to improve the land?), but it cannot be thrown out on the grounds that it fails to establish stable rights; limited rights may be as well defined as unrestricted ones. Having recognized this, we cannot advocate a principle of acquisition by appeal to the notion of desert without paying attention to the overall pattern of distribution that results from applying that principle, looking ahead into the future as well as at the present. If it is a consequence of giving A certain rights as requital for his desert that later on an equally deserving B will be unable to have similar rights, then A cannot have deserved those rights. What is required instead is an allocation of rights to A that (within the bounds of practicality) allows B and others who come later to enjoy a similar allocation.[19]

The reason for this is that justice in such contexts is a comparative notion.[20] A person can justly claim a certain proportion of goods in relation to others rather than any absolute amount. Suppose a number of people work together to make a product which is sold on the market, the selling price being the total to be divided between them. No one will be entitled to any particular reward until all claims have been compared. Nobody can say that because he has performed such-and-such a task he deserves £200. He may, however, deserve twice what B deserves or two-thirds of what C deserves. Once relative deserts have been established in this manner, the actual amounts to be received by each person can be fixed, given the available total sum. No sense can be made of everyone in the group getting too high or too low a reward, unless a tacit comparison is made with some wider reference group. Not all applications of justice on the basis of desert are comparative in this sense. Each one of a series of punishments may be in proportion to the relative gravity of the crime that has been committed, and yet the whole series may be judged too severe or too lenient, on the basis of intuitions about the 'appropriate' punishment for particular crimes. Some of our judgements about good desert may likewise be non-comparative. A helpful act deserves some expression of gratitude, and we seem able to form rough judgements about the appropriate response to

[19] I comment later on the fact that property systems cannot be expected to match ideals of justice perfectly.

[20] The distinction between comparative and non-comparative senses of justice is made by J. Feinberg in 'Noncomparative Justice', *Philosophical Review*, 83 (1974), 297–338.

different kinds of help. Someone who saves me from drowning at some cost to himself deserves more than a brief word of thanks. But in cases where property or income is being allocated as a reward for social contribution, no such absolute guidelines are available and our judgements must be comparative in nature.

It follows that once desert is admitted in justification of a system of property, it must be used to assess the overall operation of that system and cannot drop out of sight after original appropriation has been vindicated. Of course other considerations, such as efficiency, may also be used in the assessment. But given that alternative systems of property rights are possible, an important factor in choosing between them is likely to be the extent to which the allocation of rights in each corresponds to our comparative judgements of individuals' deserts.[21]

V

I have been arguing so far that a Lockean account of property acquisition, in terms of the 'mixing' of labour with objects, needs filling out in some way, but that the most plausible reconstruction, making reference to desert, undermines the proprietary theory, since it is then no longer possible to separate questions about the original acquisition of property from questions about the distributive pattern that later results from these acquisitions. Put simply, a historical theory of justice cannot afford entry to the notion of desert at any point without losing its historical character. There is, however, another way in which a proprietary theorist might try to salvage his position, taking his inspiration now from Hume rather than from Locke. He might argue that it was a matter of comparative indifference which principles of acquisition, transfer, etc. were adopted, provided that these principles were generally acknowledged by the population at large. It is, in other words, a mistake to look for a justification of the particular principles which fill out the proprietary theory; what can be justified is the system of property as a whole, not its detailed rules. In this way questions about desert need never

---

[21] I put this precept into practice in ch. 6, where market socialist arrangements are defended as distributively just on grounds of desert.

enter the picture; the Lockean principle of acquisition might be accepted not as an ethically justified principle, but as a convention whose value is that it assigns property rights in a determinate way and that it commands general recognition.

To look briefly at this position as developed by Hume: having initially identified justice with respect for the rights of property, he went on to maintain that individuals' rights to property were established by five rules of acquisition plus a rule of transfer. The rules of acquisition were: present possession, occupation, prescription, accession, and succession. Although these rules would naturally suggest themselves to anyone who had to decide on the allocation of property rights, they were neither capable of, nor stood in need of, justification in the strict sense.

That there be a separation or distinction of possessions, and that this separation be steady and constant; this is absolutely required by the interests of society, and hence the origin of justice and property. What possessions are assigned to particular persons; this is, generally speaking, pretty indifferent; and is often determined by very frivolous views and considerations.[22]

This paradoxical assertion requires some defence. In Hume's case, this is provided by (a) an account of judgement which portrays moral judgements as being neither strictly rational nor wholly arbitrary, since they are governed by the 'natural' workings of the imagination; by (b) a relatively pessimistic view of human nature, which sees people as liable to be deflected from proper observation of the rules of justice by selfishness and partiality towards associates unless kept strictly to their habitual modes of behaviour. Against this background, it makes sense to argue that the rules of property should be rigidly maintained, even though their content is no more than conventional. But take away either of Hume's assumptions and difficulties follow. If the first assumption is removed, then *either* some rules of property have a rational justification, in which case we are back to a position formally similar to Locke's, *or* the choice of rules is completely arbitrary, in which case there is no reason to prefer Hume's rules

---

[22] David Hume, *An Enquiry Concerning the Principles of Morals* in *Enquiries Concerning Human Understanding and Concerning the Principles of Morals*, ed. L. A. Selby-Bigge (Oxford: Clarendon Press, 1975), 309. For a fuller discussion of Hume, see my *Philosophy and Ideology in Hume's Political Thought* (Oxford: Clarendon Press, 1981), ch. 3.

to any other set, and the proprietary theory turns into a defence of whatever property institutions happen to exist in a given society. If the second assumption is dropped, then we have to ask why we cannot reflect on the rules of property we now have and change them when other rules seem fairer or more useful. The utilitarian case for having fixed rules of property at any time does not extend to a case for having unchanging rules unless you accept Hume's view that disturbing habitual behaviour is likely to produce social breakdown.

Hume, therefore, offers us a way of salvaging the proprietary theory, but at a cost. The cost is accepting his scepticism and his pessimism, and thereby making the theory more openly conservative than it originally appeared. It becomes now a defence of any property system which is well established, in the sense that there is general acceptance of the rules of property belonging to it. It cannot, for instance, adjudicate as between capitalist and socialist modes of ownership. We are unlikely to be convinced by the theory because we have experience of rules of property being changed gradually and deliberately, partly because they were felt to conflict with widely shared conceptions of social justice, and without the disastrous consequences that Hume predicted.

VI

Hume forms a natural bridge between the proprietary theory of Nozick and the rather different account of justice offered by Hayek.[23] Hayek, who acknowledges a debt to Hume's account, abandons the conceptual link between justice and property—a rule of justice may in theory regulate any aspect of human behaviour—and he no longer attempts to discover 'natural' rules of acquisition.[24] Instead he argues that beneficial rules of justice

---

[23] See esp. F. A. Hayek, *Law, Legislation and Liberty, ii. The Mirage of Social Justice* (London: Routledge and Kegan Paul, 1976).

[24] The contrast between Nozick and Hayek in this respect can be seen plainly in the following passage from Hayek: 'As far as the great field of the law of property and contract are concerned, we must . . . above all beware of the error that the formulas "private property" and "freedom of contract" solve our problems. They are not adequate answers because their meaning is ambiguous. Our problems begin when we ask what ought to be the contents of property rights, what contracts should be enforceable, and how contracts should be interpreted'; (F. A. Hayek, *Individualism and Economic Order* (London: Routledge and Kegan Paul, 1949), 113).

may emerge historically even though they lack any explicit rationale. The focus is on the functions of rules of justice rather than on their origins. Hayek shares with Nozick, however, a firm belief that justice is a property of procedures rather than outcomes, and an equally firm hostility to the idea of social justice. To understand Hayek's view, we need to look briefly at his fundamental distinction between spontaneous orders and organizations.

A spontaneous order is one that has emerged as the unintended consequence of many individual acts. It has a rationale, because its manner of emergence ensures that it meets human needs, but this rationale is not usually evident to any of the participants. Organizations, on the other hand, are directed by human agency and planned to fulfil a particular purpose. Hayek believes that organizations are valuable as parts of a society, but that the attempt to make society itself into an organization should be strongly resisted. This view rests in part on a belief in individual liberty, in part on the theory that a spontaneous order allows individuals to benefit from knowledge which they do not themselves possess. Organizations can only use the knowledge that can be collected by a directing agency of limited size.

A spontaneous order must be protected by rules, but rules of a particular kind. They should be general in form (apply to an indefinite number of future instances), and negative in content (prohibit behaviour rather than require it). Only rules of this type, Hayek claims, can allow individuals with differing private ends to co-operate peacefully with one another. The rules surrounding any given order emerge over a period of time, and they are changed only gradually in response to perceived inconsistencies or inadequacies. Hayek refers to these rules as 'rules of just conduct', not because they conform to any prior notion of justice, but because they define just and unjust human action. Actions which violate the rules are unjust, all other actions just. It makes no sense to comment on the justice or injustice of general patterns of distribution which result from actions conforming to the rules. For instance, if there are rules governing the exchange of commodities, individuals may act justly in their transactions with one another, but it is pointless to comment on the distribution which results from a series of such exchanges. One can only speak of the injustice of an outcome, Hayek believes, when some individual has acted unjustly by breaking a social rule.

Notions of social or distributive justice can only have place, Hayek maintains, within an organization with a specific aim. Those who insist that the overall distribution of benefits in society should be just make the mistake of regarding a spontaneous order as if it were such an organization. In a spontaneous order we should not expect the pattern of distribution to meet any particular standard of justice—desert, need, etc—for it will depend on factors such as personal whim and good fortune, as well as on people's efforts and abilities. If we try to enforce such a pattern, we must create an authority which directly controls individuals' shares and which governs not by enforcing abstract rules, but by issuing specific commands to specific persons. Hayek links the urge towards social justice with the psychological attitudes characteristic of closed societies, and classifies socialist systems together with tribal and pre-capitalist societies in contrast to the spontaneous order that he variously describes as a 'catallaxy', an 'Open Society', and a 'Great Society'.

To support this account of justice, Hayek has to provide some account of how the rules that define 'just conduct' are selected. As we have seen, he makes no attempt to find an abstract basis for the rules in the manner of Nozick. Hayek's first move is to point out that questions about the validity of any particular rule only arise in the context of an entire legal system. The first criterion in choosing a rule is coherence: it must be possible for people in general to follow the rule without infringing the requirements of some other rule or rules. But clearly this criterion is indeterminate unless we have some way of arranging rules into a hierarchy. If rule X is inconsistent with rule Y (they require incompatible forms of behaviour), we can remove the inconsistency by altering either of the two rules. We must be guided in this choice by some further criterion lying beyond the rules themselves. What might we appeal to here?

At this point we reach a bifurcation in Hayek's thought. One answer, more prominent in the earlier writings than the later, is that the development of the whole legal system should be guided by an abstract goal, namely that it should provide 'the best chance for any member selected at random successfully to use his knowledge for his purposes'.[25] In other words, when forced by evidence of incoherence to modify the system of rules, we should

[25] *Studies in Philosophy, Politics and Economics* (London: Routledge and Kegan Paul, 1967), 163.

choose rules which, as far as we can tell, will maximize the chances of a randomly selected person to achieve his aims.

It is obviously not Hayek's intention that we should draw some particular name out of a hat and then set about creating the social order in which *that* person's chances are maximized. Rather, he intends us to look at the position of every member of society, and to aggregate their chances of achieving their purposes under different sets of rules. His criterion is equivalent to a form of utilitarianism in which the goal to be aimed at is not 'happiness' in any substantive sense, but the realization of individuals' purposes whatever these happen to be.[26] As such, it faces two difficulties that will be familiar from recent general debates on utilitarianism. The first is that the criterion may select an order in which, although many people have a good chance of achieving their aims, a significant minority find that their life-chances are very poor (indeed, this is a likely outcome of the libertarian order that Hayek himself favours). Since the aim of the criterion is to define 'rules of just conduct', it is surely an embarrassment that such an outcome is on the cards. Note also that the distribution of outcomes cannot be regarded as genuinely random, in the sense of the population who have to make the choice facing a genuine lottery which will determine their personal fates. When the legal system is altered, people often have a fair idea as to how a proposed alteration will bear on their life-chances, given their skills, personal needs, occupations, and so forth.

The second difficulty goes somewhat deeper. Hayek's criterion assumes that people's purposes can be taken as given, independently of the legal system. But in fact purposes are to some degree moulded by the prevailing legal system and its behavioural consequences. Take a simple case: should a law be introduced prohibiting racial discrimination in employment? In a society with a majority of racially prejudiced whites (who prefer segregated places of work), Hayek's criterion would indicate that no such law should be enacted. If, however, the law were introduced and successfully enforced over a period of time, the experience of multi-racial employment would very likely reduce prejudice to the point where the purpose-achievement criterion

[26] It is also, it hardly needs adding, a form of rule-utilitarianism in which the criterion in question is applied to the choice of rules but never directly to individuals' choices of action.

would rule in favour of the non-discrimination rule. Thus the criterion may in many cases be indeterminate, in the sense that it will decide in favour of rule X when rule X is in force and in favour of the contrary rule, rule Y, when rule Y is in force.[27]

But it is not in any case clear how seriously Hayek takes his criterion. There is another branch to his thinking that we must now explore.[28] In this vein he rejects the need for a criterion altogether. The selection of rules of just conduct is seen not as a matter of deliberate choice but as the product of a spontaneous process of evolution. This is clearly a conservative doctrine. We should accept as far as possible the rules that already exist, since these emerge from a process somehow akin to Darwinian natural selection. What process might this be?

The story Hayek tells runs somewhat as follows. Changes to the existing system of rules are first initiated by a few individuals who, in pursuit of their private aims, act on norms that deviate from the established set. These new rules are adopted by the groups to which the deviant individuals belong. In some cases the groups in question prosper and expand, in other cases the reverse happens. Eventually the rules favoured by the successful groups obtain widespread acceptance and take their place as laws. No one makes a conscious decision to adopt the new rules because of their good results; the legal change is a by-product of spontaneous processes.[29]

The difficulty with this story is that Hayek says nothing about the mechanism which is supposed to guarantee that a rule which is beneficial to one individual is also beneficial to his group, or that a rule which is beneficial to a group is also beneficial to the whole society of which it forms a part (the form of the problem is the same in both cases). There are, of course, rules, e.g. rules of

[27] The reverse is also possible, namely that experience of rule X creates purposes best served by rule Y and vice versa.

[28] There is perhaps even a third branch, stemming from his claim that a major virtue of spontaneous orders is their capacity to make use of knowledge that is diffused among many individuals. The preferred framework of rules would here be regarded as that which allows this diffused knowledge to be co-ordinated most successfully. But on close inspection this criterion turns out to be deeply obscure. How are we to judge whether one order co-ordinates knowledge better than another, if the knowledge in question is discrete and evanescent as Hayek claims? Either the criterion is meaningless, or it turns out to be a version of the quasi-utilitarian standard analysed above.

[29] See e.g. F. A. Hayek, *Law, Legislation and Liberty*, iii. *The Political Order of a Free People* (London: Routledge and Kegan Paul, 1979), 159–63.

personal hygiene, which benefit the person who follows them, no matter how many others do. In this case it is quite plausible to suppose that the rule will be diffused spontaneously. But for that very same reason, such rules rarely need to be coercively enforced.[30] Much more common are rules which benefit the person who follows them when only a small number of others do, but whose net effect when practised universally is zero or even negative. Clipping coins may be worthwhile when only a few people engage in it, but if the practice is widespread the currency is destroyed. A good business maxim is 'send out your invoices by first-class post and pay your bills by second-class post', but as soon as all companies follow this rule the effect is no different from prompt payment all round. For a group to be successful, therefore, it cannot simply adopt the behavioural rules of successful individuals. On the contrary, it must often suppress such rules in the interest of the group. The adoption of good rules requires conscious reflection on the general interests of the group, and cannot merely be a matter of spontaneous imitation.

Similar considerations apply at the group–society level. A group may prosper by adopting practices that would be disastrous for the society at large—the Mafia is an obvious example. Such groups are parasites: their success depends on the existence of other groups who follow a different set of rules. There is no reason why such groups should not expand by attracting outsiders. Indeed it may always be in the interests of individuals to join such a group, even though each successive addition to their membership imposes a net social loss.

To sum up, Hayek provides us with no mechanism to link successful behaviour at individual level to successful behaviour at collective level, and there is no plausible way of filling in this gap.[31] On the contrary, we should often expect the effects of spontaneous changes in individual behaviour to be socially damaging. It is therefore impossible to side-step the problem of finding a criterion to govern the choice of rules by appealing to evolutionary processes. There is no need to deny the validity of

[30] The exceptions will be cases in which individuals, through ignorance or through weakness of will, fail to pursue their own best interests.

[31] See the fuller discussion in V. Vanberg, 'Spontaneous Market Order and Social Rules: A Critical Examination of F. A. Hayek's Theory of Cultural Evolution', *Economics and Philosophy*, 2 (1986), 75–100.

Hayek's claim that legal systems are best changed incrementally as new evidence comes to light, rather than reconstructed in one fell swoop. But incremental change may itself be guided by general criteria—and indeed must be if we share Hayek's wish to move society in a libertarian direction. This point is worth underlining. In adopting an evolutionary approach, Hayek is in constant danger of falling into a relativistic morass. The evolutionary account is introduced to defend the rules of liberal societies against radical attack, but in making this defence Hayek inadvertently justifies any system of rules which has developed over time, no matter what its content. His defence of gradualism would count as much against attempts to liberalize a state socialist system (e.g. the USSR) as against attempts to socialize a liberal society, since it can plausibly be maintained that the rules currently operating in the socialist systems are the outcome of a spontaneous process of evolution.[32] As noted above, Hayek's theory of justice, read in this way, appears, like Hume's, as a conservative theory whose connection with a liberal social order is far more tangential than he supposes.

VII

We have now completed our survey of procedural accounts of justice. Neither the proprietary theory of Nozick nor the evolutionary theory of Hayek stands up to scrutiny. Nozick's theory relies on an undefended conception of property and an undefended account of acquisition. Supplying the necessary defences means stepping beyond the procedural account and importing substantive criteria. Hayek faces the problem of choosing between rules in a non-arbitrary way. On the one hand, he offers an unsatisfactory, quasi-utilitarian criterion; on the other, he rests his argument on the supposedly benign effects of evolutionary processes. Once again, his theory can only be rendered

---

[32] The aim of the leaders of the Russian Revolution was undoubtedly to create a society in which all social processes were subject to deliberate planning. It is clear, however, that this aim has been systematically frustrated, and to a very great extent the rules that now prevail represent an evolutionary adaptation to economic conditions, popular beliefs and so forth. My point is that Hayek has given us no reason to view liberal societies, but not socialist societies, as products of 'genuine' evolution.

coherent by bringing in substantive criteria to guide the choice of rules. This brings us back directly to the issue of social justice, and the libertarian arguments against that concept.

These arguments can be reduced essentially to three. First, the very idea of social justice assumes that some agency can be held responsible for the distribution of benefits in society, whereas (in a market order especially) this distribution in fact arises as the unintended consequence of the activities of many individuals, each pursuing his own private aims. Second, the quest for social justice involves replacing a market economy with a stultifying bureaucracy which tries, albeit unsuccessfully, to control the flow of resources to and from individuals so that a particular distributive pattern is established. Third, maintaining this pattern over time also involves fundamental interference with personal freedom, in so far as individuals must be prevented from doing as they wish with the resources allotted to them.

How valid are these arguments? It is obviously nonsensical to treat the distribution of resources in society as though it were the handiwork of some Grand Distributor who intended to bring about the precise allocation that results. At the same time, it is equally evident that the distribution is powerfully affected by major social institutions, and that these institutions are themselves open to political modification. We have seen this already in the case of property rights. Which rights individuals acquire in the objects they own, and how these rights are acquired and transferred, plays a major part in determining the allocation of resources. So does the tax system. So do the rules which determine the validity of contracts, including especially contracts between enterprises and their employees. If there is a welfare system, it makes a big difference how it is financed and how entitlements to benefit are established. This list could be extended almost indefinitely. In appealing to social justice, we are simply claiming that any proposed institutional structure (including the one that now exists) ought to be assessed in terms of its likely distributive outcomes, measured by whatever criteria (desert, need, and so forth) commend themselves to us. There is no implication that these criteria should be applied directly to each isolated transaction or to every individual holding. The criteria are used to govern the choice of institutions—and, as we have seen throughout this chapter, there is no way of avoiding such a choice. There are no God-given rules of property or taxation. The advocate of social justice does openly what the libertarian does covertly, namely, selects those institutions which he thinks most likely to lead to the general outcome he favours.

What of the second charge, that the pursuit of social justice leads inevitably to bureaucratic control? At this point it remains an open question whether the institutional structure required by social justice includes an untrammelled market, a market controlled in certain respects, or no market at all. We have yet to specify our preferred criteria of distributive justice, and (equally important) to investigate empirically what institutional framework they require. Part of this task will be carried out in Chapter 6, and I shall suggest that the result is more favourable to markets than the libertarian argument implies—albeit not necessarily more favourable to the libertarian *version* of the market economy. It may also be worth noting that, historically, it was long argued that considerations of distributive justice pointed in favour of a market economy. If this is no longer so widely assumed, it may be because our criteria of justice have changed, or because our understanding of the workings of markets has changed, or both. There is nothing intrinsic to the notion of social justice itself which prejudices the conclusion in favour of bureaucracy.

We come finally to the third claim, summed up in Nozick's charge that 'no end-state principle or distributional patterned principle of justice can be continuously realized without continuous interference with people's lives'.[33] What Nozick has in mind is that voluntary transfers between individuals who are entitled to their holdings may upset the distribution that justice requires, so that all such transfers must be prohibited in the name of justice. The first point to make in reply is that social justice has to do with the way that resources are allocated by the major institutions, and not directly with how these resources are used by their recipients. We may decide that medicine should be made freely available on grounds of need, but it does not follow that each person must be forced to consume the medication to which he is entitled. Does this immunity extend to transfers? In principle, no, because rights of transfer are part of the institution

[33] Nozick, *Anarchy, State and Utopia*, 163.

of property, whose shape is to be decided on grounds of distributive justice. Which rights we choose to include will depend on an estimate of their likely distributive consequences. Most legal systems draw a distinction between *inter vivos* transfers and inheritance, presumably on the grounds that lifetime gifts tend to be reciprocated (and therefore have little overall effect on the pattern of distribution) whereas inheritance is likely to produce a large one-way transfer in favour of certain selected individuals. I do not think that rules limiting the right of inheritance (or taxing bequests) can be said to constitute 'continuous interference with people's lives'. Nozick's charge rests once again on the assumption that distributive justice must imply the precise calculation of individual shares by some directing agency, an assumption that we have seen to be radically misconceived.

My aim in this chapter has been to destroy the view that procedural justice can stand independently as an alternative to social or distributive justice. Put simply, we choose our procedures in the light of the general distributive outcomes that we wish to see realized. It does not follow that there is no such thing as procedural justice.[34] Once procedures are established (e.g. methods for establishing property rights or for allocating resources to the needy), people come to have fair claims under them, and it is important to honour those claims. In concrete cases there may be clashes between the fairness of the procedure and the justice of the outcome—that is, a procedure which is generally well-designed to produce a certain outcome may fail to do so on one particular occasion. For various reasons we may wish to give priority to procedural justice in such cases. The distributive outcome will therefore not match up exactly to our substantive criteria of justice, but this in no way prevents us from reviewing our procedures periodically to see whether they cannot be improved. Once we get away from the belief that certain

---

[34] Nor do I want to suggest that the justice of procedures can be reduced entirely to the justice of their prospective outcomes; procedures may have intrinsic qualities that we find commendable independently of their likely results. In evaluating social institutions, however, we are characteristically faced with a choice between various alternative practices each of which meets our criteria of procedural fairness; the choice is underdetermined unless we employ substantive criteria to assess their likely outcomes. There is a good discussion of the relationship between procedural justice and the justice of outcomes in A. Weale, 'Procedural Fairness and Rationing the Social Services' in N. Timms (ed.), *Social Welfare: Why and How?* (London: Routledge and Kegan Paul, 1980).

procedures are intrinsically just (Nozick's view), or must be accepted on evolutionary grounds (Hayek's view), we can arrive at a better understanding of the respective roles of distributive and procedural criteria in our thinking about justice.

3

MARKET NEUTRALITY

I

Much liberal thinking in recent years has been dominated by the principle of *neutrality*. According to this principle, a defensible social order must aim to deal impartially or even-handedly with the aspirations of all its members. It is not difficult to understand the appeal of such an idea. Liberalism begins from a premiss of individual diversity: each person has his own unique conception of what it is that makes life worth living, and is therefore entitled to pursue that conception to the best of his ability. A natural corollary is that social institutions should form a neutral arena in which each conception is given an equal chance of success.

If we want to convert this intuitive derivation into something more rigorous, there seem broadly two ways to set about it. The first route relies on cognitive scepticism. Conceptions of the good life are more debatable than the principles of justice that should govern the arrangements of society. Either we can say nothing at all about the relative merits of different conceptions of the good, or what we can say is not certain enough to justify building it in to the basic structure of society. This is summed up in Rawls's phrase 'the priority of the right over the good'. We can produce valid arguments in favour of principles of justice prior to resolving the contest between different conceptions of the good.

The second route makes appeal to the idea of respect for persons. Respecting a person involves, among other things, respecting the choice he has made about which plan of life to pursue, even if you happen to disagree with it. Institutional arrangements which favour some conceptions of the good at the expense of others show disrespect for all those who have opted for the disadvantaged conceptions.[1]

[1] For this argument, see A. Weale, 'Toleration, Individual Differences and Respect for Persons', in J. Horton and S. Mendus (eds.), *Aspects of Toleration* (London: Methuen, 1985).

By one or other of these routes, then, liberals are drawn towards the idea of neutrality as a regulatory principle for social institutions. For the purposes of this chapter, I assume that the neutrality principle captures an important element in our social thinking, one that socialists too will want to endorse. I do not in fact think that the principle can be accepted without reservation. Even liberals, I believe, must recognize some limits on the range of conceptions of the good life that qualify for impartial treatment under the principle. Later in the book, I argue that democratic socialists must abandon aspirations to neutrality at the point where private conceptions of the good begin to undermine the public culture necessary to a democracy. Within these limits, none the less, the principle has considerable attractions, given a society that is culturally pluralistic and at least formally egalitarian. It therefore seems worth looking more closely at its meaning and practical implications. In particular, I want to ask whether it vindicates a libertarian, market-centred version of liberalism, or something else.

In this connection it is worth noting that liberals themselves disagree sharply about the implications of the neutrality principle. Rawls,[2] Ackerman,[3] Dworkin, and Nozick are all plausibly regarded as neutralist liberals, but only Nozick believes that the principle points unequivocally in the direction of a minimal state.[4] Dworkin is equally confident that the principle would not only allow, but require, extensive redistribution in order to give unequally endowed people an equal share of those resources needed to further their respective conceptions of the good.[5] Such conflicts of opinion make clarification of the neutrality principle a matter of some urgency.

The particular libertarian claim that I want to examine holds that the market itself is a neutral device, giving it a privileged place in an ethically defensible social order; the contrast here is with the state which, it is claimed, characteristically acts in a non-neutral way. The market is neutral first of all as a means of providing

---

[2] J. Rawls, *A Theory of Justice* (Cambridge, Mass: Harvard University Press, 1971); id., 'Fairness to Goodness', *Philosophical Review*, 84 (1975), 536–54.

[3] B. Ackerman, *Social Justice in the Liberal State* (New Haven: Yale University Press, 1980).

[4] R. Nozick, *Anarchy, State and Utopia* (Oxford: Blackwell, 1974), esp. 271–3.

[5] R. Dworkin, 'Liberalism', in S. Hampshire (ed.), *Public and Private Morality* (Cambridge: Cambridge University Press, 1978).

goods and services to consumers: it circumvents judgements about the intrinsic goodness or badness of what is supplied. But it is also neutral with respect to the relationships that people choose to establish for the purpose of carrying on economic activity. It is left to each person to decide how to make use of the proprietary and contractual rights that the general rules of a free market provide. People may choose to associate in capitalist forms of organization, in which case those who become owners of capital assume a greater degree of risk and responsibility and stand to gain correspondingly higher rewards, or they may choose, say, co-operative forms, where groups of producers supply their own capital and share the profits between them. If capitalist forms are overwhelmingly favoured, as the historical evidence shows, this reveals something about most people's orders of preference. Either the bulk of the population actively wish to avoid the risks and anxieties of capital ownership, and so willingly transfer these responsibilities to the few willing to bear them; or the efficiency of the capitalist firm is such that it can pay wages high enough to compensate the work force for their loss of autonomy in comparison with the co-operative alternative.

Nozick, for example, argues that if workers' control of industry is considered a sufficiently important goal by any group of people, they ought to be prepared to take lower wages in order to join a worker-controlled enterprise.[6] The financial sacrifice would be an accurate measure of the value they find in working in a democratic environment. So even if co-operatives are less efficient as economic units than capitalist firms, they will still be established by those with the appropriate preference schedules. In this way the market responds to desires for different modes of economic organization as accurately as it does to tastes for different varieties of ice-cream. If, by contrast, a particular pattern of association were to be outlawed, as occurs in a socialist system which prohibits conventional capitalist–worker relationships, the preferences of at least some people would be ignored in the social calculus. This would not only be inefficient, but would discriminate between conceptions of the good in a way that the neutral market mechanism avoids.

This argument, if successful, would clearly have a devastating impact on the case for market socialism, for it implies that

[6] Nozick, *Anarchy, State and Utopia*, 250–3.

capitalism will spontaneously transform itself into a co-operative economy in so far as people prefer to work in co-operatives. It would then be hard to mount a case for socialist legislation, either to outlaw capitalist relations or more modestly to favour co-operative ones, unless one were willing to ignore expressed preferences in favour of some notion of 'real interests'. Since this issue is crucial to the general argument of the book, I shall examine it in some detail later on. But first we must attempt to provide an analysis of the neutrality principle itself. What does it mean to say that an institutional set-up is neutral as between different conceptions of the good life?

II

The idea of neutrality is, in fact, a fairly complex one. It has several dimensions, on each of which alternative interpretations are possible.[7] I shall restrict my attention here to two of these dimensions. First, does the idea of neutrality apply to the *reasons* that lie behind institutions or policies, or does it apply to the *effects* of those institutions or policies? Second, if we conclude that the idea applies to the outcomes of practices rather than the reasons that inform them, what is it for an institution or policy to bear neutrally on different people's conceptions of the good? Does it mean that all conceptions have an equal chance of being realized a priori, or more strongly that everyone is *in fact* equally successful in realizing his conception? Or is there some third criterion that best captures our understanding of neutrality?

Nozick offers us a reason-dependent conception of neutrality. Observing that a prohibition on rape might be represented as

---

[7] See J. Raz, *The Morality of Freedom* (Oxford: Clarendon Press, 1986), ch. 5. In particular, Raz draws attention to the contrast between neutrality as between the conceptions of the good that people actually hold, and a more extended sense of neutrality that would also embrace the likelihood of a person embracing one conception of the good rather than another. This is an important contrast. In the present discussion, I take people's conceptions of the good as given, and examine how different institutional frameworks might help or hinder their realization. It would also be possible to ask how these different frameworks affect the chances that particular conceptions will be adopted. Thus I forgo any criticism of the market on the grounds that it induces people to adopt (e.g.) commodity-based conceptions of the good, even though historically arguments of this kind have been very popular. I try to reply to libertarians on terms that they are most likely to accept.

non-neutral between potential rapists and others, he responds that the prohibition has an independent justification. Its rationale is not to make it relatively more difficult for would-be rapists to pursue their conception of the good, rather it is founded on an independent principle concerning the value of bodily integrity. Policies such as economic redistribution, by contrast, are directly intended to benefit some people at the expense of others.

But this account of neutrality is open to serious objections. To begin with, there may be difficulties, in any concrete case, in deciding what the effective rationale of an institution or policy is. It is notoriously the case that many practices are capable of being justified from different points of view. Some of these justifications will offend against the neutrality principle, others won't. The banning of public displays of pornography, for instance, might be defended on the grounds that people have a right not to have their sensibilities offended in public places (which in Nozick's terms would presumably count as an independent justification); or alternatively on grounds having to do with the inherent harmfulness of viewing pornography (which relies on a particular conception of the good, or, to be more precise, a conception of the bad). Thus it would often be difficult, using the reason-related conception of neutrality, to decide whether a particular rule or practice offended against the neutrality principle or not.

This has the further implication that such a conception of neutrality is only weakly linked to a liberal social order. A liberal order may be compatible with the neutrality principle, but so may many others, provided only that their justifying theories are of a permissible sort. It is not difficult, for instance, to think of justifications for conservatism or socialism that don't rely on the validity of particular conceptions of the good. Are there any political standpoints that can *only* be vindicated by appeal to such conceptions of the good? Perhaps there are: but it seems clear that the reason-related understanding of neutrality is not going to eliminate many possibilities.

We may also, moreover, challenge the reason-related conception directly. Why is it sufficient for an institution or policy to count as neutral that it has not been adopted *because* it favours some particular conception of the good? More generally, in order to be neutral, is it sufficient that one avoids being deliberately non-neutral?[8] I don't think so. Take the games analogy, which almost unavoidably presents itself in discussions of neutrality. The rules of a game are neutral when they don't favour any particular player or team: when they neither enhance nor diminish any player's or team's chance of winning. (Quite how this condition is to be interpreted has yet to be decided; I rely for the moment on an intuitive grasp of what it means to be neutral.) Now clearly the worst breach of neutrality is to rig the rules in order to advantage a particular competitor—say by a handicapping system that favours a particular runner. But, I want to argue, it also offends against neutrality to adopt a rule for some independent reason (say, that it will enhance the pleasure of spectators) in circumstances where it is clear that this will differentially affect the fortunes of participants. Suppose, for instance, that before the next Test series between England and the West Indies, a rule is adopted restricting the number of fast bowlers in each side to two.[9] I think this would clearly be a non-neutral rule, even if it were adopted solely on the grounds that it would make the matches more attractive to spectators.

Instead of defining neutrality in terms of the reasons underlying institutions or practices, therefore, I shall say that an institution or practice is neutral when, as far as can reasonably be foreseen, it does not favour any particular conception of the good at the expense of others. Such a definition has immediate implications for the neutrality of markets. Libertarians would wish to defend markets on the grounds that their outcomes are unplanned, so that market institutions are by definition neutral even if it turns out that some conceptions of the good are more easily realized under their aegis than others. Our definition nullifies such a defence. We are now obliged to look at the probable impact of markets on the realization of different conceptions of the good, and we will only judge markets to be neutral if all conceptions are equally favoured.

But we have yet to state more precisely what it means for conceptions of the good to have an equal chance of success. A very strong interpretation of neutrality would hold that an institu-

---

[8] Cf. ibid. 114–16.

[9] In case the point of this example should become obscure (which happily it might), I should explain that the paragraph was written in the aftermath of a series in which the English team was routed by a West Indies side containing four devastating pace bowlers.

tional framework was neutral if and only if people were all equally successful at realizing their conceptions of the good under its auspices. In other words, supposing for the sake of simplicity that people's success at realizing their chosen conceptions could be calibrated on a scale from 0 to 1, a framework would be neutral if and only if everyone ended up at, say, 0.7 on their own scale.

I believe this interpretation is too strong. A person's success at realizing his plan of life depends on factors other than the institutional framework within which he has to operate. It depends on his own capacities, other people's dispositions, and the material costs of carrying out the plan. Take the case of a mountaineer whose crowning achievement would be to conquer Everest. Whether he succeeds in doing so must depend on his own climbing abilities, the willingness and capacity of other people to collaborate with him in the attempt, the cost of the equipment he needs, and so on. His material costs will depend in turn on the scarcity of the raw materials needed to produce the equipment, the labour involved in making it, etc. Let us use 'natural factors' as a general label for all non-institutional factors such as these that bear on a person's success in realizing his conception of the good. The strong interpretation of neutrality would require a neutral framework to compensate fully for the effects of natural factors. If I have a conception that is cheap and easy to realize, and you have one that is difficult and expensive, it would require that many more resources should be allocated to you in order that we both end up with the same level of achievement.

This is an unacceptable implication. It seems quite reasonable that natural factors such as personal abilities and the physically determined costs of a project should influence levels of achievement. The games analogy may again help to make the point: a neutral set of rules is one under which the outcome of the game depends on the skills and abilities of the participants, and not one under which the outcome is always tied. Neutrality should allow the result to be affected by, say, skill at bowling, but not by extraneous factors such as a pitch which favours the team whose bowlers are of a certain type. Of course this depends on drawing a line between factors that are extraneous and those that are relevant. In the games context this is relatively easy to do, since there is usually sufficient consensus on the skills and abilities that games are meant to exhibit. Rather different considerations apply if we are trying to establish that a social arrangement is neutral. Here our drawing of the line depends on what we place within the compass of individual responsibility and what we see as a matter for collective determination. For instance, we find it acceptable that those with expensive tastes should be less successful, on the whole, in realizing their conception of the good than those with cheap tastes. That is because we see people's tastes as, so to speak, up to them. If someone is not doing well, with existing resources, in his quest for champagne, then it is up to him to decide whether to cultivate a taste for bitter instead. Plainly this is a challengeable view. The line between natural factors and the practices to which the neutrality principle applies can be drawn in different places.[10] My hunch, however, is that all of us will want to draw the line somewhere, and this is what knocks out the strong version of the neutrality principle. For strong neutrality implies that *no* natural factors shall be allowed to affect people's success at realizing their conceptions of the good; everyone must be equally successful, no matter what.

It is easy enough to show that, in terms of the strong principle, markets are non-neutral. For markets minimally involve assigning people rights over resources which they are then able to use according to their preferences. However that assignment is made, it must have a certain stability; there may be tax rules designed, for instance, to bound the inequality of the resource distribution as it changes over time, but these must be general and their incidence predictable. But then if we add to this the uncontestable fact that people's conceptions of the good vary and develop, we cannot expect a market-based resource allocation to produce a strongly neutral outcome. Even if at time t we juggle with the resource allocation so that those with, for instance, expensive tastes are fully compensated with extra resources, changes of taste between t and $t+1$ will make it very unlikely indeed that at

[10] For instance Dworkin requires a neutral state to compensate for inequalities in personal talent, but not for differences in taste, whereas I would include factors of both sorts under the rubric of natural factors. It is not easy to see how such disagreements should be resolved. In saying that we place such factors 'within the compass of individual responsibility', I don't mean to imply that people are always in a position to make deliberate choices about them: they may be as little able to do so with their tastes as with their talents.

$t+1$ everyone will still be achieving their conception of the good with equal success.[11]

Since I have already rejected the strong neutrality principle, this result is not itself a particularly interesting one. But it does help to clear the ground for what I hope is a more interesting thesis. To summarize so far: according to Nozick's weak, reason-related conception of neutrality, markets are clearly neutral, as are other undesigned institutions. According to the very strong neutrality principle, which demands equal success in achieving conceptions of the good, markets are clearly non-neutral—but again, so are most institutions that one might consider. In between these two views of neutrality there is a third, which I think is interesting and defensible. I shall try to show that on this third interpretation markets have a *qualified* neutrality; they are neutral as between certain conceptions of the good, but not as between all those we should wish to consider under the scope of the neutrality principle.

What I have been doing so far is to guard this argument pre-emptively against a certain quick, libertarian reply. The libertarian, when faced with some thesis about the non-neutrality, or limited neutrality, of markets, is apt to reply as follows:[12] 'If you mean by neutrality, equal success at realizing conceptions of the good, who could possibly suppose that markets are neutral? *Of course* beer-drinkers will generally fare better than champagne-drinkers. No-one claims that markets are neutral in *that* sense. They are neutral, though, in the sense that no-one intends the champagne-drinkers to fare worse. It just happens that they do.' The libertarian, in other words, kicks out the very strong interpretation of neutrality and offers us the weak interpretation as the only alternative. He thinks that all complaints about the non-neutrality of markets are equivalent to the observation that beer-drinkers fare better than champagne-drinkers.

But, as I have suggested, there is a third interpretation of neutrality. On this interpretation, an institutional framework is

---

[11] 'Very unlikely' rather than 'impossible' because we might conceive of circumstances in which people's changes of tastes were always exactly matched by their productive abilities: i.e. those who developed more expensive tastes were all and only those who had the talents to acquire more resources. But it would be fantastic to count on this happening.

[12] See e.g. David Gordon's reply to my argument about the disadvantaged position of co-operatives in capitalist economies in 'Miller on Market Neutrality, Co-operatives and Libertarianism', *British Journal of Political Science*, 13 (1983), 125–8.

neutral when, under its auspices, people's success at realizing their conceptions of the good depends only on natural (i.e. pre-institutional) factors. I have suggested what such factors might consist in: personal tastes (both theirs and other people's), personal abilities, and physical facts about the world, such as the comparative availability of different raw materials. On this interpretation, markets are indeed neutral as between beer-drinkers and champagne-drinkers, notwithstanding the fact that beer-drinkers are generally more successful in realizing their conception of the good. For this greater success can be attributed to the fact that they happen to have a taste which is cheaper to satisfy, and this in turn because there is more land on which to grow hops and barley than Pinot Noir grapes and/or because there is more labour involved in the making of champagne and/or because fewer people share their preference for beer.

What assumptions lie behind this claim about market neutrality? One key assumption is that people's success at realizing their conceptions of the good depends on their possession of commodities that can be privately owned and exchanged for other commodities. From this perspective, the virtue of markets is that, provided the initial distribution of resources is fair, processes of exchange will bring it about that everyone's final holdings are a true reflection of natural factors judged to be relevant e.g., the labour cost of producing an item. Indeed, it may be argued, market exchange is the only reliable way to bring this about.[13] Of course this is to assume that each person acts rationally, that markets are fully competitive and so forth. But I want to postpone questions of that sort until Part II of the book. Here I want to look instead at what happens if we introduce the idea that conceptions of the good may require conditions other than the private possession of commodities.

There are a number of possibilities to be considered here. First, and probably most familiar, are the standard cases of public goods—material benefits whose nature is such that they cannot be provided for any one person without simultaneously being provided for a substantial number of others (in the extreme case, for all members of the society in question). An example would be the benefit of living in a neighbourhood in which the streets are

---

[13] See Dworkin, 'Liberalism', 130–2.

clean, well paved, and lined with trees. Second, there are goods which consist in enjoying a certain kind of relationship with one's fellows. Again these can be more limited in scope—say, working in a democratically run enterprise—or more general—say, living in a society in which people generally behave courteously towards one another. Third, a conception of the good might involve living up to certain personal principles—e.g. of honesty, or non-sexism.

I am not suggesting that anyone's conception of the good is likely to be exhausted by these non-commodity-based elements. While not impossible, this would be an extreme case. It is much more likely that a person's idea of what makes life worth living will be complex, including the possession of certain commodities but also public, relational, and principled goods, as identified above. Indeed, it is precisely this complexity that poses problems for claims about market neutrality. People need to enter the market to earn income and to obtain commodities, but, as we shall see, this may in itself hinder their pursuit of the other categories of good.

How might a libertarian respond to the existence of non-commodity-based conceptions of the good? He might argue that market institutions, although not themselves catering for conceptions of the good of this kind, provide space in which these conceptions can be pursued in other ways—in implicit contrast to political institutions which, it is said, impose one particular version of the good life on everyone. Markets may not give people clean streets with trees, but they don't prevent people forming voluntary associations to provide them. I examine a particular argument of this kind at some length in the following chapter. Here I want to investigate a second possible response. This holds that markets can indeed cater for preferences that are not commodity-based, at least on condition that these can be satisfied in micro-environments. If your conception of the good involves non-hierarchical work relations, or religious orthodoxy, or sexual equality, you can contract into a private association that supplies these goods, with the associations themselves being linked by a market framework.[14] Of course this will not satisfy people whose desire is for *overall* religious orthodoxy, etc. But, as I shall suggest later, neutralist liberals will in any case wish to discount conceptions of the good whose realization would by definition breach the

[14] See e.g. Nozick, *Anarchy, State and Utopia*, ch. 10.

neutrality principle. So it looks as though the libertarian has a plausible case for counting out imperialistic conceptions such as these, and restricting his argument to those that can be realized on a small scale by a group of like-minded persons.

For reasons already given, I want to examine this argument as it applies to workers' co-operatives competing in an open market with capitalist enterprises. The claim to be tested is that the possibility of forming co-operatives shows that the market can accommodate desires for democratic control of the work place and the other benefits that co-operatives claim to provide. A person joining such an enterprise may have to lower his material standard of living, but this is simply the normal trade-off between different elements in a conception of the good. Against this, I will show that the exigencies of market competition are likely to pose a stark choice between economic survival and the non-material benefits of co-operation. Demonstrating this requires a short excursion into the economics of workers' co-operatives.[15]

III

A co-operative is taken to be a productive unit democratically controlled on a one person–one vote basis by everyone who works in it. Its capital may be owned, individually or collectively, by the members or leased from an outside agency, but in any case carries no rights of control. The profits of the co-operative are shared by the members according to an agreed schedule and constitute their income. How will the economic behaviour of such a unit compare with the behaviour of a technologically identical firm owned and managed on conventional capitalist lines?

To simplify the analysis, I begin by assuming that capitalists and co-operators are both interested merely in maximizing their material return from the enterprise (although later I ask what difference it makes if we attribute non-economic goals to the co-

---

[15] The analysis is presented informally and draws upon the rapidly growing body of literature on the economics of co-operatives. Readers wishing for a more formal treatment should begin by consulting the following: J. Vanek, *The General Theory of Labor-Managed Market Economies* (Ithaca: Cornell University Press, 1970); J. E. Meade, 'The Theory of Labour-Managed Firms and Profit Sharing', *Economic Journal*, 82 (1972), 402–28; A. Steinherr, 'The Labour-Managed Economy: A Survey of the Economics Literature', *Annals of Public and Co-operative Economy*, 40 (1978), 129–48; A. Clayre, (ed.), *The Political Economy of Co-operation and Participation* (Oxford: Oxford University Press, 1980).

operators). On this assumption, the capitalist's aim will be profit maximization. He will hire labour and invest capital whenever marginal return exceeds marginal cost; that is, whenever an extra labourer yields more in profit than he receives in wages, and whenever a pound invested yields more than a pound in return. This will have to be modified slightly to take account of time—a pound today being worth more than a pound in a year's time—but with this modification the assumption holds. The capitalist's wealth and the enterprise's value are one and the same, so maximizing the latter means maximizing the former.[16]

On the same assumption, the co-operative's goal is not profit maximization but maximization of income per worker.[17] Its members have no interest in increasing the overall wealth of the co-operative except in so far as this is reflected in increasing income for them. Now that does not mean that they will wish to maximize income in any one time period, say the current year; their interest is to maximize their total earnings from the co-operative. Like the capitalist, they will need to include a time discount, to reflect the lesser value of a pound a year hence; unlike him, however, they will also need to consider how long they are likely to belong to the co-operative, and how much capital they will be able to take out if they choose to leave. These factors will determine how calculations of potential income are made.

What difference does the co-operative's different maximand (income per worker) make to its behaviour? The effect can be seen easily if we compare a capitalist firm and an otherwise identical co-operative deciding whether to take on an additional worker, given a fixed quantity of capital and a fixed price for the product to be made. The capitalist, as we have seen, will hire

---

[16] I ignore here the complications that are introduced if the firm's owner, instead of managing the firm himself, employs a hired manager, whose own goal of income maximization is potentially in conflict with the owner's. For analysis of this conflict, see E. G. Furubotn and S. Pejovich (eds.), *The Economics of Property Rights* (Cambridge, Mass.: Ballinger, 1974), esp. chs. 15, 22.

[17] This is a fairly standard assumption in the economic literature. See Benjamin Ward, 'The Firm in Illyria: Market Syndicalism', *American Economic Review*, 48 (1958), 566–89; Vanek, *General Theory*; Meade, 'Theory of Labour-Managed Firms'; P. Wiles, *Economic Institutions Compared* (Oxford: Blackwell, 1977), ch. 4. It has, however, been challenged by Furubotn who argues that a long-run analysis needs to take account of the possible effects of an income-maximizing policy on the size and composition of the co-operative's membership. See E. G. Furubotn, 'The Long Run Analysis of the Labor Managed Firm: An Alternative Interpretation', *American Economic Review*, 66 (1976), 104–23.

whenever marginal return exceeds marginal cost. If the employee can be hired for £50 and makes £51 profit for the enterprise, he will be taken on. In the case of the co-operative the decision will depend on the impact of the new hiring on the incomes already being paid to members. Since the new hand can only be taken on as a full member (if the co-operative is not to degenerate into a joint-stock company), he must be paid according to a uniform income schedule. So the hiring decision depends on whether the profit he can create raises or lowers the existing schedule. Suppose for simplicity's sake that income is distributed equally, and that the rate currently paid is £55, then the extra worker will not be hired, since to do so would reduce incomes all round. One can see immediately the temptation to take on this person as a non-member for £50, which *ex hypothesi* he is willing to accept. The basic logic of hiring is likely to create self-destructive pressures in the co-operative.

We can infer from this that, *ceteris paribus*, co-operatives which remain as such will be smaller than capitalist firms. They will grow so long as there are economies of scale such that adding extra workers increases the productivity of those already in the partnership; whereas capitalist firms will grow beyond this point so long as the net marginal return remains positive. However, the biggest difference concerns not hiring but investment. This, I shall argue, is the Achilles' heel of co-operatives competing in the market with capitalist enterprises.

Consider a capitalist firm and a co-operative at the end of a time period when a net profit has been made after agreed wages have been paid out. Should the profit be consumed or reinvested? In the case of the capitalist I have postulated that investment will occur whenever the expected return is greater than the capitalist's discount for time. How the co-operative will behave depends on the structure of ownership which it has established. At one extreme the capital may be held as a collective asset with no individual having any claim to withdraw it; at the other, individual shares may be identified, with rules governing the crediting of accounts and the withdrawal of assets. There are infinitely many possibilities in between, but let us consider the two extreme cases.[18]

---

[18] Some partisans of workers' co-operatives do in fact favour mixed solutions, with assets being held partly individually and partly collectively. See e.g. R. Oakeshott, *The Case*

If assets are held collectively, then a pound invested in the co-operative is, from the point of view of any individual member, irrecoverable. Consequently he will only support the investment if he thinks that the income it will produce for him outweighs the immediate loss of revenue. As we have seen, he needs to estimate how long he is likely to remain a member—a period sometimes referred to as his 'time horizon'—to do this. It will always be true that the rate of return needed to persuade such a member to invest is higher than that needed by a capitalist. To see the magnitude of the difference, suppose that everyone's time discount is covered by a rate of return on investment of 5 per cent, so that a capitalist will invest whenever the promised yield is 5 per cent or greater. What is the minimum yield demanded by a co-operative member? If his time horizon were one year, he would require a yield of 105 per cent before investing his potential income. To take more realistic cases, a five-year time horizon requires a yield of 23 per cent, a ten-year horizon 13 per cent, a twenty-year horizon 8 per cent.[19]

Any actual co-operative will have members with different time-horizons depending on age, mobility, and so forth. If investment decisions are made by majority vote, as has been assumed, the yield required will be determined by the median voter (voters being arranged in order of ascending time horizon). If everyone expects to remain within the co-operative for the whole of his working life—say, forty years—and there is a normal age distribution, the median time horizon will be twenty years. But this is an unrealistically favourable assumption from the co-operative's point of view, and I should guess that a median time horizon of about ten years is the most one could expect. If so, we see that the necessary rate of yield is considerably higher than that required for investment by a capitalist, from which it follows that the co-operative is likely to invest a good deal less than its capitalist counterpart.

Might this unfortunate result be avoided by having assets owned individually? A share of the profit invested would be

for Workers' Co-ops (London: Routledge and Kegan Paul, 1978), 32–4, 82–4, 190–4. At best this would mitigate rather than resolve the problems identified below. For a fuller discussion, see my 'Market Neutrality and the Failure of Co-operatives', British Journal of Political Science, 11 (1981), 309–29, esp. 317–18.
[19] Calculated by Furubotn and Pejovich in The Economics of Property Rights, 240.

credited to each person's account, and could be withdrawn when the person retired or left the co-operative. Under these circumstances a member may be expected to approach investment decisions in the same way as a capitalist, investing whenever the expected rate of return more than covers his time discount. Against this, however, investment in a co-operative has two features which may make it less attractive to members than withdrawing profits in the form of income and investing elsewhere. One is the inflexibility of the investment, which prevents money being drawn out to meet current needs, obviously an important consideration for most private savers.[20] Although a capitalist may for the same reason wish to save some of his profit outside his enterprise, the amount in question will be much less than the combined total required by the n members of a similarly sized co-operative. Furthermore the capitalist is aware that, should his liquid 'cushion' fail to shield him from some large financial misfortune, he can in the last resort sell up and realize his assets; for the co-operator the existence of this option will depend on the rules of the co-operative, and therefore (in all likelihood) on finding a 'buyer' for his job with the right combination of working skills and capital. It will probably be difficult to do this quickly.

The other feature which makes investment in a co-operative relatively unattractive to its members is that such investment prevents the spreading of risk. If the co-operative should go bankrupt both income and capital would be lost, whereas a capitalist can disperse risk by investing some capital elsewhere and allowing others to invest in his own firm. As Meade has said, 'while property owners can spread their risks by putting small bits of their property into a large number of concerns, a worker cannot easily put small bits of his effort into a large number of different jobs. This presumably is a main reason why we find risk-bearing capital hiring labour rather than risk-bearing labour hiring capital.'[21] One may conjecture whether this second feature explains the observed fact that when nineteenth-century co-operators

[20] Might banks be willing to advance private loans to co-operative members, using their investment accounts as security? Only if bankers could be convinced that co-operatives were financially sound, on which see below.

[21] Meade, 'Theory of Labour-Managed Firms', 426.

began to hire labour, they often preferred to take paid employment outside the co-operative themselves.[22]

The main difficulty, however, with individualized assets is that
once the co-operative begins to lose members through retirement
or transfer, it has to require newcomers to supply capital
equivalent in amount to the withdrawals. If this requirement were
not imposed, the co-operative would be steadily drained of
capital; and, moreover, the newcomers would benefit unfairly
from the assets accumulated by the founding generation, creating
pressure for them to be taken on as employees rather than as
equal members of the co-operative. But the requirement would
quickly become a daunting hurdle as the capital per worker
increased; even if the money could be borrowed privately, it
would make the co-operative a less attractive employment prospect than a capitalist enterprise paying similar wages.[23] So
although individualized assets may reduce the co-operative's
investment problem in the short term, in the longer run the effect
will either be to deter incoming members or to cause the co-
operative to degenerate into a joint-stock company owned by the
founding generation but employing newcomers as salaried
employees.[24]

A third possible way of dealing with the investment problem is
to have the co-operative financed externally. The co-operative
would borrow all of its capital from a private bank, say, and pay
interest on its borrowing. At first sight this seems to solve the
difficulties we have been considering, for the co-operative would
invest whenever the expected return exceeded the rate of interest,
and there would be no problem created by members withdrawing
their assets. This solution may indeed be the best where it can be

---

[22] Likewise, G. D. H. Cole observed that 'workers who invested money in cotton mills
preferred not to invest it in the mills in which they were employed; for if they did this they
ran a big risk of losing both their wages and their dividends if their particular mill fell on
bad times, whereas there was more chance of avoiding the double loss by placing their
savings elsewhere'. G. D. H. Cole, *A Century of Co-operation* (Manchester: Co-operative
Union, 1945), 90–1.

[23] Nowadays professional partnerships such as those formed by solicitors may loan
incoming members the purchase price of a share, to be repaid out of income over a set
period. But these are low capital-high income enterprises, and it is difficult to envisage
such an arrangement being adopted throughout the economy as a whole.

[24] For evidence of the latter effect, see D. C. Jones, 'The Economic and Industrial
Relations of American Producer Co-operatives, 1791–1939', *Economic Analysis and
Workers' Management*, 11 (1977), 295–317.

achieved: the question is whether it is a viable solution in an environment dominated by capitalist enterprises.[25]

The question can be examined from two points of view: that of the co-operative and that of the lending agency. From the co-operative's point of view, repaying the loan will be equivalent to investing in capital, in the sense that once the loan is repaid, assets of a certain value will be held collectively. In the light of the argument so far, it will be seen that members will resist any such repayment unless the yield from their investment is unusually large. The likely outcome is that the co-operative will borrow as much as it can from the bank and repay as little as possible. It therefore faces two problems. One is that it becomes particularly vulnerable to year-by-year fluctuations in profit, having no reserves to draw on in lean years, on the reasonable assumption that bank credit has an upper limit. On the same assumption, secondly, investment ceases (in normal cases) when the ceiling is reached. So finite credit really only masks the basic problem of the co-operative structure, namely the reluctance of income-maximizing co-operators to invest in a collective asset. Of course, the masking might be effective for a considerable time, depending on the size of the credit.

Consider now the question from the point of view of the bank. Why should any bank, not influenced by ideological considerations but pursuing a profit-maximizing goal itself, lend to a co-operative when it can lend instead to capitalist firms? The bank's agents can see that the co-operators have no incentive to repay their borrowings; they can predict that the co-operative will either have to borrow ever-increasing sums, or else be outperformed by the competition and go bankrupt. Neither prospect is attractive; the bankruptcy of a firm collectively or jointly owned by a large number of individuals would be a banker's nightmare. Indeed, a rational banker would only lend to a co-operative if he could impose conditions on the loan such that the co-operative was forced to behave in a way analogous to a capitalist firm. (This kind of solution to the problems of co-operatives is considered in general terms shortly.) But why go to this trouble if he can lend to a capitalist without it? Let me reiterate that this consequence follows directly from the bank's attending to its own self-interest,

[25] See J. Vanek, 'The Basic Theory of Financing of Participatory Firms', in id. (ed.), *Self-management: Economic Liberation of Man* (Harmondsworth: Penguin, 1975).

not from any wish on the part of the bankers to suppress co-operatives or 'preserve the capitalist system'. Co-operatives are simply a worse investment from the bank's point of view.

We must conclude that the market itself provides no satisfactory solution to the co-operatives' investment problem. Each possibility we have examined—collectivized assets, individualized assets, external financing—has serious drawbacks. The likely result is that co-operatives will be unwilling to invest as heavily as capitalist enterprises, and will therefore be unable to compete in an open market whenever investment is needed to maintain technological advance. It does not of course follow that every co-operative will fail immediately. Higher levels of productivity may, for instance, offset additional investment in the short run. But in the longer term the pursuit of income-maximization by co-operators will lead to one of two unintended outcomes: competitive failure through under-investment, or degeneration into a capitalist form of organization.

IV

All of the analysis so far is predicated on the assumption that members of co-operatives are interested solely in maximizing their personal incomes. But our interest in co-operatives was aroused in the first place by the suggestion that they might provide non-commodity-based benefits for their members—primarily, democratic control of the workplace, but flowing from this other benefits such as greater flexibility in work, a more comradely relationship between workers, and so forth. Now if co-operators are interested in these non-financial aspects of industrial democracy, then of course they have an interest in the survival of their co-operative, this being the condition for enjoying the non-monetary benefits in security. Nozick relies on this idea when he argues that co-operatives should be able to survive by their members taking lower money incomes, the loss being compensated by the non-monetary rewards. This, however, only deals with the effects on productivity of workers' control and its results (e.g. the fact that more varied work might be less efficient in terms of output). It does not attack the dynamic problems we have been examining, particularly that of investment. How would a co-operative which values survival over and above its monetary rewards approach investment decisions?

One extreme possibility is that it might attempt to simulate capitalist behaviour. To dramatize this idea, imagine that the members borrow the services of an entrepreneur and ask him how he would act in each contingency as it arises, supposing that he owned the firm's capital. At the same time they bind themselves to accept his recommendations, irrespective of the effect on their own incomes. In this way, it seems, the co-operative can give itself at least as good a chance of survival as an equivalent capitalist firm.

But let us scrutinize this solution more carefully. To begin with, in order to carry out the investment decisions made by the surrogate capitalist, the co-operative will almost certainly need to raise large capital sums. For the reasons sketched at the end of the last section, it is very unlikely that a commercial bank will lend as generously to a co-operatively owned firm as to a privately owned firm. Thus there will be an investment deficit which can only be made good, if at all, by the co-operators themselves taking reduced incomes in order to create additional profit for re-investment. But income levels must have a floor. Economic security cannot reasonably become the members' overriding aim regardless of their living standards in the short or medium term. Thus it may simply not be possible for the co-operative to follow the hired entrepreneur's directives without incurring unreasonable sacrifices.

A second question is whether it is rational in the first place for the co-operators to make the indefinite survival of the co-operative their goal. The entrepreneur's recommendations will be based on his estimates of what will maximize the firm's value in the long run, allowing the usual time discount. But the current members of a co-operative cannot hope to capture all of that value. Their interest in the firm's survival is an interest in its surviving during the course of their working lives within that particular co-operative.[26] Thus it would be irrational to bind

[26] If they value the experience of co-operation, shouldn't they want to make that experience available to their successors in the next generation of workers? It depends on the way in which they value it. But even if the implication holds, it is not in general reasonable to expect people who adhere to some social goal to promote it in their private economic activity. The appropriate place to pursue such goals is the political arena. (Thus we do not generally expect people who believe in distributive justice to try to correct the

themselves to make decisions whose benefit potentially lay further in the future.

Finally, a rigid commitment to follow capitalist investment patterns would defeat the object of forming a co-operative in the first place. Decisions about investment cannot be isolated from decisions about hiring and firing, methods of production, and so forth, so that the only issues left for the assembled co-operators to resolve would be those that have no bearing on the economics of the firm. Everything else is settled by the hired entrepreneur. Participation is devalued because it is restricted to relatively trivial questions that an enlightened capitalist would allow his workforce to decide in any case. The point of setting up a co-operative was to trade non-monetary benefits off against monetary rewards in a way that the capitalist firm does not allow, but a strict adherence to the entrepreneur's recommendations would preempt any such trade-off.

It follows, then, that even the most enlightened of co-operatives would not pursue the same investment strategy as its capitalist analogue. It might treat a hypothetical entrepreneur's recommendations as a bench-mark against which to assess its own behaviour, but it would unavoidably deviate from that bench-mark to some degree. Whether an intermediate investment strategy—falling somewhere between the requirements of overall profit maximization and of maximizing income per worker —would ensure survival would depend on the particular market for which the co-operative was producing; in general, one can say that co-operatives are likely to be driven out of business whenever they face capitalist enterprises following an aggressive investment strategy.

Some readers might conclude from this discussion that co-operatives are simply unfit to take part in market competition: there is an incompatibility between the demands of the market, which constrains the producers of goods and services in the interests of consumers, and the benefits of co-operative production—democracy at work, flexible working practices, etc. I do not believe such a conclusion is warranted. What creates difficulties for co-operatives is not producing for a market in itself, but producing in competition with capitalist enterprises, institutions

current distribution of resources single-handed.) I examine the issue of altruistic concerns, and how to satisfy them, in some detail in the following chapter.

with their own built-in incentive structure. (One way of putting this would be to say that capitalist firms create externalities for co-operatives.[27]) Recall a point made in the last chapter in criticism of Hayek: it does not follow that because a group *within* a society succeeds by behaving in a certain way that the society as a whole would benefit if everyone behaved in that way. The discussion of co-operatives here demonstrates the converse of that point. Co-operatives operating in a capitalist environment may be 'unsuccessful', but a market economy made up entirely of co-operatives (with appropriate investment institutions) can be stable and efficient, and at the same time allow the members of each enterprise to make reasonable choices between income and non-monetary benefits at work. Co-operation is a practice that works better on a society-wide scale than in individual enterprises when these are in a minority.

V

The case of workers' co-operatives was chosen partly for its direct relevance to the general argument of this book (it shows why market socialism needs to be brought into being by political decision, since a spontaneous transition to a co-operative economy is virtually unthinkable), and partly for the light it sheds on the neutrality of markets. What does it show with respect to the latter? It illustrates the way in which a market economy is likely to discriminate against non-commodity-based conceptions of the good. It is not that the existence of a market makes the pursuit of such conceptions impossible; that would be too strong a conclusion. Rather, someone who wishes to pursue non-commodity ends along with commodities is likely to find that he has to make a disproportionate sacrifice of the former to enjoy the latter securely. The market has a structure and a logic, and it pays to go along with them. In the case of workers' co-operatives, we found that financial security was likely to be bought at the cost of abandoning those non-economic goals that made the co-operative form attractive in the first place.

This result can be generalized. The market favours those with

[27] Jon Elster puts it this way in 'From Here to There, Or: If Co-operative Ownership Is So Desirable, Why Are There So Few Co-operatives?', *Social Philosophy and Policy* (forthcoming).

conceptions of the good which are centred on the private enjoyment of commodities, or which have non-commodity elements which run with the logic of the market—for instance, those who enjoy competitive success for its own sake as well as for the income it brings. It penalizes those whose conceptions require behaviour that cuts against that logic—for instance, those wanting to pursue time-consuming projects outside the market, or to sustain co-operative relationships, or to act consistently on certain principles (such as religious observance). These people will be handicapped in their pursuit of the good life, not because their conceptions are naturally expensive but because of the institutional framework within which that pursuit occurs.[28]

It is important to be clear just what is being claimed here. If someone, in order to realize certain extra-market goals, were to reduce his work hours by, say, 20 per cent and thereby incur a 20 per cent cut in income, there would be no question of non-neutrality. This person would be curtailing his pursuit of his idea of the good life in one area in order to advance it in another, and choices of that kind are endemic to the pursuit of the good. The point being made is that someone who wishes to reduce his work hours by 20 per cent may have to endure an income cut of, say, 50 per cent by virtue of the structure of the market. (Think, for example, of the problems that those whose other commitments force them to work part-time face in obtaining responsible and well-paid jobs.) It therefore becomes important, from the point of view of overall self-realization, whether your conception of the good contains elements that cut into market behaviour in this way.

What does this imply in practice for a liberal committed to the idea of neutrality? I don't want to suggest that there is some other

---

[28] There is an objection to this line of argument which claims, roughly, that if enough other people had the right preferences, any conception of the good could be realized through markets alone (Nozick, for instance, contemplates worker-controlled factories succeeding because there were enough customers willing to pay higher prices for goods made in such factories). The implication is that where people are unable to realize their conceptions of the good, the fault lies with other people's preferences, not the market itself. What is overlooked here is the fact that a market economy converts preferences into behaviour in a certain way: it gives people differentially strong incentives to act on their various preferences (for instance it generally gives no incentive at all to act on preferences for public goods). In pursuing my conception of the good in a market setting, I am constrained by other people's market-channelled behaviour, not by their underlying preference.

institutional system of comparable simplicity to the market that *would* form a neutral framework. Given the variety that we actually find in people's conceptions of the good, it seems very unlikely that any simple mechanism could fully specify a neutral framework. Moreover I have already argued that markets do perform neutrally as between commodity-based conceptions of the good, and this is an important argument in their favour. Rather than looking for a simple alternative, therefore, we need to find ways of compensating for market bias.

In practice this must mean politically determined intervention in the market, whether legislative or financial. The ground rules must be adjusted to favour the disadvantaged conceptions. Consider two of the cases referred to above. The first concerns people for whom extra-market projects mean that part-time work is optimal—say parents of young children, or people with elderly relatives to look after. There are various reasons why employers are likely to discriminate against people in this position, either refusing to take them on at all or paying disproportionately low wages: with extra bodies in the firm, lines of communication are lengthened, equipment and office space is under-utilized and so forth. To compensate for these costs, employers need to be given special incentives to take on part-time workers, for instance through a reverse payroll tax that provides a subsidy when a full-time job is split into two half-time jobs.

The other case, analysed at some length above, concerns preferences for co-operative work relations. We saw that workers' co-operatives were likely to suffer a major problem of under-investment, stemming chiefly from the unwillingness of commercial banks to advance them capital. The need here is for investment agencies which are willing both to lease capital to co-operatives and to provide advice on appropriate structures of ownership and financial practice.[29] Agencies of this sort will not

[29] A model here is the Caja Laboral Popular which has been instrumental in the success of the Mondragon group of co-operatives in the Basque region of Spain. The bank was established (largely through the influence of a Catholic priest) deliberately to support the co-ops, and it is obliged by its constitution to continue doing so. For its funding it relies on the local solidarity of savers. The success of the bank depends on this particular background, without which a political initiative would be needed. Its mode of operation, however, provides valuable lessons for co-operative investment agencies generally. For description and analysis, see R. Oakeshott, *The Case for Workers' Co-ops*, ch. 10; H. Thomas and C. Logan, *Mondragon: An Economic Analysis* (London: Allen and Unwin, 1982), esp. ch. 4.

be created spontaneously by market forces. They must be public institutions, brought into being by political decision, whose brief is to foster a financially sound co-operative sector in the economy.

We need to be clear that such proposals always impose costs on the remainder of society, if only in the form of higher tax revenues to fund the necessary institutions. To achieve neutrality, we must impinge slightly on the prospects of those with market-oriented conceptions of the good in order to enhance the prospects of those with other priorities. Such a balancing of claims is inherent in the neutrality principle itself. But it brings into focus two general points that are worth noting in conclusion.

First, a neutral framework cannot be specified in advance of knowing something about the conceptions of the good that people actually hold, and this is a contingent matter. Since the point of the framework is to balance competing claims on social resources, broadly conceived, we cannot sensibly say anything about its shape until we know what claims it has to accommodate. If no-one is interested in co-operative production, there is no point establishing institutions designed to foster it.[30] Furthermore, since conceptions of the good change historically, the appropriate framework cannot be designed in a once-and-for-all manner. We need a political forum in which new demands can be heard, and the framework revised accordingly.

Second, the scope of the neutrality principle has to be limited. It cannot extend to all conceivable conceptions of the good, but at most to conceptions that strike us as intelligible, and that do not explicitly include as part of their content the frustration of other conceptions. Thus there is no reason to include (for instance) pyromaniacs or, on the other hand, people whose aim is simply to outscore others on some dimension, within the scope of the neutrality principle. Particularly if a commitment to neutrality is based on the idea of respect for persons, it must be possible to see how someone could reasonably adopt a particular conception before extending to it the protection of the principle. And although a conception should not be disqualified merely because realizing it requires a large quantity of resources, since the purpose of the neutrality principle is to mediate between the claims of different conceptions of the good, it cannot extend to

[30] I look briefly at the empirical evidence on this point in the Conclusion.

conceptions which already embody a non-neutral resolution of that contest.

These conclusions are bound to be unwelcome to liberals, who see the neutrality principle as setting the boundaries for political activity, not as a principle that needs to be implemented by politics itself. Of course, nothing has yet been said about the kind of politics that would be required to establish a neutral framework: that issue is postponed to the third part of the book. Nor have I yet attempted to identify the point at which neutrality must give way to other values. My aim here has been to clarify the principle and to consider its bearing on the role of markets. We have found that the most adequate definition—according to which a social framework is neutral when, as far as can reasonably be foreseen, it does not favour any particular conception of the good at the expense of others—has an ambivalent upshot. Markets are an essential element in a neutral framework when commodity-based conceptions are at stake; but markets taken in isolation discriminate against other conceptions, in particular those that involve co-operative work relations. Assuming that such conceptions, and others like them, are in fact widely held in the society we are considering, genuine neutrality requires a more complex framework than that which the libertarian offers us.

4

ALTRUISM AND WELFARE

I

In the last chapter I examined the general claim that a market economy of the kind favoured by libertarians dealt even-handedly with the various conceptions of the good life that individuals might want to pursue. We saw that there were good reasons to doubt this general claim. In this chapter I want to focus on a particular issue, the problem that arises if we assume that people are altruistically concerned about the welfare of others. Most people do in fact appear to manifest such concern. They are distressed if others—particularly other members of their own society—are exposed to poverty and suffering. If these feelings are universally shared, there is a strong case for a scheme of redistribution in favour of the badly-off, since such redistribution may advance everyone's conception of the good: it aids the badly-off in an obvious material sense, but it also satisfies the altruistic preferences of those who contribute to the scheme. Provided these preferences are strong enough to outweigh the material costs of contribution, we have the conditions for what economists call 'Pareto optimal redistribution'.[1]

Very few libertarians would want to deny the widespread existence of altruistic concern. They would simply deny that concern of this kind can justify *compulsory* redistribution by the state in favour of the needy. Their case might be put as follows. If people are indeed altruistically concerned about the welfare of their fellow citizens, then it is perfectly possible for them to make private arrangements to express their altruism, through chari-table giving. Indeed such charitable activity is not only a possible alternative to a compulsory scheme, but is actually superior to it in

---

[1] See H. M. Hochman and J. D. Rogers, 'Pareto Optimal Redistribution', *American Economic Review*, 59 (1969), 542–57.

two respects. First, genuine altruism has to be voluntary: forced giving, through the tax system, is no substitute for the real thing. No one likes paying taxes, whereas people generally feel good about donating money to famine relief or the church roof fund. Second, people vary both in the intensity of their altruism and in its direction. A tax-and-welfare system forces everyone in similar financial circumstances to donate the same amount to the same collectively determined ends. A voluntary system is more efficient, because it allows each person to donate the amount he chooses to the cause or causes that he favours. If Pareto-optimality is the criterion, the latter system is unequivocally better.

These sentiments would be shared by every libertarian, though not all would infer that compulsory welfare provision should be abandoned entirely. Nozick does press on to this apparently logical conclusion,[2] whereas Hayek and Friedman both pull back, conceding that the state should provide a minimal safety-net to guard against the extremes of poverty.[3] In Hayek's case the reasoning behind this appeals less to altruistic concern for the poor than to a prudential desire on the part of the wealthy to ward off social unrest. Friedman does grasp, in a slightly muddled way, the point that the supply of welfare has public-good properties that make private provision potentially ineffective (I shall explore this point in depth later in this chapter). Both authors, however, want to restrict compulsory provision to a minimum, and both favour a form of provision which interferes as little as possible with the working of the market. Hayek, for instance, advocates making insurance for old age, sickness and unemployment compulsory, and Friedman argues for a negative income tax to provide cash benefits for the poor.

What no libertarian will countenance is the creation of a welfare state as that idea is usually understood. I shall mean by a welfare state an institution with the following three features: first, it provides benefits (goods and services) to everyone in a particular society, regardless of whether they have contributed to the cost of providing them. Second, it provides *specific* benefits which are

[2] R. Nozick, *Anarchy, State and Utopia* (Oxford: Blackwell, 1974), 265–8.
[3] F. A. Hayek, *The Constitution of Liberty* (London: Routledge and Kegan Paul, 1960), chs. 17 and 19; M. Friedman, *Capitalism and Freedom* (Chicago: University of Chicago Press, 1962), ch. 12.

seen as meeting needs, rather than sums of money which can be used as the recipient pleases. Third, the institution is funded by mandatory taxation, with tax schedules having no deliberate connection with the benefits that various classes of people are expected to receive. In short the institution is potentially redistributive,[4] specific in its aims, and compulsory.

Since such an institution is an integral part of the model of market socialism defended in this book, we need to be as clear as possible about its justification. The question we want to ask is: what must be true of people's altruistic concern for others if they would prefer to see a welfare state in existence rather than relying on private charitable schemes? Why might they consent to be taxed to provide for the needy? To answer this properly, we need to look closely at the nature of altruism itself. What does it mean to be concerned about the welfare of others? How will such concern enter into the practical deliberations of each person? As we shall see, there are a number of possible forms that altruism may take, and our practical conclusions will depend on which form we expect to be prevalent. This is, of course, an empirical matter, but I shall suggest that the assumptions needed to support the libertarian position are distinctly unlikely.

I should make it clear that I do not regard the altruism argument as the best possible foundation for the welfare state. It suffers from one palpable defect: whether a welfare state is justifiable depends entirely on whether the relevant population is in fact altruistically concerned about the welfare of the poor. We may not wish our choice of social institutions to depend in this simple way on people's attitudes. Moreover there may be other reasons for regarding a welfare state founded on altruistic concern alone as flawed. A socialist is likely to argue that those in need simply and straightforwardly have *rights* to the resources which will meet their needs, independently of what others in their

---

[4] Note that this is not the same as saying that the existing welfare state is an effective agent of egalitarian redistribution. For an assessment of this claim, largely sceptical, see J. Le Grand, *The Strategy of Equality: Redistribution and the Social Services* (London: Allen and Unwin, 1982). Even existing welfare states, however, are redistributive in certain respects—from the healthy to the sick, for instance. Note further that this definition of the welfare state does not specify how the institution should be organized. We are most familiar with the welfare state in the form of a public service, its benefits supplied by employees of the state. Later in the book (ch. 12, sec. v) I examine alternative ways of providing welfare that still fall within the terms of the definition.

society believe.[5] He may also regard a welfare state as contributing in an important way to a sense of community.[6] Both of these arguments rest on premises that no libertarian is likely to accept. Libertarians deny the existence of rights to positive provision,[7] and they are sceptical about the value of community when expressed at the social level. There is a danger, therefore, that the debate about altruism and welfare provision will become a dialogue of the deaf. My purpose here is not to produce the best possible argument for the welfare state, but to show that an argument can be constructed on premises that both sides can endorse. It will, needless to say, have a conditional character: *if* people have altruistic concerns of this type, *then* they will consent to institutions of such-and-such a form. Since libertarians profess to be agnostic as to which conceptions of the good people should hold (but argue, none the less, that a market framework is always to be preferred), they cannot escape the force of such an argument.

II

We need to begin our enquiry by looking more closely at the meaning of 'altruism'. The generic sense of the term is concern for the interests of others: the altruist is someone who is affected by the level of welfare enjoyed by (at least some) others, and moved to act on their behalf. But as we shall see, this leaves open a number of possible ways in which the interests of others can enter the practical deliberations of the person in question.

A first contrast has to do with the way in which the 'interests' or 'welfare' of the others are interpreted. Does the altruist give the *preferences* of other people canonical status, or does he employ some other notion of interests: for instance, is he concerned about meeting the needs of other people as he defines them, even if the people in question would rather be aided in some other way? Collard describes altruism of the latter kind as 'meddlesome', a

---

[5] A question arises whether the view that people have welfare rights supersedes and excludes the view that the welfare state is an expression of altruistic concern, or whether the two views might be reconciled. On this question see D. Harris, *Justifying State Welfare* (Oxford: Blackwell, 1987), ch. 4.

[6] This issue is considered more fully in ch. 9.

[7] Though, as we saw in ch. 1, they may have difficulties in holding consistently to this position.

pejorative term which suggests an attempt to interfere with the way that other people run their lives.[8] Certainly a meddlesome altruist (or, as I shall describe him, a needs altruist) will want to try to prevent the recipient of his aid from converting it into a form that is preferred by the latter but valued less by the donor. So if a tramp touches me for the price of a hot dinner, I want to see that the money goes on the meal rather than on a bottle of meths.

It may initially seem difficult to make sense of this idea of needs altruism. If we are concerned about other people, shouldn't all that matters be how well off or badly off they feel? Of course our concern may extend more broadly in time: we may want to give them what makes them feel good in the long run, rather than what they most want at this moment (consider heroin addicts). It still seems that preferences ought to be the final point of reference. Preference altruism follows naturally if one interprets altruism on the lines of a Humean notion of sympathy. The other person's welfare matters to us because his happiness strikes a resonant chord in our frame: we take delight in the other's pleasure, and sorrow in his pain. But although this model obviously fits some cases of giving, it is not the only way in which altruism can be understood.

Another view would see it as a matter of recognizing obligations, with no necessary implication that psychic gratification is involved. We are altruistic because we believe that we ought to be. Obligations, however, normally correlate with specific rights on the part of other people, rather than with their subjectively defined welfare. This is clear enough in the case of promissory and contractual obligations: if I promise Jones to deliver him a certain item, I have no obligation to provide him with some other item that he prefers, even if the cost to me remains the same. There seems no reason why this should not also be true of general obligations to provide for others' welfare. We may feel that others' needs impose obligations on us, where 'need' means something like 'whatever is necessary to allow A to enjoy a decent

[8] D. Collard, *Altruism and Economy: A Study in Non-Selfish Economics* (Oxford: Martin Robertson, 1978), esp. ch. 12. From one point of view, of course, all altruistic behaviour might be described as 'meddlesome', since it alters the circumstances of the recipient. The practical contrast between meddlesome and non-meddlesome altruism, in Collard's sense, consists only in the preferred form of giving.

standard of living in this community'.[9] Here 'need' is a weakly normative notion, in the sense that its use requires us to identify a set of general capacities and opportunities that people must have to follow plans of life which are specific to them, but which fall within a certain general range. If someone wishes to follow a highly idiosyncratic project, requiring an unusual set of resources (for instance, if his idea is to experiment with the widest possible range of hallucinogenic drugs), we will not adjust our notion of need to accommodate him. Concretely, we will not feel obliged to supply him with LSD in place of medical services or decent housing.

The contrast between preference altruism and needs altruism has an obvious bearing on the case for a welfare state. Preference altruists will in general want to provide the objects of their concern with readily convertible resources, enabling them to reach their highest level of (self-defined) welfare—the simplest form of provision being cash redistribution. Thus they will be attracted to negative income tax schemes and the like. Needs altruists will want to ensure that certain specified needs are met, and will favour provision in kind, with barriers to the conversion of the resources supplied into other forms. In general, then, needs altruism will give us the clearest underpinning for the welfare state, always provided that there is consensus on the range of needs to be met. However, there are special considerations which may lead preference altruists some way in this direction as well. One has already been mentioned: if we suspect that people are liable to make choices that are bad from the point of view of their long-term welfare, preference altruists too may favour provision in kind. Suppose, for instance, that we believed that many people would underestimate the risks of serious illness, and therefore would under-insure themselves if provided with cash and left to make their own arrangements for medical insurance; then even a preference altruist would opt for a public health service, at least to cover serious medical problems.

A second consideration has to do with identifying the recipients of aid. Altruists of both varieties will be concerned about efficiency, in the sense that they will want resources to be deployed so as to bring about the greatest possible increase in the

---

[9] I examine the concept of need in greater detail in ch. 5, sec. vii.

welfare (need-fulfilment or want-satisfaction) of the badly off. Giving aid in the form of resources that the recipients can convert to the form they prefer presupposes that the extent of need can be identified prior to the giving.[10] In some instances, medical aid being again the most obvious, this may not be so. Consider the following: Jones is an altruist who has decided to lavish £100 on ten sick people of his acquaintance. The nature and extent of their illnesses is not apparent to him. Doctors charge £10 an hour for their services. Two options present themselves rather clearly. One is to present each invalid with £10, allowing him to buy up to one hour of a doctor's time. The other is to hire a doctor for ten hours, and allow the doctor himself to allocate his time between his ten patients. The merit of the second option is evident: as the doctor investigates, he discovers which patients need extensive treatment and which can be dealt with more summarily. Under the first option, the easily cured will be out of the surgery in half an hour, with £5 to spend on other items, a morally objectionable outcome for the needs altruist, but also (the point being made here) an inefficient result for the preference altruist. Providing aid in the form of a non-convertible resource (doctor's time) channels it in the direction where it can do most good.

Considerations of this kind may thus push the preference altruist, too, towards supporting institutions such as those of the welfare state, which meet specific needs. Admittedly there are pressures in the other direction.[11] To the extent that interests vary (that is, people give differing weights to the satisfaction of their socially defined needs), specific transfers will be inefficient. The medical example looks plausible because we assume that almost everyone will give a high priority to physical health. In other cases (say 'decent' housing) it may be that a significant number of people care rather little about having their needs met, and would prefer to be aided in other ways. Thus, although the argument is not clear-cut, we can say generally that welfare-state institutions will be supported most strongly by altruists of the specific or 'needs' variety.

Is there any evidence that people's altruistic concern is of this specific sort? It might seem possible to reach such a conclusion

[10] This point is made in A. Weale, *Equality and Social Policy* (London: Routledge and Kegan Paul, 1979), ch. 6.
[11] See id., *Political Theory and Social Policy* (London: Macmillan, 1983), ch. 6.

from evidence of attitudes towards the welfare state, which reveals that responses vary according to the kind of provision in question.[12] Old-age pensions, education, and the health service are strongly supported, whereas there is less enthusiasm for unemployment benefit, subsidized housing, and child benefit. It might be thought that such differentiations would only be made if people's concern for others were of the 'needs' sort, unfortunately the evidence is not decisive, for preference altruists too might have reservations about the less favoured benefits, thinking that in too many cases they were likely to be delivered to people who were not particularly badly off.[13] Child benefit, the least discriminating of these benefits, since in the British case it is available to all parents regardless of income, is also the least favoured. Thus, although it seems intuitively likely that for most people altruism does have a needs component, I know of no hard evidence to bear this out.

III

I turn now to a second contrast between varieties of altruism, this one cross-cutting the preferences/needs contrast.[14] It presupposes a context in which there are a number of possible donors able to contribute to the welfare of people that they wish to help. Each potential donor, we may assume, has a personal interest in not making a contribution; other things being equal, he would like to keep his resources to spend on himself. On the other hand, if he were the only possible donor, he would give up to a certain amount. In this context, how will people behave?

To add some rigour to the discussion, consider the following simple case. There are two altruistic individuals, A and B, facing a third person, C, who is in need to the extent of 1 unit of resources. A and B are similarly endowed; each, in isolation, would be willing to transfer 1 unit to C (although for neither would this be an absolutely trivial amount). Each can choose to give 0, $\frac{1}{2}$ or 1

---

[12] See P. Taylor-Gooby, *Public Opinion, Ideology and State Welfare* (London: Routledge and Kegan Paul, 1985), ch. 2 for a convenient survey.

[13] Or, a complicating factor, who would not be so badly off if they did more to help themselves: altruism is likely to be qualified in most cases by a principle of desert.

[14] The analysis that follows is fairly detailed, and readers who are chiefly interested in the broad contrast between libertarianism and market socialism may wish to move directly to the summary at the beginning of sec. vi.

unit of resources to C. (Other possibilities are conceivable, but these are clearly the most salient for similarly endowed givers.) There are then nine possible outcomes. Writing A's contribution first and B's second, these are (0, 0), (0, $\frac{1}{2}$), (0, 1), ($\frac{1}{2}$, 0), ($\frac{1}{2}$, $\frac{1}{2}$), ($\frac{1}{2}$, 1), (1, 0), (1, $\frac{1}{2}$) (1, 1).

Considering just A, there are potentially as many forms of altruism as there are rank orderings of these nine outcomes. Realistically, however, we can narrow the range somewhat. First, we can disregard the three outcomes ($\frac{1}{2}$, 1), (1, $\frac{1}{2}$), (1, 1): whatever else is true of them, A and B must both regard these as wasteful outcomes in which C ends up with more resources than he needs. Second, given our assumptions about A's altruism, he must give top preference to one of the outcomes in which C ends up with one unit of resources: (0, 1), ($\frac{1}{2}$, $\frac{1}{2}$), or (1, 0). Even with these restrictions, there are still a fair number of possibilities. I shall confine my attention to four.

The first I shall call the calculating altruist. He is a person who wants to see C helped, but as far as possible by someone else. If he can pass the buck, he will do so. In formal terms this means that

$$(0, 1) > (\tfrac{1}{2}, \tfrac{1}{2}) > (1, 0) \quad (> = \text{'is preferred to'})$$
$$(0, \tfrac{1}{2}) > (\tfrac{1}{2}, 0).$$

Depending on the strength of A's altruism we may either have

$$(1, 0) > (0, \tfrac{1}{2}) \text{ or}$$
$$(0, \tfrac{1}{2}) > (1, 0).$$

In less formal terms, think of the person who sees someone collapse in a crowded street. He holds back in the hope that someone else will step in, although he would help if he were the only person on hand. This person is a calculating altruist. I describe him as 'calculating' because of the way in which his behaviour depends on his assessment of how other people will behave. If he expects to be able to get away without contributing, he will.[15]

It may seem implausible to describe such a mean-spirited

---

[15] The presence of calculating altruism has been confirmed empirically in studies of reactions to emergencies. In particular, it has been shown that people's willingness to respond diminishes as the number of other bystanders increases. See e.g., J. M. Darley and B. Latane, 'Bystander Intervention in Emergencies: Diffusion of Responsibility', *Journal of Personality and Social Psychology*, 8 (1968), 377–83.

character as an altruist at all. There is, however, no reason to doubt his concern for the welfare of C. He prefers $(1, 0)$ to $(\frac{1}{2}, 0)$ to $(0, 0)$. The problem is that it is only the end-state, C's welfare, that counts: his own part in providing for that welfare is recorded as a loss. Unlike the other characters we shall consider, he has none of what Margolis has called 'participation altruism'.[16] He derives no satisfaction from the act of contributing itself.

If A and B are both calculating altruists, and if they have to decide on their contributions independently of one another, then we are immediately in the territory of games theory. Depending on how the outcomes are valued, the game may take the form of a Prisoner's Dilemma or a game of Chicken.[17] As the example has been set up, it is a case of Chicken. A would prefer B to meet C's needs; but if he really believes that B is going to pass by, then he will meet them himself. In other words $(0, 1) > (1, 0) > (0, 0)$. For B, $(1, 0) > (0, 1) > (0, 0)$. As students of Chicken know, there is no stable outcome to the game; each player makes a guess about the other's behaviour and acts accordingly.

To illustrate a Prisoner's Dilemma, suppose instead that both A and B have only $\frac{1}{2}$ unit each at their disposal; suppose also that they are both rather weakly altruistic. Both prefer $(\frac{1}{2}, \frac{1}{2})$ to $(0, 0)$ but for A $(0, 0) > (\frac{1}{2}, 0)$ and $(0, \frac{1}{2}) > (\frac{1}{2}, \frac{1}{2})$, whereas for B $(0, 0) > (0, \frac{1}{2})$ and $(\frac{1}{2}, 0) > (\frac{1}{2}, \frac{1}{2})$. Both then have an incentive to contribute 0 whatever they expect the other person to do, and we have the standard Prisoner's Dilemma case where the equilibrium outcome $(0, 0)$ is suboptimal.

In the two-person case, the psychology required to generate a Prisoner's Dilemma seems unlikely to occur very often in practice. It requires that both A and B are willing to contribute $\frac{1}{2}$ unit if this has the joint result that C's need is completely met; on the other hand, neither is willing individually to raise C from 0 to $\frac{1}{2}$ or from $\frac{1}{2}$ to 1. Suppose, for instance, that C needs a pair of gloves. A and B must be willing to collaborate to spend £1 to buy him a pair, but neither by himself will spend 50p either to buy C the first

[16] H. Margolis, *Selfishness, Altruism and Rationality* (Chicago: University of Chicago Press, 1982), ch. 2.
[17] The Prisoner's Dilemma has been widely discussed. For those unfamiliar with the idea, there is a convenient summary in M. Taylor, *The Possibility of Co-operation* (Cambridge: Cambridge University Press, 1987), ch. 1. The game of Chicken and some of its applications are explored in M. Taylor and H. Ward, 'Chickens, Whales and Lumpy Goods', *Political Studies*, 30 (1982), 350–70.

glove, or to buy him the second. There is nothing formally wrong here: 50p invested in the collaborative endeavour 'buys' more altruistic utility than either individual purchase taken separately (it makes the difference between a completely cold C and a completely warm C). All the same, the conditions are not likely to be met with only two donors involved.[18] But the likelihood of a Prisoner's Dilemma occurring rises sharply as the number of potential donors increases. If there are twenty donors, A may be willing to contribute 50p to a joint purchase of £10 of warm clothing for C, but be willing neither to buy the first glove ('he's so cold that one glove will hardly make a difference') nor to buy the last sock ('he's pretty warm now; an extra sock isn't worth 50p to me').

Thus a population of calculating altruists are liable to find themselves embroiled either in a game of Chicken or in a Prisoner's Dilemma when faced with a group of needy people. The game will be Chicken if each of the altruists would in the last resort be willing to provide for the needs out of his own pocket; Prisoner's Dilemma if he would only be willing to provide for some fraction of the needs as part of a joint endeavour. As the number of potential donors and recipients rises, a Prisoner's Dilemma becomes increasingly likely. In either case, altruists of this kind ought to be willing to enter an enforceable agreement to donate to the needy. If the game is a Prisoner's Dilemma, each can foresee that a suboptimal outcome (nobody donates) will arise.[19] If the game is Chicken, there is a fair chance either of under-provision (nobody donates) or of inefficient over-provision (more donate than is necessary). The former possibility provides, of course, the standard reply to the libertarian position

[18] The considerations that would typically make A unwilling to spend 50p on the first glove, say ('What use is a single glove? Hardly any better than no gloves at all.') ought generally to make him willing to spend 50p on a second if B buys the first; in other words, the example is likely to rely on a threshold effect of some kind, either to explain A's refusal to move from $(0, 0)$ to $(\frac{1}{2}, 0)$ or to explain his refusal to move from $(0, \frac{1}{2})$ to $(\frac{1}{2}, \frac{1}{2})$. But the threshold idea cannot be used to explain both refusals.

[19] I omit here discussion of the special circumstances in which voluntary co-operation may occur in a Prisoner's Dilemma. The essential condition is that the game should be repeated an indefinite number of times with the same group of players, in which case it may be rational for each player to adopt a (conditional) co-operative strategy. Investigating whether this condition is likely to apply in the case we are considering (public welfare provision) would take us too far afield. See Taylor, *The Possibility of Co-operation*, and I. McLean, 'The Social Contract in Leviathan and the Prisoner's Dilemma Supergame', *Political Studies*, 29 (1981), 339–51, for discussion.

on altruism: voluntary donations may fail because, although each potential donor values the outcome of giving, none values it enough to donate of his own accord.

There is, however, a short distance to traverse before we arrive at a rationale for a welfare state as a means of extracting calculating altruists from their predicament. A more obvious way out might seem to reside in a collective contract where each person agrees to provide £X on condition that a specific number of others do likewise. This would appear to solve the game-theoretical problem while retaining the advantage that each person could choose the precise direction in which his aid would be given. One might imagine specific charities approaching potential donors to ask for conditional pledges which would only be activated once the requisite number of names had been signed up.[20]

There are two sources of difficulty with this solution. One is practical, and has to do with establishing confidence. Each donor, when approached for the second time and asked to hand over his cash, needs to be convinced that the conditional contracts have been signed, and that they will be adhered to. It will be difficult (though perhaps not impossible) for a voluntary agency to generate this confidence. The second is more theoretical. For the same reason that calculating altruists will be unwilling to donate independently, they may be unwilling to sign their conditional contracts. They may hope that the charity in question can find enough other donors, so that the desired end is reached without they themselves having to dip into their pockets. Of course if there were exactly n potential donors willing to give £X, and £nX was the amount required to achieve the desired outcome, they would have no reason to hold back. But this is an unlikely state of affairs, and it is still more unlikely that anyone would know that it obtained. So, when approached, the calculating altruist will reason as follows: the chances are either that there exist $m(>n)$ donors, in which case I will hold out in the hope that some other n can be induced to sign, or there exist $m'(<n)$ donors, in which case signing up will be pointless (albeit harmless) in any case. Either way there is no good reason for me to sign.

---

[20] This possibility is canvassed in Nozick, *Anarchy, State and Utopia*, 268, though in relation to a population of reciprocal altruists (for whom the second objection below would not apply).

It may seem unreasonable to imagine an altruist reasoning in this cold-hearted way; but that would be a more general objection to the postulates that underlie calculating altruism (on which more below). The point now is that a population of calculating altruists should welcome a forcible system of transfers to the needy to which no one is exempt from contributing. For each person in the population this is the least costly way of achieving the desired outcome. Each would like to free ride on the relief scheme if he could, but since that option is impossible without destroying the scheme, it is better to force each person to provide $1/n$ of the cost. In so far as the welfare state can be seen as a mechanism of this kind, calculating altruists should welcome (and vote for) its existence.

What if the population is more mixed, containing, say, a proportion of egoists? A forcible transfer scheme is then unlikely to represent a Pareto-improvement (egoists will be made worse off by it unless they all happen to be net recipients) and may or may not maximize the overall satisfaction of preferences (depending on numbers, intensities, etc.). The altruists cannot afford, however, to opt for a scheme that includes only their own number, because by the logic outlined above each will be tempted to exempt himself by pretending to be an egoist. They must, therefore, continue to support an inclusive and compulsory scheme.

On the other hand, if each person has some altruistic feelings, but there are differences in the direction of altruism—that is, we are considering 'needs' altruists who disagree to some extent about which needs are worth satisfying—then we might contemplate a scheme by which each person (compulsorily) contributes a certain amount, but indicates at the same time how he would like the money spent. Here are no free-rider problems of the standard sort (no one is allowed to propose himself as the object of aid). There may, though, be difficulties of co-ordination. Few people are likely to want all the available resources spent in a single direction. More probably they will want money spent on medicine (say) up to a certain point, then on education (say); or else they will have preferences between these items which can be represented by indifference curves of the usual shape.[21] If donors

---

[21] I leave aside here additional problems posed by ill-informed or irrational preferences (e.g. preferences for particular forms of medical research that are unrelated to the real contribution these types of research are likely to make to the saving of life).

are only allowed to indicate a first preference, there is a risk either that the most popular items will be oversupplied or that, in anticipation of this result, an indeterminate number of people will cast their votes for items further down the list. Even if the contributors are allowed to display a more sophisticated set of preferences, there is still room for people to behave strategically and thus no guarantee that the distribution of resources that results is actually the one that corresponds best to the true preferences of the donors.

Where a welfare state is instituted, the level of contributions (the tax structure) is set by democratic decision, let us suppose, whereas the form of provision is decided by welfare professionals who make an assessment of the relative urgency of needs.[22] This will look an appealing solution to calculating altruists either (a) if they are preference altruists, unconcerned about which items in particular are provided for the needy; (b) if they are needs altruists in substantial agreement about a rank ordering of needs; (c) if despite their differences in this respect they are alive to the possible inefficiencies of an earmarking system.[23]

IV

The discussion up to this point has been premissed on the assumption that calculating altruism is a reasonable way of representing people's altruistic concerns. This assumption may well be challenged. It is certainly implausible as a general explanation of altruistic behaviour. As Margolis and Sugden have both pointed out, it would exclude commonly observed phenomena (charities that are supported by a large number of donors for example) and predict others that seem distinctly

---

[22] Clearly it would be possible to mount an empirical critique of the latter supposition, countering it with the observation that welfare professionals are likely to be governed by private interests of various sorts. The critics ought, however, to reflect on whether the same problems might not bedevil voluntary schemes. Have the organizers of charities no private interests?

[23] In the third case, one could argue that each person should be allowed to earmark a small proportion of his contribution for specific needs. The argument here would be that, with relatively small sums involved, no single item will be grossly over-supplied; at the same time, the earmarking would provide the managers of the system with up-to-date information about people's specific concerns. Such a proposal does, I think, deserve serious practical consideration; apart from anything else it might help to strengthen perceptions of the link between taxation and welfare expenditure.

unlikely.[24] For instance, it predicts that a person about to make a £10 donation to some worthy cause will reduce his contribution virtually to zero if someone else steps in and donates £10 ahead of him. Since all the would-be donor cares about is the end result (the charity being £10 richer) he should be happy to free-ride on the other person's gift.[25] Empirically, however, it is clear that people are far less susceptible than this to other people's donations, and indeed that the interactive effects may tend to operate in the other direction—that is, people may be positively encouraged to contribute by seeing others do likewise (and not only in cases where the good being sought has threshold properties). There are large areas of altruistic behaviour which the hypothesis of calculating altruism cannot explain.

It should not, however, be dismissed entirely. Some phenomena do seem to fit the model. The example I used to introduce it—bystanders waiting for someone else to go to the rescue of a person who collapses in the street—is only too familiar. The fact also that most people express their political support for the welfare state (i.e. express a willingness to be taxed quite heavily to provide welfare services) while at the same time being more or less inclined to fiddle their own contributions downwards suggests a calculating psychology. It is worth noting that in both these cases the costs of contribution are perceived as relatively high. My guess is that people who hold back when someone collapses in front of them do so out of anxiety that much time and effort will eventually be involved (will I end up escorting him to hospital?, etc.). Charitable donations, on the other hand, are typically small in relation to income, and their size is completely under control. It may be of importance that the body of experimental evidence that reveals people's willingness to contribute even when they could free-ride on the collective good being provided has been obtained using sums of money that are really quite small.[26]

The calculating altruist finds himself embroiled in Prisoner's

---

[24] Margolis, *Selfishness, Altruism and Rationality*, ch. 2; R. Sugden, 'On the Economics of Philanthropy', *Economic Journal*, 92 (1982), 341–50.

[25] This is a slight oversimplification. The intervening donation is equivalent to a £10 increment in the original benefactor's income. With this increment, he might now be prepared to give slightly more than £10 to the charity—say, an extra 50p. Even this assumes a relatively high marginal propensity to contribute. See Margolis, *Selfishness, Altruism and Rationality*, 20.

[26] See G. Marwell and R. Ames, 'Experiments on the Provision of Public Goods: I',

Dilemmas and games of Chicken because, although he values the collective outcome of giving positively, he values his own contribution negatively (as a loss of resources that would otherwise be available for private ends). The other forms of altruism I shall consider all attach intrinsic value in some way to the act of giving. They involve what Margolis calls 'participation altruism', though I shall make finer distinctions within this broad category.

The first of these sub-species to be considered is reciprocal altruism. The reciprocal altruist is someone who is prepared to contribute to the welfare of the needy, but only on condition that the other members of a designated group also contribute. In the two-person case, A will give to C provided B does also. Whereas for a calculating A the best outcome is $(0, 1)$, for a reciprocal A the optimum is $(\frac{1}{2}, \frac{1}{2})$.

Thus:

$$(\tfrac{1}{2}, \tfrac{1}{2}) > (0, 1)$$

$$(\tfrac{1}{2}, \tfrac{1}{2}) > (0, 0) > (\tfrac{1}{2}, 0) > (1, 0).$$

If B contributes $\frac{1}{2}$, A would prefer to reciprocate by giving $\frac{1}{2}$ himself rather than allow B to increase his contribution to 1. On the other hand, A will not contribute $\frac{1}{2}$ himself, much less 1, if B holds back. Thus $(0, 0)$ is a possible outcome if each expects the other not to contribute.

The reciprocal altruist is clearly moved by a notion of fairness. He sees the relief of need as something to which everyone has an equal obligation to contribute. If others do their bit, he will do his without compulsion. On the other hand, he is unwilling to be a 'sucker', to lower his own stock of resources only to find that the rest of the group have maintained theirs. Altruism of this sort may again seem mean-spirited, but it is comprehensible and, I believe, practically familiar. Its presence might be accounted for in evolutionary terms, borrowing the idea that reciprocal altruism is a stable phenomenon, whereas loftier sorts of altruists are prone to exploitation by egoists, and therefore liable to disappear in a competitive struggle for survival.[27]

American Journal of Sociology, 84 (1979), 1335–60, and 'Experiments on the Provision of Public Goods: II', *American Journal of Sociology*, 85 (1980), 926–37. N. Frohlich and J. Oppenheimer, 'Beyond Economic Man: Altruism, Egalitarianism and Difference Maximizing', *Journal of Conflict Resolution*, 28 (1984), 3–24.

[27] See R. Dawkins, *The Selfish Gene* (Oxford: Oxford University Press, 1976), ch. 10; McLean, 'The Social Contract in Leviathan and the Prisoner's Dilemma Supergame'.

If A and B are both reciprocal altruists, they find themselves playing an Assurance game. Both prefer $(\frac{1}{2}, \frac{1}{2})$ to $(0, 0)$. But each will contribute $\frac{1}{2}$ only on condition that he expects the other to reciprocate. Thus if they have to declare their contributions independently, the outcome depends on their mutual expectation. If they declare in sequence, with A going first, then B will play $\frac{1}{2}$ if A plays $\frac{1}{2}$ and 0 if A plays 0. What will A do? If he *knows* that B is also a reciprocal altruist, then he will play $\frac{1}{2}$ and all is well. If he is uncertain about B's intentions, then his choice will depend on his estimate of the probability of B's contributing (p), and his relative valuation of the two payoffs. He will contribute if $p(\frac{1}{2}, \frac{1}{2})$ > $(1-p)(\frac{1}{2}, 0)$.

Generalizing this result, a population of reciprocal altruists can arrive at an optimum by voluntary means provided they trust one another and can co-ordinate their behaviour. A compulsory welfare state would not be necessary provided that the appropriate level of contribution is established in some way, and people are able to verify that others are pulling their weight. It may be difficult to persuade anyone to make the first move since, if each reciprocal altruist demands *universal* contribution, he may be inclined to set p (the chance of everyone else doing their bit) very low indeed. This suggests that compulsion might be needed to start the scheme up; thereafter, provided contributions remain visible, no one has an incentive to pull out.

That conclusion is vulnerable, however, to complications of at least two sorts.[28] One is simply the presence of a small number of egoists or, for that matter, calculating altruists (who will generally behave like egoists in the matter of making individual contributions).[29] If the reciprocal altruist really demands *universal* participation then even one egoist will sabotage a voluntary scheme. Is that too strong a condition? Empirically it seems to be. Take the

[28] A third sort of complication, not discussed in the text, is posed for a population whose resources are unequally distributed. In the simple example, A and B are assumed to be equally endowed, and so reciprocity occurs when each contributes $\frac{1}{2}$ unit. With unequal holdings the meaning of each person 'doing his bit' may be disputed—witness the familiar debate about which form of taxation (a poll tax, a uniform income tax, a progressive income tax, etc.) best corresponds to our notion of 'equal sacrifice'.

[29] Calculating altruists will consider what chance their own failure to contribute would have on the viability of the scheme as a whole. A single calculating altruist would contribute if he believed that otherwise the scheme would collapse. Two calculating altruists might find themselves playing a game of Chicken if their joint defection would sabotage the scheme.

example of a whip-round for a departing colleague. This seems a plausible case of reciprocal altruism, in so far as most people will adjust their contribution to the 'going rate' as established by the first few donors. But such a scheme is not generally undermined by one or two recalcitrant individuals. Rather there seems to be a gradient, differently sloped for different people, whereby individuals relate their own obligation to contribute to the number of others who have contributed; below a certain point, the obligation disappears entirely ('If it's only going to be me, Bill, and Julia, let's forget the whole thing').

Note, however, that in this sort of case, the stakes involved are relatively small. As we increase them, a demand for strict reciprocity becomes more likely. Consider the following. A department of ten people is instructed to cut its budget by 10 per cent by laying off one of its members. The surviving members, altruistically motivated, offer to take a 10 per cent cut in salary to save their colleague's job. This proposal does seem vulnerable to the defection of a single participant. Most people will feel the effects of a 10 per cent salary cut quite acutely. The sight of a defector continuing to enjoy his usual standard of living may be resented strongly enough to induce further defections. Where substantial costs are involved, it may therefore be necessary to make contributions mandatory even for reciprocal altruists.

A second complication arises if the group in question is composed of people who are altruistic to different degrees. Each is willing to contribute $1/n$ of some amount $£X$ if the others do, but X varies from person to person. Under these circumstances it will prove to be impossible to obtain voluntary contributions in excess of $£X_i/n$, where X_i is the value of X for the least altruistic member.[30] Everyone else is deterred from supplying more of the altruistic good that they value by the reluctance of this person. A differentiated scheme of contributions would be more efficient. In short, relying on voluntary reciprocal altruism in a heterogeneous population leads to under-provision of need-satisfying goods.[31]

---

[30] This is on the assumption that each contributor demands universal compliance with the level of donation he makes himself. If we weaken that assumption, as in the earlier discussion, things will not look so bad.

[31] See R. Sugden, 'Reciprocity: The Supply of Public Goods through Voluntary Contributions', *Economic Journal*, 94 (1984), 772–87.

How do these complications bear on the case for the welfare state? They certainly help to show why many reciprocal altruists might favour a system which compelled them to contribute towards welfare provision for the needy. They do not of themselves show that such compulsion would be legitimate. For the substance of the argument of the foregoing paragraphs is that a voluntary system might prove highly inefficient for many altruists, in the sense that they would themselves not contributing in circumstances where they would be perfectly prepared to join a co-ordinated scheme. But what of the position of the egoist or the weakest altruist? If we take it as axiomatic that a scheme of compulsion must have *everyone's* consent (as some libertarians will stoutly maintain), then we still have no case. I ask later whether it is reasonable to impose such a unanimity criterion. Without it, considerations both of fairness and of efficiency will point reciprocal altruists towards compulsory financing of the welfare state.

There may still be some doubts as to whether reciprocal altruism really counts as altruism, even among those who recognize it as a valid account of some parts of our behaviour. If altruism is a matter of being concerned about other people's interests, then, although it is understandable enough that we should complain about (and exert moral pressure on) those who could help but don't, how can it be reasonable to make our contribution dependent on the contributions of others? Isn't it perverse of A to withdraw his donation if B fails to donate? Can he really care about C's interests if he does? (Note that this is not to be construed as a threshold case—i.e. a case where A's contribution does no good unless B also contributes.) Isn't the real altruist the person who begins by giving $\frac{1}{2}$, waits for B to reciprocate (and perhaps tries to persuade him to do so), but in the last resort gives another $\frac{1}{2}$ if B fails to donate? (That is, $(\frac{1}{2}, \frac{1}{2}) > (1, 0) > (\frac{1}{2}, 0) > (0, 0)$.)

These doubts spring, I believe, from the 'sympathy' interpretation of altruism mentioned above. Altruism here involves a sense of pleasure felt at another's happiness. This fits some cases, but it is equally possible for altruism to take the form of acknowledged obligation. In the present context, the important point is that the obligation is seen as incumbent on the group as a whole. Each person is equally obliged to help other members in so far as these latter are demonstrated to be in need. But no one is obliged to take another's share of the burden upon himself. More strongly —and this is what is required to support reciprocal altruism—no one is obliged to disadvantage himself relative to others in discharging his duties to the collectivity. (This presumably implies a background distribution which is already fair in some sense—so that if A contributes while B does not, A is disadvantaged from the point of view of this bench-mark.)

V

The reciprocal altruist can be contrasted with a third character, the conscientious altruist (or in some discussions the 'Kantian' altruist).[32] The conscientious altruist acts on a maxim which, if followed by everyone in the relevant population, would produce the outcome that he altruistically desires. He does so regardless of how other people are expected to, or known to, behave. The conscientious altruist presumably prefers others to act on the maxim as well, but this has no effect on his own behaviour. Continuing with our original example, A is a conscientious altruist if:

$$(\tfrac{1}{2},0) > (0,0)$$
$$(\tfrac{1}{2},\tfrac{1}{2}) > (0,1)$$
$$(\tfrac{1}{2},0) > (1,0).$$

The last condition differentiates the conscientious altruist from a fourth (and last) type, whom I shall call the 'superconscientious' altruist. For this person:

$$(\tfrac{1}{2},\tfrac{1}{2}) > (0,1)$$
$$(1,0) > (\tfrac{1}{2},0) > (0,0).$$

The superconscientious altruist not only does his own duty, but is prepared to do B's as well if B fails to contribute. He still, however, prefers $(\tfrac{1}{2}, \tfrac{1}{2})$ to $(1, 0)$; a person of whom the latter was not true would either be a saint, or, more likely, a person whose 'altruism' stemmed ultimately not from concern for the interests of C but from status-seeking or some such motive.

---

[32] See Collard, *Altruism and Economy*, esp. chs. 1–2.

It should be clear that a homogeneous population of conscientious altruists faces only co-ordination problems of the informational sort; there are no game-theoretical problems. To reach the desired outcome, all that is necessary is for each person to calculate correctly what proportion of his resources to donate. No one's behaviour depends on his expectations about others. Superconscientious altruists face only benign behavioural problems of the 'after you' variety (that is, if neither knows what the other's preference ordering is, they may be uncertain whether to donate $\frac{1}{2}$ or 1 and end up by over-supplying C).

It follows that conscientious altruists would have no need of a welfare state, since they would be able to achieve the same result by a system of voluntary transfers. They might find it useful to have a central co-ordinating authority, but such an authority would simply announce (and not enforce) the level of contributions. Would they positively object to a welfare state? As the case has been described so far, they would have no grounds for doing so, because the welfare state would merely compel them to do what they had good reason to do in any case.[33] Indeed, if the population was not completely homogeneous, they might welcome it as a means of compelling a recalcitrant minority of egoists or calculating altruists (assuming, that is, that they have ($\frac{1}{2}$, $\frac{1}{2}$) > ($\frac{1}{2}$, o)).[34] Note that conscientious altruists are liable to be exploited by calculating altruists (the latter recognizing that the former will contribute whatever they do themselves) and anyone may reasonably take steps to avoid exploitation of this sort ('Why should Jones sleep happily in his bed knowing that I'm looking after the old and sick?').

This reasoning breaks down, however, if the conscientious altruists are *needs* altruists with differing interpretations of 'need'. Each will then want to contribute to need as he identifies it, whereas a uniform, compulsory system will oblige him to satisfy a schedule of needs predetermined in some way (e.g. by majority

---

[33] This ignores the possibility that the act of giving might be valued only if it is a free choice, i.e. one that is not legally compelled. It is worth noting that Kant himself did not share the latter view, seeing the function of law as one of enforcing obligations that moral agents would perform out of a sense of pure duty; there was no suggestion that legal enforcement might pre-empt the moral motive.

[34] This is entailed by my initial assumption that all altruists must have as first preference one of the states in which C receives 1 unit. It is of course possible to conceive of an altruist so narrowly conscientious that ($\frac{1}{2}$, $\frac{1}{2}$) = ($\frac{1}{2}$, o). ('I've done my duty; let the others take care of their own souls.')

decision). However, this very possibility raises some doubts about the cogency of conscientious altruism as a way of representing attitudes to the needy.

The conscientious altruist, to recall, acts on a maxim that, if followed by everyone, would bring about the outcome that he (altruistically) desires, irrespective of his beliefs about how many others will actually do likewise. How intelligible a view is that? We need to investigate whether individual acts are likely to interrelate in such a way that the value of each depends on the character of the remainder. In some cases the interrelation will be relatively insignificant. If I am in a position to save somebody's life (say, by rescuing him from a cliff face) the value of what I do depends rather little on whether other people, similarly situated, would undertake the rescue. On the whole, welfare contributions are not like that . A single contribution, spread across a large number of people in need, will make very little impact. It is even possible to conceive of isolated contributions intersecting in a harmful way.[35] Here, then, the value of the act (and therefore one's decision about the right thing to do) does depend on expectations about other people's behaviour. 'Doing your bit' makes sense only if enough others are also doing theirs. This is still a different attitude from that of the reciprocal altruist. The latter objects to contributing when others don't, seeing that possibility as unfair or exploitative. The attitude I am now describing is one of wanting to do 'the right thing' regardless of others, but understanding that what 'the right thing' is may depend on how others behave. None the less, the practical effects may be rather similar.

Simple conscientious altruism makes sense where, by acting in a certain way, I can confer a visible good or avoid a visible harm (most examples of conscientious action are probably negative in character: not lying, stealing, cheating, etc.). Deprived of this certainty, people who would be conscientious are likely to behave in ways that suggest calculating or reciprocal altruism. This explains, for example, why people respond very differently to the prospect of evading taxation from that of cheating a storekeeper. In a survey, most people (66 per cent) said that they might

---

[35] If people are giving specific items, then a set of transfers may be harmful on balance, particularly if incentive considerations are included (the recipients may be given local incentives that conflict with the incentives that would eventually lead them to globally better outcomes).

consider evading value-added tax on a plumbing job, and only 35 per cent regarded such behaviour as wrong or seriously wrong.[36] By contrast only 18 per cent would pocket £5 in change given in error in a store, and 77 per cent thought such behaviour wrong or seriously wrong. In the latter case, there is a visible harm—the store is made £5 worse off. In the former case a contribution has been withheld, but there may be uncertainty about what its effect would be: perhaps the government has taken some evasion into account, so my contribution may not be important?[37] Thus we do not have to discount conscientiousness in general in order to believe that it may not provide a secure foundation for a welfare system. The problem is not necessarily that people don't have the right moral capacities, but rather that the way in which they see their relationship to others (both to other donors and to the needy) doesn't bring those capacities into play.

We might contemplate arrangements that did try to activate conscientious altruism. For instance it might be proposed that each person should donate to a specific recipient, so that a failure to contribute would have an immediate and visible effect.[38] (This, presumably, is the thinking behind charitable schemes which invite one to 'adopt' a family or a community project in the Third World.) The disadvantages of such a proposal are clear. Donations would have to be in cash (no donor could be expected by himself to provide specific aid), and it would be difficult to adjust the sums given to changes in need. We have seen already that even preference altruists might find a cash-donation system less eligible than provision in kind, depending on circumstances. Moreover if a few people default, the effects are more disastrous for individual recipients than under a pooling arrangement. Recall that, *ex hypothesi*, our conscientious altruists are concerned about the overall outcome, and therefore about others contributing, even if their chief concern is that they should do the right thing themselves $((\frac{1}{2}, \frac{1}{2}) > (\frac{1}{2}, 0))$. Unless assured of everyone's conscientiousness, this is a powerful consideration against a person-to-person arrangement.

[36] See R. Jowell and S. Witherspoon (eds.), *British Social Attitudes: The 1985 Report* (Aldershot: Gower, 1985), 123–6.

[37] Of course a similar line of reasoning might be applied to the store ('a big store' in the survey) which makes the difference in response all the more remarkable. Presumably far less than 18% would consider defrauding a private individual of £5.

[38] See Nozick, *Anarchy, State and Utopia*, 265–6.

VI

Let me now summarize our conclusions about the different modes of altruism and consider their implications for the welfare state.

1. Calculating altruists who understand their joint situation will almost certainly wish to institute a compulsory welfare system to extricate themselves from a Prisoner's Dilemma (or a game of Chicken).

2. Reciprocal altruists may wish to institute a welfare state for assurance reasons, and they will certainly wish to do so if they fear exploitation by egoists. A majority of 'stronger' reciprocal altruists will wish to impose such a system on a minority of 'weaker' altruists.

3. Conscientious altruists will in general need only a co-ordinating body, but they may also agree to a compulsory system to avoid exploitation by others.

I have suggested that although conscientious motivation in general is an important and widespread phenomenon, the character of welfare provision is not such as to bring it naturally into play. It seems better to assume that, for the most part, people will behave in this area either as calculating or as reciprocal altruists. In either case, the welfare state has a firm grounding. Although in theory a population of reciprocal altruists might manage without it, this result is fragile in a number of respects. It seems likely that voluntary reciprocal altruism could only work effectively in a small and homogeneous group.[39]

How does this bear on the libertarian claim that spurred this rather lengthy investigation? I have shown that to rely on charitable giving as a source of welfare is very unlikely to be an effective way of meeting people's altruistic concerns. If the argument is sound (as it seems to be), and if altruism in its various forms is an important fact of life, can the libertarian evade the conclusion that he should support a more-than-minimal state?

There are still at least two possible escape routes available. One involves standing firm on the inviolability of property rights.

---

[39] Cf. Sugden, 'Reciprocity', 783; M. Taylor, *Community, Anarchy and Liberty* (Cambridge: Cambridge University Press, 1982), 52–3.

If property may never be expropriated without the owner's consent, a welfare system funded by compulsory taxation must appear illegitimate even if the alternative is highly inefficient. Such a response rests on two assumptions. The first is that a convincing defence can be given of libertarian property rights. The conclusion we have already reached, in Chapter 2, is that no such defence is forthcoming. The second is that rights should be given infinite weight *vis-à-vis* considerations of social efficiency. There is nothing logically wrong with such an assumption, but it is doubtful whether even tough-minded libertarians such as Nozick are willing to rest their entire case on it. Why should Nozick try to show that a voluntary system of donation to the needy is feasible if he is impervious to the claim that altruistic concerns may make a compulsory welfare system Pareto-optimal?

A more interesting response is to question the long-run effects of the welfare state. The argument might run as follows. Once welfare provision is made compulsory, people no longer directly enjoy the experience of altruistic giving. Being deprived of that experience also means that, in the longer term, their altruism itself diminishes. They will therefore progressively withdraw their political support from the welfare state. The final outcome is that the needy receive less support than they would have received from private charity, the inefficiencies of the latter notwithstanding.

This response is interesting because it connects with certain left-wing anxieties about the impact of the state on communal practices of mutual aid.[40] But the issue that it raises is a difficult one. How far does the existence of a compulsory welfare system either encourage or discourage voluntary altruistic behaviour? At one extreme is the view that the welfare state serves as a kind of sun throwing off a multitude of minor altruistic practices.[41] At the other extreme is the view that compulsion simply replaces voluntary altruism, as we see the welfare state discharging our mutual responsibilities for us. Such limited evidence as we have suggests

---

[40] See e.g., Taylor, *The Possibility of Co-operation*, ch. 7.

[41] The *locus classicus* is R. M. Titmuss, *The Gift Relationship* (London: Allen and Unwin, 1970): 'the ways in which society organizes and structures its social institutions—and particularly its health and welfare systems—can encourage or discourage the altruistic in man' (p. 225).

that neither extreme view is correct.[42] The welfare state clearly does displace private charity in areas where it is directly involved—for instance, the provision of hospitals. But it leaves open a wide field of activity in which voluntary organizations continue to flourish. If this is so, there is no real ground for concern that our altruistic instincts will atrophy for lack of exercise. At most the libertarian argument gives a reason for confining the compulsory system to essential provision so as to leave ample scope for voluntary action of various kinds.

We have now investigated two areas in which a libertarian order appears unable to respond effectively to people's conceptions of the good. The first issue was whether orthodox markets catered adequately for preferences for co-operative work relations. The second issue was whether private charity was an effective means of expressing altruistic concern for fellow citizens. In both cases our conclusion has been that political intervention may create a social framework that is both more neutral than the libertarian framework (in the sense that it responds even-handedly to different conceptions of the good) and more efficient (in the sense that it realizes such conceptions more fully). If the libertarian replies that such intervention always involves coercion and injustice, I refer him to the arguments of Chapters 1 and 2, where the libertarian accounts of freedom and justice have been challenged. This concludes the critique of libertarianism, and I turn in Part II to the defence of markets under socialism.

---

[42] See J. Obler, 'Private Giving in the Welfare State', *British Journal of Political Science*, 11 (1981), 17–48.

PART II

A Defence of Markets

5
CONSUMER SOVEREIGNTY

I

The critique of libertarianism which I have offered in the last four chapters has been developed as far as possible from premisses that libertarians themselves should be able to accept. The case for an unrestricted capitalist economy and a minimal state has been assessed in terms of values—freedom, justice, neutrality, efficiency—to which defenders of such an order characteristically appeal. As we have seen, the case collapses on close scrutiny, or is salvageable only by introducing new and unpalatable assumptions (such as the restrictive notion of moral responsibility considered towards the end of Chapter 1). Libertarianism turns out to be indefensible even in its own terms.

In developing this critique I have also, though somewhat obliquely, been laying the ethical foundations of market socialism. For market socialism, as outlined in the Introduction, aspires to preserve the economic efficiency and freedom of choice of the market economy, but to alter the institutional framework of capitalism so as to promote other, equally important, social values. In Chapter 1 I considered the issue of freedom, and argued that widening access to productive resources would increase the freedom of those who currently lack such access. In Chapter 2 I attacked the proposition that capitalist property rights were self-evidently just, and argued that property systems should be assessed by criteria of distributive justice (preparing the way for the more positive argument of Chapter 6, in which market socialist arrangements are defended by reference to a principle of desert). In Chapter 3 I suggested that a policy that was genuinely neutral between different conceptions of the good life would require economic intervention in the market, particularly in support of co-operative work relationships. Finally, in Chapter 4, I defended welfare-state institutions on grounds of efficiency, assuming the existence of widespread altruistic concern for our fellow citizens. In each case, market socialist arrangements were presented as a better embodiment than minimal-state capitalism of the values to which libertarians appeal.

In this second part of the book, the spotlight turns on to market socialism itself. Socialists of traditional hue, while acknowledging perhaps that market socialism represents a considerable advance on capitalism, are likely to claim that *any* market economy is none the less defective in a number of respects. My aim over the next four chapters is to scrutinize the reasoning behind this basic hostility to markets as such, and to show that market socialism, at least, need not be vulnerable to such criticism. I attempt, then, to show that market socialism is compatible with the humanistic aims of the socialist tradition, as well as with libertarian ideals.

The present chapter concentrates on efficiency, or rather on one aspect of that idea represented by the slogan 'consumer sovereignty'. It is a central plank of the case for markets that they are an effective way of organizing economic life in the interests of consumers. Put simply, they are the best known means of ensuring that consumers get what they want. Now we know from the last two chapters that this cannot be unqualifiedly true. There are certain preferences which markets generically are ill equipped to meet. The cases specifically considered were preferences for certain types of personal relations (such as co-operative work relations) and altruistic preferences directed at the welfare of fellow citizens. But there are many other desires that markets tend to respond to poorly or not at all: as noted above (pp. 81–2) these will include preferences for familiar public goods such as an attractive environment. So the consumer sovereignty argument must be kept in proper perspective. Stripped of hyperbole, what it claims is that there is a range of mundane private goods—food, clothing, household items and so forth—which will be provided most efficiently by allowing markets to operate freely and obliging producers (whether individuals or collectives) to respond to the pattern of consumer demand, at the same time minimizing the cost of their inputs.

The value which is appealed to here is personal welfare, but again it is important not to spoil the case by overstatement. The assumption is that people are better off when they are able to obtain goods in the quantities and qualities that they prefer. One need not assume anything about the proportion contributed by consumption of any sort to 'real' or inner happiness. Such evidence as we have suggests that the major sources of personal happiness lie elsewhere—in family life, leisure activities, and so forth. In particular, there is no observable general increase in human satisfaction as a society's material standard of living increases, suggesting that absolute levels of consumer goods are not of great importance from this point of view.[1] But to conclude from this that economic arrangements are irrelevant from the point of view of welfare is to set the stakes too high. Even if such arrangements only contribute a small amount, they represent the portion over which we have the greatest degree of collective choice. That is why debate over the relative efficiency of markets and planning has raged so fiercely.

There are broadly two ways to challenge the claim that markets, with the qualifications noted above, are an efficient means of satisfying the desires of consumers. One is to take issue empirically with the standard theorems of welfare economics, which show (for instance) that the competitive equilibrium towards which a properly functioning market will gravitate is always Pareto-optimal. Here the critic may point out various competitive failures—tendencies to monopoly, distorted information, cycles in production—which in the real world drive markets away from the text-book results. This is economists' territory, which in general I have no wish to encroach upon, although I touch upon certain aspects of the problem in Chapter 7. There is, however, another line of attack, which begins from the observation that most of the desires people manifest in market economies are artificially induced. They are not rooted directly in human biology or psychology. Instead they are fostered by the process of production itself, either deliberately, for instance by advertising, or incidentally, as when the very appearance of a new product creates a demand for it. This observation appears to cut the ground from beneath the efficiency argument for markets. On the face of it, the very idea of efficiency presupposes an independently given set of wants in terms of which the comparative effectiveness of different systems of production could be estimated. If markets create the demands that they then proceed to satisfy, the argument becomes damagingly circular. As Gal-

[1] See R. E. Lane, 'Markets and the Satisfaction of Human Wants', *Journal of Economic Issues*, 12 (1978), 799–827.

braith once put it, applauding the market is rather like applauding a squirrel for keeping abreast of a wheel that is propelled by its own efforts.[2] Many critics of the market would conclude that the much-vaunted superiority of markets to economic planning is for this reason largely illusory.

My strategy in this chapter will be to look at a number of ways in which individuals' wants may change, and to separate out those cases where the change might seem to have worrying implications for the general efficiency argument for markets. I shall also ask whether in these cases it is possible to conceive of political intervention producing a better outcome. In order to do this, it is necessary to appeal to an idea of welfare that can accommodate changes in desires. That is, we must be able to make comparative judgements about how well off a person is in two states of affairs, even if his preferences are different in the two situations. We might, for instance, judge that Smith is better off in S_2 with preferences P_2 than he was in S_1 with preferences P_1. How should such judgements be interpreted? For present purposes we may set aside questions about the quality of different desires; there is no need to introduce Mill-like distinctions between higher and lower pleasures, or to consider the issues raised by immoral or anti-social preferences. The notion of welfare we shall employ will depend solely on the quantity of preferences that are satisfied.[3] But this notion still stands in need of interpretation. Suppose, for example, that Smith acquires some new desires in S_2 without losing any of those that he had in S_1. Should we compare his welfare in S_1 and S_2 by the relative *proportion* of his preferences that are satisfied in the two states, or should we try to total up the *volume* of preferences that are fulfilled in each? If, say, he has three new desires in S_2, of which one is fulfilled, then the first criterion might give $S_1 > S_2$ and the second $S_2 > S_1$. The first suggestion sees welfare as a matter of how close a person comes to achieving his overall goals, the second regards it as an aggregate of satisfying experiences. Each interpretation has some

---

[2] J. K. Galbraith, *The Affluent Society* (Harmondsworth: Penguin, 1962), 132. See also Penz's discussion of 'evaluation circularity', in G. P. Penz, *Consumer Sovereignty and Human Interests* (Cambridge: Cambridge University Press, 1986), ch. 6.

[3] I postpone consideration of the view that it is not the satisfaction of *preferences* but the fulfilment of *needs* that matters from the point of view of welfare until the end of the chapter.

immediate plausibility, yet on reflection neither seems acceptable as an index of welfare in all conceivable cases.[4]

Since we are employing a desire-based notion of welfare, the obvious course is to appeal to Smith himself to decide whether he is better off in S_2 with preferences P_2 or in S_1 with P_1. This seems to me a compelling solution in cases where his judgement tallies under both P_1 and P_2. For example, starting with P_1 he engineers a change to P_2, believing that he will be better off as a result, and after the change he judges it to be a success. Suppose he decides to cultivate a taste for fine wines, believing that the exquisite sensations he will experience will more than outweigh the extra cost of his new drinking habits. Or suppose he recognizes that one of his present desires is an expensive obsession, preventing him from pursuing a number of other activities that he values, and he undergoes therapy to escape it. Where his judgements before and after the event agree, we have the best possible evidence that Smith's welfare is higher in S_2 than in S_1.

Matters are more complicated when his judgements under P_1 and P_2 differ: for instance if he prefers P_1/S_1 when he has P_1 and P_2/S_2 when he has P_2. In some cases we might want to discount one or other of these judgements. We might believe, for instance, that he just fails to remember how well off he once was with P_1 in S_1, or he suppresses that memory in order to justify his present situation to himself. Presumably such a belief on our part would be supported by comparing observable signs of frustration and so forth in the two situations. On the other hand, he may have quite a clear view of the facts of the case, under both sets of preferences. His judgements diverge because he aggregates want-satisfactions differently under the two sets of preferences: that is, when summing over a number of discrete satisfactions in order to reach a general verdict on how well off he is in S_1 and S_2 respectively, he varies the relative weight attached to each. In changing his wants, he also changes his sense of how important it is to satisfy wants of

---

[4] The case which makes the proportionality criterion seem most problematic is that of the stoic who tailors his desires to his circumstances in such a way that all are fulfilled. Conversely the volume criterion looks least satisfactory in the case of a person whose routine wants are all satisfied, but who has a burning ambition that he is completely unable to fulfil. For wider discussion of the difficulties involved in making comparative welfare judgements when individuals' preferences change, see A. Buchanan, *Ethics, Efficiency and the Market* (Oxford: Clarendon Press, 1985), ch. 2, and Penz, *Consumer Sovereignty*, ch. 7.

different kinds.[5] Here it seems impossible to arrive at a judgement of welfare except by imposing some external view about how different sorts of want-satisfaction are to be aggregated. This case is similar to (though no worse than) one in which interpersonal comparisons of welfare have to be made.

If we wish to make welfare comparisons between situations in which different sets of preferences prevail, therefore, we cannot always rely on the judgements of the agents concerned. At the same time I believe we should follow these judgements when they consistently point to the same conclusion, in keeping with my general policy of interpreting welfare in want-regarding terms. With this proviso in mind, we are now in a position to embark on the main task of this chapter, which is to consider the various ways in which consumers' wants may change, and to see what the implications are in each case for the general efficiency argument for markets.

II

I shall begin with the most uncontentious kind of change—that in which a new instrumental want is acquired, i.e. a want instrumental to the satisfaction of a pre-existing desire. For instance, the demand for dishwashers may be plausibly seen as instrumental to existing goals, namely cleaner dishes and less housework. If a dishwasher is an efficient means to these ends (i.e. the cost of the dishwasher is more than compensated for by the time and effort it saves), then one is uncontroversially better off when one has this demand and has it satisfied.

In so far as markets multiply and satisfy demands of *this* kind, therefore, there is no possible objection to be raised. A problem might arise only if people were misinformed about the

---

[5] A simple illustration might clarify this point. Suppose that under $P1$, Smith's tastes are for bread and beer. In $S1$ he is able to satisfy 0.8 of his desire for each. He also rates eating and drinking equally highly. Under $P2$, his taste for beer is replaced by a taste for wine. In $S2$ he can satisfy 0.6 of his desire for bread and 0.9 of his desire for wine. But under $P2$ his relative ranking of food and drink has changed; he now rates the pleasures of drinking three times more highly than the pleasures of eating. If he is now asked to compare $P1/S1$ with $P2/S2$, we get the following outcome (using the proportionality criterion for the sake of illustration):
Under $P1$, $U(P1/S1 = \frac{1}{2} \times 0.8 + \frac{1}{2} \times 0.8 = 0.8$; $U(P2/S2) = \frac{1}{2} \times 0.6 + \frac{1}{2} \times 0.9 = 0.75$.
Under $P2$, $U(P1/S1 = \frac{1}{4} \times 0.8 + \frac{3}{4} \times 0.8 = 0.8$; $U(P2/S2) = \frac{1}{4} \times 0.6 + \frac{3}{4} \times 0.9 = 0.825$.
Thus with preferences $P1$, $P1$ $S1$ is preferred to $P2/S2$, and vice versa with preferences $P2$.

instrumental value of the object demanded. It is likely that dishwasher manufacturers will exaggerate the value of owning one. In the case of items that are bought repeatedly (disposable razors, say), the market itself provides a remedy, since no one is likely to go on buying commodities that are not worth the outlay. With consumer durables such as dishwashers, the problem is more acute. Even here, however, we may look for a remedy within the market in the form of a consumer advice service. Admittedly consumer advice in practice partially displays the character of a public good, since it is difficult to confine the information to those who pay to receive it. There may therefore be a case for political support for such services. But there is hardly a case for political intervention to stop new products being produced and marketed on the grounds that consumers might buy unwisely. Of course, if people were concerned that they might be literally helpless in the face of a certain advertising technique, they would want to protect themselves against that.

III

The second case I want to consider is that in which a person simply acquires a new taste. In other words he tries something, finds that he likes it, and thereafter includes it in his demand schedule. One might think of avocados or hang-gliding. A change of this kind might be beneficial, neutral, or detrimental. Suppose that the person's income remains the same, so that the new want has to be satisfied by cutting back elsewhere. The change may still be beneficial if the new experience is judged to be more enjoyable than what has been forgone. The person who takes up hang-gliding may decide to give up golf to do so; on balance he considers this an improvement.

Many such changes are, however, likely to be neutral, in the long term especially. The new taste simply displaces an older one, to no genuine advantage. Many changes in tastes for food seem to be of this kind. When a new version of salami appears on the market, one's palate may be tickled, but it is not clear that, once one has settled down to buying the new brand in preference to what one bought before, there is any real gain in satisfaction. One symptom of this would be cyclical changes of taste, where one switches from W to X to Y to Z and then back again to W.

Precisely because these changes are neutral, however, they are not subversive of the argument for a market. If a market economy turns out to be the most efficient way of satisfying whatever wants consumers have at any given time, this will not cease to be true merely because over time the market has the side-effect of inducing a number of neutral preference-changes. The only defence of the market which might be undercut by the idea of neutral changes in wants is that which holds up the sheer profusion of commodities that market economies generate as a consideration in their favour. Anyone who has visited cities in Eastern Europe will have been struck by the limited range of goods available on the shelves of supermarkets compared with those in the West. If, however, the diversity of the Western shops were not a response to a pre-existing variety of tastes, but merely had the effect of inducing new ones, it would not seem much of an advantage.[6]

Finally, and more worryingly, changes in taste may be detrimental. This will be so if the new taste is more expensive to satisfy than the one it replaces, so that, overall, the person concerned is less able to fulfil his desires with a given income. How might such a change come about? Consider this case: a family which for many years has been taking its annual holidays in Bournemouth wins a sum on the pools and decides to spend it on a fortnight in the Seychelles. The effect of this delightful experience is that the old routine comes to seem tawdry. Given their budgetary constraints, they now have to choose between two possibilities: an annual visit to Bournemouth (pleasant, but no longer very satisfying), or an exotic holiday abroad once every three years (better than Bournemouth ever was, but not three times as good). Whichever choice they make, they will be worse off on balance than they were before the unfortunate pools win.

This is clearly the kind of case that feeds Galbraith's metaphor of the squirrel and the wheel. The market economy extends production, but may at the same time induce detrimental changes in consumers' tastes, so that the net effect is nil. Could we begin

---

[6] This is not intended as a defence of the Communist economies, for the visitor is made equally aware that people very often aren't able to obtain what they want. The point is simply that, for some value of n, an economy which satisfies n tastes may be as efficient as one that satisfies $n+m$ tastes, once neutral changes of preferences are brought into the picture.

to build here a case for political intervention in the market, with the aim of preventing such deleterious changes from occurring? (Should holidays in the Seychelles have a Government Health Warning on the booking form?) The problem is going to be one of knowing in advance which preference changes will be detrimental for which consumers. Another family might win a holiday in the Seychelles, and this might have either a neutral or a beneficial effect on their desire schedule (they might not enjoy Bournemouth any the less, but merely save in other ways to have an occasional exotic holiday). Unless there is a general reason to believe that exposure to a particular new commodity or experience is going to be harmful, there is no defensible ground for abandoning the market. In practice, people's tastes and reactions vary so much that we are rarely in a position to make such a judgement. The most likely instances are provided by the special cases considered below.

IV

New desires may come to be felt as part of what I shall call 'status oriented consumption'. The familiar idea here is that the possession or consumption of certain goods is seen as conferring status, so a person wishing to achieve or maintain a given social position will need to acquire whatever goods that position demands. Typically the list will extend over time (or its component items will become more expensive), so one has to consume more and more in order to stay socially in the same place.

It is important to differentiate between two criticisms that may be offered of this phenomenon. The first is that there is something unhealthy about the desire for status itself, so that the particular desires which flow from it are contaminated by the source. As a general criticism this is not persuasive: status, after all, may refer not only to superior status—status in the sense of standing above some other group of people who are regarded as common or vulgar—but to equal status; one may simply wish not to exclude oneself from the normal practices of social life by appearing to be a pauper. No doubt someone who is obsessed with the niceties of social position is an unattractive creature, but this is a relatively minor aspect of the phenomenon we are considering. The second, and more telling criticism, focuses on the public goods aspect of the search for status. If the goods which confer status have no intrinsic value—or at least no greater intrinsic value than other, cheaper goods which do not—then everyone would be better off if the link could be severed. The consumption in question is unproductive in the sense that if one weren't obliged to buy expensive goods or live in an exclusive district to keep up appearances, more income would be released for fruitful consumption.[7] It would be better, from everyone's point of view, if status were based entirely on income.

For a variety of reasons, this uncoupling of status and consumption is hard to bring about. It cannot be achieved by any one individual coming to understand the linkage—I may see quite clearly that a particular commodity is worth having only for the prestige that it confers, and yet seek to have it all the same. Nor is it enough if everyone understands this, for there would still be no mechanism for bringing it about that possessing such-and-such an object carried no special status. We might perhaps expect such a collapse to occur if the object in question really had no extra consumption value. But in fact this is very unlikely to be true. Two cases spring immediately to mind. The first occurs where the high status object *is* slightly more satisfying to possess and use than its low status equivalents—Rolls-Royces are, I believe, somewhat more comfortable to ride in than ordinary saloon cars. So it is not possible to undermine the prestige of owning a Rolls by simple ridicule, as it might be in the case of a hypothetical pure prestige object. The second case occurs when status between households builds upon status within households. An example may explain this. Many households possess more than one set of crockery, with one for everyday use, and another for use on special occasions. The second set is the best set, not more useful in the ordinary sense than the other, but finer and more expensive. The distinction is needed to mark the special occasions.[8] Another household, then, whose *everyday* crockery resembles the fine china of the first household will have achieved a higher consumption status. The upward spiral that this implies cannot

---

[7] Cf. the more general discussion of 'positional goods' and the limits their emergence places on the value of economic growth in F. Hirsch, *Social Limits to Growth* (London: Routledge and Kegan Paul, 1977).

[8] For an illuminating discussion of the use of consumption goods to mark status, see M. Douglas and B. Isherwood, *The World of Goods* (New York: Basic Books, 1979).

be halted by all households agreeing that earthenware is a perfectly adequate material for serving food, because (as indicated) each household will wish to make one or more status distinctions internally.

For these reasons, status-oriented consumption is likely to prove an intractable problem. What are the implications for the efficiency argument for markets? Notice first that the source of the problem does not lie in markets as such, but in the private possession of objects of consumption. Thus status-oriented consumption might equally well emerge under a planned economy, provided only that income differentials remained, so that the possession of certain valued objects could be seen as a badge of status. Indeed, there is ample evidence that this is true of existing planned economies. The only direct solution is to transfer high-status objects from private to public ownership: if sought-after paintings are hung in public galleries, no one can acquire kudos through owning them. But although this might be desirable on quite independent grounds for objects of certain kinds (e.g. Old Masters, which are naturally as well as socially scarce), it is difficult to conceive of it as a wholesale solution to the problem we are considering. There are an enormous number of items which, for quite familiar reasons (chiefly having to do with differences in individuals' tastes) are best purchased privately by consumers, and there is no way of telling prior to the event which of these may acquire high consumption status. For the same reason, no political authority could be in a position to forestall status-oriented consumption. It is no good at all waiting to see which items take off as indicators of status and then suppressing their production. This would merely ensconce the position of those who were lucky enough to have bought them at the beginning. And although it might be possible to remove the status element from a particular good by arranging to have it mass-produced, this would simply serve as an invitation to the status-conscious to switch their attention to some other commodity.

An indirect solution, canvassed by Hirsch[9] along with the direct solution, is to reduce the size of income differentials. To take the extreme case, an egalitarian economy would offer no scope for status-oriented consumption, since there would be no superior achievement to be displayed by the show of goods. (I take

[9] Hirsch, *Social Limits*, Ch. 13.

it that status-oriented consumption aims to display one's success as an income generator, not simply one's deftness at transforming income into specific consumption goods.[10]) In less extreme cases, the limits of such consumption are set by the gap between the highest and lowest incomes. Income redistribution, therefore, tends to release a greater proportion of income for fruitful consumption, even among the status-obsessed. *A fortiori*, market economies will evade the problem of status-oriented consumption to the extent to which they distribute income in an egalitarian fashion, and market socialist systems will be less open to this criticism than capitalist systems.

V

I turn next to changes in tastes which I shall refer to generically as 'addictive'. The common feature of all cases of addiction is that a person's desire for a commodity changes systematically as a function of his past consumption. There are two main sub-categories to consider. In the first, which I shall call benign addiction, a person's desire for, and enjoyment of, a commodity increases the more of it he consumes, at least up to a certain limit. This might, for instance, be the case with certain foods or drinks whose taste or texture is offputting at first, but which one enjoys increasingly as one's taste buds are educated. It might also apply to forms of art such as opera which require education of a different kind to be fully appreciated. The second category comprises cases of malign addiction, where what was originally a desire turns into a compulsion, in the sense that the desire itself becomes increasingly strong, but the satisfaction achieved (for a given expenditure) diminishes. Familiar cases here would be drug addiction and certain kinds of sexual perversion. Putting the contrast in economic terms, with benign addiction each additional unit of expenditure yields an increasing amount of satisfaction, whereas with malign addiction, ever greater expenditures are necessary to maintain a given level of satisfaction.

[10] It is true that there is also modishness, which has to do with spending income in the 'right' way, and which in theory could thus persist under equality. My hunch, however, is that modishness can very largely be explained as a side-effect of status-oriented consumption. For instance 'young Fogeyism' (riding around on old bicycles in battered tweed jackets) seems to be a defensive reaction on the part of professional people who lack the income to enjoy the life-style they would really like to have.

The possibility of people's tastes changing addictively doesn't, of itself, pose any special problems for the efficiency of a market economy. Obviously there will be cases in which people would be better off (more satisfied) if they could become benignly addicted to some commodity, and cases in which they would be worse off if they were to become malignly addicted. But some of these cases can be handled satisfactorily within a market context. Take benign addiction first. This will come about quite spontaneously if either of two conditions are met: (*a*) the person's first experience of the commodity in question is at least enjoyable enough to make him want to try it again; or (*b*) although the first experience is not enjoyable, he knows about the commodity's benignly addictive properties, and so is willing to persist. Most of us become benignly addicted to beer, either because the first pint tastes all right or (more commonly, I suspect) because our friends tell us that it's a taste worth acquiring. For malign addiction *not* to occur, the reverse conditions must hold: either (*a*) the first experience is not enjoyable enough to make one want to continue experimenting; or (*b*) one knows enough about the commodity's addictive properties to want to avoid embarking on the downward spiral.

The corollary of this is that there is a prima facie case for political intervention when (*a*) a commodity is not rewarding enough on the first encounter to make people purchase it again, *and* (*b*) people are unable or unwilling to persist while the process of benign addiction occurs. (For malign addiction there is a corresponding conjunction.) Why might (*b*) hold? There must be a failure of rationality, which might be of two kinds: either the person is not convinced that the addictive change will come about, despite the general evidence that it will, or he is unable to act in what he recognizes to be his own long-term interests. That is, faced with a choice between commodity X and commodity Y, he chooses Y which is more immediately satisfying, even though he would be better off in the long run by sticking to X and acquiring a taste for it. Political intervention might take the extreme form of compelling him to consume X until the addictive process had worked, or the less extreme form of subsidizing the price of X so that it becomes an immediately attractive purchase. For malign addiction, the corresponding policies would be an outright ban and a consumption tax.

Arguments of this nature are not unknown in politics, particularly in the area of culture and the arts. The Reith view of broadcasting seems to have embraced the idea that by feeding people a relatively highbrow diet (whatever they appeared immediately to want) one was fostering tastes that would be beneficial in the long run.[11] Again, an argument sometimes offered for subsidizing forms of art such as opera is that to some extent they are acquired tastes, demanding a period of cultivation, and that at market prices very few people would be willing to embark on the process. On the reverse side, the banning of drugs such as heroin is standardly justified in this way (i.e. people who enjoy them at first will later regret having become addicted). In practice, addiction arguments tend to be conflated with arguments to the effect that certain commodities are inherently good or inherently bad—arguments which I have already excluded from the scope of this discussion —but in principle they are quite distinct; they are at base want-regarding arguments.

There are, however, two difficulties with political intervention in cases such as these. First, an authority embarking on such an intervention would have to be sure that the addiction effect would occur in the great majority of cases, if it was to avoid the accusation that the proposed tax or subsidy simply constituted a transfer from those with one set of tastes to those with another. The Reith argument now looks flimsy because rather few people seem to be susceptible to having their tastes cultivated in the way that he had in mind. The most plausible cases are obviously going to be those of malign addiction essentially involving physiological factors, such as drug addiction. (Even here, though, there may be disputes about whether the change that has occurred is actually deleterious, as can be seen from the various discussions of cigarette smoking.) Second, a general policy of compulsion, ban, subsidy, or tax is going to hit too broad a target. If opera subsidies are justified on addiction grounds (not on 'inherent goodness' grounds), they ought to be directed only towards those people still undergoing the addiction process. A general subsidy also benefits people who have acquired the taste and who ought therefore to be paying the full market price. Analogously, in cases of malign

---

[11] John Reith was managing director, and later director-general, of the BBC from 1923 until 1938. For his views about the functioning of broadcasting, see J. Reith, *Broadcast Over Britain* (London: Hodder and Stoughton, 1924).

addiction, the policy ought to be to deter people at the top of the spiral, but to allow a normal supply of the commodity in question to the confirmed addicts. (Of course, this supposes that the spiral reaches a lower limit, which may not be so in the case of certain drugs such as heroin.) So the policy will only be justifiable if it can be targeted selectively. This might be achieved in the case of opera by providing cheap seats to everyone below a certain age, or by giving each person a specified number of price-reducing vouchers. Whether intervention is permissible in any given case will depend on the practical question of whether such targeting is feasible. So although addictive tastes (in my broad sense) are undoubtedly important, there may turn out to be rather few instances in which we can justify abandoning consumer sovereignty in practice in favour of a politically determined choice-set.

VI

Finally, there are what I shall call, following Elster, 'adaptive preferences'.[12] Generically speaking, preferences are adaptive when they vary according to the perceived range of choices open to the agent. There are two possible types of adaptive preference formation, which can be labelled 'sour grapes' and 'green grass'. In the sour grapes case, a person places a lower value on some commodity or experience when he believes it to be unattainable than he otherwise would. Suppose he has to choose between two houses, X and Y. When he thinks that both are available to him, he values them at £70,000 and £90,000 respectively. If, however, he comes to believe (rightly or wrongly) that Y is no longer available (say he believes that someone else has purchased it), his estimate of the value of Y declines—say to £80,000 ('it doesn't matter, it was overpriced anyway.'). 'Green grass' refers to the opposite effect: the option which is perceived as unattainable has its value enhanced relative to those options which are in the feasible set. For instance, a person may always think that he

---

[12] The terminology used here has not yet been standardized. In some discussions (e.g. Von Weizsacker, 'Notes on Endogenous Change of Tastes', *Journal of Economic Theory*, 3 (1971), 360–3), 'adaptive preferences' is used to refer to preferences which change as a function of past consumption, in particular those cases I have referred to as 'benign addiction'. For Elster's analysis, see J. Elster, *Sour Grapes: Studies in the Subversion of Rationality* (Cambridge: Cambridge University Press, 1983).

would be better off in some job other than the one that he currently holds, no matter which job that happens to be.

Why might adaptive preferences pose problems for consumer sovereignty and the argument for markets? The problem with 'green grass' preferences is relatively easy to see. A person with adaptive preferences of this kind may incur a good deal of wasteful expenditure trying to alter the feasible set to include alternatives that he currently values highly. For instance, the person described above may pay out large sums of money to train for a succession of careers, only to find out in each case that the grass still looks greener in the next field. It is even theoretically possible to return to one's starting point with a lighter purse—the phenomenon which Elster describes graphically as 'improving oneself to death'. Clearly there is a loss of welfare here which could be avoided if the person were able to dispense with his adaptive preferences and rank all the alternatives as though they were equally feasible.[13]

At first glance, 'sour grapes' preferences suffer from no such defect, and might be seen as a psychologically healthy (albeit irrational in one sense) way of coping with the realities of one's position. There is more to be said, however, and I shall look at the issue in terms, first, of personal welfare and, second, of personal autonomy. From a welfare point of view, there is no loss if a person places a lower value on some conceivable state of affairs that really is outside the feasible set—say, if a person of limited physical ability pooh-poohs the delights of mountaineering. Very often, however, 'unfeasible' does not mean 'physically impossible' but 'impossible in the light of choices already made by the person in question or by other people'. Here sour grapes may indeed imply a welfare loss. Consider, for instance, a child of poor parents who believes that he will never be able to become a doctor (despite having the necessary aptitude) because the costs of training are too great for his family to bear. As a consequence he values a doctor's life no more highly than, say, a bank clerk's.

---

[13] In saying this I disregard the possibility that each new career—and more generally each new choice—may have a novelty value, so that change itself contributes to the person's welfare. If this is so, then what initially appear to be 'green grass' preferences may be better described as an (unconscious) reaction to boredom.

Given these preferences it would of course be irrational for him to try to become a doctor. But if he were able to escape from his adaptive preferences, he might then see that it would be worth borrowing up to a certain sum in order to become a doctor—and, provided he could borrow the necessary amount, he would be better off as a result. Or suppose that currently no manufacturer is making a particular commodity—say a car that can be serviced and repaired by an amateur handyman. Because of adaptive preferences, consumers surveyed place this relatively low on their list of priorities. Given this information, it may indeed not appear financially feasible to manufacture such a car—although if the car were actually put into production, a different set of preferences would be revealed, and the car would sell, profitably. In the first case, adaptive preferences mean that a person calculates his own costs and benefits wrongly; in the second, he reveals a distorted demand schedule to another agent. In both cases there is a damaging interaction between the options making up the feasible set and the person's preference order, with a consequent loss of welfare.

The personal autonomy argument is rather different. The suggestion here is that adaptive preferences are formed in a way that is undesirable in itself, irrespective of any implication for welfare (in the sense of want-satisfaction). Elster contrasts adaptive preference formation with 'character planning'; in the former case, the preference change occurs through causal processes of which the subject remains unaware, whereas in the latter one decides to shape one's personality in the light of what one sees as the feasible options ahead—for instance, a person who for some reason has to live in the remote countryside decides to cultivate a taste for bird-watching and to abandon interest in avant-garde cinema. I should prefer to draw the moral lines differently. Although character planning may, in the light of a certain ideal of self-determination, seem to be the optimum way of forming one's preferences, adaptive preference formation doesn't appear to be morally repugnant *unless* it involves manipulation by other parties. The objectionable cases are those in which the apparent feasible set is engineered by someone else with a view to getting me to change my preference ordering in a way that suits him. Where this is not so—in ordinary cases of sour grapes, for instance—the main undesirable aspect of adaptive preference formation is its possible effect on welfare.[14]

How might political intervention help to cope with (undesirable) adaptive preferences? It is difficult to imagine anything of this nature being done for people suffering from the green grass syndrome. (Personal counselling might be the answer.) Sour grapes, on the other hand, might be susceptible to treatment by getting people to expand their vision of the feasible. We might place this interpretation on some programmes of positive discrimination, where it is said that by placing members of a certain social category (women, ethnic minorities) in roles that they would not otherwise occupy, others in the same category will begin to include these roles in their range of possible choice, and will then be able to make less distorted career decisions. Proposals of this kind may impose an overall loss of welfare in the short term, since they require that jobs should be given to people who are slightly less qualified to hold them, but it is possible to argue—as, for instance, did J. S. Mill—that in the long run the tapping of a new pool of ability will more than compensate for this.[15] Another example might be subsidies offered to induce people to move out of areas with declining industries into new areas with better employment prospects. The rationale for this would be that the people concerned regarded such moves as impossible, and hence were inclined to downgrade the benefits offered by the new locations. If the subsidy had the effect of widening the feasible set to include this option, a number would

---

[14] This may also indicate the response I would make to the more general charge that many of the wants in a market economy are 'manufactured' by producer interests. It is worth distinguishing three cases: (a) A producer manipulates my wants in a way that benefits him and harms me. This is the worst case, involving both manipulation and exploitation. (b) A producer manipulates my wants without leaving me any worse off. This offends against an ideal of positive freedom: I am made into an instrument of his will without recognizing it. (c) A producer causes me to have certain wants, without manipulation (e.g. he doesn't intend that I should have them, or he does intend this, but goes about it openly). Here the only issue, apart from the welfare issue, is whether I am enough of a 'self-made man'. The difficulty is that I find it hard to conceive of a person as being 'self-made' all the way through; part of our nature has simply to be regarded as given to us, whether by biology or by social influences. Self-making has to go on within these natural limits.

[15] I don't intend this observation to settle the issue of positive discrimination, since there are still questions of justice to resolve, and these may be taken to trump considerations of general welfare. It is, however, worth noting that the welfare argument may go in this direction if the groups to be favoured have been held back by adaptive preferences.

choose to move. In the right circumstances, it is even possible for a subsidy of this kind to be Pareto-optimal, because the cost can be recaptured in tax from the increased earnings of the workers concerned.[16]

The problem here will be to know which preferences are adaptively formed. This has at least two aspects. First, there is a danger that an engineered change in the feasible set will simply induce an alternative set of adaptive preferences, which are then mistakenly regarded as 'true' preferences. For instance an authority might forcibly transfer a group of people from one setting to another, and justify its action by pointing out that (after a suitable interval) the people in question said that they preferred their new location. But this might come about simply because they had given up any hope of returning to their old homes, and had therefore downgraded that option. A second danger lies in confusing adaptive preferences with simple changes in taste. Measures designed to encourage the members of a social category to enter new occupations might not so much release them from adaptive preferences as give them a taste for the modes of life in question. This might still be advantageous on balance, but it would depend on whether the change in taste itself was beneficial or detrimental (see above, Section iii). There is a common fallacy in social theory to the effect that if a person prefers X to Y when he has only experienced X, and Y to X when he has experienced both, his original taste for X must somehow have been defective, and exposure to Y was in his interests. But this is not always the case. Exposure to Y may merely bring about a neutral or detrimental change of taste.

Can we decide whether a given set of preferences is adaptive just by looking at the structure of the set—i.e. without enquiring into the mental processes underlying it? (Opinion polls and consumer research, for instance, normally reveal preferences but not the beliefs underlying those preferences.) Elster suggests that a good piece of evidence that a set is not adaptively formed is that at least one of the top preferences lies outside the feasible range. 'If . . . there are many things that I want to do, but am unfree to do,

---

[16] This is shown in Weizsacker, 'Notes on Endogenous Change'. Von Weizsacker's example is actually one of benign addiction, in the sense that the workers' tastes change as a result of their exposure to the new location in a manner that constitutes an improving sequence, but the formal proof is not affected if one thinks instead of preferences in the old location as being adaptive in character.

then this indicates that my want structure, including the things that I want to do and am free to do, but not free not to do, is not in general shaped by adaptive preference formation.'[17] There is something in this, though it does seem possible for a person's preferences to be adaptive in one sphere (say concerning job opportunities) while not being adaptive in another (say concerning consumer goods), so one cannot give a preference ranking a clean bill of health, as it were, merely by discovering one utopian aspiration in it. A more serious problem (recognized by Elster) is that deliberate character planning might also mean that the top preference was in the feasible set. He suggests that one way of distinguishing this from adaptive preference formation would be by observing a tendency in the latter case to 'overshoot' in the direction of downgrading the unattainable alternatives. Again this seems plausible: when we hear (for instance) someone who has failed to get to university railing violently about the uselessness of university education, we immediately suspect sour grapes; whereas someone who has consciously moulded their desires to their opportunities can often speak dispassionately and realistically about the possibilities forgone. The problem is that information of this kind cannot easily be captured in official statistics.

VII

This brings us back to the general question that this chapter is addressing. Even granting that markets are less than wholly efficient, because the desires they are responding to are less than optimal from the point of view of the agent's welfare, can we imagine a better outcome occurring in practice? If we look to a political solution, we run up against the fact that no political authority has direct access to the psychic processes that lie behind consumers' expressed preferences. There is no certain way for such a body to identify adaptive preferences, or indeed the other types of distorted desire we have considered. The best sort of information, in practice, is obtained by looking for uniformities in the behaviour of large numbers of people, on the assumption that similar processes of preference formation are at work. This is the ground on which it may be possible, for instance, to defend

[17] Elster, *Sour Grapes*, 129.

policies of discrimination in favour of women or ethnic minorities in the job market, or subsidies to encourage workers to move to new areas to find employment. But it is a very far cry from specific interventions of these sorts to a wholesale replacement of the market by political provision of goods and services. The principle of consumer sovereignty turns out to be fairly robust. Even where the arguments supporting it break down in theory, it is often difficult to devise a more efficient alternative policy.

Some readers might be disposed to challenge the fundamental assumption on which the argument of this chapter has been based. The aim of all production, they might argue, should be to respond, not to wants or preferences at all, but to something else, namely *needs*. To assess the force of this challenge, we must first be clear about the conceptual distinction between needs and wants[18], and then consider how it bears on the choice between market and non-market provision of goods and services.

I suggested in the last chapter that a person's needs might be defined as whatever is necessary to allow him to lead a decent life in the community to which he belongs. Let me expand a little on three aspects of this definition. First, the items that a person needs are the items that are *in fact* necessary for him to live decently, not the items that he believes, perhaps mistakenly, to be necessary. In some cases—medical needs, for instance—it may require extensive investigation to discover precisely what a person's needs are. Second, needs are assessed by reference to an implicit notion of what is involved in living a decent life. In general this will be worked out in terms of a set of capacities and opportunities; a person must be able to use his body freely, to qualify for work, to engage in normal social intercourse, and so forth.[19] The lives that people choose to lead are of course very varied, but almost all will require at least these capacities and opportunities to be carried through satisfactorily. The concept of

---

[18] I have discussed the distinction between needs and wants more fully in *Social Justice* (Oxford: Clarendon Press, 1976), ch. 4. I should add that I now regard the conception of need developed there as over-extensive, in particular for failing to draw a distinction between basic capacity and the full set of resources required to carry out one's plan of life. The latter view of need no longer seems to me viable as a basis of social policy.

[19] An account of 'need' along these lines has been spelt out briefly in A. Sen, 'Equality of What?' in his *Choice, Welfare and Measurement* (Oxford: Blackwell, 1982) and at greater length in D. Braybrooke, *Meeting Needs* (Princeton: Princeton University Press, 1987) ch. 2.

need does not, however, bend to accommodate any plan of life whatsoever, as I indicated in Chapter 4 with the example of the drug addict. Third, the notion of a decent life is itself relative to a particular community. Although there are some very basic needs—biological needs especially—that are invariant across societies, many other needs only count as such because of the notions of decency and self-respect that prevail in a particular time and place. It follows immediately that needs will change as social standards and expectations change. I shall return to consider some of the political implications of this point in Chapter 12.

If this account of 'need' is accepted, then very often we will find that people want what they need. There is no reason to introduce any categorical separation between people's revealed preferences and their 'real' needs as defined by some abstract theory of human nature. Needs are identified by reference to the concrete forms of social life that people engage in. In specific cases, however, people may want things that they do not need. They may simply make mistakes in estimating what is necessary to secure a minimally decent life—for instance they may dose themselves with the wrong kind of medicine. They will almost certainly have tastes and preferences for items that are not basic enough to count as needs—for champagne and caviar, say, as opposed to mere sustenance. Finally some desires may, if satisfied, subvert the fulfilment of needs, as when people choose to engage in activities that damage and eventually disable them.

Suppose, then, that we take the view that needs and wants may on occasion pull apart, and that where this happens we should give precedence to needs. What practical implications follow, and in particular what follows for the general argument for markets in terms of consumer sovereignty discussed in this chapter? First, we must adopt a distributive policy which ensures that everyone has adequate resources to satisfy their needs, in advance of other resources being made available to meet non-basic desires; bread for all must take precedence over jam for the few.[20] This does not

[20] This of course assumes that it is feasible to aim for an outcome in which all needs are met with at least some resources left over for other purposes. Such an assumption is generally reasonable in the case of the advanced societies, although there are problems to be faced in the case of medical needs (for a discussion, see Braybrooke, *Meeting Needs*, sec. 8. 3). I have considered the implications of the need principle in situations of scarcity in 'Social Justice and the Principle of Need' in M. Freeman and D. Robertson (eds.), *The Frontiers of Political Theory* (Brighton: Harvester, 1980).

so far amount to an argument for abandoning markets, but rather for framing the market in such a way that primary income is more equally distributed, with special supplements for those who are unable to earn an adequate income in the labour market. This chimes closely with the egalitarian aims of market socialism as set out in the Introduction. With market socialist institutions in place, people will be able to meet most of their needs through normal market purchases.

There are, however, some cases in which relying on markets would be an ineffective way of responding to need. I gave an example on p. 104 of a medical case in which it would plainly be more efficient to provide medical care collectively than to rely on each individual purchasing it separately. Meeting needs is a collective obligation of social justice; but the obligation is only to provide for those in need in the way that encroaches least on general social resources. It is quite reasonable, then, in deciding on the *manner* of provision to take account of the relative efficiency of market and non-market provision in fulfilling a particular need. Where non-market provision does better—say because the extent of need cannot be adequately determined in advance of the treatment designed to meet it—it should obviously be chosen.[21]

Switching from wants to needs as our point of reference, then, will cause us to revise our attitude to markets in certain respects. We shall be concerned about the distribution of resources as well as with overall levels of satisfaction; and we shall be alive to the possibility that some needs may best be met by collective provision. But noting these limits is very different from dismissing markets outright. On a reasonable construal of 'need', there is still a large area of economic life which is concerned simply with the satisfaction of desires, and if markets are shown to be an efficient means to that end, that is a strong argument in their favour. My main aim in this chapter has been to show that such a conclusion is not fundamentally upset by the observation that consumers' desires are malleable. The fact of malleability does not of itself drive a wedge between preference satisfaction and personal welfare. Even where, in theory, a person's welfare might be better promoted by means other than responding to his present preferences, it is much harder in practice to devise an

---

[21] I return to this question briefly in chapter 12, sec. v.

alternative policy. Thus there is no good reason to reject the general efficiency argument for markets on the grounds that desires are created rather than innate. Whether other anti-market arguments are more powerful remains to be seen.

6

DISTRIBUTIVE JUSTICE

I

Is it possible to envisage a market economy that meets substantive criteria of distributive justice? This is a relatively venerable question, much discussed in nineteenth-century handbooks of political economy, but it is clearly crucial to any normative assessment of markets. In general, the socialist tradition has answered it in the negative. Some socialists have been willing to tolerate markets on other grounds, arguing that their distributive results can be corrected by political intervention.[1] Others, more radical, have seen the injustice of market allocations as a major reason for dispensing with them altogether.

At the other end of the political spectrum, libertarians have increasingly abandoned the attempts of their liberal predecessors to demonstrate the substantial justice of *laissez-faire* capitalism. As we have seen, modern libertarians embrace a procedural theory of justice according to which it is permissible to ask whether the framework of rules surrounding a particular market is just or unjust, but nothing can properly be said about the justice or injustice of market outcomes themselves.

It is interesting to note that neither of these views accords with that of the man in the street, who is inclined to see markets as materially fair, and indeed to have a higher opinion of the justice of market allocations than that of political allocations.[2] Whether the man in the street could possibly be right remains to be seen; I shall argue here that his view is likely to be seriously in error at least as far as *capitalism* is concerned. The fact that it is held, however, is of the utmost importance as far as the legitimacy of

[1] A good specimen of this view would be C. A. R. Crosland, *The Future of Socialism*, (London: Cape, 1956), although Crosland does in places allow that some market-based inequalities of income may be socially just.

[2] See R. E. Lane, 'Market Justice, Political Justice', *American Political Science Review*, 80 (1986), 383–402.

markets is concerned. It seems certain that a belief in the justice of market economies is a major reason why people are prepared to support them in practice. As the neo-conservative Irving Kristol has remarked, '. . . in the same way as men cannot for long tolerate a sense of spiritual meaninglessness in their individual lives, so they cannot for long accept a society in which power, privilege, and property are not distributed according to some morally meaningful criteria.'[3] If this is so, neither the libertarian view, nor the more moderate socialist view referred to above, will be viable as a public ideology. Hayek himself has shown some awareness of this point.[4] Proponents of markets will need once again to take on the task of showing that they can be substantially just, if they want their ideas to obtain any kind of mass hearing.

In investigating this issue, it is plainly important to beg as few questions as possible about the institutional structure of the market at the outset. We shall want in particular to contrast the likely distributive results of market socialism with those of capitalism; but this broad contrast itself leaves open many questions of detail about the framing of the market under either system. We do, however, need to say something about how people can be expected to behave in market transactions. The assumption I shall make is that each participant will try to maximize the value of his holdings, taking into account his tastes, and also his desires or aversions for different sorts of labour. We need not make any further assumptions about his underlying motives. If he chooses finally to give his resources away to his family or to Oxfam, this is best regarded as an irrelevant extra-market transaction. To understand market behaviour, we need not postulate egoism in the narrow sense but merely what Wicksteed called 'non-tuism':[5] participants in market transactions are assumed to be concerned about the extent of their own holdings (for whatever ultimate reason), but to have no direct concern for the welfare of their contractual partners.

Does this assumption itself place any constraints on the distributive outcome of a market economy? Some egalitarian

[3] I. Kristol, ' "When Virtue Loses all her Loveliness": some Reflections on Capitalism and "The Free Society" ', *Public Interest*, 21(Fall, 1970), 8.

[4] See F. A. Hayek, *Law, Legislation and Liberty, ii. The Mirage of Social Justice*, (London: Routledge and Kegan Paul, 1976), 73–4.

[5] P. H. Wicksteed, *The Common Sense of Political Economy*, ed. L. Robbins (London: Routledge, 1933), B. I, ch. 5.

critics of existing market economies have proposed divorcing the allocative and distributive functions of the market more or less completely. Market prices are to govern the allocation of resources between alternative uses, but they need not also govern the distribution of income between persons, since this is potentially open to political determination. The state has discretion in deciding how to tax personal incomes, and in the extreme case it might choose to tax all incomes above the minimum wage at 100 per cent, leaving post-tax incomes perfectly equal. This is compatible with the use of market mechanisms provided that producers continue to maximize their pre-tax incomes. As DiQuattro puts it, distinguishing between the (pre-tax) gross wage and the (post-tax) net wage:

In the interest of efficiency, it is important that workers seek to maximize the gross wage even though they receive only the politically determined net or fair wage. In this way, justice holds sway in the sphere of distribution while efficiency reigns in the sphere of production. In market socialism the market is used to allocate resources but not to distribute wealth and power. Accordingly, the use of the market is perfectly compatible with the egalitarian and compensatory principles of socialist justice.[6]

Such proposals raise two main problems. First, is it plausible to suppose that producers will continue attempting to maximize their pre-tax incomes if in the end they receive no material benefit from doing so? Second, will the surrogate motivating force that is required allow the market to perform its allocative function unimpaired? Is it possible, in other words, to simulate monetary incentives without actually providing them?

This second question has been tackled with great ingenuity in a recent book by Joseph Carens which seeks to prove that an egalitarian market economy is indeed a possibility.[7] Carens proposes that 'individuals be taught during late childhood and early adolescence that they have a social obligation to earn as much pre-tax income as they can'. Provided such socialization could be made effective, post-tax incomes might be equalized.

[6] A. DiQuattro, 'Alienation and Justice in the Market', *American Political Science Review*, 72 (1978), 879.

[7] J. Carens, *Equality, Moral Incentives and the Market: An Essay in Utopian Politico-Economic Theory* (Chicago: University of Chicago Press, 1981).

He then tries to show that a market economy operating on these premisses would be as efficient as an orthodox market economy using monetary incentives. To make the argument work, he has to find an equivalent in the egalitarian system for the satisfactions provided by income in the orthodox system. This is necessary because in an orthodox economy, the latter satisfactions are usually traded off against work satisfactions, leisure, and so forth. People, in other words, don't attempt simply to maximize their incomes, but are willing to take a lower income for more free time, more interesting work, and so forth, the balance differing from person to person. It is obviously desirable that similar trade-offs should occur in the egalitarian system. Carens's proposed equivalents are 'social duty satisfactions', which vary according to the relationship between a person's actual pre-tax income and the maximum income that he would earn if he worked flat out at the highest-paid job for which he had the necessary qualifications. If people could be induced to value these satisfactions to the same degree as they currently value income-derived satisfactions, the egalitarian economy will in most respects[8] function in an identical manner to the orthodox economy—thus a rise in the price of a certain kind of labour will have the same effects as in the latter system, and so forth. In this way, Carens is able to show that the standard efficiency theorems can be transferred from an orthodox economy to his model egalitarian economy.

How plausible are the motivational assumptions that Carens requires to make his model work? Let us assume for the sake of argument that people might in principle become as powerfully motivated by social duty as they currently are by financial incentives. Observe, however, that if social duty is to become the moving force of a market economy, it has to yield graduated satisfactions that can be traded off against satisfactions of other kinds. (If such trades were not made, and everyone *per impossibile* worked like a Stakhanovite, goods would be over-produced in relation to leisure, etc.) Can we imagine duties having this character? We need here to distinguish between the internal and external aspects of duty: between the inner satisfaction gained

---

[8] Though not in all; for instance social duty satisfactions will be affected by changes in the price of the labour which represents a person's maximum earning potential, whereas income-derived satisfactions will not. See Carens, *Equality, Moral Incentives and the Market*, ch. 2 for a full discussion.

from knowing that you have carried out your obligations, and the applause and recognition which social contribution brings with it.

Consider the external aspect first. Here there is no difficulty in conceiving of a graduated response such that contributions were psychologically rewarded according to their magnitude. The problem, however, is that in Carens's system, social duty satisfactions are supposed to be proportional not to a person's actual pre-tax income but to actual income *divided* by maximum possible income. So, for example, a lecturer earning £10,000 whose maximum earning potential is to be an accountant earning £15,000 must receive less social duty satisfactions than a craftsman earning £5,000 whose maximum earning potential is to be a machinist earning £7,000 (since $\frac{10}{15} < \frac{5}{7}$). If these satisfactions are to be supplied externally (through the praise and recognition of others) these others need to know not only how much the person in question is actually earning, but what he could earn if he chose. This seems practically impossible. The likelihood is that praise, etc. would be awarded according to actual contributions (measured by pre-tax income), so that the distribution of satisfactions would be inegalitarian, more going to those who through skill, effort, luck, or whatever were able to earn higher incomes in the market. In this case the inequalities of the orthodox economy would be reproduced, with 'psychic' satisfactions replacing income-derived satisfactions.

If, therefore, Carens wants the final outcome to be genuinely egalitarian, he must rely on internally derived social-duty satisfactions. Assuming that each person is aware of his maximum earning potential, his level of satisfaction must vary according to the percentage of that maximum that he achieves. But even granting that this idea of a graduated duty is intelligible, it seems certain that the most powerful conscientious motives are brought into play in all-or-nothing situations; that is, situations in which 'the right thing to do' is plain to see, and in which the choice lies between doing that right thing and not doing it. (A similar consideration underlay my earlier claim that conscientious altruism is not an adequate foundation for a welfare system.[9]) Where duties are variable in content, their motivating force is far less strong: it is easy for people to find ways of mentally enhancing the

[9] See above, Chapter 4, sec. v.

value of their contribution relative to their maximum potential. So even if we are convinced that social duty might, in general, become a more powerful motive than it now is, it is far less clear that it could replace financial incentives as a means of allocating labour between alternative possible uses in a market context.

It remains an open question how large these financial incentives need to be. The stronger Carens-style social-duty satisfactions become, the more feasible it will be for politically determined income taxes to redistribute income in an egalitarian manner. Market socialist arrangements, in particular, permit co-operatives to choose their own internal pattern of distribution; the more highly skilled members of each enterprise may decide, as an act of solidarity, to forgo some part of the additional income that they could command by competing in the labour market. But rather than counting on the elimination of all income inequalities in our assessment of markets, it seems preferable to assume that some inequalities of this kind will remain, and to see whether they can be reconciled with a suitable criterion of justice.

How should we try to establish this conclusion? One method, at first sight the best, would be to specify our conception of justice first, and then see whether a market economy, suitably framed, could hope to instantiate it. I prefer to adopt a more oblique strategy, in which the conception of justice and the character of the market are adjusted to one another, as it were, until eventually they rest in equilibrium.[10] This may sound like cooking the books. My first line of defence is that conceptions of justice are in any case controversial. As we well know, there are many intuitively plausible ways of spelling out the idea of a just distribution of resources. It is far from clear how we should go about deciding between them. It doesn't seem absurd, therefore, that we should be guided in our choice, to some extent at least, by the institutions that we want to justify. Of course it *would* be absurd if we simply took the full institutional structure for granted and tailored our conception of justice to fit. But this is not how I intend to proceed. We may hope that in the course of working out a suitable conception of justice, we shall also be able to establish which set

[10] The idea I am employing here is similar to Rawls's notion of reflective equilibrium, although the subject matter I am applying it to is different. For Rawls's notion, see J. Rawls, *A Theory of Justice* (Cambridge, Mass: Harvard University Press, 1971), 19–21, 48–50.

of background rules is most likely to generate a just market economy.

Perhaps the rationale for this approach will become clearer if I say that the conception of justice required here must be a desert conception. If we want to show that market allocations can be substantively (and not merely procedurally) just, the only possible way forward is to demonstrate that each participant receives what he deserves by some criterion of desert.[11] But we have often been reminded by careful investigators that the idea of desert is a complex one.[12] In particular, the basis of desert—the characteristics in virtue of which people are said to deserve this or that—appears to change according to the kind of benefit in question. Compare, for instance, what is involved in deserving a prize with what is involved in deserving a reward. So there is some room, at least, for debate as to what the basis of desert should be for income and the other benefits that markets provide. At the same time the concept of desert is not completely malleable. In particular, it would overstretch its boundaries if we were to allow people's deserts to vary according to outside events not reflected in the appropriate way in their own characteristics; for instance, if something that you did could, of itself, make me more or less deserving. So we should think of desert as having certain fixed conceptual features, and other features that are more open to negotiation. Our question must be whether we can give an account of market justice that respects the fixed elements while filling in the debatable elements in a way that seems plausible.

I propose to tackle this question by considering a series of objections to the idea that market allocations can be socially just. I begin with the most abstract objections and move towards problems that have more to do with empirical features of markets as we see them in operation. The earlier difficulties can only be met by conceptual argument; as we move forward, there is increasing scope for proposing adjustments to the framework of the market to meet the objections raised. We should not, of course, require

---

[11] I hope that this is more or less self-evident. I have already pointed out (ch. 5, sec. vii) that we should not expect markets to allocate resources on the basis of *need*, the main alternative criterion of substantive justice. I do not count utilitarian arguments in favour of markets as arguments of justice, for reasons that there is no space to spell out here (for discussion, see my *Social Justice* (Oxford: Clarendon Press, 1976), 31–40).

[12] One of the best investigations is still J. Feinberg, 'Justice and Personal Desert', in id. *Doing and Deserving* (Princeton: Princeton University Press, 1970).

markets to achieve results that we know, empirically, they cannot possibly achieve; but at the same time it would be a serious error to regard all of the features of present-day capitalism, say, as intrinsic to markets as such. At this pole of the argument, too, we need to distinguish between what must be taken as given and what is more open to debate.

II

It may be said, firstly, that a person's desert depends on the moral character of his activity—either on the pure quality of will that he displays, or on some broader notion of 'realized virtue' that takes account not only of quality of will but also of success in altering the world in the desired direction. Thus people are said to deserve reward for their justice or their benevolence, or for some other moral virtue. However, it is a characteristic of markets that they 'reward' people for behaviour that is typically self-interested or at least not virtuous in the relevant sense. When people produce or exchange they do so for reasons that (normally) have nothing to do with the general moral values that their actions might realize. It is therefore impossible to see a market as an institution within which deserts are by and large rewarded.

In reply, I should say that not all desert is moral desert in the sense which this objection presupposes. There is an important distinction that needs to be kept in mind here. It is true that all, or nearly all, desert claims are moral claims. If I say 'John deserves a pay rise', or 'Mary deserves to be elected', my statement in each case has moral force. I am saying that, other things being equal, John ought to get more pay or Mary ought to be given office, the 'ought' here being the familiar moral 'ought'. This is not to say, however, that the properties in virtue of which people come to deserve things are necessarily themselves moral properties. It is possible to deserve on the basis of moral qualities—this, presumably, is one criterion for beatification or sanctification—but equally possible to deserve for other reasons. John may deserve a pay rise simply because he's a hard and conscientious worker, and Mary her office because she has the intelligence to make good decisions once elected. But neither may be virtuous in the moral sense: John may have worked hard simply in order to make more money, and Mary may be seeking office because she anticipates that she will enjoy holding it.

Not only is it in fact the case that we frequently make judgements of desert which have a non-moral basis; I cannot think of any plausible argument which would show that the exhibition of moral virtues was the only basis on which people could appropriately deserve benefits.[13] So although it is easy to show, as Rawls and others have done, that markets do not and cannot reward desert in this narrow sense, we are given no reason to suppose that desert in general is irrelevant to the justification of markets, as Rawls goes on to argue.[14]

III

A second objection, which is sometimes I think confused with the first but needs to be kept separate, is that people deserve reward in proportion to the value they create, whereas markets, at best, reward people according to the demand for their goods or services. The point being made here is not about agents' motives, but about how to assess the value of what they do. The suggestion is that desert should be based on the real or intrinsic value of someone's activities, as opposed merely to the amount that people are prepared to pay in practice for their performance. In support of this suggestion, it might be pointed out that, in market contexts, people may demand things which are not in their best interests, or the demands they express may be demands which the producers themselves have helped to manufacture. As F. H. Knight put the point:

The product or contribution is always measured in terms of price, which does not correspond closely with ethical value or human significance. The money value of a product is a matter of the 'demand', which in turn reflects the tastes and purchasing power of the buying public and the availability of substitute commodities. All these factors are largely created and controlled by the workings of the economic system itself. . . .[15]

To assess this objection, it is important to separate the overall assessment of economic systems from what might be called a

---

[13] One might perhaps reach this conclusion by combining two theses: that desert must be based on characteristics subject to voluntary choice, and that moral choices were the only genuine (i.e. non-determined) choices that people ever made. I discuss the first thesis briefly below.   [14] Rawls, *A Theory of Justice*, 310–12.

[15] F. H. Knight, 'The Ethics of Competition', *Quarterly Journal of Economics*, 37 (1922–3), 597–8.

humanistic perspective, from the much more specific question that concerns us here, namely the relative assessment of individual deserts (and thus of distributive justice). Some may believe that a relevant criterion for judging economic systems is the extent to which the benefits they provide are real benefits according to a standard of intrinsic value. I have indicated already, in the previous chapter, that I am unwilling to contemplate any such *wholesale* severance of value from want-satisfaction, even though, as we saw, there are a number of specific cases in which we would wish to apply a distinction between what a person desires and what it is good for them to have. Suppose, though, that our critic is willing to make such a radical divorce between value and want-satisfaction. Does it follow that *desert* should be based on a person's success in creating 'real' value? It seems to me not to follow, and one reason is that doing so would separate personal desert in an unacceptable way from personal responsibility.

Let me try to elaborate this thought. I believe that we want to see a close connection between what a person deserves to have and the choices and efforts that he makes. We want it to be possible for people to become deserving through directing their activities appropriately. I shall argue later that we don't necessarily want to base desert *entirely* on these voluntary choices, etc. Nevertheless it would be anomalous from the point of view of our conception of the person if people acquired deserts, or failed to acquire them, through processes lying beyond their conscious control.[16] Now if that thesis is accepted, we have one good reason why the value of people's activities should be measured primarily in terms of their capacity to meet desires rather than in terms of an intrinsic standard of value. For value in the former sense is empirically detectable. I am in a position to judge how much value I will create by doing X rather than Y because I can observe the relative demand for the two activities, measured in a market context by the prices people are prepared to pay. (The problems created by uncertainty about the future are discussed later.) If

[16] In this respect our contemporary concept of desert may differ from older ideas of merit, which were less closely tied to notions of personal choice and responsibility. See, for example, the analysis of moral judgement in Homeric Greece in A. W. H. Adkins, *Merit and Responsibility* (Oxford: Clarendon Press, 1960). Here merit was based primarily on military prowess, the skills needed for war together with actual success in deploying them. As Adkins points out, this made intention more or less irrelevant to the assessment of merit.

customers will pay twice as much for a beaver as for a deer, this provides evidence that the activity of trapping a beaver is twice as valuable as that of hunting a deer. If, on the other hand, we tried to estimate value in terms that made no reference to overt demand, it seems inconceivable that we should be able to light on a publicly available standard—i.e. one that was generally acceptable and could at the same time feasibly be applied empirically. In the absence of such a standard, the agent would be in no position before the event to estimate how much desert he would acquire by performing this or that task. Although it would still be open to you or I or anyone else to make judgements of desert using whatever criteria we found most appealing, there would no longer be a practice of rewarding desert, in the sense of a practice that connects what the agent is in a position to discover before embarking on a course of action with what will happen to him afterwards.

Let me be clear about what this argument does and does not assert. It does not claim that the economic market is the only sphere which can support a practice of rewarding desert. Obviously there are well-established practices of requiting desert to be found elsewhere—in competitive sports, in religious communities, in public service, and so forth. My argument has only to do with the superiority of market-determined value over other standards of value as a basis for judging general social contributions. Moreover, it is meant to apply in the context of modern, culturally plural societies in which there is very unlikely to be agreement about intrinsic criteria of merit (as there may have been in simpler and more homogeneous communities).[17] On the other hand, the argument aims to avoid the error of conflating deserts with entitlements—i.e. the claims that people have under existing conventional rules.[18] The point is not that a market-based criterion of value is appropriate for estimating desert because this is the practice that now prevails. It is rather that if we want desert to form the basis of a social practice—rather than being an idea that is used merely to form a series of idiosyncratic judgements—we need a non-arbitrary public standard to

[17] For instance Homeric Greece as described by Adkins, or the Buddhist Sherpas of Tibet studied by Fürer-Haimendorf, with their well-defined criteria of religious merit; see C. von Fürer-Haimendorf, *Morals and Merit* (London: Weidenfeld and Nicolson, 1967), ch. 7.
[18] The distinction between entitlement and desert is well drawn by Feinberg in 'Justice and Personal Desert'.

measure it. In this light, the attraction of a market-based criterion is very considerable.

If, therefore, we want to keep something like our present concept of desert and the practices that go with it, there is much to be said for using overt demand as a way of measuring the value of output. Even if, from a spectator's standpoint, we think that our whole social system is producing goods which have little or no real value, we should not expect an individual producing within the system to take up such a lofty vantage-point. From the participant's perspective, which is also the appropriate perspective for making desert judgements, it is a mistake to try to look behind consumers' demands in an effort to discover their 'real' needs (by some criterion).

IV

A third objection, advanced for example by Hayek, is that market receipts don't in any case measure general 'social value' even if value is interpreted in a want-regarding manner. At best, they measure the value of my services to whoever happens to purchase them. Since 'the values attached to the different services by different groups of people are incommensurable', the idea of a 'value to society' is wholly fictitious.[19] And if there is no value to society, Hayek concludes, the idea of assessing the justice of market remunerations according to how closely they correspond to values contributed makes no sense.

It is worth separating two ways in which my receipts may be determined by the particular individuals to whom I sell my services. First, whatever it is I am offering may have some special feature that especially commends (or fails to commend) it to the customer in question. I may, for instance, have made some article that has a fairly standard market value—say, an oak walking-stick—but made it from wood whose markings happen to appeal greatly to a particular buyer. This may give me the opportunity to sell the article for more than the standard value. There is as far as I can see no prospect of showing that the surplus is in any sense deserved. (Note that this is different from the case of someone who is in the business of turning out individually tailored articles,

[19] Hayek, *Law, Legislation and Liberty*, ii, p76.

where fitting the object to the customer's needs or whims is precisely the relevant skill, and therefore the appropriate basis of desert.) But although in the particular case there is a departure from strict justice, over the longer term we would expect such windfall gains to accrue randomly to everyone producing items of the type in question. Provided that it makes little difference when the windfalls arrive, the deviation from justice may not be serious. I shall return later to the general issue of windfall gains and their implications for distributive justice.

There is, however, another way in which my services may be sold to particular individuals: it may turn out that the items I am providing are purchased exclusively by one section of the population. This seems to be the possibility that chiefly motivates Hayek's argument. He cites as an example commodities sold only to women.[20] The point here is that if you and I are selling items to mutually exclusive groups of customers—none of your customers ever wishes to buy products of the kind that I produce and vice versa—there seems to be no way in which the relative value of our services can be measured. There is no common denominator which would allow us to say that your services were more or less socially valuable than mine.

What should we make of this? In one obvious sense the idea of a 'value to society' must be spurious if is taken to require a personified 'society' to do the valuing. But there is no need to interpret it in this way. We may instead use 'value to society' as a shorthand for the aggregate value each person creates for all the other individuals making up the population in question. Talk of a person 'benefiting society' is therefore strictly speaking meta-phorical, inasmuch as the benefits one creates are actually benefits for a discrete number of individuals, except in the very rare cases where the advantage actually touches everyone. But why should this matter from the point of view of desert? It matters only if the discreteness of individuals somehow makes it imposs-ible to compare the value created by supplying goods and services to different people. I have argued already that the relevant standard of value, for this purpose, is personal welfare. Now the general problem involved in making interpersonal comparisons

[20] Ibid.

of welfare is well known. There is no certain way of telling how much satisfaction A derives from a certain good as compared with B. The market 'solves' this problem, in a sense, by equating £1 worth of goods sold to A with £1 worth of goods sold to B. Value is measured by equilibrium price. Clearly this neglects personal differences between A and B which might mean that A derived more welfare from his £1 worth of goods than B did from his. From the point of view of distributive justice, however, this is irrelevant. When we measure desert by the value of the resources each person creates, the standard of value we invoke is value in general, not the particular, unique value that an item has for any given customer. (That is why, a moment ago, we had to allow that producers might make undeserved windfall gains when selling to particular clients.)

It seems, then, that the market itself resolves the problem of aggregating values for discrete individuals into a general measure of value. But are there any cases where we would expect market prices to provide a distorted assessment of welfare? Suppose that A and B have unequal disposable incomes, and suppose also, as we generally do, that the marginal utility of income diminishes: B's income may be five times A's, but his welfare will only be, say, twice as great. *Ceteris paribus*, therefore, an item sold to B will produce less welfare than an item sold to A; this is not because of any personal peculiarities of A and B, but because of general facts about human beings. Now if there are items sold only or primarily to the rich, and other items sold only or primarily to the poor, there must then be a presumption that the money prices of the former items will overstate their welfare value, and conversely with the latter items.

It is important to be clear what is at stake here. As I have already argued, it is irrelevant to a producer's deserts that a commodity he produces may have different welfare values for each of the customers he deals with. A baker doesn't deserve more for supplying a loaf to a poor person than to a rich person; the fact that, as individuals, they may derive different amounts of utility from consuming the loaf is beside the point. The problem arises only in so far as the commodity bundles purchased by the rich differ systematically from those purchased by the poor: in the extreme case, when there are items bought only by one or other class. Where this is true, we might expect the money incomes of those who cater primarily or exclusively to the tastes of the rich to exaggerate the value they create.

How well founded is this expectation? Note that it depends on assuming the diminishing marginal utility of income. What makes *that* assumption plausible, however, is the idea that the rich will buy more of the same things as the poor. If someone presents me with a series of oranges, there will come a point in the series beyond which each extra orange will bring me progressively less enjoyment. But if the rich are using their high incomes not to buy more and more oranges (or whatever) but to substitute, say, mangoes in their fruit bowls, why suppose that they are not reaching a higher level of welfare? To the extent that consumption is stratified, then, we have less reason to suppose that the marginal utility of income will diminish. This substantially mitigates our problem. The charge was that the providers of luxury goods would be systematically over-rewarded in relation to the providers of basics, but we now see that this charge rests on two assumptions that pull against each other, namely stratified consumption and the diminishing marginal utility of income.

V

I come now to what might be termed the argument from contingency. This points out that the rewards I can reap in a market context depend on a number of contingent facts, especially the tastes of consumers for goods of different sorts and the availability of various skills and abilities in the workforce. The point can be made most dramatically if we consider what happens when one of these parameters changes: if the taste for my product diminishes, or more competitors enter my branch of production, my income will fall; but, as Sidgwick remarked, 'it does not seem that any individual's social Desert can properly be lessened merely by the increased number or willingness of others rendering the same services'[21], and the same argument might be advanced with respect to changes in demand.

Again, I think there is a distinction that must be drawn here if we want to weigh the force of this objection properly. We need to distinguish between the short-run effects of fluctuations in

---

[21] H. Sidgwick, *The Methods of Ethics* (London: Macmillan, 1907), 288.

market conditions and the long-run implications of such changes. Take the case of an increase in the supply of some service: say, a large number of manufacturers switch more or less simultaneously into making pocket calculators. The product is oversupplied at the prevailing price, and the price falls until eventually a new equilibrium is reached—perhaps restoring the original price, perhaps not. What of the position of Smith, who has been making calculators all along? His income falls, but how have his deserts lessened? The answer is that they *do* lessen when the supply of calculators increases. If desert is based on value created, that value cannot be estimated without taking account of what others have produced; the notion that the service you render has the same value regardless of what others do is absurd. This is easily illustrated. If every month I clean the windows of my elderly neighbour's house, I deserve considerable gratitude; but if one month her grandson has forestalled me, I can't expect to be thanked as warmly if I go through my usual routine. Desert isn't merely a matter of good intentions; it also has to do with how much benefit you create for the recipients of your services, and in nearly every case that depends on the configuration of the world outside. A fall in the price of a commodity or a service not only acts as an incentive to shift to some other line of business, but it is also a signal that the good or service in question has become less valuable, in the short term at least, as a result of what other people have decided to do.

But we have still to consider the long-term issue. When equilibrium is reached, the price of any commodity will depend on consumers' tastes, and also on the willingness or unwillingness of producers to supply it. How much do people want pocket calculators, and how ready are other people to make them? These are contingent facts, and yet they will affect Smith's long-term receipts. But how can his *deserts* depend on such contingencies? Surely, it may be said, Smith's deserts must depend solely on facts about Smith. If Smith has the knack of wiring up pocket calculators, but very few others do, his receipts will be increased; but does this make him any more deserving? As Knight puts it, 'It is hard to see how it is more meritorious merely to be different from other people than it is to be like them .'[22]

[22] Knight, 'The Ethics of Competition', 599.

Knight goes on immediately, however, to qualify this remark in one respect: 'except again, possibly, if the capacity has been cultivated by an effort which others refused to put forth'. And surely this qualification, at least, needs to be made. Even if the distribution of tastes and abilities is a contingent matter, Smith can respond to it in various ways when deciding e.g. what skills to acquire. If he chooses to become skilled at a task which he rightly foresees will become essential to the production of a valuable commodity, then he is surely properly rewarded for making that choice. And that remains true even if a factor in his calculation is the number of others likely to acquire the same skill. Smith is, if you like, being entrepreneurial when he decides to specialize in electronic circuitry *because* most of his contemporaries are learning to play rock music, but again entrepreneurship of that kind creates value and deserves reward.

There still remain two major problems to consider, and these form the bases of the fifth and sixth objections. First, personal abilities and tastes are not wholly a result of deliberate cultivation, but to some extent a product of biology and social conditioning for which the person concerned can claim no credit. Second, even in the case of deliberately cultivated abilities, it is often partly a matter of luck that the capacities you have chosen to develop are the capacities for which there turns out to be a large social demand. Few people are far-sighted enough to be certain that the skills they are acquiring will be permanently valuable.

VI

The fifth objection raises the much-discussed question whether desert may be based on involuntary capacities, or whether its basis is properly limited to features such as effort which are potentially subject to the conscious control of the agent in question. The case for the latter view is sometimes put in a misleading way, for instance by Rawls, who claims that 'no one deserves his place in the distribution of native endowments' and then takes this as a reason for holding that he does not deserve the material advantages achieved through having those endowments.[23] But against this it has been argued, convincingly I think,

[23] Rawls, *A Theory of Justice*, 103–4.

that the basis for a judgement of desert need not be a personal feature that is itself deserved.[24] So any case against basing desert on involuntary capacities must rest on other grounds. The key consideration, I believe, is our wish to link personal desert to personal responsibility. We want to see people as deserving on the basis of features for which they can be held responsible. Where certain capacities are innate, or at least brought into being by external forces beyond our control (I shall subsequently use the term 'native abilities' to cover both these possibilities), we cannot be held fully responsible for the results of their exercise. This view rests on a conception of human agency which is admittedly fairly fragile, since it is open to the determinist riposte that we are not responsible in the relevant sense for *any* of our doings.[25] But it is none the less a view of agency which in practice commands widespread support.

This appears to generate a major objection to the thesis that markets can be socially just. For market receipts clearly depend on native abilities as well as on other features of our behaviour. I shall not attempt to rebut this objection directly, but instead try to weaken its force in a more roundabout way.

Observe to begin with that the voluntary control principle doesn't draw a line between capacity and effort, as is sometimes suggested, but between voluntary and involuntary personal characteristics of whatever sort. In particular, capacities acquired as a result of deliberate choice—say, a choice to train for a certain profession—would remain an appropriate basis of desert under this principle, as would choices about the direction in which one's capacities were later to be exercised.[26] Thus entrepreneurship in the sense discussed above—say a decision to acquire unusual skills which one guessed would be in demand in the future— would still rightly bring its rewards. This means that it will be impossible in practice to separate the results of voluntary and involuntary characteristics in the way that the principle demands. Given someone's existing set of capacities, there is no feasible

[24] See R. Nozick, *Anarchy, State and Utopia* (Oxford: Blackwell, 1974), 213–27; A. Zaitchik, 'On Deserving to Deserve', *Philosophy and Public Affairs*, 6 (1976–7), 371–88; G. Sher, 'Effort, Ability and Personal Desert', *Philosophy and Public Affairs*, 8 (1978–9), 361–76.
[25] I have looked briefly at the relationship between determinism and the idea of desert in *Social Justice*, 95–102.
[26] The argument here draws on *Social Justice*, 109–10.

means of deciding which are the results of previous voluntary efforts and choices. Abilities do not divide themselves neatly into those that are always native and those that can only be acquired by conscious effort.

A further implication is that there is no realistic possibility of bringing market allocations into line with the voluntary control principle by means of an ability tax. Such a tax has occasionally been proposed as a means of offsetting natural inequalities in endowment; unlike more conventional income taxes, it would have no disincentive effects, since a lump sum would be levied on personal ability irrespective of how the person in question chose to exercise that ability. But, quite apart from the issues of equity that this proposal raises[27], it is clearly open to the objection that native ability in the relevant sense cannot be detected by external observation; nor would the person to be taxed have any incentive to reveal the extent of his native endowment, even supposing that he himself could disentangle it from acquired capacities.

The upshot is that any economic system (and this applies to non-market systems too) that attempts *inter alia* to reward desert may require a choice between two imperfect solutions. On the one hand, we can measure desert by value created, recognizing that that this will depend partly on native ability; on the other hand, we can take a voluntary feature such as effort as the basis of desert, remunerating people according, say, to the number of hours they work (or some more sophisticated variant of this).[28] The second solution, however, ignores the extent to which people's efforts are turned in a socially useful direction, and also the value of the skills they have chosen to acquire, and this is surely paradoxical from the point of view of justice (as well as potentially inefficient). Neither solution, therefore, perfectly matches the requirements of the voluntary control principle; the question is, which gives the closer approximation? Is it less

---

[27] John Roemer, for example, shows that the mechanisms which have been proposed to offset inequalities in natural endowment are likely to leave the well endowed worse off than the poorly endowed in terms of welfare. See J. Roemer, 'Equality of Talent', *Economics and Philosophy*, 1 (1985), 151–87.

[28] In theory we might favour a mixed solution, measuring desert partly by value created and partly by effort expended, but it is difficult to see what social arrangements such a conception would require. It might just be possible to interpret the familiar combination of market-determined incomes and progressive income taxes in this way, if we took the view that high incomes were predominantly attributable to native ability—but this is pushing towards the limits of credibility.

distorting to include native ability as a determinant of desert, or to exclude acquired ability and choices made about the direction in which to exercise that ability? It may therefore turn out that even someone who is wedded to the voluntary control principle will come to see the first solution, which measures desert by value created, as the better means of realizing distributive justice in practice.

Finally, and still without attempting to attack the voluntary control principle head on, it may be worth observing that in other cases where desert is at stake—for instance, cases of personal gratitude—it matters that the result is brought about by conscientious effort, but does not seem to matter that native ability is also a pre-condition. Thus if I rescue my neighbour's cat from a tree, I deserve gratitude only if it takes some effort on my part to do so, but the fact that I am naturally agile may rightfully bring me greater thanks than my brother, who tried as hard but wasn't able to bring off the rescue. In other words, although we might feel misgivings about attributing desert *solely* on the basis of native ability, we seem prepared to ascribe it in cases that blend involuntary attributes with voluntary efforts. Perhaps, then, we might interpret the voluntary control principle as providing a necessary condition for successful desert claims, rather than as a complete determinant of such claims.

VII

The sixth objection points to the major part played by luck, or chance, in determining market outcomes. A useful way of thinking about this problem is to envisage the market as operating over a series of discrete time-intervals, and participants as having to make, at the beginning of each period, investment decisions which are irrevocable for the period ahead. These might concern the acquisition of a new skill or the purchase of a piece of equipment. Because of the rigidity this introduces, unanticipated shifts in market conditions—say, a change in consumers' tastes—will boost the incomes of some producers and cut those of others in a random manner. Although this model is obviously artificial in some respects, it does capture the salient point that no one is in a position to respond with complete flexibility to market fluctuations; indeed, major decisions, such as training for a career, may involve a lifelong commitment.

Conceiving of the market as operating over discrete time-periods also helps us to think about the effects of luck on distributive justice. If the periods were numerous, and the gains and losses relatively small and randomly distributed, then each person's long-run level of benefit might not deviate significantly from their deserts. The market would resemble a football league where, although the result of each game depends to some extent on chance factors, over the season points accumulated represent a fair assessment of merit. But this is not a good model of most existing markets. The random gains and losses in any period may be carried over to the following period in the form of new investment. Players in this game do not start each new period on an equal footing; they are unequally endowed with value-creating assets as a result of their success or failure in the previous period.

The extent to which this is so depends of course on the structure of the market. Capitalist markets amplify the role of luck by allowing participants, if they choose, to carry their winnings forward in the form of capital investment. Inequalities that emerge in the initial period may then be amplified very rapidly. Some apologists for capitalism would argue here that investment of this sort represents a fair gamble that will appeal only to those with a taste for winning or losing big stakes; but this apologia overlooks the fact that capital as a scarce resource commands a premium over and above the gains and losses accruing to particular investments. In contrast, market socialism tends to spread the windfall gains of economic success more widely, since profits are shared throughout the membership of each enterprise, and (for the reasons sketched in Chapter 3, section iii) they are unlikely to be converted into capital investment in succeeding periods. Thus, market socialism seems likely to correspond more closely to the football league model than existing capitalist markets, for which, if we are looking for a games analogy, the most appropriate might be Monopoly, where the player who gets ahead in the early rounds usually moves inexorably towards complete domination of the game.

It needs to be said that there is no feasible way of correcting completely for luck in a market economy. It is impossible to separate the effects of chance from shrewd entrepreneurship—that is, the making of wise investment decisions in circumstances of uncertainty. This cannot be done because, as the Austrian economists have argued, the knowledge needed for entrepreneurship is dispersed, local knowledge. No public authority could be in a position to decide how far a successful outcome was the result of chance, and how far the result of the producer's intelligence and insight. The idea of a general tax on windfalls is therefore a non-starter. (We may of course wish to implement a policy of taxing windfalls of particular kinds, such as the unanticipated discovery of valuable raw materials under someone's land.) What we *can* do is try to ensure that the results of luck are non-cumulative, so that its distributive effects are as far as possible genuinely random. As I have suggested, this depends on which background institutions we choose to frame the market.

VIII

My reply to the sixth objection leads naturally to the seventh and final critique of the idea of justice in markets that I want to consider. All of the analysis up to this point has been based on the assumption that markets gravitate towards a competitive equilibrium in which each factor of production receives the equivalent of the value it creates.[29] But, the seventh objection runs, this view of markets is largely mythical: the stringent conditions required for perfect competition are never actually realized. As a result, receipts in real markets are strongly affected by the particular assets that a person holds, both by their quantity and their quality. Even if we envisage a market economy starting from an equal distribution of resources, so that income in the early periods bears some relation to desert, at later points this relationship is attenuated as the assets people have been able to acquire increasingly determine their receipts.

Consider two ways in which real markets may diverge radically from our idea of a competitive equilibrium. One has to do with non-reproducible resources: that is, either scarce natural

---

[29] Strictly speaking each factor receives the equivalent of its marginal product. This might create a problem for the use of market value as a measure of desert if there were reason to think that some particular factor was always treated as if it were the last to be hired. When speaking here of producers receiving the value of their output, I have assumed that, over the long run, this value is averaged over all circumstances of supply, ranging from the first to the last quantum to be purchased. However, this assumption may not always hold; Jon Elster, for instance, has pointed out that, in the absence of collective bargaining on the workers' side, capital may be able to exploit labour by treating each worker as if he were the marginal employee. See J. Elster, *Sour Grapes* (Cambridge: Cambridge University Press, 1983), 146.

resources, or man-made resources that for one reason or another cannot be replicated (paintings, antiques, and so forth). As demand for such resources increases, those who hold them can extract a surplus from consumers. In a technical sense there may be no departure from competitive equilibrium, since the income received may simply reflect a market-clearing price. In the sense that concerns us, however, where equilibrium prices are being used to measure desert, these surpluses are anomalous since they reflect no input on the part of the asset-holders. This is true whether the particular assets in question were acquired by chance or deliberately.[30]

These possibilities pose serious problems for market justice. Notice that the problem arises not only in the case of resources that are invested as capital, but also with land and other commodities held for private use that are non-reproducible. Thus it is not circumvented fully when capital holdings are transferred to social ownership, as in the case of market socialism. It is possible to treat some other holdings in the same way: for instance, it may be proposed that land and certain other valuable assets, such as Old Masters, should be publicly owned. An alternative approach is to attempt to recoup the surplus, through a capital gains tax. But clearly, restoring justice here requires fairly extensive intervention in the market by a political authority.

A second form of deviation from competitive equilibrium arises from the process of production itself. Technical factors such as economies of scale may mean that particular industries reach equilibrium with only a small number of competing enterprises, since would-be entrants find themselves unable to compete effectively with large, established firms. Under such conditions of oligopoly, tacit or overt price-fixing will allow each firm to reap profits in excess of the value they create (as measured by prices at a competitive equilibrium). Although private ownership of capital is likely to exacerbate this problem, it may quite conceivably arise even where the enterprises in question are worker's co-operatives using socially owned capital.

To deal with these problems, we need to examine the condi-

---

[30] We should distinguish genuine entrepreneurship, which deserves reward because it creates value, from the spurious entrepreneurship involved in, say, collecting rare items whose value increases over time; in the latter case the 'entrepreneur' merely syphons off a portion of the value that would be created whatever he did.

tions under which markets will fail to reach competitive equilibrium, and explore ways of minimizing such departures. In particular we need a theory of *exploitation*, that is a theory about the circumstances in which participants in a market are able to use power of some kind to take advantage of those in a weaker position. This is the subject of the following chapter. I end here by noting simply that an account of justice in markets must eventually cover not only the distributive results of markets that are perfectly competitive, but the additional problems posed by competitive failure.

We are already in a position, however, to reach one firm conclusion: any market economy that aims to achieve, or even approximate to, distributive justice must be regulated by a politically controlled agency (or set of agencies). Nor is it sufficient merely to set ground rules (for instance, concerning the terms on which people can hold capital) and then allow the market to operate spontaneously. The relevant authority must be prepared to monitor the development of particular markets and to intervene in a fairly *ad hoc* way to rectify major inequities. One can see why libertarians, who believe that social systems require only a simple set of ground rules to operate effectively, are wise to eschew the attempt to show that unfettered markets can be socially just. Aiming to avoid both this conclusion and its socialist mirror-image—namely, that distributive justice is something to be achieved entirely outside market contexts—I have attempted so far primarily to establish three theses: first, that there are no deep conceptual grounds for thinking that markets cannot allocate resources in accordance with personal deserts; second, that there are good positive reasons for taking equilibrium prices as indicators of value when measuring desert; but third, that a market economy will only gravitate towards an equilibrium in the relevant sense if it is given an appropriate regulatory framework. What such a framework should consist in, and how it might be created politically, are matters requiring further discussion.

7

EXPLOITATION

I

I concluded the last chapter by noting that a theory of market justice needs to be completed by a theory of exploitation. If we aim to show that a suitably framed market can conform to our principles of distribution, we must at some point assess the factors which deflect real markets away from competitive equilibrium—or, more precisely, from an equilibrium of the kind that our theory of justice demands where each agent receives on average, the equivalent of the values he has created. This, essentially, is what a theory of exploitation does. Exploitation is best regarded as a particularly repugnant form of injustice. It implies not only that the final distribution of resources as between exploiter and exploited is unjust, but that this imbalance arose through the exploiter's use of power of some kind: both the process and the outcome are objectionable. Thus a theory of exploitation links together the issue of market power with that of the final distribution of resources.

There is another evident reason for considering the issue of market exploitation. It has been a central claim of the socialist tradition (associated particularly with Marx, but not confined to him) that capitalism involves the systematic exploitation of workers by their employers. By implication, a valuable feature of socialism is the disappearance of exploitation. It then becomes of critical importance to see whether market socialism ensures this, or whether exploitative relationships might re-emerge under such a system. To put the matter very crudely, we need to discover whether the source of exploitation is to be found in the private ownership of capital or more generally in the market economy as such.

It would be tempting here to *define* exploitation in such a way that it could only arise under capitalism, but this would be a hollow victory. If our analysis is to carry conviction, we need to unearth the basic intuition that lies behind charges of economic exploitation, without at this stage committing ourselves as to the kind of system that could avoid it. The conclusion I shall reach, to anticipate, is that market socialism is not characterized by *systematic* exploitation in the way that capitalism is, although particular instances of exploitation remain possible under that system and need to be guarded against. But before drawing such conclusions, we must get clear about the notion of exploitation itself, and examine critically some recent accounts of the conditions for exploitation in markets to occur.

We need straight away to separate two basic senses in which markets may be said to be exploitative.[1] First, what may be at issue is the fact, already acknowledged here, that market transactions are non-tuistic. Each party, in other words, engages in them for reasons that have nothing to do with the welfare of the other party. Such transactions may be thought to offend against a certain ideal of human relationships, for instance a belief about what constitutes respect for persons. Notice that exploitation here may be mutual: A may exploit B, and be exploited by him, in the very same transaction. Both may be moved entirely by private concerns and have no interest in the other's welfare.

Exploitation in this first sense will be considered in the following chapter as part of the more general charge that personal relationships in market economies are inhuman and alienating. Our interest in this chapter will be in exploitation in a more specific sense: taking advantage of someone, benefiting at their expense. Exploitation in this narrower sense is always asymmetrical: in every such relationship there is an exploiting party and another that is exploited. As I have noted already, all cases of exploitation are also cases of distributive injustice, but in attaching the term 'exploitation' we are also saying something more specific about how the injustice arose. We are saying that the exploiter already enjoyed some position of advantage on which he capitalized in order to benefit unfairly from the present transaction.

If exploitation has this general character, it may at first sight seem puzzling how it can occur at all in market transactions, since

---

[1] See J. Elster, 'Exploitation, Freedom and Justice', in J. R. Pennock and J. W. Chapman (eds.), *Nomos XXVI: Marxism* (New York: New York University Press, 1983), 278; also A. Buchanan, *Ethics, Efficiency, and the Market* (Oxford: Clarendon Press, 1985), 87–95.

such dealings are by definition voluntary, both parties engaging in them in the hope of improving their material situation in some respect. They are to be distinguished from coercive interactions, where A forces B to part with some of his material resources by threatening to inflict damage of still greater magnitude on B. The exploitation involved in coercion is easy to see: there is a one-way transfer of value caused by A's power in relation to B—his capacity to harm the latter. But market exploitation is harder to pin down. When A exploits B through a market exchange, the transaction seems to hover uneasily between voluntariness and involuntariness. B would rather exchange with A than do nothing at all; at the same time, there is some third hypothetical transaction that he would prefer to engage in still more, forming a bench-mark against which we judge the actual exchange to be exploitative. If I run into someone out walking on a hot day, miles from the nearest source of liquid refreshment, and offer to sell him a bottle of beer for £5, he would rather engage in this transaction than not, but would prefer still more to buy the beer for £1, the price that I paid for it that morning in the shop. I am (it appears) exploiting him to the extent of £4, the difference between the terms of the actual exchange, and the terms of the hypothetical bench-mark exchange. The problem, however, is to decide on the appropriate bench-mark. Out of all the possible exchanges that B prefers to the actual exchange, which one should be singled out as privileged from the point of view of demonstrating exploitation?

II

Two approaches to this question have been dominant in discussions of exploitation. The first, associated with Marx, focuses on the actual transfer of value between A and B. Assuming an objective criterion of value, the view maintains that exploitation occurs whenever the value transferred by B to A exceeds the value transferred from A to B; in other words, the appropriate bench-mark is a transaction in which the flows of value in either direction are exactly equal. In Marx's case, of course, the focus was on exchanges between labour and capital, and the measure of value used was the labour-time socially necessary to produce each commodity, but the approach itself can be widened beyond these particular limitations.

There are, however, several basic difficulties with such an approach.[2] Here I draw attention to the fact that focusing on the transfer of value alone abstracts from the motives of the agents concerned in an unacceptable way. Take, for example, the purchase of lottery tickets or insurance policies. Suppose that the purchaser turns out not to win a prize or to make any claim on the policy he has purchased. There is then a unilateral transfer of value from B to A, but it is hard to maintain that B, the purchaser, has been exploited. The reason is, of course, that the transfer has been made under circumstances of risk which B assesses in such a way that he is willing to go ahead with his purchase.

To this it may be objected that there is indeed a reciprocal transfer of value—namely (to take the lottery case), a $\frac{1}{n}$ chance of a prize of a certain amount, together with whatever psychological satisfaction B gains from participating in the gamble. But such a response immediately shifts the argument away from observable transfers of value measured by an objective criterion towards subjective questions. We are now talking not about the value of transfers to and from B, but about the value of such transfers as perceived by B. And this suggests that there may no longer be a strict correlation between the value that A attaches to the items involved and the value that B attaches. Consider once again the bottle of beer that I sell to the thirsty hiker for £5. We know from this transaction that the hiker values the beer at not less than £5, and that I value it at not more than £5. But we cannot derive any more information than that from the transaction alone. We need more information to decide whether the exchange is exploitative. If we see it as exploitative, it is because we assume that the value of the beer to me is the £1 that I originally paid for it. But of course it may be that I too would pay up to £5 for a beer in present circumstances, in which case I am not exploiting the other party in exchanging at that figure, despite the £4 cash profit I have made.

Once, therefore, we allow the subjective value attributed to items to diverge from their objective value (according to some criterion), we can no longer take one-way flows of objective value

[2] For difficulties of other kinds, see G. A. Cohen, 'The Labour Theory of Value and the Concept of Exploitation', *Philosophy and Public Affairs*, 8 (1978–9), 338–60; R. Goodin, 'Exploiting a Situation and Exploiting a Person', in A. Reeve (ed.), *Modern Theories of Exploitation* (London: Sage, 1987); P. Van Parijs, 'Some Problems with the Labour Theory of Exploitation', Working Paper No. 8212, Institut des Sciences Économiques, Université Catholique de Louvain, 1982.

as a sufficient condition for exploitation. It may be worth adding that this result does not depend on the assumption that each of us has a unique psychology. Even if our underlying preferences were all identical, the values we placed on particular items might differ because of circumstances, past consumption, etc. For instance, everyone may be willing to pay an extra £1 for a bottle of beer for each five miles that he walks on a hot day.

So quite apart from the familiar difficulties with the labour theory of value, an objective-value theory of Marx's type is unable to provide a general account of exploitation in the market. It might provide an approximation to such an account, if we knew we were dealing with a range of situations in which subjective valuations of objects closely corresponded to their objective values; but that is the best that could be said for it.

III

A second approach to exploitation attempts to identify it in terms of the background distribution of resources against which an exchange is made. Suppose that with the current distribution of resources d, A and B make an exchange e. Under an alternative distribution d' which is regarded as equitable, a different exchange e' would have occurred. Suppose that B holds less resources under d than under d', and that e is less favourable to B than e'. Then B is exploited to the extent of the difference between e and e'. Exploitation is assessed according to what would have happened under an alternative (and morally privileged) set of circumstances.

This approach has recently been interestingly fleshed out in two rather different ways by Hillel Steiner[3] and John Roemer.[4] Steiner offers a 'liberal' theory of exploitation which explains exploitation in terms of prior violations of rights. The core idea is that an unequal exchange of value between A and B counts as exploitative if it can be attributed to a prior violation of the rights of some third party C, either by A or by a fourth party D. Steiner cites cases in which C would be willing to make an equal

[3] H. Steiner, 'A Liberal Theory of Exploitation', *Ethics*, 94 (1983–4), 225–41.

[4] J. Roemer, *A General Theory of Exploitation and Class* (Cambridge and London: Harvard University Press, 1982); id., 'New Directions in the Marxian Theory of Exploitation and Class', *Politics and Society*, 11 (1982), 253–87; id., 'Property Relations vs. Surplus Value in Marxian Exploitation', *Philosophy and Public Affairs*, 11 (1982), 281–313.

exchange with B, but is forcibly prevented from doing so either by A or by D. This leaves B no alternative but to make a less favourable exchange with A. The exploitative transfer itself does not involve a rights violation (the transfer is voluntary and no rights of B's are violated), but it results from one. (As indicated, the exploiter A may or may not himself be responsible for the rights violation.) On this version, then, the question whether an exchange is exploitative depends on a history, on whether among its historical antecedents there is a violation of rights that worsens the bargaining position of one party.

Steiner's theory is subject to a number of difficulties, of which two in particular are important for the argument of this chapter.[5] The first is that we need an objective standard of value if we are to distinguish exploitative exchanges from other exchanges that are not exploitative, even though their terms are affected by earlier rights-violations. Why is this so? Consider the situation of A, B and C as described in the last paragraph. Without an objective standard of value, we would be unable to tell whether the actual exchange between A and B exploits B, or whether the exchange that would otherwise have occurred between B and C was simply a particularly favourable one from B's point of view. Suppose I own an item standardly valued at £5. For some reason (urgent need, a liking for that particular specimen, a desire to curry favour) Jones will buy it from me for £10. If Harris forcibly prevents this transaction, and I later sell the item for £5 to someone else, I haven't been exploited (though my rights have been violated). But to reach this conclusion we required the standard valuation.

Steiner's theory promises to avoid difficulties of the kind that I raised earlier in relation to value-transfer theories of exploitation, but without tacit appeal to an objective standard of value it loses touch with any intuitively plausible idea of exploitation in exchange.[6] The second difficulty is that Steiner takes too narrow

---

[5] I leave aside here the question whether, as Steiner claims, exploitation always involves at least three parties (the exploiter, the exploited, and the victim of the rights-violation). For the contrary view see my 'Exploitation in the Market', in A. Reeve (ed.), *Modern Theories of Exploitation* (London: Sage, 1987), 151–2; and S. Walt, 'Comment on Steiner's Liberal Theory of Exploitation', *Ethics*, 94 (1983–4), 242–7. For Steiner's reply, see H. Steiner, 'Exploitation: A Liberal Theory Amended, Defended and Extended' in Reeve (ed.), *Modern Theories of Exploitation*.

[6] Steiner might of course simply *define* as exploitative any exchange which is under-

a view of the necessary pre-history of exploitation. For the sake of simplicity, let us continue to assume that we can establish objective values. Return to the case in which B would have made an equal exchange with C, but following an intervention by A he instead makes an unequal exchange with the latter. Steiner regards the latter exchange as exploitative only when A's intervention takes the form of a rights violation. But suppose instead that A induces C to withdraw from the proposed exchange in some other way: for instance he offers him a bribe, or feeds him false information, or threatens him with some future harm.[7] Why, from B's point of view, should it matter which kind of intervention has occurred? The relevant considerations are: *a*) he is now receiving less than the full value of the goods he is exchanging; *b*) he would have received the full value but for A's intervention. From C's point of view, of course, it matters a good deal which form the intervention takes: rights violations are generally unwelcome, other modes of intervention may be positively welcome. But C isn't the victim of exploitation: B is. It seems natural to identify exploitation in terms relevant to the victim and his exploiter.

taken in lieu of a better exchange that a rights violation has prevented. But if, say, I discover B about to sell C some item under false pretences (a forged Old Master, for instance), immobilize C while I persuade him of his error, and later buy the forgery from B at some much lower price, it is very implausible to say that B has been exploited, whatever view one takes about the propriety of my course of action as a whole. In 'Exploitation: A Liberal Theory Amended', Steiner focuses exclusively on various ways in which C ('White' in his example) may be prevented from exchanging with B ('Red')—essentially separating rights violations from other cases—without considering whether *in all circumstances* the fact that a potential higher bid has been eliminated is relevant to demonstrating exploitation.

[7] In 'Exploitation: A Liberal Theory Amended', Steiner argues that no rational person could aim to exploit another by means of bribes or threats directed at third parties, even in cases where what is threatened involves a rights violation. The argument, in a nutshell, is that A must lose as much to C as he stands to gain from his exchange with B. However, the premises of this argument are far too narrow, especially in the case of threats. The cost to A of threatening C is not at all easy to calculate. It depends in the first place on whether A feels obliged to carry out his threat in case of non-compliance—to protect his future credibility, say (if not, the cost is essentially zero). Otherwise, let the probability of C's complying be p, the probability of A's being punished after the threat is carried out be q, the gain to A from violating C's rights be G, and his loss in case of punishment be L: then the expected cost of issuing the threat is $(1-p)(qL-G)$. For C, there is a corresponding calculation to make. Supposing the benefit to A of exploiting B is E, the value to A of issuing the threat is:

$$pE-(1-p)(qL-G).$$

Since the probabilities involved can only be estimated subjectively, I can see no general reason to expect this quantity to be negative.

To make this analysis fully convincing, we need to say more about how A is able to make the intervention that disadvantages B. As I shall argue later, exploitation presupposes that the exploiter enjoys some special position of advantage on which he is able to capitalize. But enough has been said to show why the rights analysis isn't powerful enough to get a proper grip on the idea of exploitation. Rights violations are neither a necessary nor a sufficient condition for exploitation to occur. They are not sufficient because rights violations can occur, and yet all participants in the market may be left with sufficient partners to make non-exploitative exchanges. They are not necessary because other types of intervention in the market may also create circumstances of exploitation.

Roemer's approach to exploitation is rather different. He first of all fixes a comparative bench-mark: a distribution of resources that is equitable by some criterion. He then looks at groups of people under existing conditions to see whether they are faring worse or better than they would under the bench-mark distribution. Various bench-marks are possible, but the appropriate comparison point for identifying capitalist exploitation, Roemer argues, is a state of affairs in which alienable goods are equally distributed. The conditions under which a group S is capitalistically exploited by its complement S' are set out as follows.

1. If S were to withdraw from the society, endowed with its per capita share of society's alienable property (that is, produced and non-produced goods), and with its own labour and skills, then S would be better off (in terms of income and leisure) than it is at the present allocation;

2. If S' were to withdraw under the same conditions, then S' would be worse off (in terms of income and leisure) than it is at present;

3. If S were to withdraw from society with its *own* endowments (not its per capita share), then S' would be worse off than at present.[8]

Condition 1 requires that the exploited group should be better off under the equitable distribution; condition 2 requires that the exploiting group should be worse off; condition 3 requires that the exploiting group's advantages should depend on the exploited group, so that if the latter were simply to disappear from the scene, leaving capital intact, the exploiters would be worse off.

[8] Roemer, 'Property Relations vs. Surplus Value', 285.

What are the difficulties with an approach of this kind? I shall focus on two, leaving aside the many fascinating questions which Roemer's book (and associated articles) raise. The first has to do with complementarities in production.[9] It is clearly often the case that two or more producers, by pooling their assets, can generate a collective product that is greater than the sum of their individual products were they to produce separately. In these circumstances, no producer may be able to gain by withdrawing from 'society' with his share of assets, and on Roemer's definition no one can be regarded as exploited in situations of this type. Roemer initially develops his model by reference to a technology where there are no increasing returns to scale—he thinks of producers using infinitely divisible seed corn as capital. Once increasing returns to scale are introduced, he recognizes that there may no longer be anyone who is individually exploited by the criteria set out above—no-one can benefit by withdrawing with his $\frac{1}{n}$ share of society's assets. To deal with this problem, he introduces the broader idea of 'vulnerability'. An individual is said to be vulnerable if he belongs to a minimal exploited coalition. A minimal exploited coalition is in turn defined as a group satisfying the criteria of exploitation which contains no redundant members: if any member were to be deleted, the group minus that member would no longer meet the criteria. In other words, even where the technology of production is such that 'lumps' of capital are needed to produce efficiently, it will be possible to find potential groups of producers of such a size that they would do better if they withdrew from existing arrangements with their per capita shares of collective assets. Members of these groups are quasi-exploited or 'vulnerable'. (Members of complementary groups are quasi-exploiters or in Roemer's term 'culpable'.)

This generalization of the exploitation criterion appears likely to work successfully for large economies where, although complementarities of production will undoubtedly exist, they will not be so all-encompassing that no vulnerable groups emerge. It will, in other words, be possible to find groups of moderate size who would benefit from withdrawing with their proper share of alienable assets. On the other hand it may be more difficult to

[9] See also P. Van Parijs, 'Thin Theories of Exploitation', Working Paper No. 8213, Institut des Sciences Économiques, Université Catholique de Louvain, 1982.

apply Roemer's criterion to individual exchanges. That is, if exploitation can occur not only globally (say, between employers as a class and workers as a class) but also locally (say, between one factory and a second factory which supplies components to the first), applying the vulnerability notion may become more problematic. For how would we construct the relevant counterfactual here? Suppose that the employees at Factory 2 could not benefit by withdrawing with their per capita share of assets (because they would form too small an economy for efficiency). Might they nevertheless form part of an exploited coalition? The difficulty is to see how the prospects of a withdrawing coalition should be assessed. Presumably the employees in question would not continue in precisely their present lines of production in the hypothetical economy. That economy contains a segment of the human skills and preferences present in the actual economy. If we imagine it reaching an equilibrium, the type of work performed and rewards received by each person may be quite different from the current distribution. (To aid imagination, think of what happened when convicts were shipped out to form new colonies.) It may be that when the reshuffling has finished most members of the withdrawing coalition are better off, a few are worse off. This would defeat Roemer's criterion. For exploitation to be identified under that criterion, all members of S must be better off if they withdraw with their per capita share of assets.[10]

The second problem with Roemer's analysis is of a rather different sort. Roemer identifies (capitalist) exploitation by comparing how people are faring currently with how they would fare under an equal distribution of alienable assets. The application of this criterion at any point in time will depend on how people have accumulated assets up to then. Some accumulations may not seem to raise questions about exploitation. Think of two neighbouring market gardeners, each of whom begins with the same initial endowment of land. One improves the land, erects greenhouses and watering systems, etc.; the other works less hard

[10] Roemer himself takes the criterion to be whether S as a whole does better under existing or under bench-mark arrangements; and in one place in his book he explores how coalitions will form on varying assumptions about the function they will attempt to maximize (Roemer, *General Theory*, 226–33). However, it makes little sense to speak of a person as exploited merely because he forms an indispensible part of a coalition which would do better under alternative arrangements if the person himself won't also do better under these arrangements.

and/or less skillfully, and his plot remains more or less in its original condition. They exchange surplus products to their mutual advantage. Applying Roemer's criterion, the first gardener exploits the second. For (*a*) Gardener 2 would be better off if allowed to withdraw with his per capita share of current assets—viz. half the improved plot and half the unimproved plot; (*b*) Gardener 1 would be worse off under these circumstances; (*c*) Gardener 1 would also be worse off if Gardener 2 withdrew with just his own plot, because the exchange of products would then not occur. (That is, one assumes the products were exchanged because Gardener 1 preferred to grow more tomatoes, say, and receive cabbages from 2 than to grow cabbages himself—perhaps there are economies of scale; now he must grow his own cabbages.) But it seems very implausible to regard this relationship as exploitative. Gardener 1's advantages stem from his own labour and skill, deployed over time.

Roemer (rightly, in my view) resists arguments of this kind when offered in defence of capitalism against charges of exploitation. But the point about these arguments is that they are empirically implausible, in general. The advantages enjoyed by capitalists are not simply the stored-up advantages of labour and skill. So we may accept that capitalism cannot be defended in this way and still find Roemer's criterion of exploitation inadequate. The basic flaw with a counterfactual account of exploitation such as this is that it disregards the processes whereby the final distribution of resources has come about.[11] All that matters is whether some coalition could now be made better off by redistribution of assets. It may therefore include as exploitative resource-distributions that have arisen in quite unobjectionable ways, while at the same time excluding other states of affairs where groups of producers are deprived, on the grounds that there is no withdrawal scenario under which these particular groups would do better.[12]

[11] For a further discussion of this point, see J. Elster, *Making Sense of Marx*, (Cambridge: Cambridge University Press, 1985), 196–204.

[12] In his most recent writing, Roemer claims that exploitation is not the appropriate object of moral concern (for Marxists in particular), since it is really only an imperfect proxy for what does matter, namely differential ownership of productive assets; see J. Roemer, 'Should Marxists Be Interested in Exploitation?', *Philosophy and Public Affairs*, 14 (1985), 30–65. However, this analysis is predicated (as indeed was Marx's own) on the assumption that markets are perfectly competitive. If this condition obtains, then the only

If Roemer's analysis is too indifferent to history, Steiner's is historical in too narrow a way. Steiner, as we have seen, holds that exploitation cannot occur except as a result of rights violations in the past. This implies that if we begin with a fair allocation of resources (which for Steiner would mean an equal allocation)[13] and allow markets to operate over time, then, in the absence of fraud, theft, or other interference with rights, we can be certain that no subsequent transactions will be exploitative. But this overlooks the fact that, as markets evolve, some participants may gain advantages that enable them to strike bargains that are quite as disadvantageous to their contractual partners as the bargains that would be struck following rights violations. There is no reason to single out one particular feature of the historical background to a current exchange and tie exploitation to that feature alone.

IV

Our discussion of Steiner and Roemer has, however, helped to bring out what we are looking for in a theory of market exploitation. In order for us to identify a transaction as exploitative, two conditions must be fulfilled. First, the transaction must typically be more advantageous to the exploiting party and less advantageous to the exploited party than some bench-mark transaction which we use (tacitly or explicitly) as a point of reference.[14] Second, the actual transaction must have come about through some special advantage that the exploiter enjoys, upon which he capitalizes to induce the exploited to engage in this relatively less beneficial exchange. Both the terms of the exchange and the causal history leading up to it are necessary ingredients in

morally relevant factor affecting the final distribution of benefits is the initial distribution of productive assets. My argument here is that failures of competition are in themselves an important source of differential benefit, and this gives us good reason to hold on to the idea of exploitation as a more general critical tool than inequality in productive assets.

[13] See H. Steiner, 'Liberty and Equality', *Political Studies*, 29 (1981), 555–69.

[14] In the standard case, the exploiter gains and the exploited loses relative to the bench-mark. One can envisage non-standard cases where one or other of these conditions is not satisfied. In contrast to Goodin, (see Goodin, 'Exploiting a Situation'), I believe that the more crucial of the two conditions is that the exploited party should be made worse off by the exploitation. Where this is not so, it is likely that 'exploitation' is being used in the broader sense of 'using unethically', rather than in the stricter sense of 'taking unfair advantage' which is relevant to the present discussion.

identifying a case of exploitation. Let us examine each condition in turn.

The bench-mark transaction, I suggest, is one that occurs at equilibrium prices, understood in the following way. Under conditions of free exchange, every commodity (including human labour if there is a labour market) will gravitate towards an equilibrium price determined by factors of two kinds; first, natural facts about the world, such as the amount and type of labour needed to extract raw materials and convert them into useful products, the tastes of the population (including its tastes and distastes for various types of labour), and the availability and distribution of skills and talents; second, the entitlements of individuals participating in the market, including entitlements to natural resources and personal assets, as determined by an appropriate set of ground rules. Including factors of this second kind clearly introduces a normative element into our definition of equilibrium price, which differs in this respect from the notion of equilibrium commonly used in economics. For the purposes of understanding exploitation, we are interested not merely in the prices that will emerge starting from current entitlements, but in the prices that would emerge given entitlements that we regard as morally defensible. This last clause shows why the notion of exploitation is potentially contestable. Socialists, for example, may regard transactions between labour and capital as exploitative on the grounds that capitalists are not entitled to the assets that they bring to these transactions, whereas libertarians will take a different view.

There may be no dispute here that the market has reached an equilibrium given the prevailing set of entitlements. The question at issue is whether *this* equilibrium is the appropriate one for arriving at verdicts about exploitation. I will return later to the question of how a competitive equilibrium should be defined for these purposes. Supposing that we have such a definition, how do we decide whether the transaction we are considering is exploitative? The first point to notice is that this cannot be true of any exchange that actually occurs at equilibrium prices. This is perhaps not quite as trivial as it seems. Consider a case in which a temporary shortage of some good causes its exchange price to rise above the equilibrium price. Say that coal, which normally sells at £80 per ton, rises to £100 per ton during the shortage. B persuades A—say, by feeding him false information—to sell him coal at £80 per ton. Under these circumstances B is not exploiting A. He is merely depriving A of the chance to profit from holding a commodity that is in short supply.[15] B's behaviour may well be unethical, and there may be some sense in which A is being unfairly treated; however, A is not being exploited in being persuaded to exchange at the equilibrium price. (Note further that B may well go on to exploit some third party C if he resells the coal at £100 per ton.)

Exchange at non-equilibrium prices is therefore a necessary condition for exploitation; it is not, however, sufficient. There are at least three circumstances in which exchanging above or below the equilibrium price is non-exploitative. The first is genuine ignorance on both sides. If neither A nor B knows what an item is worth, but they succeed in agreeing a price, the one who turns out to gain from the deal (when the equilibrium price is revealed) is not an exploiter. Exploitation requires an asymmetry between the parties: A must in some sense be better placed than B in order to exploit him. Now in cases of two-way ignorance, questions of fairness may perhaps arise at a later point. Consider the classic case of the old lady who sells to an antique dealer a picture that turns out to be worth thousands of pounds. The dealer, we are supposing, bought in genuine ignorance of the picture's worth. Many would nevertheless feel that the old lady is hard done by unless the dealer turns over some part of the windfall gain. I share this feeling, but would still insist that the dealer has not exploited her whatever he later does.

A second circumstance in which exchange away from equilibrium prices is non-exploitative is one where both parties value the good at the price for which it is sold. Suppose that in a shortage I buy coal at £100 per ton (because I need coal to keep my boiler alight, and it is worth paying the higher price). I don't exploit my neighbour if I sell him some at the same price, so long, that is, as I continue to value the coal at £100 per ton. (If I know that next week I shall be able to purchase new coal at £80 per ton, and I decide to make a killing on my existing stock, I may exploit my neighbour.) The test is whether the selling party would be

---

[15] What if A had himself bought the coal at £100 per ton? He was then (probably) exploited by some agent(s) in the chain of exchanges leading up to this sale. The exchange with B underlines this earlier exploitation; it doesn't add to it.

willing to buy at the non-equilibrium price, in cases where this stands above the equilibrium price. (In the opposite case, a price below the equilibrium price, the test is whether the buyer would also be prepared to sell at that price.)

The third circumstance is simply one in which the person who loses out (by comparison to the equilibrium exchange) is willing to lose out. That is, the losing party either prefers exchanging at Y to exchanging at X, or is at least indifferent between these possibilities. Why might this be? The exchange might conceal a gift: A may decide to help B by buying his goods at over-the-odds prices. Or the differential between X and Y might be very small in relation to A's resources, so A may simply not care about paying the higher price. (Thus it is hard to accept that very rich people are exploited by tradesmen who charge a higher price for their services in this knowledge.) Or A might have some extraneous reason for wanting to be seen to pay the higher price. It may be important to A to impress C with his wealth. Making a show of indifference between paying X and Y for the item in question might be an effective way of doing so. Thus, a rich young man may take a girl out to a restaurant which he knows charges outrageous prices for its wine.[16]

V

To decide when exchanges at non-equilibrium prices involve exploitation, we must therefore turn to the second condition, namely the factors by virtue of which the exploiting party is able to bring about the exchange that actually occurs. Broadly speaking, these factors fall into two categories: asymmetries in information, and asymmetries in bargaining power. Take asymmetries in information first. I can exploit someone by selling an item to him for more than the equilibrium price if I know that the equilibrium price is X and he mistakenly believes it to be $Y (Y > X)$; conversely I can exploit by buying at below the equilibrium price. Are all such

---

[16] This case must be distinguished from one in which A, faced with a demand for Y for some item, must appear not to mind paying over the odds (for some extrinsic reason). An example would be a young man who pretends to be wealthy and mistakenly chooses a restaurant where the prices are excessively high. He is being exploited. He can't afford to walk out (with his impressionable girl), but he'd prefer not to be there at all.

cases instances of exploitation? The clearest case is one in which A causes B to have the mistaken belief; e.g., A produces fraudulent information which indicates that the item is selling down the road at Y. What if B's belief arises without A's intervention? I think our verdict here will depend on whether A and B are equally or unequally placed as far as gathering information in this area is concerned. At one extreme, we have the antique dealer who spots a (probable) Renoir in the old lady's loft. He doesn't mislead the old lady (this would be the clearest case), but he allows her to act on her belief that the picture is a piece of Victorian rubbish; and buys it for £25. This looks like exploitation, because the dealer is trained to spot Renoirs, whereas the old lady wouldn't be able to do so without bringing in expert advice (and she might not know where to go, or might not even have any idea that valuable paintings can turn up in this way). At the other extreme there is the case where I buy an overpriced good because I can't be bothered to shop around; in this case it is relatively easy for me to obtain the information, so if I choose not to do so it seems to indicate that I care rather little whether I buy the item for £100 or £120, say. (The case would be different if I have to buy an item urgently, so have no time to discover its equilibrium price; here the possibility for exploitation exists.) In other words, for asymmetrical information to lead to exploitation, it has be rooted in the circumstances of the two parties. A has to be better placed than B either because he has skills and capacities which allow him to obtain information that B can't obtain, or because he has somehow been provided with information that is not available to the other (thus I can exploit you by taking a bet on some event whose outcome I already know). If the asymmetry is easily rectifiable by B, the case begins to look more like the third circumstance above, where B is simply indifferent between exchanging at Y and exchanging at X, and so isn't exploited when he pays over the odds.

The other major category of exploitation is exploitation stemming from objective features of the market, in circumstances in which both parties have full knowledge of equilibrium prices. The opportunity for exploitation occurs, that is to say, because the market has not reached a competitive equilibrium in the sense defined above. Of the various ways in which this may occur, I shall consider three. The first is a short-term imbalance between supply and demand, caused, let us say, by a sudden contraction in supply, or a change of taste that increases demand. There is an unavoidable time-lag before additional workers switch to making the product in question, and in the meantime those already producing it can sell their output at an inflated price. A second case arises where there are economies of scale in the production of certain goods, so that the market achieves stability with only a small number of firms (or, in the extreme case, a single firm) making these goods. Knowing that potential entrants will find it difficult to compete, the existing producers are able to restrict their output and raise prices above the competitive level. The third case concerns monopolies of natural resources, where either a single owner or a small group of colluding owners can charge a premium for access to the resources that they control. As in the second case, the market may be stable without having reached a competitive equilibrium in the sense that we are looking for.

These three cases obviously differ in important respects, and as we shall see later our response to each of them may also be different. But is important to see what they have in common. In each case a departure from competitive equilibrium provides the beneficiaries with a certain kind of market power *vis-à-vis* those consumers who need to use the resources in question. Exploitation occurs when the favoured parties use their position to extract a surplus return from those who have no alternative but to deal with them. It seems not to matter whether the state of disequilibrium was deliberately engineered or arose fortuitously. What does matter, from the point of view of exploitation, is whether the situation provides the beneficiaries with any freedom of manœuvre, and whether they choose to use it in the manner indicated. Exploitation is an active relationship: an exploiter must actually do something to deserve the label.

This point may be brought out most easily by considering the first of the three cases, a short-term imbalance between supply and demand. Suppose that television sets sell for £300 a piece in a fully competitive market. There is a sudden contraction in supply—say, a major manufacturer goes out of business. The remaining producers find that they can dispose of their output at £400 per set pending an increase in production which takes, say, a year to accomplish. Are they in the meantime exploiting their customers?

It is useful here to distinguish two polar cases. Suppose on the one hand that demand for televisions is highly elastic. When the price rises to £400, the market clears and everyone who is willing to pay that price is able to obtain a television. Here the price rise has performed a useful rationing function. Even though the producers themselves have made a windfall gain, their response has simply created a temporary equilibrium pending the restoration of a genuine competitive equilibrium. Note that if a public authority decided to nationalize the television industry as a response to the shortfall, it would still need to allocate the available sets somehow. Although other rationing devices might be proposed (e.g. first come, first served), price rationing might well seem the most appropriate. So although the windfall raises questions of distributive justice,[17] the television manufacturers cannot plausibly be seen in this case as exploiters.

Suppose on the other hand that demand for television sets is highly inelastic. Most people regard a television as a necessary part of their lives, and they are willing to pay up to a fairly high limit to have one. In these circumstances, virtually as many televisions will be sold at £400 as would be sold at £300. Here the rationing function must be performed primarily by some factor other than the price rise (e.g. a queueing system, with people waiting months to receive their sets). As a result, the price rise looks exploitative. It would have been feasible to hold the price at £300 and to allow the shortfall in supply to have been handled entirely by the informal queueing system. But, finding that they could easily dispose of sets at £400, the manufacturers have seized the opportunity to exploit their customers.

This example also illuminates another aspect of exploitation. Exploitation is possible because the vulnerable party 'must' (in some sense) engage in the transaction in question. Inelasticity of demand is a sign of this necessity. In the particular example, we assumed that consumers counted televisions among their needs. The necessity does not have to be so permanent. I can exploit someone who requires some item urgently, even though in normal circumstances there would be no chance of his paying the inflated price I am now demanding. Moreover the 'need' in question may not be a basic consumption need. Consider the case in which one enterprise buys virtually all of the output of a second enterprise. This relationship may become exploitative if the

---

[17] See above, ch. 7, sec. vii.

second firm is unable to find potential alternative buyers for its products, or unable to find them within a short enough period. The first enterprise may drive down the price of its purchases, knowing that the second would go out of business if the contract were withdrawn. Here the necessity is economic rather than physical or psychological, but in the relevant sense the second enterprise unilaterally 'needs' the first, and this is sufficient to pave the way for exploitation.

VI

The discussion so far has focused on the conditions under which a particular market transaction can be regarded as exploitative. I have argued that there are two essential conditions. First, the terms of the transaction must deviate in the exploiter's favour from the terms that would obtain at a (suitably defined) competitive equilibrium. Second, the deviation must be brought about by some advantage that the exploiter already enjoys, whether of information or of bargaining power. The first condition shows why exploitation always involves injustice; the second condition picks out what is distinctive about exploitation, as opposed, say, to the making of windfall gains through market fluctuations.

This focus on particular transactions has been deliberate. Most theories of exploitation are concerned with systemic issues, such as the question whether a capitalist economy is necessarily exploitative. Although these macro-questions must eventually concern us, starting with them may lead to crude over-simplification at the level of theory, and a corresponding naïvety at the level of policy. We may be encouraged to believe that some simple dramatic change in the ground rules of the market would eliminate exploitation once and for all. In contrast, an approach which highlights the way in which exploitation may emerge in particular segments of the market at particular times may help us to think more realistically about the regulatory framework that would be needed to forestall this possibility.

But the large issues cannot be avoided. Have we any general reason to believe that capitalism is exploitative in a way that market socialism is not, or should we conclude that both systems are, to the same degree, contingently liable to exploitation? I shall argue that, with one qualification, the first of these positions is the correct one.

Exploitation under capitalism centres on the economic relationship between employer and worker, notwithstanding the fact that it may also occur elsewhere. The terms under which individuals agree to be employed by owners of capital characteristically exploit those employees. Now we have already rejected the Marxian account of this relationship, since it rests on an unsustainable theory of value. To bear out the charge that the employer/worker relationship is exploitative, we need to show that it fulfils the two conditions identified above, viz. that its terms deviate from the terms that would obtain under a competitive equilibrium, and that the deviation is to be explained by reference to the advantaged position of the capitalist. The relevant competitive equilibrium is identified for us by the theory of justice in markets worked out in the last chapter. In equilibrium, each person's holdings will depend solely upon (*a*) natural facts about the world—the availability of resources, their physical properties, human tastes and aptitudes etc.; and (*b*) personal facts about him—the choices he makes, the skills he possesses, the effort he expends. The bundles of goods held by each person will not normally be identical (since tastes differ, market exchanges will continue until each person holds the resources that suit him best), nor will they be equal in value (purchasing power will vary according to a person's aptitudes, choices and so forth). None the less the differences in holdings that result will be directly traceable to factors of the two kinds referred to above, and this is sufficient to show the equilibrium allocation meets our criterion of justice.

Why do capitalist transactions violate this condition of equilibrium? The owner of capital is able to command a premium which reflects simply the social scarcity of the resource he brings to the transaction, not natural facts about the world or personal facts of the appropriate kind about himself. Since he can command more, the employee must accept less than he would obtain under a competitive equilibrium. The bargain is skewed in the capitalist's favour: the first condition of exploitation is met.

Apologists for capitalism resist this conclusion by pointing to facts about the capital owner that, they claim, legitimize the premium he commands. They point out that he must defer consumption in order to advance his capital, that he takes risks by investing it in an enterprise, that he displays entrepreneurship by choosing to invest it in one kind of enterprise rather than another. There is no need to deny the relevance of these facts to the justification of returns to capital. For instance, it is a fact about people's preferences that they are generally not indifferent about the time at which consumption takes place, so someone willing to defer consumption will, in equilibrium, obtain extra resources by so doing. But the facts cited do not, even when taken together, add up to a complete explanation of the premium that capital commands. Some part of that premium is attributable entirely to the scarcity of capital as a resource. In somewhat the same way, someone who owns a collection of Monets can charge for the privilege of viewing them, the charge not being reducible to the labour involved in preserving them, the costs of insurance, and so forth. If you have Monets in your possession, you can extract a rent simply because Monets are scarce in relation to the demand for looking at them.[18]

There is, however, also a difference between the owner of capital and the owner of the Monets, namely that the latter's relationship to his customers is not, under normal circumstances, exploitative. The collector's returns are unjustified, but he does not take advantage of the people who want to see his pictures. The reason, of course, is that the second condition for exploitation is not met: the customers do not, in the relevant sense, need to look at the Monets. With exchanges between capital and labour, however, it is reasonable to assume that workers must have access to the productive resources that capital provides. Without this access, their lives will be seriously restricted. The availability of unemployment benefit and other such benefits mitigates but does not fundamentally alter this fact. A worthwhile life still requires productive work, and in capitalist societies this normally means striking a bargain with an employer. The worker's needs and the employer's command of resources together create the power relationship that culminates in exploitation.

[18] The scarcity of Monets is itself a natural fact, in the sense that if enough people could paint as well as Monet, it would no longer be possible to charge a premium for looking at his pictures. What takes the case away from a competitive equilibrium is not the scarcity of Monets but the fact that they are privately held. The capacity of the owner of the Monets to extract rent from art-lovers cannot be explained by personal facts of the relevant sort (cf. my remarks in ch. 6. n. 27 about spurious entrepreneurship).

Two riders should be added to this outline account of capitalist exploitation. The first is a note that capitalist relations may emerge, over time, from a starting point that is itself a competitive equilibrium, and without anyone's rights being violated. It is not part of the account that the scarcity necessary to capitalist exploitation must be coercively engineered: in that sense, we can envisage the immaculate conception of capitalism. I laid the ground for this proposition when I argued earlier, against Steiner, that violations of rights are neither a necessary nor a sufficient condition for exploitative transactions to occur. It is enough that inequalities of bargaining power should materialize—for instance, because technical change reduces the value of the resources held by certain individuals to the point where they cannot live an adequate life without access to means of production held by others. So although monopolies of natural resources, for instance, might be one possible source of capitalist exploitation, it would be a serious mistake to conclude that an exploitation-free economy can be guaranteed simply by setting the economy running with an initial distribution of resources that meets the criteria for a competitive equilibrium.[19]

The second rider I want to add is that it is possible to conceive of a non-exploitative capitalism or, more precisely perhaps, of a non-exploitative society in which capitalist relationships predominated. The condition for this would be that any worker who wanted to could readily obtain access to his own capital—presumably from public sources—so that capitalist employment would represent a genuine choice.[20] Under these circumstances the second condition for exploitation would not be met, since the terms of engagement would no longer derive from the unequal

[19] These strictures apply not only against Steiner, but also against Dworkin's proposal that goods should be allocated by means of a Walrasian auction at which each participant is given the same number of tokens with which to bid. See R. Dworkin, 'Equality of Resources', *Philosophy and Public Affairs*, 10 (1981), 283–345. Dworkin's complete theory is more complex than this, since he uses the idea of a hypothetical insurance market to justify redistributive taxation in order to compensate for inequality of talents. He does not, however, consider the problem posed by temporal changes in the value of resources for the Walrasian auction.

[20] A critic might want to argue that this description in fact fits contemporary capitalism, since workers do indeed have other options than working for private employers—for instance, they can set themselves up in co-operatives. In response, I refer to the argument of ch. 3 concerning the special disadvantages suffered by co-operatives in economies dominated by capitalist firms.

bargaining power of the two parties. (Indeed, it seems unlikely that the first condition would be met either, since if workers choose in this situation to take paid employment, this must presumably reveal something about their preferences.[21]) Thus, it is not entering a relationship of a certain form that constitutes capitalist exploitation, but entering that relationship on terms set under conditions of unequal bargaining power.

In the light of this account of capitalist exploitation, it should be reasonably clear that market socialism avoids the systematic exploitation that characterizes capitalism. In a socialist market economy, capital is treated as a social asset allocated to co-operatives by investment agencies. It remains, of course, a scarce resource, so charges for the use of capital will reflect that fact. But the revenue from leasing capital accrues to public funds, which are themselves earmarked for distribution according to criteria of justice. Under market socialism, individuals can acquire resources only through engaging in productive activity,[22] and these resources, once acquired, cannot be converted into private capital. People can save, and receive interest on their savings that reflects a time discount, but they cannot lease their assets to other individuals on terms that represent a return to the assets themselves. Capital investment remains the prerogative of the public agencies.

This is not to say that exploitation is impossible under market socialism. Although the central source of exploitation under capitalism has been removed, there remain other areas in which exploitative exchanges might emerge. No real-world economy can be expected to approximate at all times to a competitive equilibrium. For instance, interruptions in the supply of essential goods may give some enterprises the opportunity to charge their customers exploitative prices. Again, we might envisage one co-operative becoming economically dependent on another—if, for instance the second enterprise buys the entire output of the first—and this leading over time to exploitative terms of trade. These are forms of exploitation which market socialism might be expected to share with capitalism. In general, they should be less

---

[21] A similar thesis can be found in J. S. Mill: see the passages cited in S. Hollander, *The Economics of John Stuart Mill* (Oxford: Blackwell, 1985), 818.

[22] As opposed, that is, to owning resources of certain kinds; I leave aside for the sake of simplicity entitlements to welfare provision.

severe under the former system, since (as noted earlier) its component enterprises will tend to be smaller and more numerous. Provided that adequate arrangements are made to facilitate the creation of new enterprises, a market socialist economy should come closer to fulfilling the requirements of perfect competition than its capitalist counterpart.[23] Whether this happens in practice will depend on the economic policies pursued by the state: in particular, whether it pursues policies to counter the emergence of monopolies and encourage new entrants to industries in which competition is weak. The point about the market socialist framework is not that it provides us with a foolproof recipe for an exploitation-free economy. It is rather that it removes exploitation to the realm of contingency: whether it appears at all depends on the effectiveness of public policy.

Someone might conclude from this discussion that the only general solution to market exploitation is the abolition of markets. In a narrowly analytical sense, this is of course true: if there are no market transactions, no one can be exploited through engaging in them. In a wider and more substantive sense, however, the problem is shifted sideways rather than resolved. Suppose we envisage a planned economy in which both incomes and prices are fixed by collective decision. Each person receives an income from his work which he then uses to purchase his preferred bundle of goods. It seems clear that exploitation can occur in such an economy, although to demonstrate that this was so we should need to introduce some measure of value. Suppose, simply by way of illustration, that we measure the value of all goods by the labour-time necessary to produce them.[24] We could then identify as exploited all those individuals who, by virtue of the income and pricing decisions that are taken, have no choice but to receive less value in their consumption bundle than they create through labour. In the light of past experience of economic planning, there is no reason to expect such exploitation to be an infrequent occurrence.

The upshot of my argument, therefore, is not that market

[23] See J. Vanek, *The General Theory of Labor-Managed Market Economies* (Ithaca: Cornell University Press, 1970), esp. ch. 6.

[24] I choose this measure of value because it may appeal to those who believe that all and only market economies are exploitative; earlier in the chapter I indicated some objections to using it. I also assume that all produced goods are distributed to producers—i.e. that there is no net investment and no welfare system.

economies are uniquely subject to exploitation. On the contrary, I should argue that the appearance that this is so arises mainly from the ready availability of a bench-mark, in the form of equilibrium prices, against which exploitative transactions can be judged. In a non-market economy, it will always be more difficult to select and apply a suitable measure of value to substantiate a charge of exploitation. My conclusion is rather that the likelihood of exploitation is strongly dependent on the way in which the market is framed, in particular on the forms of ownership made available by the legal system. There is nothing incoherent in the attempt to establish an economy that is market-based but exploitation-free; though we should not be misled by simple-minded theories into underestimating the complexity of this task.

8

ALIENATION AND COMMUNISM

I

Of the various charges that socialists have levelled at market economies, perhaps the most fundamental of all concerns the intrinsic quality of human relationships under markets of whatever kind. Markets, it is said, necessarily embody acquisitive and competitive social relations, in diametric opposition to the communal solidarity which socialist principles demand. They encourage people to see themselves as self-sufficient atoms, disguising each person's material dependence on his fellows, and they transmute all human intercourse into exchanges in which each party seeks to use the other for his own private ends. These charges, it appears, apply as much to market socialism as to capitalism. Thus, economic markets are intrinsically anti-socialist, and at best can be tolerated as part of a transitional stage leading to socialism proper, or communism, which is characterized by co-operation, planning, communal existence, and so forth.

It would be too strong to say that the source of this fundamentalist critique was Marx, since elements of it can be found in the work of the early socialists whom he called 'utopian'. But Marx articulates it in its strongest and most convincing form, grounding it (especially in his early *Economic and Philosophical Manuscripts*) in an elaborate theory of human nature and human community. An investigation of Marx's writings thus enables us to grasp both the strengths and the limitations of this critique. In particular I want to argue here that Marx's overall position, including his subtle and often misunderstood attitude to capitalism, does not hold unambiguously for communism as against a market version of socialism. Of course Marx nowhere explicitly defends market socialism as an ideal, and it would be absurd to try to recruit him as a whole-hearted advocate. The point, rather, is that while certain of his ideas appear to count against it, others, when properly understood, tell for it and against communism. It is a tribute to the depth of Marx's social theory, albeit a backhanded one, that the socialist who is usually held up as the foremost critic of the market economy in fact produced arguments that can be shown to favour it.

For the purpose of this discussion, I shall simply take Marx's idea of communism at face value, leaving aside familiar questions about whether such a system is economically viable, particularly in the circumstances of an advanced industrial society.[1] Marx notoriously failed to elaborate this idea in any detail (for good and not so good reasons), and we have to extrapolate its main outlines from cryptic remarks in the *Economic and Philosophical Manuscripts*, the *Critique of the Gotha Programme*, and elsewhere.[2] Here communism is defined primarily as a negation of the leading features of capitalism. Wage labour, commodity production, and the market are all abandoned. Production takes place according to a socially determined plan, though each person is allowed to choose the kind of work he performs. The division of labour is broken down, each person being permitted to work at a succession of different tasks. People are allocated goods from the common stock according to need. Economic competition disappears, and social relationships become communitarian.

The question to be addressed in this chapter is how Marx's critical attitude to capitalism bears on the choice between market socialism and communism. In order to answer it I shall use Marx's pronouncements about human nature and social relations as a source of ethical standards in terms of which the three systems can be assessed comparatively, bypassing the familiar debate about whether and in what sense Marx had an ethical theory.[3] Marx, of course, often castigated those who thought that socialism was a matter of developing some ideal model of the

---

[1] For a summary of the problems, see my *Anarchism* (London: Dent, 1984), 51–7, 171–3.

[2] For a fuller account, see B. Ollman, 'Marx's Vision of Communism: A Reconstruction', *Critique*, 8 (1977), 4–41.

[3] Steven Lukes, among others, has argued that Marx did hold an ethical theory in the broad sense which encompasses social and political ideals as well as principles of personal conduct. See S. Lukes, *Marxism and Morality* (Oxford: Clarendon Press, 1985). On the related question of whether Marx had a view of human nature, the arguments of N. Geras, *Marx and Human Nature: Refutation of a Legend* (London: Verso, 1983) seem to me conclusive.

good society whose attractions would be such that everyone would immediately set about realizing it. The fact remains that he did present his own version of communism as 'the solution to the riddle of history', and even if one interprets him as holding that the downfall of capitalism will be brought about largely through economic crises, there is still the question why people should choose to move forward from his 'first phase of communist society' (which resembles market socialism, in certain respects)[4] to communism proper. There is no plausible materialist argument for this conclusion to be found in Marx, so the only reasonable answer is that people will move forward because they are convinced of the ethical superiority of communism.[5]

Marx's implicit anti-capitalist arguments fall into two main categories: those that rely on the idea of exploitation, and those that rely on the idea of alienation (though as we shall see, the two critiques cannot be completely divorced). In the previous chapter, I gave reasons for rejecting Marx's concept of exploitation (as the unilateral transfer of labour-determined value). The same general conclusion will, however, follow from the use of that concept, namely that market socialism avoids the systematic exploitation that is characteristic of capitalism, without eliminating the possibility of exploitation altogether. But that is true of communism as well, as I showed at the end of the last chapter. A communist system might operate in such a way that, for instance, some individuals were called upon to perform excessive quantities of labour. Seen in the light of the Marxian theory of exploitation, therefore, communism and market socialism are on all fours.[6] In both cases, exploitation appears as a contingency

---

[4] For analysis of this point, see J. H. Elliott, 'Marx and Contemporary Models of Socialist Economy', *History of Political Economy*, 8 (1976), 151–84.

[5] There is a convincing argument to this effect in S. Moore, *Marx on the Choice Between Socialism and Communism* (Cambridge: Mass and London, Harvard University Press, 1980). See also S. Avineri, 'Marx's Vision of Future Society', *Dissent*, 20 (1973), 323–31.

[6] A possible counter-argument here would hold that the communitarian attitudes and values fostered by communism would make it very unlikely that anyone under this system would in fact make exploitative demands of the kind described, even if in a position to do so. Market socialism, by contrast, since it relies to some degree on material incentives to motivate people to produce, encourages acquisitiveness and makes it more likely that people who are faced with opportunities for exploitation will in fact grasp them. An adequate answer to this would need to examine the mechanisms available under market socialism to bind people morally to the ground rules of the system, an issue explored at length in Part III.

liable to distort a system that does not essentially require it, whereas, in Marx's view and in mine, the exploitation of workers by capitalists is a central and unavoidable feature of a normal capitalist economy. Thus the exploitation argument bears neutrally on a choice between the two versions of socialism.

It may seem that matters are quite different with the alienation argument. Doesn't Marx's diagnosis of the alienation suffered by workers under capitalism point unambiguously in the direction of a communist society? The difficulty here is that Marx's argument is multi-faceted, and needs careful unpacking if its true force is to be appreciated. 'Alienation' as a generic term refers to a condition where a subject finds himself separated from some feature of his context, this separation being regarded as damaging in human terms. But Marx claims that workers under capitalism are alienated in a number of quite specific ways, and it is not clear that these forms of alienation are all traceable to the same source. Since the theory of alienation has been worked over pretty thoroughly, I shall proceed quickly.

II

Marx argues first that the producer sees his product as an alien and hostile force. It is alien because, rather than remaining under his control, its behaviour is determined by external forces. It becomes a commodity, and is therefore subject to the laws of the market. Furthermore, it is seen as hostile because it helps to reproduce the conditions under which his exploitation occurs. His product is sold, and the profit returns to the capitalist, who is then in a position to renew the unequal wage bargain.

Second, the producer is distanced from, and at odds with, his own activity. He works not out of desire for the activity, but to remain alive. Work, in other words, is instrumental, 'not the satisfaction of a need, but only a *means* for satisfying other needs', as Marx puts it.[7] Further, work under capitalism is often dirty, boring, physically exhausting, and so forth.

Third, the producer is alienated from his human essence. According to Marx, each person recognizes in himself certain

---

[7] K. Marx, *Economic and Philosophical Manuscripts*, in *Karl Marx: Early Writings*, T. B. Bottomore (ed.) (London: Watts, 1963), 125.

potentialities which would unfold in a humanized form of production. Two are particularly significant. First, each person can work creatively and flexibly. Rather than being confined to a preordained task, he can set his own targets and adapt his activity to them. Second, he could also work communally, in the sense that he could find his satisfaction in work that aimed directly to meet the needs of others, and in that way bound him to the community. Thus, each person's potential is to work creatively and communally, whereas under capitalism he is forced to work routinely and for selfish ends.

Fourth, the absence of communal work means that each person is alienated from all the rest, whom he regards merely as partners in exchange and as competitors. He does not treat them as ends, but as means to his own satisfaction. In Marx's words, 'the result of my production as such has as little direct connection with you as the result of your production has with me, that is, our production is not production of man for man as man, not *socialized* production . . . Our mutual production means nothing for us as human beings.'[8]

Fifth, the collective results of human activity assume an incomprehensible and alien form. Men fail to understand the social world they have created; it seems to them to move according to its own inscrutable laws. In particular commodities take on a mysterious or, as Marx puts it, 'fetishistic' character. They appear to be animated by a will of their own. The producers' 'social action takes the form of the action of objects, which rule the producers instead of being ruled by them', Marx claims.[9]

The difficulty in assessing this account of alienation is to decide which aspects are to be attributed to which causes. Certain aspects appear to stem directly from the fact that, under capitalism, work is controlled by an exploiting overlord. Marx's remarks about the degrading character of work and about the hostility with which the worker regards his product rely on the premiss that the work relationship is simultaneously a relationship of exploitation. Alienation of this type is specific to capitalism, and would

---

[8] Id., *Excerpt Notes of 1844*, in *Writings of the Young Marx on Philosophy and Society*, eds. L. D. Easton and K. H. Guddat (Garden City, NY: Anchor, 1967), 278.
[9] Id., *Capital*, vol. i. (London, Glaisher, 1909), 46.

disappear in a socialist market economy, as well as in communism. Where work is organized co-operatively and the profits of enterprises are shared among all the members, there is no reason for work to be monotonous or physically unpleasant, nor will workers be estranged from their products, given that they benefit directly from the sale of these products in the market-place. Thus the economic arrangements of market socialism immediately eliminate some aspects of alienation as diagnosed by Marx. Conversely, other aspects of alienation appear to be deeply rooted in the idea of work as a social activity—so deeply rooted that no mere change of economic organization, however radical, could extirpate them. For Marx implies that fully human work is both a means of creative fulfilment for the producer and a means of establishing a communal tie between him and the user of his product. Unless we assume that the needs of producers and consumers dovetail perfectly, these two requirements are in tension with one another. In deciding what to produce, should I give precedence to my own creative impulses, or to others' needs as I perceive them? If I decide to make whatever best expresses my own nature at any time, then, even if the product is of some use to others, it is not likely to be the most useful thing I could have made. Conversely, if I decide to make what I judge to be the most needed item, then my work has assumed a partly instrumental character—not in the sense that I am performing it for some private advantage, but in the sense that it is undertaken in deference to an end external to itself, rather than merely as 'the satisfaction of a need'. Insofar as he implies that this dilemma is soluble, Marx's theory of alienation takes on a metaphysical character.

For our purposes, the problematic aspects of alienation are those which, on Marx's account, stem directly from capitalism's character as market economy, and which therefore appear to apply with barely diminished force to other market systems, including market socialism. Three such aspects can be identified.

First, under all market economies, goods are primarily produced as commodities, and producers have to be concerned about the exchange value of what they make. Of course, this point cannot be pushed too far because no commodity can sell unless it answers to a human desire, and it is only on Marx's rather peculiar theory of exchange value that use value (i.e. the extent to which a product meets wants and needs)[10] becomes irrelevant to a commodity's market price. Yet although producers know what they are making ministers to human needs, there is a sense in which the exchange system comes between their work and this outcome.[11] Their direct aim is to sell the product and maximize the exchange value they receive, and they must regulate their production in the light of this goal; for example, they may have to lower the quality of their product in order to match their competitors' prices even though they believe that the new version represents worse value than the old. If Marx is right to claim that 'humanized' work involves responding directly to others' needs, then any market system stands as an obstacle.

Second, markets not only establish relationships between goods but also constitute and condition relations between human beings; thus social relationships in a market society take on a certain character. Partners to an exchange transaction are at best indifferent to one another's interests; at worst there is an active conflict of interests between them, and each will seek to benefit at the expense of the other. The simplest case is probably haggling over price between buyer and seller where no clear equilibrium price exists. Consider also competition between buyers to attract sellers, which may well involve the making of fraudulent claims, malign persuasion, and so forth: human relations in the market are typified by competitiveness, mutual suspicion and, at worst, chiselling at the other's expense. This is not fundamentally altered if, in place of private individuals, transactions are conducted between groups, or between groups and individuals. It does not seem to be true in general that groups behave more ethically or considerately in their economic dealings than private persons. The fact, then, that under market socialism the sellers of commodities would typically be associations of workers does little to offset *this* feature of the market.

---

[10] Marx himself does not make anything of the distinction between wants and needs, and normally uses 'needs' as an inclusive term for human desires. Since I am offering a critical reading of his ideas, I shall follow this practice in the remainder of the chapter. (My own preferred usage was explained in ch. 5, sec. vii.)

[11] Contrasting capitalism and communism, Marx says: 'In the first case the social character of production is *posited* only *post festum* with the elevation of products to exchange values and the exchange of these exchange values. In the second case *the social character of production* is presupposed, and participation in the world of products, in consumption, is not mediated by the exchange of mutually independent labours or products of labour.' K. Marx, *Grundrisse* (Harmondsworth: Penguin, 1973), 172.

Third, alienation from the collective results of human activity seems to be a feature of all market economies merely in virtue of the fact that they are unplanned. It is an essential property of markets that a collective outcome, which may indeed have certain desirable properties, is reached through a myriad of individual actions and decisions, none of the individuals concerned being aware of, or able to control, the whole picture. No one decides that so many million tons of steel are going to be produced, or that steel will exchange with corn at such-and-such a ratio. If a fall in the price of steel forces steel-workers to change jobs, none of those involved can, or even perhaps could, trace the causal sequence that led to this outcome. In this sense man is, in Marx's terms, 'the plaything of alien powers' in a way that he seems not to be in an ideal planned economy where every outcome is directly related to a human decision, and social relations become (again in Marx's words) 'transparent'.

These, then, are the three charges which appear to apply to market socialism as well as to capitalism, but which communism, at least in Marx's ideal version, claims to avoid. Under the market economy, the relationship between production and human need is distorted by the intervention of exchange value; human interactions take on a detached and potentially hostile character; and the whole economic system slips out of people's theoretical and practical grasp. Now the force of these charges depends, of course, on our willingness to accept the theory of human nature from which they derive. Libertarians might be inclined simply to dismiss the Marxian argument on the grounds that it relies on a spurious understanding of human needs.[12] Socialists, on the other hand, are likely to be sympathetic to the communally orientated view of the person which the argument invokes, even if they are not convinced by the precise way Marx develops the idea. An ethical defence of market socialism ought, therefore, to try to accommodate the Marxist critique of capitalist alienation. Moreover, the accommodation cannot merely take the form of

---

[12] This would, however, be a risky line of argument for libertarians attracted to the principle of neutrality analysed in ch. 3. The Marxian theory of alienation clearly rests on a particular conception of the good life for man; but so equally does a response which denies that self-realization at work, communal production, etc. are authentic human goals. Anyone who wishes to preserve a neutral stance must allow the conditional force of the Marxian argument: *if* people have these needs *then* they will be alienated in market settings.

conceding the alienating character of markets while pointing to beneficial features that offset this defect, such as economic efficiency. It would obviously not be difficult to counter the Marxian argument by mounting an economic critique of communism—pointing, for instance, to the conflicts it would generate between people, especially over the form that collective consumption should take. But this would leave us in the unhappy position of choosing the lesser evil. Although my general strategy in the book is to defend market socialism on the grounds that it embodies an optimal trade-off between important social aims, not that it achieves every conceivable goal, the case for it would be seriously weakened if we could not respond at all to Marx's claims about the alienating character of markets.

I intend, therefore, to continue for the moment with Marx himself, trying to show that the Marxian theory of human nature has a more ambivalent bearing on the choice between markets and communism than so far suggested. I shall, in fact, try to extract from that theory a humanistic defence of market socialism. Since Marx was selected as the most powerful socialist critic of market economies, it is of considerable significance to my argument to establish this conclusion.

III

The key to this undertaking is to pin down as precisely as possible how Marx's standpoint differs from romantic anti-capitalism. By 'romantic anti-capitalism' I mean the view that rejects capitalist society as alienating, exploitative, and so forth in the light of an ideal of human community drawn from the pre-capitalist period; for example, in terms of an idealized picture of the medieval village (though it is not essential to the view that it should have some particular referent in mind). The point about this position is that it dismisses capitalism as unequivocally a negation of all genuine human relationships; so the proposed alternative, whether socialist or conservative in flavour, simply negates in turn the main features of capitalism. Marx, although afflicted to some extent by the romantic anti-capitalist outlook in his early writings, including the *Economic and Philosophical Manuscripts*, had at least by the time of writing *The Communist Manifesto* in 1847 broken with it decisively.[13] That work, somewhat oddly it may seem for a revolutionary tract, celebrates capitalism as much as it condemns it; and in the later sections Marx and Engels distinguish their own revolutionary communism from various brands of socialism that fail to recognize the radical transformation of human relationships brought about by capitalism, and are therefore to a greater or lesser extent reactionary in content. Marx adhered to this perspective in all of his later writings, especially the *Grundrisse* and *Capital*.

For Marx, then, communism does not involve any straightforward rejection of the achievements of capitalism; instead it involves taking over those achievements and adding to them. The crucial question is: what are the achievements of capitalism that are to be preserved under communism, and how is this preservation to be accomplished? In other words, what is it about communism as Marx sees it that prevents it from being merely a reversion to pre-capitalist forms of society?

The answer to this question most familiar to readers of Marx is that communism takes over the productive forces of capitalism, including its *human* productive forces. That is, communism inherits the machinery, the productive techniques, the scientific know-how, the co-operative organization of work that capitalism has developed. Communism seeks to avoid the problem of material scarcity and all that follows from it by unashamedly borrowing and extending productive methods evolved by its predecessor. Marx makes a great deal of this idea, and castigates all forms of socialism that seek to return to pre-capitalist methods of production and an ascetic way of life.

Since we are not here considering the economic problems of communism, I shall leave aside the difficulties raised by this claim. Of greater relevance to our enquiry is a second achieve-

---

[13] Did he at the same time abandon the theory of alienation? Although Marx spoke less about alienation after about 1845, it is doubtful whether his primary reason for doing so was an awareness that the idea was bound up with a romantic anti-capitalist attitude that he wished to discard. It seems rather that he came to regard the term as embodying a residue of idealism and therefore as incompatible with a materialist outlook. His reasons, in other words, were primarily methodological rather than substantive. For convincing evidence that the idea did not disappear entirely from Marx's thought, see J. H. Elliott, 'Continuity and Change in the Evolution of Marx's Theory of Alienation: From the *Manuscripts* through the *Grundrisse* to *Capital*', *History of Political Economy*, 11 (1970), 317–62.

ment unique to capitalism (according to Marx), namely its creation of what might be termed developed individuals. Along with its unprecedented expansion of the forces of production, capitalist society ushers in a new kind of human being: one who is an individual in the sense that he enjoys a certain kind of independence from material and social ties, and who is developed in the sense that his powers and needs are continually being expanded and enriched. Before examining the problems this poses for Marx's account of communism, we need to look more closely at what is involved in each aspect of this achievement.

To see how capitalism produces the independent individual, we need to examine the contrast Marx draws between production in pre-capitalist societies and work under capitalism. In pre-capitalist societies, Marx says, labour is 'naturally' divided. 'Natural' here is far from being a term of commendation. Marx's meaning is that people are assigned functions, by physical necessity or custom, which they then look upon as natural aspects of themselves; that is, they regard themselves as tied by nature to this plot of land or that occupation. They also see themselves as tied naturally to the community; they cannot conceive themselves as standing outside of the communal group of which they are members. Let me cite Marx's words:

the original conditions of production appear as natural presuppositions, *natural conditions of the producer's existence* just as his living body, even though he reproduces and develops it, is originally not posited by himself, but appears as the *presupposition of his self* . . . These *natural conditions of existence*, to which he relates as to his own inorganic body, are themselves double: (1) of a subjective and (2) of an objective nature. He finds himself a member of a family, clan, tribe, etc.—which then, in a historic process of intermixture and antithesis with others, takes on a different shape; and, as such a member, he relates to a specific nature (say, here, still earth, land, soil) as his own inorganic being, as a condition of his production and reproduction.[14]

In this passage Marx takes the analogy of the relation between the self and the body to bring out the indissoluble link between the producer and his conditions of production. He can no more think of himself as separated from these conditions than he can imagine

[14] Marx, *Grundrisse*, 489–90.

himself dissociated from his body. Jerry Cohen has illuminatingly described this relationship as one of engulfment.[15]

In later pre-capitalist societies, the tie is not always between the producer and the soil, but sometimes between the producer and his instrument of production, as occurs under systems of craft labour.[16] The medieval craftsman, Marx says, 'was completely absorbed in his work, had a contented, slavish relationship to it'.[17]

This natural division of labour, mediated through the community, can only be broken down by the growth of a generalized exchange economy. Under capitalism, the worker is hired more or less at random by the capitalist, and given a task. There is no chance here that he will regard this productive role as a natural extension of himself. On the contrary, he will regard his work as an accidental encumbrance, something into which he was thrown by chance. Nor, on the other hand, is there any sense in which his work appears to him as a communal task. The community disappears from view; the only force directing him is the cash nexus.

Looked at from one side, this merely recapitulates the theory of alienation in work which we examined earlier. But we see now that Marx also regards the exchange relationship as conferring a kind of freedom. Which kind? Not full freedom, clearly, for the worker is externally constrained by the laws of the market, and unable to develop his full individuality. He does, however, enjoy a limited measure of negative freedom, and a degree of autonomy. He sees that his choice of work is a contingent matter, and within the compass of the capitalist market he can exercise that choice. As Marx puts it, 'he sells the particular expenditure of force to a particular capitalist, whom he confronts as an independent *individual*. It is clear that this is not his relation to the existence of capital as capital, i.e. to the capitalist class. Nevertheless, in this way everything touching on the individual, real person leaves him a wide field of choice, of arbitrary will, and hence of formal freedom.'[18]

---

[15] G. A. Cohen, 'Marx's Dialectic of Labour', *Philosophy and Public Affairs*, 3 (1973–4), 235–61. Cohen's article has been an important influence on the argument advanced here.

[16] See Marx, *Grundrisse*, 499–500.

[17] K. Marx and F. Engels, *The German Ideology*, in *Writings of the Young Marx*, ed. Easton and Guddat, 446.

[18] Marx, *Grundrisse*, 464.

Along with this limited kind of freedom goes a limited kind of equality. Individuals meet in the marketplace simply as bearers of exchange value, and as such they are necessarily equals. People in pre-capitalist societies, by contrast, defining themselves by their work and their position in the community, also regarded others as their 'natural' superiors or inferiors. Marx, of course, argued that the formal exchange of equivalents in the market concealed a real inequality in the transaction between worker and employer. Capitalism's inner secret was exploitation; however, it appeared immediately as a set of relations between equals, and this formed the basis for the various egalitarian ideologies that flourished under it—for instance the ideology of natural rights. People became individuals, then, not only in the sense that they saw themselves as independent of any particular place, type of work, or social grouping, but also in the sense that each saw himself as fundamentally the peer of all the rest. Marx regarded the achievement of this status as a historic step forward from the ordered communities of the pre-capitalist period.

Being an individual means having achieved a certain social status and self-understanding; being a developed individual, on the other hand, is not a final achievement but a process. Such a person not only possesses an enlarged set of powers and needs, but continues to expand them all the time—in Marx's view, there seems to be no upper limit to the capabilities of human beings. How, then, has capitalism created developed individuals? It has not done so deliberately, but as an accidental by-product of market forces. Although the worker is likely at any moment only to have a simple, restricted task to perform, changes in supply and demand will force him to drop one line of work and take up another. Marx, in *Capital*, cites the experience of a French printer visiting America who found to his astonishment that he was capable of working as a miner, typographer, slater, plumber, etc. 'In consequence of thus finding out that I am fit for any sort of work, I feel less of a mollusk and more of a man', he wrote.[19] Modern industry, Marx argued, requires 'the fully developed individual, fit for a variety of labours, ready to face any change of production, and to whom the different social functions he performs, are but so many modes of giving free scope to his own natural and acquired powers'.[20]

[19] *Capital*, 493.   [20] Ibid. 494.

Equally, capitalism creates new needs; competition between capitalists means that each vies with the rest to develop new products to tempt consumers. A romantic anti-capitalist would write this off as the creation of false desires. Not so Marx: in his view, most human needs are not biologically given but created historically, as an offshoot of production, and the greater the extent of needs in a society, the wealthier that society has become.[21] The unique feature of capitalism is that its capacity for revolutionizing production knows no bounds. Earlier forms of production were limited precisely by the fact that the aim of production was to satisfy pre-existing needs. Because capitalist producers are only concerned with expanding exchange value, they are not confined to any particular form of use-value.[22] Provided they can create a market for their products, they are happy to manufacture anything.

IV

Reflecting on Marx's idea of the developed individual, two points stand out. First, it is the system of exchange through the market that appears crucial both to individuality and to development. Employment on a market basis breaks down the 'natural' division of labour and communal dependence, and market exchange gives rise to the belief in intrinsic equality. Moreover it is what one might call the indirect quality of production in a market economy—the fact that the immediate aim of production is exchange, not the fulfilment of need—that leads spontaneously to the expansion of powers and needs. In other words, it is capitalism's character as *market* economy, rather than its character as specifically *capitalist* economy, that is critical. Second, Marx clearly implies that developed individuality is to be preserved and indeed enhanced under communism: he speaks of the goal of communism being 'free individuality, based on the universal development of individuals'.[23] Such phrases are meant to convey,

---

[21] See id., *Grundrisse*, 527. In his early writings, however, Marx sometimes claims that the needs created by capitalism are false; e.g. 'the expansion of production and of needs becomes an *ingenious* and always *calculating* subservience to inhuman, depraved, unnatural and imaginary appetites'; *Karl Marx: Early Writings*, ed. Bottomore, 168. The mature Marx argues instead that the needs capitalism engenders are genuine enough, although that is clearly not the capitalist's own reason for fostering them.

[22] See Marx, *Grundrisse*, 541.   [23] Ibid. 158.

among other things, that communism will not involve a return to the personal engulfment of pre-capitalist societies, and that the expansion of powers and needs will continue. 'What is wealth', Marx asks in a well-known passage, 'other than the universality of individual needs, capacities, pleasures, productive forces etc., created through universal exchange?'[24] The question this immediately raises is how developed individuality is to be preserved in the absence of the market mechanism that first brought it into existence.

As far as I can see, there are only two ways in which Marx might have responded to this question. First, he might have argued that capitalism has brought about an *irreversible shift* in human personality, such that people in post-capitalist societies will unavoidably continue to exist as developed individuals. Second, he might have argued that communism will embody *alternative mechanisms* that sustain this achievement, in place of the market.

The irreversible shift answer would model the transfer of capitalism's human achievements to communism on the transfer of its material achievements—the expanded forces of production, etc. The difficulty is to see how aspects of human personality can be transferred in the same way as physical objects, or even as scientific knowledge. Consider the emergence of the individual, as described by Marx. Crucial to a person's existence as an individual is a certain kind of self-understanding. Individuals are independent because they interpret their relation to their work as one of potential separation; they do not regard themselves as 'naturally' members of a social grouping, etc. It is not easy to see how such forms of self-understanding can be transmitted across the revolutionary divide that separates capitalism from communism, particularly if we are influenced by the canons of historical materialism. Marx wisely shows no inclination to adopt the Hegelian view that successive forms of consciousness always constitute an ascending spiral, the later forms incorporating the advances of the earlier. Nor, on the other hand, could individuality plausibly be grounded in material factors alone. There is no necessary relationship between the development of the forces of production and the emergence of particular forms of consciousness. Marx's most convincing arguments in this area relate forms of consciousness to relations of production, not forces of produc-

----
[24] Ibid. 488.

tion. But communism dispenses with the contractually based relations of production that created the developed individual under capitalism. The fact that it inherits forces of production from capitalism provides no guarantee that it will also inherit forms of personal self-understanding characteristic of the capitalist epoch.

If the irreversible shift answer looks weak, how does the alternative mechanisms argument fare? It might seem straightforward enough. The arrangements of communist society are chosen by people, now for the first time in control of their own destiny, precisely in order to realize the ideal of free individuality. These arrangements (to remind ourselves) involve: collective planning of production to meet human needs; voluntary work; rotation of tasks; a direct link between production and use-value. We need, however, to look more closely at how these arrangements would foster the developed individual.

How, to begin with, would they prevent people from lapsing back into that immediate identification with the social group that Marx calls the consciousness of the herd? As in primitive societies, labour is once again directly social, i.e. directly aimed at meeting the needs of society. In future communism, of course, work will be voluntary and tasks will be rotated. It is not clear, however, that these features alone are sufficient for individuality. To say that work is voluntary is to say that no one is obliged to perform it, either by command or by material necessity, but this does not exclude the possibility that people will work in a spirit of simple identification with their task and their social group. Indeed if we look back again to what Marx has to say about early forms of society, his argument is not that men were herd animals because they were *forced* to work for society, but because they failed to grasp the arbitrary nature of their social role—they looked on it as a 'natural' extension of their personality.

Now it might seem that the difference between pre-capitalist and post-capitalist society is precisely that in the latter people consciously choose their lines of work, so they are always aware of the willed character of their role identities. But my point is that there is nothing in communist practice to sustain that consciousness. It is after all a familiar fact that people who begin by choosing their occupations, styles of life, and so forth may later reach a point where they can no longer imagine themselves making different choices. There seems no reason why the same process cannot happen at the collective level, once we have rejected the Hegelian idea of a necessarily ascending spiral of consciousness.

Might rotation of tasks avoid this danger? Can people possibly identify naïvely with their social function if they are switching around all the time? This seems to be Marx's thought in the famous passage where he speaks of being able to 'hunt in the morning, fish in the afternoon, breed cattle in the evening, criticize after dinner, just as I like, without ever becoming a hunter, a fisherman, a herdsman, or a critic'.[25] One can read this passage as saying that neither I nor anyone else has a chance to think of me as a hunter because by the time the thought is formed, I'm off fishing, etc.

This argument seems successful in its own terms, but it creates two further difficulties for Marx's position. First of all, rotation may prevent people from developing certain of their talents to the full, and by implication from contributing as much as they otherwise might to the community's welfare. The playful tone of the hunting, fishing passage ('just as I like') can be contrasted with Marx's later remark that when labour becomes a means of self-realization it is by no means 'mere fun, mere amusement'. 'Really free working, e.g. composing, is at the same time precisely the most damned seriousness, the most intense exertion.'[26] If this is so, then, to become a good composer, I may need to devote most of my time to music. If obliged to divide my hours between composing, hunting and fishing, etc. I will create less benefit for the community than I am capable of creating.

A second difficulty is that the rotation of tasks must be compulsory to circumvent the original problem. It is possible, of course, that everyone might agree to such a compulsory scheme, consenting to be compelled at some later time in order to avoid becoming narrowly absorbed by a single job. But even accepting this possibility, social relations would no longer display the transparency and perfect voluntariness Marx sought. If compulsory rotation is allowed in on this basis, why shouldn't market relations also be permitted since (as I shall argue later) they may

[25] Marx and Engels, *The German Ideology*, in *Writings of the Young Marx*, ed. Easton and Guddat, 425.
[26] Marx, *Grundrisse*, 611.

be rationalized in much the same way—as a device for bringing about shared ends in an oblique manner?

The reader may, however, be impatient with the idea that under communism people would identify too closely with the community, and so might become absorbed one-sidedly in a particular role. After all, the vulgar argument against communism is precisely the reverse of this: without individual incentives to do useful work, people will suit themselves and essential needs will go unmet. Wouldn't it be more realistic to assume that people will strike some kind of balance between their personal satisfaction and the needs of society, doing useful work but not always the most useful work they were capable of? As a report about human nature, this is probably (on average) about right; however, there are particular difficulties in people behaving in such a way under communism. As I have argued already,[27] in the absence of an exchange system there is no readily available standard of value that would enable each person to measure his productive contribution (he can calculate his hours of work, of course, but not the relative utility of working at task X or task Y). Thus there is no possibility of norms emerging which would indicate the value of the work each person must perform to discharge his social obligations. That is, one can't say to a person: our needs will be met provided everyone creates at least so many pounds' worth of useful products; if you are worried about fairness, choose whatever work you like subject to that constraint. One can't say it because in the absence of a market there is no adequate and non-arbitrary way of measuring value.

The advantage of a market system, from this point of view, is that it allows people to assess the relative contributions they would make in different lines of work, and so to balance their social contribution against their personal needs. Such potential contributions will be signalled, albeit imperfectly, in the prices that labour can command in different branches of production. Under market socialism the labour market takes on a special form, since workers belong to co-operatives which distribute their profits according to schedules that are applied uniformly to all members. Since membership is voluntary, however, we may expect these schedules to reflect, to some extent at least, the scarcity prices that different sorts of labour can command. Thus

[27] See ch. 6, sec. iii.

workers will be given choices of two kinds. First they must choose whether to remain in their present co-operative, or to move to another which may offer them a higher return for their skills. Second they must participate in a collective choice as to the nature and intensity of the production their co-operative will engage in, given prevailing product prices. Both choices allow and encourage the producer to balance social contribution, indicated by income, against other factors such as leisure time, pleasure in work, and so forth. The existence of a market makes such an assessment possible and protects the individual against being swallowed up by his work role.

So far I have been looking at the difficulties communism poses for Marx's idea of the individual. What, now, about the developed individual? What in communism would replace the revolutionary thrust of capitalism which constantly expands human powers and needs? People might regard it as abstractly desirable that powers and needs should be increased, but is there any mechanism that would produce this result in a practical way? The difficulty is that communist production is aimed directly at meeting needs, without the mediating role of the market. This seems inevitably to give it a conservative slant. The needs that will feature in the planners' schedules will be existing needs — needs revealed either by past consumption, or through consumer surveys, or however. If new needs appear spontaneously, then of course the plan should be altered to take them into account. But there is no impetus for producers to foster new needs. Consider the position of a planner, or producer, in a communist system contemplating making a product for which there is no existing demand. Going ahead with such a plan is inherently risky. It may turn out that there is indeed no need for the product, so the labour expended will have been socially wasteful. Even if the product eventually finds consumers, it may not be clear that this shift in taste constitutes a genuine enrichment.[28] Thus in order to fulfil Marx's ideal of labour as the communal bond linking producer and consumer, the optimum course is to ensure that the product meets a visible need.

Somewhat the same may be said about the development of powers. If I am to engage in what Marx calls human production, it is crucial that my activities should correspond to the needs of

[28] See ch. 5, sec. iii.

others. Although, within the limitations of the plan, I am free to develop new talents and skills, there is no positive incentive to do so. Such experimentation is risky; it may turn out that I simply haven't the ability to work as a cabinet-maker or a nuclear physicist, so the time and energy spent trying to acquire these skills will be wasted. Once again, the safest course is to continue in lines of work that I know I can undertake successfully. Under communism there is no external pressure to force the snail out of his shell.

Some may be tempted to respond to this charge by pointing to the theory of human nature implicit in Marx's account of history. Isn't it an essential element in the story Marx tells about human progress that men are inherently creative beings, always searching for new ways of meeting their needs, and enlarging their needs and powers in the process? Marx does tell such a story, but he tells it about people who are forced to produce by external pressure; he acknowledges, in his comments on primitive communities, that where a society's needs are matched by the natural resources available to it, the society will simply stagnate until externally disrupted.[29] 'Human nature' alone is not a sufficient guarantor of progress.

Thus there is a serious risk that communism, as Marx describes it, will be a stagnant and stultifying society. It carries the danger that people will become immersed in particular lines of production, and that production itself will be conservatively organized.[30] Merely giving people the freedom to distance themselves from their work, to develop new needs and new powers, doesn't ensure that these things will come about. Communism lacks any institutions with an inbuilt dynamic thrust; it cannot plausibly be seen as the inheritor of capitalism's revolutionary character.

V

Let us now stand back from Marx and consider the implications of our analysis for the theory of market socialism. We find

---

[29] Cf. G. A. Cohen, *Karl Marx's Theory of History* (Oxford: Clarendon Press, 1978), 23–4.
[30] For similar doubts, see J. S. Mill, *Principles of Political Economy*, Bk. iv, ch. 7, sec. 7, in *The Collected Works of John Stuart Mill*, (Toronto: University of Toronto Press, 1965), 795.

ourselves caught in a theoretical dilemma. On the one hand, we have unearthed a powerful argument to the effect that a market economy is a necessary, if not sufficient, condition for developed individuality, an achievement to which we must attach consider-able value. On the other hand, the price of this achievement appears to be alienation, in particular the alienation of people from their work, from one another, and from the results of their collective activity. Must we conclude, then, that personal auto-nomy and personal development can only be bought at the cost of human self-estrangement? Or can we find anything in the idea of market socialism that might suggest a way out of this quandary?

Let us proceed by way of a thought-experiment. Suppose that the threshold to socialism has been crossed, and the people, now consciously controlling their future existence in a democratic manner, have to decide what economic arrangements to establish. Having read both *The Wealth of Nations* and the *Grundrisse*, they opt for market socialism. In other words, they are impressed both by the efficiency arguments for markets con-tained in the texts of classical economics and by the humanistic arguments of Marx. They want their society to be dynamic and innovative, for people to preserve their independence and individuality. They believe, however, that this can be achieved without reverting to capitalism, through adopting a socialist market economy of the kind outlined at the beginning of this book. This belief is subject to regular debate in the democratic forum; as are more specific issues of policy, such as the position of the boundary between the market and public sectors of the economy.

Under these circumstances, would economic life still be alienating? The new idea that this thought-experiment has intro-duced is that the market might be consciously chosen as an economic device; it might represent an expression of collective will. Even so, the immediate nature of market transactions remains unchanged; people act instrumentally, treat one another as competitors, have no control over collective outcomes. The question this raises is whether social relations in such circum-stances might have a dual character such that their underlying quality as communal relations would offset the alienating effect of their immediate quality as market relations.

It is not difficult to think of relationships that can sustain such a dual character. Typically these are cases where the underlying objective can only be achieved by indirect (and apparently contrary) means, or at least can be achieved most effectively by such means. Consider, for example, a game of tennis between two friends, each of whose main objective is to give pleasure to the other. Since what each most enjoys is battling hard on the tennis court, the only way to achieve the objective is for each to play as hard as he can. On the surface the relationship is competitive, each trying his best to win; underneath the game is a co-operative enterprise for mutual enjoyment. Both players understand this, and understand the other's point of view. Here the co-operative character of the relationship seems well able to survive its immediate competitive quality. Or again, consider two altruists each holding a varied stock of goods and wishing to make transfers that will benefit the other person. Making reasonable assumptions about the character of their altruism and their informational capacities, it can be shown they ought to barter with one another as though they were egoists.[31] If they try to behave directly as altruists—in other words each tries to bestow on the other those things that he thinks the other will most enjoy—they will miss their target. Once again it seems quite possible for the bartering to be conducted in the knowledge that its underlying purpose is altruistic.

The suggestion now is that social relations under market socialism might not be alienating because their deeper character was fully understood. That is, work would appear to be merely instrumental—in Marxist terms, the production of exchange values—but at an underlying level would be seen as communal, because everyone would understand that the system of exchange led to beneficial results. Again, social relations would appear competitive, but it would be understood that competition was the most effective way for each to contribute to the welfare of the rest. What about the third element in the theory of alienation, the claim that people have lost control over the collective results of their actions? Introducing a market does indeed imply that *particular* outcomes are unplanned; nevertheless, if the overall

---

[31] For this result, see D. Collard, *Altruism and Economy* (Oxford: Martin Robertson, 1978), ch. 2. See also S.-C. Kolm, 'Altruism and Efficiency', *Ethics*, 94 (1983–4), 18–65 for discussion of the conditions under which the result holds. It assumes in particular that, to use the terminology employed in ch. 4, the two people in question are preference altruists.

shape of the economy is planned—as it is in the sense that property rights are allocated in a specific way and so forth—must these results be experienced as alien? One might look for support here to cases of *planned spontaneity*; that is, cases where an activity is set up in such a way that it will lead to unexpected results: an encounter group, or a piece of experimental theatre, for example. For people participating in these activities, the unpredictable nature of the outcome is a major attraction. It does seem possible to understand such practices as designed and controlled in their overall shape, but deliberately unplanned in their precise working out. If so, the theory of alienation will need to be modified so as no longer to equate spontaneity with estrangement.

It is integral to the proposal being advanced here that the market should be an object of collective *choice*; it is not enough that people should grasp intellectually the reasons for having it. There is an important difference between recognizing as justified something that exists independently of our choice, and seeing that thing as an expression of our will—important, anyway, if we accept the view of the human subject implicit in the notion of alienation. But this reliance on collective choice introduces a further set of problems. A political system of some kind is the necessary medium through which the collective will can be expressed. What must the political system be like if each member of society is to regard the social arrangements that are chosen as somehow an expression of his own individual will? Even if we envisage a participatory system in which each person is given an equal status, how can conflicts between different interests and different opinions be overcome? It looks at first sight as though an attempt to solve the problem of alienation through an appeal to politics creates as many difficulties as its removes.

This challenge is taken up in the third part of the book where I explore in greater depth the socialist commitment to community and attempt, in Chapter 10, to outline a conception of politics which will meet the requirements of the last paragraph. I also try to identify the institutional structure that would make non-alienating politics possible.

Let me finish here by summarizing the argument of this chapter. Marx saw that markets were a liberating force, creating what I have termed developed individuals. However, he excluded them from his ideal communist system on the grounds that they were inherently alienating. My suggestion has been that the desirable properties of markets might be preserved under social-ism, provided their alienating properties were countered. For this to occur, the market must appear as an expression of collective will. People must both understand the reasons for having markets and act on those reasons when they legislate for their existence through a democratic assembly. Moreover, this decision must always be open to reversal. Under these circumstances, I have claimed, economic relations may take on a dual character, being at one level instrumental, competitive, and spontaneous, but at another level 'human', co-operative and planned. Only in this way can we conceive of overcoming alienation without relapsing into the personal engulfment of pre-capitalist societies.

PART III

The Politics of
Democratic Socialism

9

COMMUNITY AND CITIZENSHIP

I

The aim of the last four chapters has been to defend market economies—in particular, market socialism—against various ethical charges that are often laid against them. I have tried to show that markets, when suitably framed, may satisfy consumers' desires efficiently, may be distributively just, may avoid exploitation and alienation. In each case, however, there has been a caveat. To achieve these desirable aims, markets must be complemented by agencies of government that regulate their outcomes, and more generally express the collective will. The belief that markets will do everything we want, provided only that we set them running from the right starting point, is chimerical.

A defence of market socialism must, therefore, address the question of how these desirable policies may be achieved. This means examining the nature of the political system. It is no use viewing government as a benign perpetual motion machine that will turn out whichever policies we deem to be appropriate. We must give some account of the human agents who have in practice to turn its wheels (who they are, how they are related, what motivates them). Moreover we must do this in the knowledge that most ordinary citizens will also be actively engaged in market relations, as producers and consumers. We cannot turn a blind eye to the interests and beliefs that this will unavoidably generate in them, and begin our account with purely political animals.

In short, we need a socialist theory of politics to complement our socialist theory of economic markets. The purpose of this final part of the book is to begin formulating such a theory. The next chapter looks at the nature of politics itself, and the two following ones at aspects of the question whether and in what respects the role of government ought to be limited.[1] Here I

---

[1] Many important issues are left undiscussed—the problem of bureaucracy, to name just one.

tackle a wider issue arising directly from the discussion of alienation in the last chapter, namely that of community.

It is often said that proposals for market socialism effectively abandon the traditional socialist commitment to community.[2] Socialism cannot be understood simply in terms of policy outcomes—the distribution of consumption goods and so forth. It is also fundamentally concerned with the quality of human relationships in so far as these are affected by social institutions. I argued at the end of the last chapter that the apparently anti-communitarian character of market relations might be offset if the market were made the subject of deliberate political choice. This argument does not take us the whole way. It shows that where community exists, and finds political expression, the presence of markets need not destroy it, but we have still to show how community is possible in the first place in modern, economically developed societies. Markets alone cannot provide it, even if they can be contained within it.

At the same time, we need to probe the commitment to community itself. What does it mean for relationships to be communitarian, and why should their being so be valued? How, in particular, does a socialist view of community differ from conservative and liberal views?[3] We must allow the possibility that some forms of community are in fact antithetical to other equally important, socialist ideals, so that socialist communitarianism must be discriminating. We must even consider whether socialists should abandon communitarian commitments altogether. These questions answered, we can return to the practical issue of how community can be realized, and what, in particular, it implies for the politics of socialism.

It may be helpful to begin with the most radical vision of community found in the socialist tradition, that associated with thinkers like Marx, Morris, and Kropotkin.[4] This may serve as a

---

[2] See e.g. A. Buchanan, *Ethics, Efficiency, and the Market* (Oxford: Clarendon Press, 1985), 106–9.

[3] For the contested character of the concept of community, see R. Plant, 'Community: Concept, Conception and Ideology', *Politics and Society*, 8 (1978), 79–107. For the breadth of its appeal, see R. Nisbet, *The Quest for Community* (New York: Oxford University Press, 1953). For an assessment of the recent revival of communitarian thought from a socialist perspective, see my 'In What Sense Must Socialism be Communitarian?', *Social Philosophy and Policy* (forthcoming).

[4] What follows is a reconstruction which I hope captures the larger area of agreement between these thinkers without attempting to do justice to the philosophical and political

touchstone against which other versions of community can be tested. It seems safe to assume that when market relations are attacked by socialists as inherently anti-communitarian, this is the ideal to which appeal is openly or tacitly made.

II

What, then, are the characteristics of community as depicted in the writings of these radical socialists? First, each person identifies with the social group in the sense of seeing both his origins and his destiny as bound up with those of the group as a whole. Capitalism creates the illusion of the self-made man, the person who has formed his own character and is able to control his own fate. In community these hard lines of separation are eroded; we would see ourselves as integral parts of a larger organism.

Second, our sentiments towards others would be those of solidarity, or fraternity, or fellowship (different writers use different terms). We know about one another, enter into each other's concerns, rejoice at others' happiness and grieve at their pain. People's lives are not lived in private compartments, but are out in the open for all to share in. Marx saw this foreshadowed in the associations of communist artisans: 'Their association itself creates a new need—the need for society—and what appeared to be a means has become an end . . . Smoking, eating and drinking are no longer simply means of bringing people together. Society, association, entertainment which also has society as its aim, is sufficient for them . . .'[5]

Third, solidarity finds practical expression in a general willingness to act on others' behalf, to engage in practices of what Kropotkin called 'mutual aid'. We assist others in their projects in the general expectation that they will help us when we are in need, although without this becoming formalized on a person-to-person basis. (The system envisaged, in other words, is what

issues that divide them. Major sources are K. Marx, *Economic and Philosophical Manuscripts*, in *Karl Marx: Early Writings*, ed. T. B. Bottomore (London: Watts, 1963), W. Morris, *News from Nowhere* (London: Longmans Green, 1918), P. Kropotkin, *The Conquest of Bread* (New York: Vanguard Press, 1926). See also the helpful discussion in C. McCulloch 'The Problem of Fellowship in Communitarian Theory: William Morris and Peter Kropotkin', *Political Studies*, 32 (1984), 437–50.

[5] *Karl Marx: Early Writings*, ed. Bottomore, 176.

anthropologists would call 'generalized reciprocity'.[6]) Because of our sense of communal interdependence, we make no distinction between aiding a particular person and aiding the community in general. 'We are beginning to think of society as a whole, each part of which is so intimately bound up with the other that a service rendered to one is a service rendered to all.'[7]

Fourth, the institutional embodiment of solidarity is common ownership with distribution according to need. Although no doubt certain items would be used primarily by particular people, to attribute rights of private ownership would be to reintroduce that very separation of persons that community overcomes. Need as a distributive criterion follows naturally from the idea that each concerns himself with the welfare of others as if it were his own.

Fifth, the community is egalitarian, not only in its distribution of material resources, but through the absence of hierarchies of status and power. It is this feature that most obviously differentiates the socialist view of community from, in particular, conservative views which link community to the idea of each person having his proper station in life. Socialists may differ somewhat over the question whether specific, functional forms of authority are permissible or not. (I am thinking here of Marx and Engels's dispute with the anarchists over whether authority relations might be needed to organize industry.[8]) What is not in dispute is that relationships between people should embody a fundamental equality of respect, and that positional inequalities may arise only (if at all) through common consent.

Sixth, relationships within the community are unitary, in the sense that people do not have specific role-relations with one another. We interact with one another in the course of a multitude of concrete activities (working, playing, debating, etc.), but in each of these interactions we relate simply as person to person, our relationship exemplifying the general qualities described above. Raymond Plant has drawn attention to the contribution made by the German Romantics to this theme: 'It was widely felt by the Germans that the idea of community involved

---

[6] See M. Sahlins, *Stone Age Economics* (London: Tavistock, 1974), ch. 5. M. Taylor, *Community, Anarchy, and Liberty* (Cambridge: Cambridge: University Press, 1982), ch. 1.

[7] Kropotkin, *The Conquest of Bread*, 26.

[8] See e.g. F. Engels, 'On Authority', in K. Marx, F. Engels, V. Lenin, *Anarchism and Anarcho-Syndicalism* (Moscow: Progress Publishers, 1972).

some notion of the whole man, in which men were to be met by other men in the totality of their social roles and not in a fragmented or segmental way.'[9] In particular, genuinely communal relationships preclude relations of economic exchange in which the common good is pursued, if at all, by indirect means. As Marx expressed this idea: 'Let us assume *man* to be *man*, and his relation to the world to be a human one. Then love can only be exchanged for love, trust for trust, etc.'[10]

Seventh, community should exist at all levels of society: there is no juxtaposition of community at one level and something else at another (as there often is in liberal thought, for example). The radical socialist view does not necessarily deny that the most intense communal relationships would be enjoyed with friends, neighbours, and workmates; the point is that our relations with other people would be of the same essential kind, albeit with weaker linkages. Society should be a community of communities. For purposes of practical organization, the primary unit might be a small geographical area (a village or a neighbourhood), but such units would be linked to one another by the same feelings of solidarity, the same practices of mutual aid, as link persons at primary level. Ideally this communal solidarity should extend globally. In the view I am delineating, national communities have no special status; either they would disappear altogether, or they would remain merely as one link in a chain that begins with the household or group of friends and ends with mankind as a whole.

I want to enter two critical remarks about the idea of community just sketched. The first of these points to an incoherence in the idea which appears particularly in the juxtaposition of the first and the seventh features in the above list. If we look at actual cases in which people identify with their community (and there is no reason to dispute that such identification does in fact occur), we see that they identify with it as a concrete and distinct object. If a community is to make a claim on my allegiance, it must represent a distinct way of life; there must be something about the community and its members that makes it *my* community. It would be too strong to say that it is necessary to the very idea of community that there must be outside communities in competition, so to speak, with the one with which I identify. Nevertheless

---

[9] R. Plant, *Community and Ideology* (London: Routledge and Kegan Paul, 1974), 16.
[10] *Karl Marx: Early Writings*, ed. Bottomore, 193.

there seems to be a well-supported empirical connection between the strength of people's attachment to their own community and their awareness of rival collectivities. Again, it does not follow that there must be active hostility between communities. Attitudes to the outside group may vary from incomprehension through disdain through indifference to a cheerful kind of rivalry.[11] What goes by the board, however, is the idea of a community of communities, of inter-communal relations as merely a less intense version of intra-communal relations. Communities which make strong claims on their members' allegiances need to be linked together by a framework of a different, non-communitarian kind.

If this argument is accepted, adherents of the radical version of community are faced with a painful choice. Either one opts for small, intense communities and then faces the problem of how, compatibly with socialist principles, these communities are to be related;[12] or one opts for more inclusive communities, but at the cost of a dilution of those elements which were presented above as constitutive of (socialist) community—solidarity, simplicity of relationships, and so forth.

I shall return to this issue later. My second critical remark stems from the analysis of the last chapter, and is directed especially at the sixth feature of community indicated above: the notion that communal relationships must be unitary. The question is whether unitary relations leave adequate space for the development of individuality. To put the matter in somewhat Hegelian terms, we appear to need a moment of separation, where people set themselves apart from the community and see themselves as distinct individuals each with his own projects to pursue, as well as a moment of universality, where people can identify with the community and recognize what they do as contributing to its good. I have already argued for the importance of markets as agencies of separation. The unitary community

[11] Taylor's conclusion is somewhat more pessimistic. 'We have no grounds for believing that growing up and living in a community necessarily engenders a tolerant, pacific and co-operative disposition towards outsiders. It is true that many primitive anarchic communities lived at peace with their neighbours (though having little contact with them and invariably taking a dim view of them); but many did not, and the world is a great deal more crowded now' (*Community, Anarchy and Liberty*, 167).

[12] For a practical example, see the discussion of anarchist collectives in Spain in my *Anarchism* (London: Dent, 1984), ch. 11; for the general issue, see McCulloch, 'Problem of Fellowship', 446–50.

must exclude markets, and it provides nothing in their place to encourage individual self-assertion.

I do not see how the force of this criticism can be avoided by the radical socialists I have cited. There are some communitarian views—for instance, certain religious views—which see the obliteration of the self as a positive feature of community life. But Marx, Morris, Kropotkin, and others in their tradition all see individuality as an integral part of their goal; their aim is to reconcile individual self-development with communal solidarity, not to extinguish the former in the name of the latter.[13] This points unavoidably to a looser form of community in which direct communal ties co-exist with other relations between people, including market relations.

III

The question we must now ask is whether the quest for overall community is really an essential part of the socialist project. Faced with the difficulties raised above for the radical communitarian vision, it is tempting to look instead for a social framework in which people are able to choose the form of community they prefer (or none at all) rather than making community an integral part of the framework itself. An extreme version of this view is Nozick's claim, examined and rejected in Chapter 3, that an unfettered market does itself form such a framework. We saw that this claim overlooked the bias in market relations towards non-communitarian conceptions of the good. A more moderate view would see the fostering of partial communities as a proper function of the state. In this way, the quality of human relationships valued by the communitarian would be promoted, while the difficulties posed by the idea of overall community would be avoided. As Plant puts it: 'Communities can exist within a society, but whether there can be a society-wide conception of community in anything like the present industrial set-up is highly dubious. Within these smaller communities in which the full details of individual need are known there will always be a place for generosity and altruism, and the vision of society as one pared down to procedure with no importance

---

[13] As I argued at length in the case of Marx in ch. 8.

attached to motive and character in the distribution and receipt of welfare is a false one.'[14]

What reason might we have to reject this attractive-sounding compromise between liberal individualism and the radical vision of community? What is important about overall community that is missing in this vision? There are essentially two considerations, one having to do with the intrinsic value of overall community, the other to do with its implications for distributive justice. Neither is uncontroversial.

To grasp the intrinsic importance of overall community, we must begin with the claim that personal identity is partially constituted by communal attachments. That is, people see themselves not merely as individuals with essentially private interests and concerns, but as tied to social units in such a way that in answer to the question 'Who are you?' they will say, among other things, 'I belong to . . .' [15] Community is not merely a matter of sentimental attachment to other persons, but enters deeply into identity in such a way that, cut off from the relevant community, a person's life would lose an important part of its meaning.[16]

'Part of' needs to be stressed here. Whereas the radical communitarian vision sketched above would sink personal identity into an undifferentiated form of community, the view I am advancing sees people as complex creatures, typically having allegiances to smaller and larger groups as well as pursuing personal projects that may be entirely idiosyncratic. The disappearance of overall community need not mean that the person concerned loses all of his bearings. Something essential is, however, lost, which cannot be compensated for by these other commitments.

Why cannot this need for identity be met through partial

[14] R. Plant, H. Lesser and P. Taylor-Gooby, *Political Philosophy and Social Welfare* (London: Routledge and Kegan Paul, 1980), 243.

[15] I express this in a way that deliberately blends empirical and normative claims; that is, people both do in fact have identities that are constituted in this way, and it is desirable that they should. Some would wish to sever this connection—for instance, Hayek in his denunciation of 'tribal sentiments' that unfortunately refuse to disappear in a 'Great Society'; F. A. Hayek, *Law, Legislation and Liberty, ii. The Mirage of Social Justice* (London: Routledge and Kegan Paul, 1976), 133–4. I am not sure how to argue with someone who sees no value in common identities.

[16] The contrast between 'sentimental' and 'constitutive' notions of community is developed in M. Sandel, *Liberalism and the Limits of Justice* (Cambridge: Cambridge University Press, 1982), ch 4.

communities? To the idea that identity is partially constituted by community we must add the (equally contentious) idea that the identity involved is an activist one. We see ourselves not merely as the inheritors of traditional ways of doing things, but as shaping our common world in line with our aspirations. The world that we create bears the imprint of human consciousness and will. This is a characteristically modern idea, articulated especially in the writings of Hegel and (as we noted in the last chapter) in Marx's theory of alienation.[17] To some it appears heretical, an arrogation to humanity of a prerogative that belongs properly to God. I see it as a natural consequence of two other beliefs, the first that human arrangements are mutable, and therefore to some degree a matter of choice, the second that we can understand enough about social causation to be able to shape our institutions in the way that we collectively desire. Given these premises, acquiescing in institutions and practices that are merely *de facto* must come to seem irrational.

Once again, this idea needs qualification. We saw in the previous chapter that there were good reasons to endorse institutions, especially markets, which operate spontaneously to produce outcomes that no one has intended. In other words we may use our power of control to protect areas of social life in which that power is not exercised directly, just as an individual may plan his life in a way that leaves scope for impulse and spontaneity. Provided that the overall framework remains subject to collective control, particular unplanned outcomes need not be experienced as alien or irrational. Rather, they may be recognized as the effect of making room for people to pursue private projects and plans that may not dovetail neatly with one another.

In short, the idea of overall, activist community need not be totalitarian in its implications. What gives it value is the sense that each participant may have of shaping the world in which he lives, moulding it to fit shared understandings and desires. For this to be possible, communal identification must occur at the level at which most major decisions affecting the shape of a society are

---

[17] The intellectual background has best been captured in Charles Taylor's discussion of 'expressivism' in his *Hegel* (Cambridge: Cambridge University Press, 1975), chs. 1, 20. Note, however, that expressivism weaves together several strands of thought not all of which are necessary to support the idea of community I am discussing. I have assessed Taylor's own position in 'In What Sense Must Socialism be Communitarian?'

made—meaning, in practice, at the level of the nation state. Although smaller-scale forms of community may provide the most intense experiences of solidarity, these communities will have little power to shape their environment.[18] They will inevitably be subject to market forces and to political decisions taken at national level. To the extent that the activist element in collective identity is important, therefore, these lesser forms of community will be inadequate.

So far I have been trying to show why overall community is an inherently desirable aim; I have not yet attempted to show how it is possible in what Plant calls 'the present industrial set-up'. What does collective identity mean in a society with millions of members? How can people have a (non-illusory) sense that they are participating in shaping their common world? I return to these issues shortly. The present topic is whether the quest for overall community is worth undertaking in the first place. In case the argument in the previous paragraphs should seem unduly abstract, I turn to a second consideration having to do with the distribution of welfare.

Our point of departure is the socialist commitment to the principle of distribution according to need. Some part of society's resources, at least, is to be allocated on that basis. What are the conditions that make this possible? At first sight it may seem that all that is necessary to achieve this goal is to set up a welfare bureaucracy with the appropriate policy directives. But in fact such a proposal would be quite inadequate unless it were backed up by a popular consensus about the distributive principle in question. For, to begin with, we may take it that the welfare system should be democratically supported and not merely the work of a high-minded élite. More subtly, the relationship between those who are at any moment the recipients of welfare and those who contribute, directly or indirectly, to its provision will alter according to the generally prevailing ideology of welfare. We should like to see recipients viewing their claims as matters of justice rather than as benevolence or charity. This requires that the prevailing view among both recipients and donors should be that distribution according to need is a requirement of social

---

[18] By the same token, however, each member will be able to make a correspondingly greater impact on collective decisions within the community. I return to the problems that the size of modern states poses for the ideal of activist community in secs. v and vi of ch. 10.

justice. Now although almost everyone would acknowledge a general humanitarian obligation to aid people in life-and-death situations, the much stronger idea of distribution according to need—where 'need' is stretched beyond biological survival to include items that are necessary only from the point of view of a socially defined manner of life—is rooted in a social context. All the evidence suggests that people give greater weight to this notion to the extent that they see themselves as bound to the beneficiaries of the principle by common ties. The more communal the relationship, the more need displaces merit (in particular) as a criterion of justice.[19] Thus the kind of underpinning for a welfare state that socialists will look for can only be provided through a widespread sense of common membership throughout the society in question.

It is once again worth stressing that this common identity must exist at national level. Small-scale or local communities may of course practise distribution according to need internally, and there is ample historical evidence of this occurring.[20] But there is no reason to believe that separate distributions at this level will add up to a just distribution overall, when one takes into account local and regional variations in productive wealth, population profile, and so forth. Only a national distributive mechanism can guarantee fairness; and this requires ideological support at the same level. For the reasons given on p. 232, we cannot anticipate such support in a society that is merely a congeries of smaller communities. The obligations of justice we are invoking extend in scope only as far as the group which forms the focus of identity.

IV

The promise of overall community, then, is that it allows people to regard themselves as active subjects shaping the world accord-

---

[19] There is, for example, evidence from empirical social psychology that people give less weight to merit and more weight to equality in distribution when they believe that they will be interacting with their partners over a period of time (the experiments were not set up in such a way as to allow differences in need to affect the outcome). See E. C. Shapiro, 'Effect of Expectations of Future Interaction on Reward Allocation in Dyads: Equity or Equality', *Journal of Personality and Social Psychology*, 31 (1975), 873–80; M. J. Lerner, 'The Justice Motive: "Equity" and "Parity" among Children', *Journal of Personality and Social Psychology*, 29 (1974), 539–50.

[20] See M. Walzer, *Spheres of Justice* (Oxford: Martin Robertson, 1983), ch. 3.

ing to their will; and that it undergirds the distributive arrangements to which socialists (especially) are committed. But now we
must begin to ask how, if at all, this promise can be fulfilled in the
advanced industrial societies on which our discussion is focused.

The collective identities that people currently possess are
predominantly national identities. Here, if anywhere, it seems,
the promise of overall community must be redeemed.[21] But the
socialist tradition has been overwhelmingly hostile to nationality
as a source of identity, usually regarding it merely as an artificially
created impediment to the brotherhood of man. And, of course,
the historical conjunct 'national socialism' is rightly regarded
with the utmost abhorrence.

Despite the weight of this tradition, I believe we need to mount
a rescue operation on behalf of nationality if we are to have any
hope of providing a socialist theory of community that respects
the limits already identified. This operation will have two phases.
First, I separate the idea of nationality itself from various accre-
tions that have given nationalism a bad name, on the left especially. Second, I try to defuse the charge that nationality is an
essentially irrational phenomenon, and therefore an inadmissible
basis on which to found a socialist project that aspires to be
rational.

What does it mean for people to have a common national
identity, to share their nationality? It is essentially not a matter of
the objective characteristics that they possess, but of their shared
beliefs:[22] a belief that each belongs together with the rest; that this
association is neither transitory nor merely instrumental, but
stems from a long history of living together which (it is hoped and
expected) will continue into the future; that the community is
marked off from other communities by its members' distinctive
characteristics; that each member recognizes a loyalty to the
community, expressed in a willingness to sacrifice personal goals
to advance its interests; and that the community should enjoy a

---

[21] Socialists need not take a stand on the question whether it is ultimately preferable for
there to be a plurality of national communities or a single global community. The point is
that a feasible form of socialism must begin from the communal identities people actually
have, not those which it might be abstractly desirable for them to have. There is presently
no sign that national identities are on the wane. Insofar as there is any movement, it
appears to be in the direction of smaller, more intense forms of nationality rather than
towards cosmopolitanism.

[22] See B. Barry, 'Self-Government Revisited', in D. Miller and L. Siedentop (eds.),
The Nature of Political Theory (Oxford: Clarendon Press, 1983).

measure of political autonomy, normally (but not I think necessarily) in the form of a sovereign state.[23] Where these beliefs are widely held throughout the population in question, we have sufficient grounds for saying that a nation exists.

What needs underlining is how little this definition includes. It contains no assumption that nations are, as it were, natural kinds marked off from one another by physical characteristics. It can easily accommodate the historical fluidity of national identities, and recognize the extent to which nations are brought into being by extraneous circumstances such as conflicts between states. Nor is there any assumption that people who share a nationality will share objective characteristics such as race or language.[24] It is indeed possible that people's *beliefs* about these characteristics may form part of particular national identities—for instance that it is part of (French) people's understanding of what it is to be French that one should speak the French language—but this is quite a different matter. Moreover, the salient characteristics may vary from case to case: one nation may define itself by race, another by religion, a third by nothing more than common history. (In fact these examples are too simple. If we think about existing national identities, we quickly realize that they are almost without exception made up of an array of characteristics, none of which is regarded as strictly necessary to being Italian, Japanese, etc.)

The definition is minimal in another respect too. It embodies no assumptions about how nations ought to behave towards one another. In particular, it does not include the idea that nations are ethically unrestricted, so that powerful nations may justifiably impose themselves on the weak. All that nationality, as such, includes is the idea that one owes a special loyalty to one's compatriots. Now it is certainly true that acknowledging a loyalty of this kind means favouring the interests of members of the group at the expense of outsiders in certain circumstances. That is what loyalty means: talk of impersonal loyalty, or loyalty to the human race as a whole, is meaningless, except in science fiction

---

[23] I hope there is no need to labour the conceptual distinction between a state (a political institution) and a nation (a group of people with shared beliefs of the appropriate kind), nor to dwell on the reasons why most nationalities aspire to form their own sovereign states.

[24] For the sake of argument I assume that race *is* an objective characteristic, though clearly this might be disputed.

cases. But to acknowledge loyalty to a group need not imply being ethically indifferent to outsiders, much less being willing to trample on their interests in the name of the group.

Most socialists see the value in attachments to primary groups.[25] They see that owing a special loyalty to your workmates or your neighbours does not exclude caring about and supporting wider constituencies. (Indeed, as I argued earlier, they have often taken such a rosy view of this relationship that they have ignored the structural problems of inter-group relations.) Why, then, should national loyalties be looked on with disfavour? Perhaps it is the fact that national groupings are normally co-extensive with states, so that the group has the organized power to inflict damage on outside groups, if it so wishes. But this, it seems to me, is simply an unavoidable corollary of the feature which should make nationality *attractive* to socialists as a form of community. It is precisely the conjunction of nation and state that makes it possible for national communities to approach the ideals of self-determination and distributive justice sketched in the previous section. Only a politically organized community can aspire to shape its own future and to distribute resources throughout its membership according to need.[26] Unfortunately, the power which enables it to do this will also, if misused, allow it to damage other communities in ways that are too familiar to need rehearsing.

My strategy so far has been to separate nationality, as the idea that socialists should hold on to and favour, from nationalism—a rather inchoate notion, often thought to encompass (*a*) the idea that nations are distinct, immutable chunks of humanity, and/or (*b*) the idea that national allegiances are to be fostered at the expense of all other commitments, whether wider or narrower, and/or (*c*) the idea that nations may aggress against each other as

[25] Most, but not all. Godwin was the best-known exponent of the view that one must be rigorously impartial in one's treatment of fellow human beings. But Godwin was in any case an odd sort of socialist, if indeed one at all.

[26] Obviously nation-states are constrained to a varying extent by the international economic and political environment in which they have to act. I do not mean to imply that any nation can be fully self-determining in the sense of facing no external impediments at all. Nor would I deny that some nations are constrained to an extent that makes their nominal self-determination fairly meaningless. I would simply reiterate that nationality, where it works, holds out a promise that socialists should find very attractive, in a world that falls far short of utopia.

forcefully as they are able. These latter ideas may all lead to repugnant conclusions, but their connection with nationality as such is no stronger than, say, the connection between football violence and loyalty to one's chosen team. All particularist loyalties create at least the *potential* for objectionable behaviour towards outsiders, but to conclude that we should never pledge ourselves to anything less than humanity as a whole is to overlook everything that is valuable in these special commitments.[27]

There is, however, a further issue that we must consider before allowing nationality to stand as our idea of overall community. A socialist view of community, unlike certain conservative views, must embody a condition of rationality. Members of the community must be able to subject their relationship to critical scrutiny without destroying it. This follows from socialist egalitarianism—there is no privileged caste holding the rest of society in intellectual thrall—together with the idea that the community is an active agent reshaping the world in accordance with its purposes. Now it is often suggested that national 'communities' are in one important sense fictitious, for it is characteristic of nations that their identities are not formed through spontaneous processes of self-definition, but primarily according to the exigencies of power—the demands of states seeking to assure themselves of the loyalty of their subjects. Nationality is to a greater or lesser degree a manufactured item. This is brought out in Anthony Smith's recent study of the formation of nations out of older ethnic communities.[28] Smith distinguishes broadly between two cases. In the first, the nation is based on a single dominant ethnic group, and the culture of that group is imposed more or less successfully on ethnic minorities falling within the territorial boundaries of the emergent nation. In the second, a dominant culture is lacking, and has to be forged in order to create a nation out of a series of disparate ethnic groups. In both cases, but especially the second, nation-building is a work of

---

[27] For explorations of the value of such commitments, see A. Oldenquist, 'Loyalties', *Journal of Philosophy*, 74 (1982), 173–93; J. Cottingham, 'Partiality, Favouritism and Morality', *Philosophical Quarterly*, 36 (1986), 357–73; P. Pettit, 'Social Holism and Moral Theory', *Proceedings of the Aristotelean Society*, 86 (1985–6), 173–97. I have looked more fully at the ethical issues raised by national allegiances in 'The Ethical Significance of Nationality', *Ethics*, 98 (1987–8), 647–62.

[28] A. D. Smith, *The Ethnic Origins of Nations* (Oxford: Blackwell, 1986).

invention, in particular the invention of a common national past. As Smith puts it:

If the nation is to become a 'political community' on the Western territorial and civic model, it must, paradoxically, seek to create those myths of descent, those historical memories and that common culture which form the missing elements of their ethnic make-up, along with a mutual solidarity. It must differentiate itself from its closest neighbours, distinguish its culture from theirs, and emphasize the historic kinship of its constituent *ethnie* and their common ties of ideological affinity. This is done by creating or elaborating an 'ideological' myth of origins and descent.[29]

Let us take it, then, that nations require histories which are to a greater or lesser degree 'mythical' (as judged by the standards of impartial scholarship); and that those stories are not only needed at the time during which a national identity is first being created, but pass into that identity itself—so that in order to understand what it means to be French or Greek, one has to accept (some version of)[30] the common story. Do these facts imply that national loyalties cannot withstand rational reflection?

To answer this question, we need to make a distinction between beliefs that are constitutive of social relationships, and background beliefs which support those constitutive beliefs. To illustrate the former, consider the example of friendship. For A and B to be friends, it must minimally be true that each is willing to put himself out for the other. Suppose that A believes this of B, but in fact the belief is false. B is merely a fair-weather friend: should an occasion arise on which he is called on to sacrifice something for A's sake, he will certainly renege. A's loyalties to B are then drained of their value, since the reciprocal attitudes that constitute friendship are not in place. An indicator of this is that A, if he is rational, must want to be informed if indeed it is the case that his 'friendship' is not being reciprocated.[31]

---

[29] Ibid. 147.

[30] Very often political disputes within a nation will surface as disputes about the precise character of the national past—e.g. the intense competition between 'Whig' and 'Tory' accounts of English history in eighteenth-century Britain. But the competing accounts will recognizably be different versions of the same general story, with many basic facts not in dispute.

[31] If A resists the passing on of this information, then the emotion he feels for B is not friendship but love, which (proverbially) is blind.

But now consider a different case. Suppose there is a family, call them the Smiths, who exemplify all the best features of that relationship: there is love, mutual support, and a wide range of activities performed in common. If asked what it was that made these attitudes to one another appropriate, the Smiths would point, among other things, to the fact that members of the family were biologically related. Suppose now that owing to some dreadful mix-up at the hospital, one of the Smith children is in fact not a Smith. We can then say that the family relationship is backed up by a false belief: the love and concern they feel for one another is supported by a supposed genetic connection which in one case fails to obtain. But a falsity of this kind doesn't mean that the attachment of each member to the family is itself valueless. The *constitutive* beliefs are all in order; each does genuinely identify with the family unit, and his beliefs about the others' attitudes are correct. In contrast to the first case, it would not be rational in these circumstances to want to have the false belief brought to light.[32]

If we apply this distinction to the case of nations, the imagined national past, which as we have seen appears to be an essential element in the process of nation-building, must count as a background (rather than constitutive) belief. It does of course matter (given my definition on pp. 238–9) that nations should see their identities as extending over time, but the constitutive belief is only that there should be some national past. The particular story which a nation tells itself about its past is a background belief. It is important that the story should be generally believed—or to put the point more precisely, that there should be substantial convergence in the versions of the story that are believed[33]—but not that it should be historically accurate.[34]

[32] Some may think that it is always rational to divest yourself of irrational beliefs, but this is a superficial view. Here we are on Jon Elster territory; see, e.g. the discussion of 'decisions to believe' in his *Ulysses and the Sirens* (Cambridge: Cambridge University Press, 1979), sec. ii. 3. The essential point is that there may be beliefs which it is valuable for a person to have in the light of his underlying goals, in which case it is rational for him to set up mechanisms which ensure that he has them (and if necessary protect the beliefs from later rational scrutiny).

[33] See n. 30.

[34] Not important from the point of view of constituting the nation. In a wider perspective, it may make a good deal of difference how far removed the national myths are from historical truth. If the distance is great, this may have serious repercussions for scholarly research and intellectual toleration generally.

Indeed, since the story is told for purpose of self-definition, and since the nation's self-definition bears on the goals that its members will try to pursue in the future, we should expect a dynamic nation, actively engaged in critical debate on its common purposes, regularly to reinterpret the past as well.

But there may be doubts whether the distinction I have invoked can do all the work that it is needed to do. For even if we can successfully interpret the national past as a background belief, we may not be able to do the same with the national present. Nations need a common view about what they now are; a view about what distinguishes membership of this nation from membership of others. To use an old-fashioned phrase, they need some conception of 'national character'. But, it might be urged, these beliefs are also to a large extent mythical, in the sense that they attribute a spurious homogeneity to a set of people who, if looked at objectively, vary enormously in values, lifestyles, cultural attributes and so on. And this observation destroys a *constitutive* belief, because it is constitutive of national identity that members of a nation should have characteristics in common which make it appropriate for them to be lumped together politically, rather than parcelled out in some other way. Take away 'national character' and all we are left with is *de facto* boundaries between states.

To meet this objection, we need to be able to draw a distinction between a public culture that is shared by all who belong to a particular nation and the various private cultures that may flourish inside it. Since we have rejected objective definitions of nationality, 'national character' must be interpreted in cultural terms—in terms of beliefs and attitudes, ritual observances, and so forth. But given the cultural variety that we observe in most modern nations, it is also clear that the common culture we are looking for must be of a relatively thin kind—it cannot embrace all the rich cultural attributes that particular sections of the society may possess. This raises the issue of how such a public/ private distinction can be drawn. Is it possible to have a viable sense of nationality without trespassing in the realm of private culture, or will there be areas in which we have to choose between maintaining national identity and encouraging cultural pluralism? I address this difficult issue in Chapter 11 below. Here I have tried to sketch in a minimalist view of nationality which on the one hand is substantial enough to serve as an idea of community, but on the other hand is sufficiently free of irrationalist elements to allow socialists to consider stomaching it.

V

Nations are the only possible form in which overall community can be realized in modern societies. But a nation needs the right kind of political organization if it is to satisfy socialist ideals. I shall describe this organization in terms of citizenship. Nationality and citizenship complement one another. Without a common national identity, there is nothing to hold citizens together, no reason for extending the role just to these people and not to others. Without citizenship, nationality cannot fulfil the activist idea of a community of people determining its own future; it is at risk of becoming a merely traditional form of association in which received ways of doing things are continued without critical scrutiny. Nationality gives people the common identity that makes it possible for them to conceive of shaping their world together. Citizenship gives them the practical means of doing so.

Citizenship here must mean something more than merely being subject to the laws of a state, which is often how the term is now understood. It must be a social role which is partly, but not wholly, defined in terms of rights.[35] Let us take the rights first. It is conventional to distinguish analytically between three kinds of rights that citizens enjoy. First, there are protective rights, rights safeguarding the private freedom and security of each citizen against invasion by others. Second, there are political rights, rights to take part in decision-making in whatever political arenas the society in question provides. Third, there are welfare rights, rights guaranteeing a level of provision of goods and services that admits the citizen to full membership of his community.[36]

[35] I assume for the time being that this is an appropriate way of understanding citizenship. In ch. 12 I consider the general question of rights under socialism, and conclude that the relationship between state and citizen is indeed best formalized in terms of rights.

[36] The best-known analysis of citizenship as a status linking the three kinds of rights is T. H. Marshall, 'Citizenship and Social Class', in *Sociology at the Crossroads and Other Essays* (London: Heinemann, 1963). The implications of citizenship for social policy are drawn out in J. Parker, *Social Policy and Citizenship* (London: Macmillan, 1975). The best critical analysis of the tradition as a whole is D. Harris, *Justifying State Welfare* (Oxford: Blackwell, 1987).

The distinction here is analytical only, because the whole thrust of the citizenship idea is that the different kinds of rights support each other. Protective and welfare rights provide a secure basis upon which the citizen can launch into his political role. The sense of common membership that the exercise of political rights (together with nationality) fosters underpins the obligation to provide for the welfare of fellow citizens. Taken together, the rights confer an equality of status upon citizens which, it is claimed, bolsters their self-respect. Although inequalities of other kinds may persist, each can draw comfort from the fact that, in the basic political arrangements of his society, he is treated as an equal.[37] Testimony to the force of this idea is provided by the popularity, even in present-day political debate, of the phrase 'second-class citizen'. To say that someone is a second-class citizen is to say that, although nominally holding citizen status, he is deprived in some way that robs him of self-respect—hence he is not, in the full sense, a citizen of this society. It is an argument for adding a new right to the definition of citizenship, or for ensuring that an existing right is properly protected.

This observation may also, however, create anxieties about the whole idea. Isn't the notion of citizenship so amorphous that it can be appealed to in order to resolve any and every issue of social policy? Recall that we are trying to translate the idea of community into a form that leaves room for a sphere of 'civil society' in which private associations and market relations hold sway. How can we be sure that the contents of this sphere will not have to be determined politically in the name of citizenship?

Certainly some forms of private association seem incompatible with the citizenship idea. The most obvious case is slavery. The subservient position held by the slave excludes him from citizenship, as the Greeks understood. A more pertinent case for us is that of people subject to wide-ranging paternalism, such as the inhabitants of Pullman, Illinois under the hegemony of George Pullman. Michael Walzer concludes that Pullman's well-meaning domination of the lives of the workers who lived in his town ('his' because all the property and the services were owned by Pullman) was incompatible with democratic citizenship. 'George

---

[37] This argument is found in J. Rawls, *A Theory of Justice* (Cambridge, Mass.: Harvard University Press, 1971), 544–5, though Rawls resists extending its scope beyond civil and political rights to welfare rights.

Pullman hired himself a metic population in a political community where self-respect was closely tied to citizenship and where decisions about destinations and risks, even (or especially) local destinations and risks, were supposed to be shared.[38] Citizenship requires independent citizens who are not continually forced to conform their wills to other people's outside the political realm, but have sufficient autonomy in their private lives to gain experience in exercising judgement.[39] It has, therefore, social preconditions.[40] But it does not follow that every aspect of civil society must be geared to the production of citizens, or that there is no space left for market relationships. Under normal circumstances, the independence of action that people enjoy in market contexts is compatible with the requirements of citizenship.[41]

Citizenship, however, is not just a matter of possessing rights, even if these are broadly interpreted. It is also a matter of belief and behaviour. The citizen has to see himself as playing an active role in determining his society's future, and as taking responsibility for the collective decisions that are made. He must be politically active, both in the sense of informing himself about the issues currently under discussion and in the sense of participating in decision-making itself. Moreover he cannot regard politics merely as an arena in which to pursue his private interests. He must act *as* a citizen, that is as a member of a collectivity who is committed to advancing its common good. We have said that, for the socialist, the sought-after common identity must be an activist

---

[38] M. Walzer, *Spheres of Justice* (Oxford: Martin Robertson, 1983), 297.

[39] The argument here can, of course, be run in either direction. I am assuming the value of universal citizenship and inferring that social life ought to be ordered in such a way that everyone develops the capacities of a citizen. An earlier generation of liberals took social relations as given, and argued for the restriction of citizenship to those who were competent to exercise it. See my 'Democracy and Social Justice', *British Journal of Political Science*, 8 (1978), 1–19, repr. in P. Birnbaum, J. Lively, and G. Parry (eds.), *Democracy, Consensus and Social Contract* (London: Sage, 1978).

[40] These are explored in D. S. King and J. Waldron, 'Citizenship, Social Citizenship and the Defence of Welfare Provision', *British Journal of Political Science*, 18 (1988), 415–43.

[41] The structure of enterprises will be of considerable significance here. If workers are directly involved in the making of economic decisions, as they are under market socialist arrangements, they are more likely to be active in politics, and hence better prepared for citizenship. For empirical confirmation of this, see E. S. Greenberg, 'Industrial Democracy and the Democratic Citizen', *Journal of Politics*, 43 (1981), 964–81.

one. This has now to be cashed out as a specific way of engaging in politics.

In the following chapter, I look more closely at the form of politics which is demanded by the citizenship ideal, and ask whether it is a realistic possibility. At this point, we need only consider the feasibility of the ideal in general terms. Note first that, although the rights of citizenship must be distributed equally to everyone, it isn't necessary that each person should display the same level of political activity. Citizenship requires *some* level of political involvement (and equal opportunities beforehand) but it can allow for differences in taste. Michael Walzer has reminded us that there are ineradicable variations in people's desire for participation, and it would be intolerable to try to iron these out by making a high level of involvement compulsory.[42] There is no need to do so. Citizens can regard themselves as equals, and regard their common status as important, even though they are active to different degrees, just as members of a club can attach equal weight to membership even though they make varying use of the facilities provided.

But can citizenship be an important status in the first place? Scepticism about this claim extends from Marx's somewhat abstract argument that, so long as the division between civil society and state remains in existence, man's membership of the political community must be illusory—'man is the imaginary member of an imaginary sovereignty, divested of his real, individual life, and infused with an unreal universality'[43]—down to Robert Lane's empirical critique of the Rawlsian assertion that the possession and exercise of political rights is an important source of self-esteem.[44] What unites Marx and Lane, unlikely bedfellows in other respects, is the conviction that what really matters to people is the world of work and immediate personal relationships. For Marx, genuine communal relationships must be rooted in the sphere of production; for Lane, it is work, leisure, and family life that provide the major sources of self-esteem. The realm of politics is too distant and intangible for participation in it to be personally meaningful.[45]

[42] M. Walzer, 'A Day in the Life of a Socialist Citizen', in *Obligations* (Cambridge, Mass.: Harvard University Press, 1970).

[43] K. Marx, 'On the Jewish Question', in *Karl Marx: Early Writings*, ed. Bottomore 13–14.

[44] R. E. Lane, 'Government and Self-Esteem', *Political Theory*, 10 (1982), 5–31.

[45] Lane's claim is that as a matter of psychological fact political life is of marginal

It is tempting to write off these criticisms (and others like them) as merely a response to the limited form of citizenship available in capitalist societies—intuitive in Marx's case, empirically-grounded in Lane's. Certainly we need to envisage very different institutions of citizenship—in particular, many more arenas of participation—if the ideal I have been sketching is to become a reality. But one essential contrast between private (including economic) life and political life would still remain. Broadly speaking, in the former realm, we experience the results of our activity personally and directly—we see the object we have made, we bear the costs of our own decisions—whereas in the latter realm our voice is always one among many, and our collective decisions normally have quite a remote impact on our lives. Isn't it this almost truistic observation that finally justifies Marx's and Lane's scepticism?

In fact, although the observation is truistic, to infer from it that politics must always play a peripheral role in people's lives is to make a contestable assumption about human nature. The assumption is that material activity, activity which has immediate and tangible results, always counts for more than expressive and symbolic activity. This tenet has only to be spelt out for its frailty to be evident. If it were true, many things would be difficult to explain—the pre-eminent role of religion in many societies, for instance, or the motivating power of nationalism as an ideology capable of stimulating enormous self-sacrifice on behalf of the fatherland. That we find such experiences alien (and usually alarming) is a fact about the public culture of liberal societies, not the reflection of a truth about human nature. In liberal culture the person who is deeply engaged in politics is regarded with suspicion—either he is a fanatic, the victim of irrational impulses, or he is an opportunist, cloaking his ambition in idealist rhetoric. In ancient Greece, by contrast, this presumption was reversed: the person who *withdrew* from normal political life was seen as deficient, as 'idiotic'.[46]

importance to citizens. Marx, writing in a somewhat different context, insists rather on the unreal quality of citizenship (the analogy with religion is used throughout). That is, political life may seem important to the citizen, but in believing this he is somehow deceived. (Marx doesn't explain why the belief is illusory; perhaps he is anticipating his later view that the state appears to act independently, but is in reality subordinate to the needs of civil society.)

[46] See C. Berry, 'Idiotic Politics', *Political Studies*, 27 (1979), 550–63, and more generally H. Arendt, *The Human Condition* (Chicago: University of Chicago Press, 1958), ch. 2.

None of this addresses the practical difficulties involved in revivifying the role of citizen for the inhabitants of large, modern societies. To do so requires the exercise of some imagination.[47] The effort will be worthwhile only if the case made above for valuing citizenship is accepted. If so, we should not be deterred by current, disparaging attitudes towards political life. We should take a broader view.

VI

How does this vision of community, combining nationality with citizenship, fare when tested against our original touchstone, the radical communitarian vision of Morris and Co.? We have abandoned the idea that communal relationships must be unitary. Instead people are related to one another in a number of different ways—as friends, as competitors in the market, as citizens, and so forth. This introduces an element of artifice into the relationship. We have to decide whether, on a particular occasion, our interaction should be governed by the norms of economic competition, say, or political loyalty. We will need markers to separate the various realms of existence from each other.[48] The transparency and simplicity of human intercourse in the radical vision is replaced by something more familiar, but not, I believe, less attractive. There is in the end something rather flat and insipid about life in the communist utopia, where all dealings between people are informed by the same sentiments of universal good will. Perhaps the idea of role-playing, and of coping with the dilemmas that arise when role-requirements are felt to conflict, will seem on reflection to be integral to our idea of a mature human being.

Also abandoned is the idea of fraternity as an emotional bond linking members of the community, at least if that is understood literally, on the model of brotherhood. The new version still makes room for loyalty and emotional attachments, but the object of attachment is more abstract—a nation, the embodiment of a

---

[47] I return briefly to this issue in the following chapter. For fuller discussions, see B. Barber, *Strong Democracy* (Berkeley: University of California Press, 1984), ch. 10 and P. Green, *Retrieving Democracy* (London: Methuen, 1985), ch. 9.

[48] Bob Goodin's discussion of how the moral realm is kept free from contamination by more mundane motives illustrates this idea. See R. Goodin, 'Making Moral Incentives Pay', *Policy Sciences*, 12 (1980), 131–45.

public culture. I may feel strongly attached to Britain, but it is absurd to suppose that I could feel fraternally towards every individual Briton. Size alone would ensure this, even if complexity of relationship did not. Reasoned conviction is also given a larger role to play in generating ties. I am committed to my compatriots partly because I am committed to the principles and policies that we have worked out together politically. (I return to this proposition in the following chapter.)

Some elements in the radical vision are preserved. We have held on to the claim that a person's identity should be constituted, in part, by his membership of a collectivity, and shown how nationality and citizenship together can meet this demand. We have also seen how citizenship embodies an equality of status, and to that extent meets the radical ideal of egalitarian community. Finally citizenship provides a moral underpinning for distribution according to need, and at the same time the practical means for realizing this ideal on a society-wide basis.

Whether the form of socialism I have sketched should be described as 'communitarian' is in the end a matter of definition and taste. To the extent that 'community' conjures up a 'natural' form of association, based on physical proximity and traditional ties—Tönnies' idea of Gemeinschaft[49]—some other term is preferable. Again, if community is thought to imply unitary relation ships in the sense explained earlier, our proposals do not embody it. If, however, we follow recent debates in assuming that community has centrally to do with the constitutive role of social relationships in personal identity, then we have gone some way towards showing that market socialism can indeed be communitarian. Our next task is to look more closely at the form of politics that is needed to give substance to the idea of citizenship.

---

[49] See F. Tönnies, *Gemeinschaft und Gesellschaft*, translated as *Community and Association* (London: Routledge and Kegan Paul, 1955).

10

POLITICS AS DIALOGUE

I

The socialist tradition has never developed an adequate theory of politics, in the sense of an account of what the nature, scope, and purpose of political activity should be. Perhaps this is due to the long shadow cast by positivism, in its nineteenth-century sense. The positivist slogan was the replacement of government by administration. Social questions could be resolved by scientific enquiry, and the solutions implemented by benevolent administrators. The influence of this doctrine on socialists of the Fabian school is evident enough, but Marx too, although less élitist in his view of administration, adhered to an ideal of social organization that was essentially non-political. Politics was exclusively a phenomenon of class societies: 'political power, properly so called, is merely the organized power of one class for oppressing another'[1] Once conflicting class interests had been eliminated with the abolition of classes, the only remaining question was how best to advance the shared interests of all the members of society. This was a technical, rather than political, question.

The naïvety of this view is now quite apparent. Many, perhaps most, political issues would survive in a recognizable form even such a radical transformation of social relationships as that envisaged by Marx. Consider just one example: a society which now generates most of its energy using coal-fired power stations deciding whether to switch instead to nuclear power. What makes this a political question? Assume that we have all the facts at our disposal. We know that, with coal power, energy will cost so much per kilowatt to generate, so many men will find employment mining and burning the coal, of whom some proportion will, on average, be killed or injured in each year. With nuclear power, the cost per kilowatt will be some other figure, employment will fall to some lower level (let's say), there will be so much anticipated

---

[1] K. Marx and F. Engels, *The Communist Manifesto* in *Selected Works*, vol. i (Moscow: Foreign Languages Publishing House, 1962), p. 54.

radiation released into the environment, and there will be a slight risk of a major disaster affecting thousands of people. There is no 'scientific' way of making this choice. Which option is preferred will depend on our attitude to risk—do we choose to incur the certainty of a small number of deaths and injuries through mining coal or the possibility of a much larger number through nuclear accident?—as well as on ethical questions. (Is it relevant that the risks associated with coal power are voluntarily assumed whereas those of nuclear power are for the most part externally imposed? How should we weigh any of these risks against the benefit of employment, the cheapness of energy, etc.?)[2] Although the parameters may change somewhat, the essential nature of the choice remains the same whatever the social system: it is not greatly different in the USSR than it is in the UK or the US. Moreover, it is a choice that must be made collectively: I assume here that we need to have a general energy policy and cannot segment the choice into a series of private decisions by individuals through the device of a market.[3]

Decisions of this kind are necessarily political. We must find some means of agreeing on a policy in circumstances where there is no 'right' answer in the scientific sense.[4] There is no reason to expect spontaneous agreement at the outset. People will be affected differently by the various possible policies, and quite apart from that may have conflicting opinions as to which is preferable. Politics, as I understand it here, is a process whereby, starting from such an initial situation of disagreement, a collectivity arrives at a common policy outcome which is generally accepted as authoritative and enforced in the face of dissent.[5] The

[2] For a discussion of these issues, see R. Goodin, 'No Moral Nukes', *Ethics*, 90 (1979–80), 417–49.

[3] Energy decisions will almost certainly have significant external effects reaching beyond the immediate producers and consumers of the energy source—for instance, most current forms of energy involve a significant level of pollution. This places them outside the scope of the arguments for consumer sovereignty sketched in ch. 5.

[4] For a fuller discussion of the nature of politics, emphasizing this point, see B. Barber, *Strong Democracy* (Berkeley: University of California Press, 1984), 120–31.

[5] Politics as a process makes no sense unless, in general, those who engage in it regard the decisions reached as authoritative, i.e. as providing reasons for acting over and above the private judgement of each participant. Whether politics strictly requires enforcement of these decisions is more moot; but in practice it is highly improbable that people would continue to recognize the authority of a political system if they were not satisfied that its decisions would be enforced against dissenters. A forum in which people met from time to time to see whether they could agree on a common course of action, but without any sense that decisions reached had a binding quality, would not count as political in the sense employed here.

question now arises: what kind of process? I don't at this stage want to consider mechanical questions (such as voting procedures, definitions of the relevant constituency, and so forth) but a more basic issue: what is supposed to be going on when a multitude of different interests and opinions are consolidated into a single collective outcome? Here I think it is useful to distinguish between two conceptions of politics, each representing this process in a very different way. I shall label the two conceptions politics as *interest-aggregation* and politics as *dialogue*.[6] I shall also argue that the first of these conceptions associates naturally with a liberal political outlook, whereas the second is more appropriate to socialists. But first let me elaborate the distinction.

II

Politics as interest-aggregation sees the political process in roughly the following way. People enter the political arena with interests that they want to promote. These interests may be essentially selfish—people may want to channel, through politics, a larger stream of material benefits towards themselves—or they may extend to a wider group or cause—for instance, some may want to encourage the practice of a particular religion. Such interests are consciously recognized and, for the purposes of politics, fixed. The need for political engagement stems from the fact that the interests in question are not universally shared, while at the same time they can best be promoted by collective action. Politics, therefore, is the process whereby a multitude of conflicting interests are aggregated into one single outcome. Precisely how this occurs will depend on the procedures employed, but let's suppose for the sake of illustration that decisions are made by a majority vote of the constituency in question. Essentially what will happen is that individuals and groups will bargain with one another until a compromise policy emerges that commands the support of at least 51 per cent of the constituency. No one may regard this as the best possible outcome but, if the procedure has

---

[6] For a similar distinction see J. Elster, 'The Market and the Forum' in J. Elster and A. Hylland (eds.), *Foundations of Social Choice Theory* (Cambridge: Cambridge University Press, 1986).

worked effectively, each of the 51 per cent will regard it as the best attainable result, in the sense that no preferred alternative could have commanded the necessary majority.

Politics as dialogue offers quite a different view of the process. According to this conception, people enter politics with conflicting opinions about what ought to be done over matters of general concern. What then ensues is a process of persuasion in the course of which spokesmen for the different points of view articulate reasons for the beliefs that they hold. A dialogue develops within which people may be led to revise their original opinions radically. Arguments are trumped by better arguments, until eventually a consensus emerges. What shape this consensus must have—whether or not it must amount to unanimity, whether everyone's considered opinion counts equally, or whether differential weights are assigned—varies according to the precise conception being employed. The important point is that people's adherence to the consensus view does not depend on its proximity to their original opinion, nor on strategic considerations, but on the strength of the arguments that have been offered for it. Once consensus is reached, it is formally adopted as common policy.

The first of these conceptions is the more familiar, and may well seem the more down-to-earth and realistic. As I have suggested, it will appeal naturally to liberals: it takes people as they come, so to speak, and it assumes that, as a matter of course, their interests will conflict in a way that rules out genuine convergence (as opposed to compromise). It also sees politics as a sort of market-place. The political arena is distinguished from the market proper by its contrasting ground rules, and is therefore capable of achieving different results, but in both spheres individuals are expected to act instrumentally in pursuit of their interests rather than to search for common ends. Yet despite its apparent realism, politics as interest-aggregation faces a number of serious difficulties. Some of these are internal, in the sense that they remain within the compass of liberal political theory. I will briefly consider three.

First, if interest-aggregation is to be an acceptable means of reaching collective decisions, we need to be assured that all interests will be pressed with equal force; only in that way will the outcome represent a fair compromise between the claims of everyone affected by the decision. But we know, empirically, that this condition is difficult, perhaps impossible, to achieve. Politics as interest-aggregation favours those with the resources and the incentives to press their interests politically.[7]

Second, the political process understood in this way is necessarily blind to the *quality* of the interests that are being pursued. Since all that counts is the strength of an interest (as indicated by a person's willingness to sacrifice other interests to promote it) and the number who share it, there is no chance to discriminate between interests that have a clean bill of health, so to speak, and those that are defective in one way or another.[8] Among defective interests we might count the following: interests that are in the most straightforward sense irrational, in the sense that people are demanding things that are not really in their interests (e.g. people lobbying for a power plant in their neighbourhood which they hope will increase employment, but which in fact will only add to pollution); interests that are based on objectionable moral attitudes, such as racial prejudice; interests that are based on non-autonomous desires (e.g. desires that people have been manipulated into having by powerful groups or individuals who stand to benefit from the interests in question being advanced).[9] To distinguish expressed interests of any of these sorts from

[7] This is, of course, the standard difficulty faced by pluralist theories of democracy and pressed home by critics of pluralism. For a balanced discussion, see R. Dahl, *Dilemmas of Pluralist Democracy* (New Haven and London: Yale University Press, 1982).

[8] In my discussion of consumer sovereignty, in ch. 5, I deliberately set this issue aside, focusing on the question whether markets are an efficient means of satisfying preferences, regardless of quality. Why, then, raise it here? The problem of defective interests is far more salient in political contexts than in market contexts, for two reasons at least. (a) In political contexts, decisions reached have a wide-ranging impact, so if some people act on irrational preferences (say), others may bear the brunt of their error. (b) In political contexts, decisions are much more likely to be one-off and irreversible, so the feedback mechanism which tends to improve individuals' choices in the market has no chance to operate. It is more important in politics to make the right decision first time round.

[9] Some readers might wish to make a distinction here between interests and preferences: irrational or manipulated 'interests' are not interests at all, but merely subjective states which in these cases do not correspond to genuine interests. This distinction is perfectly valid, and I should make it clear that when discussing interest-aggregation as a form of politics I am concerned only with *expressed* interests, which may indeed not be genuine. A wholly satisfactory terminology cannot be found: if 'interests' has too narrow a meaning for our purposes, 'preferences' has too broad a meaning, since it embraces ethical preferences (e.g. opinions about which policy is fair or in the common interest) as well as selfish ones, and so is liable to blur the distinction between the two conceptions of politics. For discussion of the concept of interests, see A. Reeve and A. Ware, 'Interests in Political Theory', *British Journal of Political Science*, 13 (1983), 379–400, which also footnotes earlier contributions.

'healthy' interests, we need to go behind the demands themselves to the reasons that people would offer to support them (for, in general, knowledge of the bare demand will not allow us to make the discrimination). But a pure politics of interest-aggregation allows no room for such reasons to make their appearance.

Third, even if we assume that the interests people express are all wholesome, there is now a large body of literature devoted to the impossibility of finding an acceptable aggregation procedure. The problem is roughly this: if we assume that we want a single procedure to handle all cases, if we lay down no more than a rather weak set of conditions for acceptability, and if we make no a priori assumptions about the distribution of policy preferences in the relevant constituency, then no such procedure can be found. This is the gist of Arrow's impossibility theorem.[10] Those who believe that Arrow problems rarely if ever occur in the real world of politics should refer to William Riker's recent book *Liberalism against Populism*.[11] Riker's central point, illustrated by concrete examples, is that where there are three or more policy options to choose between on a given issue, the outcome that actually emerges is liable to depend in arbitrary fashion on the procedure used to reduce the range of options to a final choice of two.

All of these represent potentially serious internal flaws of the interest-aggregation model. They indicate that although a political process of this kind may work, after a fashion, to produce an outcome, the result may be difficult to justify even in terms of liberal political principles. Supporters of the model may of course offer various responses to the objections I have outlined. But rather than pursue this debate any further, I want to raise a problem of a somewhat different kind.

What reason has anyone to accept the decision that emerges from the process of interest-aggregation? In particular, why should anyone whose interests in this instance have not been successfully advanced regard the outcome as legitimate? Clearly, all the weight of legitimation must in these circumstances be carried by the procedure itself. If people accept the outcome, it is because they regard the mechanism used to reach it as fair or

---

[10] See K. Arrow, *Social Choice and Individual Values* (New Haven: Yale University Press, 1963).
[11] W. Riker, *Liberalism against Populism* (San Francisco: Freeman, 1982).

commendable. They have been given no reason to accept the *content* of the decision; no one will have tried to persuade them that this policy is itself a good or fair one. The reason that its supporters have for favouring it remains opaque: perhaps it is simple self-interest, perhaps a more far-sighted pursuit of sectional interest involving strategic considerations (open or tacit deals with other groups, etc.), perhaps some more elevated motive.

Now it would clearly be wrong to suggest that decisions can never be legitimated in this procedural way. Most of our contemporaries, for instance, are strongly committed to democratic procedures, and are willing to accept the outcomes of such processes even when their own interests are affected quite adversely; at other times other procedures have won acceptance. But we should note that this form of legitimation cuts against another powerful modern ideal, namely that when people are called upon to act, they should be given reasons to justify what they are asked to do. Doing so respects their claims as rational creatures. Since complying with a political decision that you disfavour normally imposes some cost, political processes which do not involve giving general reasons for the decisions that are taken seem to fall foul of this ideal.[12] The point I am making should not be confused with the anarchist thesis that people are only rationally autonomous when acting on the balance of reasons as they themselves see it. This thesis, which is straightforwardly destructive of all forms of political authority, is in my view absurdly strong.[13] The present claim is rather that people should be *presented* with the reasons for the course of action that has been decided on, even if they themselves assess the balance of reasons differently. In this way the decision becomes rationally intelligible. The contrast is between being commanded to do something, with no reasons given, and being presented with an intelligible justification which you can recognize even though you might not have reached the same conclusion yourself. What I am suggesting is that this provides a way of legitimating the *content* of

---

[12] This has the further implication that a society whose politics comes close to the pure model of interest-aggregation may need an expanding coercive apparatus to obtain compliance with the decisions reached. The point is developed in W. Connolly, 'The Public Interest and the Common Good', in *Appearance and Reality in Politics* (Cambridge: Cambridge University Press, 1981).

[13] See D. Miller, *Anarchism* (London: Dent, 1984), ch. 2.

decisions which is potentially more powerful than mere procedural legitimation.[14]

There is one further point to be made here. We saw, in the last
chapter, that communal identity in modern society must, for the
socialist, take the form of citizenship in a nation-state. Moreover
this identity was to be interpreted in activist terms: people should
look on the social world as something that they themselves had
helped to create. Now the manner in which political decisions are
reached is clearly of crucial importance in bringing this about.
Where people are presented with the justifying reasons for a
decision, they can identify themselves with the decision in a way
that seems impossible where bare procedures are involved. This
must depend, of course, on how closely the reasons provided are
aligned with the considerations that would move the person
himself in any case. We won't identify with a policy of apartheid
merely because we understand how it flows logically from racist
assumptions. But this is an extreme case. More often our
disagreement with the outcome of a political process will have to
do with the relative weights to be attached to various values that
we share with the supporters of the decision. Here the experience
of participation may lead us to regard the decision taken as our
own, even though it is not the decision we would have come to in
isolation. Peter Laslett has put this well:

When we attend the meeting of a committee, hear and take part in the
discussion, vote for or against the final resolution, and afterwards find
ourselves obliged to defend that resolution whether we agreed with it or
not at the time, then the phrase 'general will' does seem to mean
something to us. We can concede that something embodied in the
decision is general in the sense that the will of all is not general; we can
even concede that this something is, or began by being, a minority
opinion, or held by one man alone. Surprisingly often it corresponds to
no-one's opinion at all. The interplay between the group of personalities

---

[14] To avoid misunderstanding, I should make it clear that I do not intend to express
general scepticism about the idea of procedural legitimation. There are large areas of
social life in which people are generally willing to accept outcomes, even ones which
significantly damage their interests, provided they are convinced that proper procedures
have been followed—I am thinking of the law, employment, sport, and so forth for
evidence see R. E. Lane, 'Procedural Justice: How One Is Treated vs. What One Gets'
(unpublished). The argument here is about *political* decisions and the extent to which they
can be rendered legitimate simply by procedural devices, such as majority voting, in the
absence of debate about the reasons behind the decisions.

in committee, in fact, can discover a consensus which all of them feel to be outside their own personalities, and after the decision it is remarkable how often it is accepted as if each personality had 'willed' it for himself. It is significant, too, that this 'general will' is felt to be rational . . . .[15]

To sum up: where politics takes the form of interest-aggregation, the political system remains a piece of external machinery. Subjects have in general no reason to identify with its output, and the decisions reached are legitimated only through the validity of the procedures that the system employs. It would be wrong to suggest that a system of this kind is inevitably going to be unstable, but I hope to have shown why the alternative model, politics as dialogue, can make greater claims on behalf of the political sphere. I have suggested, in particular, that the socialist idea of citizenship exerts powerful pressures towards the form of legitimation that politics as dialogue promises to provide. Where dialogue succeeds, the citizen's rational capacities are respected, and he is able to align himself with the decisions that are reached.

Yet it may appear that, in modern societies, there are insurmountable obstacles in the path of any such idea of politics. The enormous diversity in individual plans of life, carrying with it equally diverse systems of belief and value, may seem to rule out completely any notion of arriving at a reasoned consensus on political matters. Political debate may take on the appearance of dialogue, but if each speaker is simply articulating a position whose underlying premisses are incompatible with those of the other speakers, then no genuine convergence can occur, and any formal vote will merely record the numbers falling on either side of the issue being debated. In order to weigh the force of this seemingly crucial objection, I want to look briefly at the ideas of Arendt and Habermas, both of whom offer us versions of the dialogue model of politics, but, in terms of the problem we are considering, diametrically opposed versions. I shall suggest that neither version is adequate, but that reflection on their respective weaknesses can help us in formulating a more defensible view.

---

[15] P. Laslett, 'The Face to Face Society' in id. (ed.), *Philosophy, Politics and Society* (Oxford: Blackwell, 1956), 169–70. I should make it clear that Laslett himself does not regard this conception of politics as appropriate to large 'territorial' societies.

III

Arendt's view of politics can reasonably be described as existentialist, though this is not a label she would have welcomed herself. She sees the political realm as a medium of individual self-disclosure. Men reveal their individuality in speech, and the political forum is an arena in which they can display this unique identity to an audience, thereby ensuring themselves immortality of a sort. For Arendt, a prime example of a public realm having this character was the Greek *polis* which, she says, 'assures the mortal actor that his passing existence and fleeting greatness will never lack the reality that comes from being seen, being heard, and, generally, appearing before an audience of fellow men . . .'[16] Here the stress is laid on the *authenticity* of political activity. Arendt obviously considers it important that each person's opinion is formed through confrontation with conflicting opinions, but this is to ensure that opinion is grounded in authentic reasons rather than merely being prejudice absorbed from the mass. She does not explain how conflicting opinions might be synthesized to produce a single outcome. Indeed, it is not clear that Arendt regards politics as having an outcome at all; the debate itself is what matters. This is indicated, for instance, by the esteem in which she holds the political clubs in Revolutionary France who '. . . regarded it as their main, if not their sole task to discuss all matters pertaining to public affairs, to talk about them and to exchange opinions without necessarily arriving at propositions, petitions, addresses, and the like'.[17] There is an obvious connection between this conception of politics as essentially a matter of talk, and Arendt's wish to exclude from the political sphere all social and economic issues, which she regards as unwarranted intruders from the realm of necessity into the realm of freedom.

The weaknesses of Arendt's conception are all too apparent. We must find it archaic to suppose that the scope of politics could

[16] H. Arendt, *The Human Condition* (Chicago: University of Chicago Press, 1958), 198. The importance to Arendt of the theatrical analogy which this quotation displays is well brought out in M. Canovan, 'Politics as Culture: Hannah Arendt and the Public Realm', *History of Political Thought*, 6 (1985), 617–42.

[17] H. Arendt, *On Revolution* (Harmondsworth: Penguin, 1973), 243.

be narrowed to exclude all socio-economic problems, and one could press this point further by asking what, on Arendt's view, *are* the appropriate topics for political dialogue (the texts give us no clear answer). Moreover, if politics is to have a practical outcome, we need some account of what lies between argument and policy. The more stress is laid on individual distinctness and authenticity, the less likely it seems that the upshot of political debate will be a policy commanding all-round assent. And this immediately raises a third difficulty: what is it that holds Arendt's citizens together in a body politic, each of them recognizing the legitimacy of public decisions? Her somewhat oblique remarks on this question suggest that she looks for an answer towards a mutual promise or contract—which is essentially a mechanical device for binding together discrete individuals into a fictitious unity.[18] Politics itself never appears as an integrating activity.

If Arendt's version of the dialogue model is existentialist, Habermas's may reasonably be described as rationalist. Here I take Habermas's account of the 'ideal speech situation' as a model of politics, even though the author himself seems to regard it primarily as a general device for justifying moral norms. Yet at the same time he presents the ideal speech situation as a solution to the problem of *legitimation* and he offers no separate account of political rationality. So it seems safe to conclude that Habermas effectively identifies the issues of moral justification and political legitimacy. The norms that would be generated in the ideal speech situation are binding on us both as moral agents and as citizens. I shall argue in a moment that this assimilation constitutes a major difficulty in Habermas's conception.

Habermas claims that legitimate norms are those that would emerge from an unconstrained dialogue between equals. An unconstrained dialogue means one in which no participant can force or induce another to agree to a proposition by means other than argument itself. The equality condition is essential here, guaranteeing in particular the absence of relations of domination that would enable one person to pressure another into accepting an outcome for extrinsic reasons. Habermas assumes that, under these conditions, consensus can be reached only through the identification of interests that are common to all parties, and this ensures the validity of the norms that emerge. 'The discursively

[18] Id., *Human Condition*, 243–5.

formed will may be called "rational" because the formal properties of discourse and of the deliberative situation sufficiently
guarantee that a consensus can arise only through appropriately
interpreted, *generalizable* interests, by which I mean needs *that can
be communicatively shared.*'[19]

The meaning of this last phrase is not altogether clear, but I
interpret Habermas to be saying that, in the process of trying to
convince others of the validity of his claims, each participant's
understanding of his needs is transformed in such a way that
eventually we are left only with universally shared needs. These
would, of course, form the basis for a genuine political consensus.
But if the model is interpreted in this way, its practical prospects
seem very dim indeed. For if we envisage the dialogue as taking
place simply between competent language-users, each with his
own conception of the good life and defining his needs initially in
terms of that conception, why should we anticipate any substantial degree of convergence? What rational resources have you to
persuade me not merely that *your* needs are such-and-such, but
that I should define my needs in such a way that our needs will be
common to us both? The chances of arriving at consensus about
anything beyond the most basic of biological needs by rational
argument alone appear to be slight.[20]

In his more recent writing, Habermas appears to accept the
validity of this criticism. He acknowledges that the ideal speech
situation is appropriate only for deriving abstract norms, while
there are more concrete political questions that cannot be
decided in this way. In particular he recognizes that there are real
differences of interest between sectional groups in present-day
society which cannot be reconciled through dialogue. 'When only
particular interests are at stake, conflicts of action cannot be
settled, even in ideal cases, through argumentation, but only
through bargaining and compromise.'[21] But this honest admis-
sion leaves Habermas's theory of politics—which, I should
repeat, remains implicit, since unlike Arendt he has no clear and

[19] J. Habermas, *Legitimation Crisis* (London: Heinemann, 1976), 108.
[20] Cf. S. Lukes, 'Of Gods and Demons: Habermas and Practical Reason', in J. B.
Thompson and D. Held (eds.), *Habermas: Critical Debates* (London: Macmillan, 1982).
For a sympathetic reading of Habermas which tries to deflect this line of attack, see S. K.
White, *The Recent Work of Jurgen Habermas* (Cambridge: Cambridge University Press,
1988), ch. 4.
[21] J. Habermas, *Autonomy and Solidarity*, ed. P. Dews (London: Verso, 1986), 176.

distinct conception of the political—in disarray. On the one hand we have the ideal speech situation as a criterion for the legitimacy of norms; on the other, we have a fairly straightforward endorsement of the interest-aggregation model of politics wherever sectional conflicts are involved. These two conceptions are not knitted together in any coherent fashion; we are not told which political disagreements are properly resolved by dialogue and which by bargaining and compromise.

IV

What, then, can we learn from Habermas's difficulties? Principally, I think, that a viable conception of politics as dialogue will need a sharper specification than Habermas provides of the proper *scope* of politics. It will need to move in a liberal direction by conceding that there is a range of issues which fall outside the ambit of political debate, not only on the grounds that this is important to personal freedom but also because the chances of a successful dialogue are actually improved if its scope is restricted. Two sorts of issues in particular should be excluded in this manner.

First, questions about everyday consumption—the food people should eat, the clothes they should wear, the forms of entertainment they should favour. These are matters that are both adequately and properly handled by market mechanisms; political dialogue serves to set the parameters of the market, thus regulating the resources people have available for consumption, but there should be no attempt to determine how these resources are to be converted into particular items. Not only would this offend against ideals of personal freedom and individuality, but it would be a fruitless enterprise. There is no chance of collectively persuading beer drinkers that wine is a better tipple, or jazz fans that rock music is really to be preferred. This is obvious enough, and requires saying only because talk in Habermasian vein about 'needs that can be communicatively shared' appears to overlook this extensive realm of tastes and desires in which political dialogue is simply out of place.

Second, questions of personal belief and morality—for instance religious convictions, and more generally the codes of

behaviour that people choose to follow in their private lives. Here
again, substantive dialogue would be both inappropriate and
pointless. The proper role of dialogue is to establish a framework
of toleration, marking out the area within which people should be
free to pursue ideals and beliefs whose value or validity is not
itself a matter for political discussion. Not that this is an easy task:
I shall return in the following chapter to the questions that
toleration poses from a socialist perspective. We must therefore
make a much sharper separation between personal morality and
politics than Habermas provides for with his ideal speech situation which, as already noted, is presented as an all-round device
for generating legitimate norms. If this is the point that Arendt is
making when she says that the aim of political dialogue is opinion
rather than truth, then her conception is to be preferred to the
excessive rationalism of Habermas.[22]

In contrast, dialogue may usefully proceed in two major areas.
The first is the identification of interests common to all members
of the collectivity in question, and specification of the best means
of realizing those interests. Included here would be debate about
the provision of public goods in the economists' sense, and also in
the somewhat wider sense discussed in Chapter 3. The second is
the adjudication of competing claims to resources in terms of
shared standards of justice; that is, the assessment of claims
advanced by groups or individuals that they are entitled to extra
benefits of one sort or another in terms of general criteria, such as
those of special need, which are common ground among the
participants in the dialogue in advance of the particular case at
issue. There is, of course, no guarantee that either of these forms
of dialogue will be successful. The identification of common
interests depends on there being some degree of convergence in
individuals' plans of life, such that they are able to identify general
conditions which are necessary to the success of all (or virtually
all) plans—environmental conditions, for instance. Equally, there
is no a priori reason to assume a convergence in standards of

[22] See H. Arendt, 'Truth and Politics' in P. Laslett and W. G. Runciman (eds.),
Philosophy, Politics and Society, 3rd ser. (Oxford: Blackwell, 1967). Habermas's response to
Arendt on this issue can be found in J. Habermas, 'Hannah Arendt's Communications
Concept of Power', *Social Research*, 44 (1977), 3–24. There is a helpful analysis, bringing
out the basic differences in the two theorists' understanding of the political, in M.
Canovan, 'A Case of Distorted Communication: A Note on Habermas and Arendt',
Political Theory, 11 (1983), 105–16.

justice. But it is far more likely that agreement can be reached in these areas than over questions of personal taste or conviction.

What does it mean for dialogue to be successful, and what should happen when it fails? Without attempting a precise answer to the first question, one can say roughly that political dialogue succeeds when a proposal emerges that commands the support of a large majority, and which the minority can also accept—that is, although they are not in favour of the proposal itself, they grasp the reasons behind it, and do not regard them as outlandish. If no such consensus emerges, then a decision must still eventually be taken by majority vote (subject to qualifications to be introduced in Chapter 12). It is not a necessary part of the dialogue view that the status quo should prevail unless and until a new consensus emerges.

Note, however, that such a dissensual outcome may arise in two different ways. One involves a sincere difference in opinion, where attitudes eventually crystallize around separate poles. Here the dialogue has still probably done useful work in refining the opinions that end up in the majority. The other, more sinister, occurs when opinions, at least on one side of the debate, are really dictated by interests. This sabotages the dialogue model, for, as Elster has pointed out,[23] a combination of disinterested dialogue and interest promotion may produce even less satisfactory results than straightforward interest-bargaining all round. I return to the issue of degeneration at the end of the chapter.

There is a further respect in which Habermas (and a similar point could be made about Arendt)[24] makes the requirements of dialogue more arduous than they need to be. His discoursers are conceived simply as rational agents, constrained only by the demands that language use itself places on their reasoning. They are not seen as belonging from the outset to a particular society with a distinct cultural tradition.[25] They cannot appeal in their

---

[23] J. Elster, *Sour Grapes* (Cambridge: Cambridge University Press, 1983), 38–9.

[24] As indicated above, Arendt sees political dialogue as occurring between individuals held together only by the force of mutual promises. She stresses the *originality* of political activity: the chance it affords of breaking with the past and starting something new. This conception appears to exclude the possibility of dialogue that involves the interpretation of a shared tradition.

[25] Habermas appears to accept the force of this observation in his more recent work; see e.g. 'A Reply to My Critics', in Thompson and Held, *Habermas*, and the Editor's Introduction to Habermas, *Autonomy and Solidarity*, esp. pp. 18–20.

dialogue to the received opinions of the community as carrying any sort of weight. They are, in other words, seen as Kantian moral agents, legislating for the whole of mankind. Against this, it seems clear to me that a successful form of dialogue would have to draw heavily on the ethical traditions of the participants, which would form a point of reference to which all speakers could appeal. It is important to recall, therefore, that the political dialogue we are envisaging takes place between the citizens of a nation-state, bound together by a common public culture. Of course ethical traditions are never homogeneous, and there will always be room for speakers to offer conflicting interpretations; but at least these interpretations are interpretations of *something* which can be presumed to be common ground among all participants.[26]

V

Even if we can specify the subject-matter of political dialogue in a way that does not exclude a reasoned consensus emerging from initially conflicting opinions, there may still be serious doubt whether *politics* is an appropriate way of arriving at such a consensus. We have become accustomed, in this century, to thinking of politics as a sphere in which emotional and affective thought-processes predominate to the detriment of rational argument, a view for which there appears to be ample empirical evidence. Joseph Schumpeter summed up a whole body of literature when he wrote: 'The typical citizen drops down to a lower level of mental performance as soon as he enters the political field. He argues and analyses in a way which he would readily recognize as infantile within the sphere of his real interests.'[27]

Now we might accept Schumpeter's verdict on the citizen's

[26] It follows from this that when the aim of dialogue is said to be a *rational* consensus, what is meant is that the participants adhere to the consensus for good reasons, and also that they have arrived at their opinions by rational means—i.e. by reflecting critically on the range of arguments advanced in the debate. Rationality rules out, for instance, the manipulation of opinion that occurs when A succeeds in getting B to accept a position for some specious reason. But rational consensus does *not* imply that the reasons which finally count with the members of a particular collectivity are universal reasons, in the sense of reasons which must weigh with any intelligent being.

[27] J. A. Schumpeter, *Capitalism, Socialism and Democracy* 5th edn. (London: Allen and Unwin, 1976), 262.

current performance while finding his overall position damagingly circular. The ordinary citizen, on Schumpeter's view, is fit only to choose between competing teams of leaders, not to debate and decide policy. But since he is currently given no opportunity to debate and decide, why should we expect him to form reasoned opinions on matters over which he has no influence? The resolution of political issues, after all, often requires a great deal of research and cogitation. Normally we should expect people to concentrate their time and energy in areas where they can make some impact. But to this it might be objected on Schumpeter's behalf that no ordinary citizen in a mass public can anticipate making more than the tiniest impact on collective decisions. Neither his voice nor his vote can be more than a drop in the ocean.

Clearly, if citizens take an instrumental view of political activity, assessing each intervention through a calculation of its likely costs and benefits, this objection will hold, and the division of labour between leaders and ordinary citizens that Schumpeter describes will represent a sensible economy. But it is a thin view of rationality that reduces all rational action to instrumental action.[28] Indeed, it is doubtful whether present-day democracies could subsist on instrumental rationality alone: as has often been pointed out, even the decision to vote in elections is hard to make sense of in strict cost–benefit terms. To some extent already, citizens are prepared to acknowledge political responsibility, that is to behave as though their own ballot was going to decide the outcome. The dialogue model is in one respect more demanding than this, for it requires citizens to think responsibly about a whole range of issues, as opposed to reaching an on-balance verdict about two or more packages of policies offered by parties. It demands that more time and attention be devoted to politics. At the same time, the process of debate itself applies a certain kind of moral pressure to participants. People who are going to stand up and argue for positions have to be prepared to offer supporting reasons of a general kind, connecting the policy they favour to an

[28] In particular such a reduction would exclude most principled moral behaviour. For discussion of the limits of instrumental rationality, see Elster, *Sour Grapes* pt. i; A. Sen, 'Rational Fools: A Critique of the Behavioural Foundations of Economic Theory', *Philosophy and Public Affairs*, 6 (1977), 317–44 repr. in *Choice, Measurement and Welfare* (Oxford: Blackwell, 1982); M. Hollis, *Models of Man* (Cambridge: Cambridge University Press, 1977), ch 6.

idea of justice or common interest.[29] This in itself requires them to think through the ramifications of their position, if they are not going merely to look foolish. Furthermore, people will be answerable for their views, in the sense that if the policies they have advocated prove to be disastrous, others will later remind them of this fact. Although neither of these factors *guarantees* responsibility, both will encourage it.

It may, however, seem that the sheer size of modern states defeats these arguments. It has for centuries been an axiom of political science that participatory politics of the type I have been describing could only exist in small republics. Aristotle, who can plausibly be seen as the founding father of the tradition, in particular for the connection he drew between man's membership of the *polis* and his capacities for speech and moral knowledge, likened the concord (*homonoia*) that exists between good citizens to a species of friendship. *Homonoia* means practical agreement about matters of common concern among people who know one another—something more than mere convergence of judgements.[30] Aristotle therefore took it for granted that the *polis* must be a city-state of modest size, not only for the physical reason that all citizens must be able to assemble within earshot of one another in order to debate, but so that they should form a society of friends rather than strangers.[31] This tradition extended down at least as far as Rousseau, whose *Social Contract* was based on the same assumption that citizens ought to know one another.

But the augustness of this tradition should not lead us to conclude that intimacy is always an asset from the point of view of political dialogue. Remember that the aim of dialogue is not consensus at any price, but rational consensus—i.e. an informed collective judgement based on premises that all can assent to. In very small groups, pressures to conform may silence dissent prematurely, with the result that proposals are never given a

[29] See R. Goodin, 'Laundering Preferences', sec. 3 in J. Elster and A. Hylland (eds.), *Foundations of Social Choice Theory* (Cambridge: Cambridge University Press, 1986); and Elster, *Sour Grapes*, 35–7. Elster does, however, go on to express some doubts about the strength of this argument. The questions raised on pp. 37–42 of his book are crucial for the dialogue conception of politics.

[30] Aristotle, *Nicomachean Ethics*, trans. J. A. K. Thomson (London: Allen and Unwin, 1953), 243–4.

[31] This aspect is well brought out in R. Beiner, *Political Judgement* (London: Methuen, 1983), ch 4.

proper critical assessment. This is the phenomenon of 'group-think', an idea used by the American psychologist Janis to explain various catastrophic decisions made by small committees responsible for US foreign policy. The characteristics of groupthink that Janis points to include the filtering out of new information that would upset the policy already favoured by a majority of the group, social pressures exerted upon those who advance vigorous dissenting arguments, and an unquestioning belief in the morality of collective decisions.[32] It may seem that Janis's examples are drawn from groups too small to be relevant to our question. But it is interesting here to compare Jane Mansbridge's study of town meetings in a New England town of around five hundred people.[33] Mansbridge notes that the mode of decision-making was largely consensual; but she also notes that to some extent conflicts of interests were artificially suppressed, in order to forestall rifts that might damage the social fabric of the community. She observes, too, that some inhabitants of the town avoided taking part in the meetings, preferring not to be drawn into potentially rancorous and divisive argument. This suggests that groups held together literally by friendship are not likely to be optimal for rational political dialogue. Such dialogue needs to be impersonal, in the sense that hearers should be moved only by the force of the arguments advanced, and speakers should not be inhibited from expressing their sincerely held views by personal loyalties. As dialogue proceeds, people will build up political relationships: they will find that they are closer in basic outlook to some speakers than to others; some participants are proved to be shrewd judges of events, others less so; and so forth. But these relationships are best kept separate from more intimate social relationships, in which other criteria come into play: personal compatibilities, common tastes and pursuits. A tightly knit community is for this reason not necessarily the best basis for political discussion. Its members will find it difficult to maintain the social distance that impersonal dialogue requires.

---

[32] I. Janis, *Groupthink*, 2nd ed. (Boston: Houghton Mifflin, 1982), esp. ch. 8.
[33] J. J. Mansbridge, *Beyond Adversary Democracy* (Chicago and London: University of Chicago Press, 1983).

VI

This further implies that the dialogue conception of politics may be less hostile to a certain sort of representation than we might at first imagine. Representation allows a political forum of a size small enough to allow genuine dialogue to occur to be formed out of a larger community, at the same time allowing political relationships to develop separately from social relationships in general. The usual objection to representation is of course that it confines dialogue to those who are chosen to serve. Perhaps it might be possible to circumvent this objection by ensuring that people took it in turns to act as representatives—say via a system of sortition (random lottery), the device used routinely in antiquity to select individuals for public service.[34] This would not be representation as it is normally now understood: the person selected would not be asked to represent the opinions or interests of any specific constituency, but simply to act as a 'representative person' for the whole collectivity in question. The deliberative assembly would be a microcosm of the wider community. Provided that those not currently serving as representatives could continue to be drawn into the debate as listeners, encouraged by the thought that it would sooner or later be their turn to participate actively, we could envisage the dialogue successfully discharging its legitimating function.

It is still much easier to think of this solution as working on the scale of classical Athens or Rousseau's Geneva than of the modern nation-state. Whereas in the former a single deliberative assembly could serve for the whole polity, in a modern state we would need to envisage primary assemblies at local level, and then further tiers of representation, perhaps at regional and national levels. Representatives at these higher levels would serve as carriers of the judgements reached in the primary assemblies: the standard argument against mandating representatives to vote for specific policies, which has some validity when what is being

---

[34] For instance the Athenian council was chosen in this way; see A. H. M. Jones, *Athenian Democracy* (Oxford: Blackwell, 1964), p. 105. There has recently been renewed interest in sortition after centuries of neglect; see J. Burnheim, *Is Democracy Possible?* (Oxford: Polity Press, 1985); Barber, *Strong Democracy*, ch. 10; and Jon Elster's Tanner Lectures, University of Oxford, 1987.

transmitted by the deputy is merely an aggregate of privately formed opinions, has far less weight in the case of collective views that have already been dialogically formed. On the other hand, we ought not to rule out the possibility that fresh arguments might be produced in the higher level assembly which would lead the deputy rationally to revise his view, so strict mandating is excluded. Under these circumstances the representative would be obliged on returning to his primary assembly to explain his change of judgement. But clearly the distance we have unavoidably now introduced between the primary forum and the eventual policy decision brings with it the possibility of alienation between centre and periphery, as well as the more mundane difficulty that particular representatives may not act as conscientious servants of those they represent.

The nation-state brings with it not only problems of size, but of diversity of interests. We must expect the members of a modern state, left to their own devices, to form themselves into factional groups on the basis of occupational, leisure and other interests, moral causes, and so forth, and to press these objectives politically. I assume that it would be unthinkable to attempt to suppress these associations.[35] The strength of the interest-aggregation conception is that it takes this fact for granted and tries to create a common interest out of the diversity of partial interests by devising suitable political machinery. The dialogue conception, by contrast, must try to separate a person's role as participant in the public dialogue from his role as promoter of a particular interest. It cannot deny the latter role: particular interests are, after all, in large measure the raw material of politics, the claims that need to be adjudicated in terms of shared standards of justice. There has to be a mechanism whereby these claims are brought into the political arena. The problem is to prevent the advocate's role from taking over the judge's. How can we create an environment in which people see it as their business to stand back from the particular interests with which they are associated and to act as representatives of the public as a whole, assessing particular claims from a detached point of view?

One inviting way forward is to take up Hayek's suggestion of a constitutional arrangement which, in effect, cordons dialogue

---

[35] This issue is explored more fully in the following chapter.

and interest-aggregation into two separate compartments.[36] Hayek proposes one body to enact legislation—meaning, general rules applicable to an indefinite number of future cases—and a second body to process requests for specific government funds and services. The first body could not dispense aid, the second could not prohibit conduct of any kind. This appears to recognize, realistically, that governments cannot avoid being subject to lobbying by various particular interests, while reserving an arena in which more abstract principles of justice can be brought into play. The fatal theoretical weakness in Hayek's proposal, however, is his assumption that legislation is not itself a distributive activity, i.e. an activity which potentially always has a differential impact on different sections of society. So the idea that interest groups will channel their efforts entirely towards the second chamber, or that members of the first will be oblivious to distributive considerations when debating legislation, is unfounded.

What *can* be salvaged from Hayek's proposal, on the other hand, is the thought that political dialogue stands a better chance of success in so far as the questions under consideration are of a general and long-term kind, so that their net impact on particular groups is less clear-cut. I take it this was Rousseau's thought when he maintained 'that the general will, to be truly what it is, must be general in its purpose as well as in its nature; . . . and that it loses its natural rectitude when it is directed towards any particular and circumscribed object . . .'[37] It follows from this that the dialogue conception demands a differentiated and therefore a constitutional form of government in which, in particular, a distinction is made between legislation of a general nature and the application of that legislation to particular cases, which is better devolved to specialist administrative bodies. In this way a case could be made out for the separation of powers, here primarily seen not as a device for the protection of individual citizens, but as a way of providing the preconditions for successful dialogue in the legislative assembly.

Ultimately, however, politics as dialogue has to rely on the

---

[36] See F. A. Hayek, *Law, Legislation and Liberty*, vol. iii. *The Political Order of a Free People* (London: Routledge and Kegan Paul, 1979), ch. 17.

[37] J.-J. Rousseau, *The Social Contract*, trans. M. Cranston (Harmondsworth: Penguin, 1968), 75.

prevalence of a political culture in which disinterested debate on public matters is taken as the norm. We shall look in the next chapter at ways of protecting such a culture from degeneration. There is, however, no ultimate guarantee that these attempts will succeed, and this may account for the resigned tone that from time to time creeps into the writing of advocates of this conception. To cite Rousseau again:

when the state, on the brink of ruin, can maintain itself only in an empty and illusory form, when the social bond is broken in every heart, when the meanest interest impudently flaunts the sacred name of the public good, then the general will is silenced: everyone, animated by secret motives, ceases to speak as a citizen any more than as if the state had never existed; and the people enacts in the guise of laws iniquitous decrees which have private interests as their only end.[38]

In such moments of pessimism, we may fall back on to interest-aggregation as the most feasible form of politics in a large and diverse society, and look for ways in which the effectiveness and fairness of the aggregation process can be increased. Certainly, if the choice lay between interest-aggregation and a crude form of majoritarianism in which majorities simply imposed their preferences on minorities without engaging in genuine dialogue, there would be good reason to prefer interest-aggregation.[39] Much will depend here on how seriously we take the claim that politics as dialogue, when successful, allows people to identify with public decisions even in cases where they have opposing interests or private opinions, and so reconciles them to their social environment. Liberals, who tend to regard the human subject as constituted by private aims and interests, may not be very impressed by this claim. Socialists, on the other hand, for the reasons given in earlier chapters, must look to politics as the arena in which collective identity and will are expressed; they, I suggest, must pursue the promise of the dialogue conception, notwithstanding

[38] Ibid. 150.
[39] I have developed this argument in 'The Competitive Model of Democracy', in G. Duncan (ed.), *Democratic Theory and Practice* (Cambridge: Cambridge University Press, 1983), esp. sec. v. That essay was more pessimistic about the chances of successful dialogue than the present chapter, and urged the merits of interest-aggregation from a liberal perspective.

the formidable difficulties it faces under modern conditions,[40] and continue to search for the constitutional arrangements which give it the greatest chance of success.

[40] In stressing the difficulties, I should not wish to overlook compensating advantages which may make dialogue more feasible: generally higher levels of education, the development of mass media which allow political debates to be transmitted nationally, and so forth. Radicals often focus optimistically on the technical feasibility of participatory politics, while overlooking cultural factors in modern societies which threaten to destroy its virtue. I shall leave it to others to identify the appropriate technology for democratic dialogue.

11

TOLERATION

I

Let me begin with a traveller's tale, set in the mid-1980s, that may bring out the political relevance of the topic addressed in this chapter. A visitor from the West to, let us say, Moscow will observe a number of unfamiliar features in his new surroundings. He will notice, for example, the absence of *The Times*—unless he happens to be on the streets in the early hours of the morning, during that brief interlude between one van delivering the papers and another collecting them for transmission to the government department that has purchased all the copies. This he will probably have anticipated. He may, however, be a little more struck by the lack of cultural variety in his surroundings. There are no ostentatious youth subcultures; no quarters of the city where ethnic shops and restaurants flourish; no streets where gay pride is on show, or bookshops barred to men. Religious practices have not entirely disappeared, but church and synagogue are very largely the preserve of the elderly and there are no orange-robed monks parading in the streets. In short, the impression received is of a society where not only opinion but also culture is pressed as far as possible into a single mould that bears the label 'socialism'.

Back home again, and opening *The Times* over breakfast, our traveller is quite likely to be confronted by a large advertisement from the Greater London Council, fighting for its survival, and the standard-bearer of what is currently referred to as 'municipal socialism'. The ad may perhaps be the one that lists 167 organizations whose survival (it is claimed) has been ensured by cash handouts from the Council. Looking down the list he finds the Black Londoners' Action Group, the Lesbian Feminist Writers' Conference, the Union of Turkish Workers, the London Gay Teenage Group, the Chilean Cultural Committee, the Conference of Ethnic Minority Senior Citizens—to say nothing of the Welsh Harp Society, and many other such organizations.

This is a puzzling contrast. In the East, socialists discourage minority cultures, either suppressing them forcibly or exerting pressure of a more discreet kind (in the job market, for instance) to dissuade potential adherents. In the West, socialists encourage a hundred flowers to bloom—with cash subsidies. Now there are two simple-minded responses to this paradox that I want to reject. One maintains that what our traveller has experienced is nothing more than the contrast between socialists in and out of (effective) power. Socialists sign up racial, sexual, religious, and other minorities in the service of the revolution; once the great event has occurred, they reveal their true colours and stamp down hard on their erstwhile allies. That is the first response. The second, diametrically opposed, maintains that cultural oppression in the East has nothing to do with socialism as such. It is an excrescence resulting from the economic backwardness of the socialist states, from the despotic political tradition of Russia, or from some other such factor. Authentic socialism, it is implied, is really a superior version of liberalism. Despite liberal claims that cultural diversity flourishes best under liberal institutions, it is in fact only with a socialist transformation that hitherto repressed minority cultures will enjoy equal status with the dominant culture. Socialism will deliver what liberalism only promises.

In my view this second response is no more adequate than the first. It fails to consider how a shift from liberal to socialist principles changes the manner in which the issue of toleration is addressed. The task of this chapter is to examine that issue in the light of the ideas developed in the last two chapters: the idea that citizenship in a nation-state may provide citizens with a common identity that overcomes the divisions of private and economic life; and the idea that this identity can be made active through a continuing political dialogue on matters of justice and common interest to which each citizen is potentially able to contribute. If we embrace these ideas (as I have argued socialists should), to what extent can we consistently advocate toleration of minority beliefs and practices? How would a socialist policy of toleration differ from a liberal one? Before getting to grips with these questions, I need to say a brief word about the idea of toleration itself.

First, although the issue of toleration first arose in relation to matters of belief, especially religious belief, it clearly extends to many other aspects of human life—including, for instance, personal dress and appearance, social practices of various kinds, forms of art, and so on. In all these areas, toleration means permitting activities to flourish that diverge from those that the tolerator himself regards as correct or valuable. Second, although the simplest way to be intolerant is to suppress the disapproved-of activities by force—that is, either through direct physical force, or through the force of law—toleration as an ideal appears also to exclude other ways of discouraging deviant behaviour; for instance, withholding benefits or services from those who engage in certain practices in cases where there is no internal connection between the practice itself and the benefit or service that is refused (an obvious case would be the exclusion of Catholics from public office in England prior to 1829). Third, to extend this line of thought still further, the values that underlie toleration appear to point beyond toleration itself towards the idea of a society that is equally hospitable to all the beliefs and activities that its members espouse, at least in so far as these beliefs and activities do not impinge adversely on the lives of other members; in other words, to an image of society as a neutral arena in which the success or failure of different forms of life depends only on factors internal to those forms of life, with social institutions themselves not being biased in favour of any practices in particular. Although a view of this kind does admittedly go beyond mere toleration, if we base our commitment to toleration on, for instance, the idea of respect for persons, this seems to require arranging our institutions so that, as far as possible, they do not discriminate between the plans of life that people have chosen—since discrimination would imply that the favoured plans of life and/or their adherents were seen as more worthy of regard than the disfavoured.[1]

We have already, in Chapter 3, explored some of the difficulties in implementing this ideal of institutional neutrality. I draw attention to these matters here because, in approaching the question of socialism and toleration, it seems preferable to begin with as broad an understanding of toleration as possible. Socialists, after all, often point out that to treat issues of freedom and

---

[1] For an example of this position, see A. Weale, 'Toleration, Individual Differences and Respect for Persons', in J. Horton and S. Mendus (eds.), *Aspects of Toleration* (London: Methuen, 1985).

tolerance in relation only to legal permissions and prohibitions is to ignore all those other factors—economic factors especially—that promote or discourage particular practices and forms of thought.[2] A tolerant society must do more than provide the legal freedom to engage in unconventional activities. But now we must begin asking whether socialists ought to value unlimited toleration in the first place.

II

The central area of difficulty is not that of freedom of speech and its limits. Far more important, for the socialist, is the issue of how to respond to cultural diversity. By cultural diversity I mean the co-existence within a society of distinct patterns of belief and behaviour such that normally a person is a participant only in one subculture. These subcultures are sustained by social pressures of various kinds; people may be born into them or decide to become participants at some later point, but once inside it becomes costly to move out, in the sense that one will be regarded as a traitor or a lost sheep by those remaining inside whose comradeship one values. (I don't mean that the costs are always deliberately imposed.) Now why should cultural diversity pose any problem for socialist ideals? In the light of the discussion in Chapter 9, the answer is easily anticipated. Subcultures threaten to undermine the overarching sense of identity that socialists are looking for. They are liable to do so in two ways: they give participants a narrower focus of loyalty that may pre-empt commitment to the wider community; and by way of reaction people outside a particular sub culture may find it difficult to identify with those who are seen as in some way separated off.

These claims are made by way of hypothesis at the moment, and I shall return to the arguments for and against them later. Let me now put some flesh on these rather abstract bones by considering the example of ethnicity, which I think poses the most acute problems for socialism. Ethnicity involves two elements: first, a belief in common descent, leading to a historically given identity; second, possession of a common culture, involving belief

[2] See G. Duncan and J. Street, 'Marxism and Tolerance' in S. Mendus (ed.), *Justifying Toleration* (Cambridge: Cambridge University Press, 1988).

and behaviour that sets the ethnic group off from the larger society to which it belongs. Precisely how this cultural separation is manifested will vary a great deal from case to case. In some cases the key element will be language (French and English communities in Canada), in some cases religion (Hindus, Muslims, Sikhs in India), in some cases the weight will largely be carried by descent plus social rituals (Jews and Italians in America). Race may become an element, but it is important not to confuse race with ethnicity as such. Ethnicity is centrally a matter of a person's beliefs about his cultural identity, whereas race is assigned 'objectively' without reference to belief.[3] In theory it is always possible to discard an ethnic identity by ceasing to have the beliefs in question. In practice there may be difficulties posed by other people's beliefs. A black Englishman, for example, who wants to see himself simply as English may be hindered by others, black and white, who identify him as a West Indian. Even here, however, it is clear that in the last resort no one can have an ethnic identity foisted on him against his will.

As far as I can see there is nothing in the idea of ethnicity as such that a socialist should find objectionable. Historically, many socialists (like many liberals) have been inclined to see ethnic identities as involving a sort of false consciousness, to be dissolved away painlessly with the coming of a Rational Society. But the cause of socialism is not harmed by abandoning this profoundly mistaken belief. Socialists can afford to be agnostic as to whether it is intrinsically better to have a culturally homogeneous society or a society with a rich ethnic patterning, just as they can over other questions of private taste and belief. It is not ethnicity as such that should concern them.[4] What they should be concerned about are the possible political effects of ethnic divisions.

There are two, partially separable, sources of difficulty. One is the relation between ethnic identity and communal identity *qua* member of the wider society. There is no reason, of course, why narrower loyalties should not serve to strengthen wider ones, as

---

[3] I put 'objectively' in scare quotes to accommodate the view that racial distinctions are socially constructed. Even on this view, the contrast I am drawing still holds. Once there is agreement on the characteristics by virtue of which a person is assigned to this or that racial group, racial identity becomes an objective matter.

[4] They may of course be concerned about particular ethnic practices, such as the subordination of women in traditional Muslim families, that appear to be incompatible with the general principles underlying socialism.

commonly happens in the case of local and national attachments. Burke made this point:

We begin our public affections in our families. No cold relation is a zealous citizen. We pass on to our neighbourhoods, and our habitual provincial connexions . . . so many little images of the great country in which the heart found something which it could fill. The love to the whole is not extinguished by this subordinate partiality. Perhaps it is a sort of elemental training to those higher and more large regards, by which alone men come to be affected, as with their own concern, in the prosperity of a kingdom.[5]

But here it is important that the small should be made in the image of the great. With ethnic identities this may not always be the case. The clearest example is where the ethnic identity contains within it a loyalty to some other community in another place. Familiar examples here would be Jews in the Diaspora and Israel, the Asian communities in Britain and parts of the Indian subcontinent, and more generally people who, say as a result of the redrawing of national boundaries in war, find themselves on the wrong side of a border. But the problem goes somewhat further than this. Communal identity is not merely an abstract notion; it needs to be embodied in particular symbols, practices and beliefs. Where one ethnic group is dominant, it is almost certain that the form in which communal identity is expressed will embody elements of the majority culture. Where the dominant group is Christian, for example, Christian rituals will be used to mark important national occasions (for instance, remembrance of war victims). To the extent that maintaining ethnic identity requires rejecting such cultural practices, members of minority groups will be alienated from the rituals, and will find it correspondingly harder to identify strongly with the wider community.

I do not want to make more of these points than they deserve. It is clearly possible to feel strong loyalties to more than one place; for example, it is a matter of common observation that many Jewish people are strongly committed both to Israel and to the country they inhabit. Equally it may be possible to forge a national identity that draws rather little on the beliefs and practices of any

[5] E. Burke, *Reflections on the Revolution in France* (London: Dent, 1967), 193.

one ethnic group in particular. In some respects the US might serve as an example here, since it combines deep ethnic cleavages with a strong sense of national allegiance.[6] Here the focus of loyalty is fairly abstract: the Constitution and the 'American way' (involving opportunities for individuals to strive for success), rather than any more substantial vision of what it means to be an American. It would therefore be wrong to regard the identity problem as completely insoluble; but equally wrong to suppose that there is no problem in the first place.

The second difficulty posed by ethnicity is one of distributional conflict. On the assumption that the state will be a major distributor of resources, whether in the form of direct employment, or capital investment, or of welfare benefits such as subsidized housing (an assumption which all socialists—even those who endorse the extensive use of markets—must make), ethnic divisions are likely to lead to political competition to enhance the share of resources flowing to each group. Two main outcomes are on the cards, depending on whether or not a single ethnic group can establish a dominant position. If it can, a likely outcome is exploitation of the minority community or communities by the dominant community, a case classically illustrated by Northern Ireland in the period before direct rule was imposed; the power of the state is used to direct a disproportionate share of resources to members of the majority group. If no single group is dominant, the response may well be a general agreement, born of mistrust, to starve the state proper of resources, and instead to organize distribution on a community basis, either through local government or through voluntary organizations within each ethnic group. In this way each group retains control of the resources that broadly speaking it raises itself—a solution that, as I noted in Chapter 9, does nothing to correct underlying imbalances in the living standards of the various communities. This is often advanced as at least a partial explanation of the low level of

---

[6] The difficulty with using the US as an example is that national loyalty rarely appears to translate into effective political action on behalf of fellow citizens, as I note below in relation to welfare provision. From a *practical* point of view ethnic affiliations remain paramount, no matter how strongly American hearts may beat when flags are raised or anthems sung. Perhaps the key to the paradox can be found in Alasdair MacIntyre's observation that Americans inhabit 'a country and a culture whose *Sittlichheit* just is *Moralität*'; in other words, one in which the cause of the nation itself is identified with a liberal morality of individual rights. See A. MacIntyre, *Is Patriotism a Virtue?* Lindley Lecture (University of Kansas: 1984), 19.

welfare expenditure on the part of the federal government in the US.[7]

Besides these two unattractive possibilities, there is a third, namely consociational democracy (a model developed by the Dutch political scientist Arend Lijphart to explain the relative stability of democratic regimes in socially divided European nations, especially Austria, Belgium, The Netherlands, and Switzerland).[8] The essence of the consociational model is collaboration between political élites representing the various communities to ensure that each has its vital interests safeguarded when government policy is made. It may also involve some devolution of decision-making to political bodies in which one or other community is dominant—e.g. a form of federalism. In this way, it appears, distributional conflict can be handled in such a way that each community gets its fair share of resources, with the state still playing a large role in resource allocation. The magnitude of welfare state expenditure in The Netherlands and Belgium could be cited as a supporting example.

For a socialist, this third alternative is clearly preferable to either majority rule by the dominant community or contraction of the distributive role of central government. The cost, however, is rule by élites. The consociational solution depends on bargaining between a small number of decision-makers, each holding an informal power of veto in case a decision appears to him to damage seriously the interests of the group he represents. This conflicts in two respects with the ideal I have been sketching of a society whose political decisions are made through a dialogue in which each citizen is potentially a participant. First, the form of politics involved is interest-bargaining. Resources are allocated to each ethnic group on the implicit understanding that its representatives are willing in their turn to support policies that favour other groups when necessary. Although by this means a rough form of justice may emerge, such an outcome depends entirely on the balance of power between the various groups. Second, the bargaining can only be carried on successfully if the

---

[7] For a good presentation of this argument, see G. M. Klass, 'Explaining America and the Welfare State: An Alternative Theory', *British Journal of Political Science*, 15 (1985), 427–50.

[8] A. Lijphart, *Democracy in Plural Societies* (New Haven and London: Yale University Press, 1977). For a critical appraisal, see B. Barry, 'Political Accommodation and Consociational Democracy', *British Journal of Political Science*, 5 (1975), 477–505.

spokesmen for each community are left to act unhindered by their clients. Control from below would threaten accommodations that can be reached only through personal contact between representatives, and that cannot normally be spelt out in public. The consociational model excludes widespread participation in public affairs. Thus for socialists it can only be seen as a second-best solution, a realistic way of coping with cleavages that forestall the emergence of a more participatory form of democracy.

If we want both to have democracy of a more radical kind and envisage a fairly extensive redistributive role for the state, it is essential that people should participate politically, not as advocates for this or that sectional group, but as citizens whose main concerns are fairness between different sections of the community and the pursuit of common ends. This means that participants must share a common identity as citizens that is stronger than their separate identities as members of ethnic or other sectional groups. Thus we now have a second argument to set alongside the first. The first argument, to recall, was that ethnic divisions may directly undermine the overall sense of common membership that socialists value; the second is that they may foster a factionalized form of politics which, at best, amounts to horse-trading between the various groups. The solution to both problems must lie in creating and maintaining an overarching identity which is more salient for all communities than their separate ethnic identities. But this immediately raises a further problem, addressed in the remainder of the chapter, namely whether there must be any limits to the toleration that can be extended to subcultures and their expression.

III

There are two areas in which socialists ought to value toleration at least as strongly as liberals. One is freedom of speech, in particular freedom to express dissenting political opinions. The dialogic conception of politics outlined in the last chapter assumes that each person can participate in political debate on an equal footing, and with an equally authentic voice. Plainly, any bar on the expression of political views would offend against that assumption and discriminate against those whose opinions were suppressed.[9] Moreover the dialogue itself stands to benefit from the introduction of fresh opinions. The aim of dialogue is not simply to allow participants to air their views, but to reach the best possible decision on matters of general concern. Provided that political debate really is debate—provided those engaged in it are willing to modify their views when superior contrary arguments are produced—the greater the pool of opinion on which it draws, the greater the chance of finding this best solution. So freedom of expression is not only a claim that individuals can make in their capacity as equal citizens, but a precondition for successful dialogue itself. In so far as a socialist policy will differ from current liberal practices in this area, it will be in the direction of providing each person with the resources to participate effectively in political discussion—through education, access to information, and opportunities to use the media of communication to put his views across.[10]

The second area is what one might call the realm of private culture; how a person chooses to dress, what lifestyle he adopts, what sexual relationships he engages in, what religious beliefs he holds, and so forth. The reason for toleration here is simply that socialists hold no brief in this area; they recognize (or ought to recognize) the value of the private realm, but they have nothing directly to say about its substantive content. This point is sometimes expressed by saying that socialism embodies no conception of the good life. Such a formulation is potentially misleading, because, as I have been at pains to stress, socialism does contain a clear view about the importance of citizenship to human fulfilment; but it carries no judgements about specific modes of life within that setting.

There is, however, an important qualification to be entered here. Socialists may be indifferent to what occurs in the private realm itself, but they are plainly interested in the impact that private culture may have on the public realm. It is likely that particular subcultures will generate demands on the state for special forms of support—for legislation that makes it easier to

---

[9] I omit any discussion of the special case of views whose expression threatens to subvert the conditions for future dialogue. This is the familiar problem of whether toleration should be extended to the intolerant; my sense is that the socialist will address it in much the same terms as the liberal.

[10] For a fuller discussion of this point, see T. D. Campbell, *The Left and Rights* (London: Routledge and Kegan Paul, 1983), ch. 8.

engage in certain practices, or for financial assistance for modes of life (such as living on remote islands) that would otherwise be very costly. It is tempting to try to keep this particular genie very tightly stoppered up, to say that the proper distributive policy should be to give each person the same basic set of resources and leave it to him to decide what style of life to follow. But this response cannot really be sustained, for reasons that emerged in Chapter 3. It is impossible to specify a set of exchangeable resources that are equally basic for all modes of life in a culturally plural society.[11] Besides commodities, people will require, to varying degrees, relational and public goods, which in general cannot be provided other than by direct political means. It must therefore be open to those who share such a mode of life to make out a case for support in the political arena, a case that will ideally be judged according (a) to the depth of commitment to the mode of life that its adherents evince, and (b) to the reasonableness of the form of support requested. But this in turn implies that people may have to act politically as spokesmen for a particular form of private life, raising once again the spectre of a factionalized form of politics in which people participate not as citizens but as group representatives.

This places socialists in a quandary: they recognize (a) that it may well be desirable for many forms of private culture to flourish; b) that fairness may require differential support for these subcultures; and (c) that nevertheless politics should not take the form of bargaining between competing interests. To escape from it they need to rely on a sense of common citizenship that transcends cultural differences. But such an understanding of political life will not simply appear spontaneously; it must be fostered through appropriate background institutions. Here; at least, socialists have an advantage over liberals. For whereas liberals tend to regard cultural identities as given, or at least as created externally to the political system, socialists have usually possessed a stronger sense of the malleability of such identities, that is, the extent to which they can be created or modified

[11] Witness the criticisms attracted by Rawls's attempt to couch the problem of distributive justice in terms of a set of 'primary goods' that are supposed to be equally essential for each person's plan of life. Representative examples include B. Barry, *The Liberal Theory of Justice* (Oxford: Clarendon Press, 1973); M. Teitelman, 'The Limits of Individualism', *Journal of Philosophy*, 69 (1972), 545–56; A. Schwartz, 'Moral Neutrality and Primary Goods', *Ethics*, 83 (1972–3), 294–307.

consciously. The practical question is: which institutions are likely to be crucial in fostering the sense of citizenship?

IV

First, the institutions of politics themselves: how political activity is arranged will influence the way in which participants regard their roles. Consider as an example the impact such arrangements may have on political parties. Parties in their now familiar form have evolved as a direct response to electoral systems in which large constituencies of voters have to choose candidates to represent them without direct knowledge of the individuals in question. The institutions sketched in the last chapter would have representatives chosen by and from primary assemblies in which their qualities were better known, so the party as a device for mobilizing electoral support would become obsolete. Nevertheless, it is hard to conceive of political debate and decision-making in a large society without people who share, broadly speaking, the same set of beliefs forming organizations to promote them. How, from the point of view of citizenship, should we regard political parties in this broader sense?[12] There is no cause for concern in the case of parties that approximate to Burke's classical definition: 'a body of men united, for promoting by their joint endeavours the national interest, upon some particular principle in which they are all agreed'.[13] Such parties, to underline the point, are held together by principles, and their aim is to promote the public interest as it appears to them in the light of these principles. Very different considerations apply where parties become no more than umbrella organizations for advancing a range of sectional interests, or worse still for advancing one

[12] Some theorists of deliberative democracy argue that parties are essential to the proper functioning of democratic dialogue, since they increase the coherence of debate by crystallizing opinion around a limited range of alternative policies. For this view see B. Manin, 'On Legitimacy and Political Deliberation', *Political Theory*, 15 (1987), 338–68; J. Cohen and J. Rogers, *On Democracy* (New York: Penguin, 1983), ch. 6. Against this, however, must be set the fact that parties are likely to develop their own hierarchical structures, and political arguments will be distorted as they are turned into weapons in internal power struggles. On balance the citizenship ideal suggests a neutral response to parties of principle, neither positively encouraging them, nor attempting to hinder their formation.

[13] Burke, *Thoughts on the Present Discontents*, in *The Writings and Speeches of Edmund Burke*, vol. ii, ed. P. Langford (Oxford: Clarendon Press, 1981), 317.

particular sectional interest. In this case the party, instead of serving as a bridge between personal beliefs and public principles, will tend to strengthen sectional identities at the expense of shared ones. Suppose that someone belongs to a Muslim minority in a predominantly Christian society. If a party is formed that aims explicitly to promote the interests of Muslims, which he joins, he will find his political experience shaped by that purpose. He will interpret his political role as one of advancing a minority interest; he will not be encouraged to see himself as a citizen who has to make principled decisions on a wide range of issues facing his society as a whole.

Such possibilities are a proper cause of concern for socialists committed to the ideal of citizenship. Sectional parties are more corrosive of that ideal than simple interest groups, such as associations representing the workers in particular industries. In the latter case, we will always face the practical problem of encouraging the members of such associations to place their concerns as citizens over and above their concerns as interest spokesmen. But there is little real danger of the two roles being confused. Despite Charles Wilson's famous adage, it is unlikely that anyone will genuinely be unable to distinguish between the interests of car workers and the interests of his country. The menace of sectional parties, in contrast, is that they offer a political identity which can supplant citizenship. So although we should be completely tolerant and even-handed in our dealings with parties of principle, it is a legitimate aim of constitutional design to discourage sectional parties.

How, in practice, might this be done? It would probably be unwise to attempt to ban such parties outright, for two reasons. First, it is difficult to legislate for such prohibitions in a way that does not exclude legitimate forms of association. Second, sectional identities may already have become so strong that what we have is really two separate nationalities living side by side, in which case the best outcome is ultimately likely to be the secession of one community. Here a sectional party will be the natural expression of the national aspirations of the secessionist community. Short of an outright ban, however, it may be possible to discourage the growth of sectional parties by, for instance, disqualifying their members from serving as political representatives, by refusing to support their activities with public funds or tax concessions, and so forth.

Such policies will always be hard to implement fairly, and it is clearly preferable to belong to a society where citizen identity is so strong and/or sectional cleavages are so weak that they become unnecessary. Perhaps we should think of these provisions as reserve powers, contained in the constitution but only to be brought out if the political arena becomes factionalized. It is not part of my argument that socialists should seek out occasions on which to be intolerant, but it is important to see how the idea of citizenship we have been developing changes our view of toleration. In some respects, as I have argued already, it enlarges our understanding of what toleration requires; in other respects it narrows its scope, in principle at least.

V

Let me now turn to a second institutional locus that is likely to be important for citizenship, the education system. In particular, I want to ask how far socialists should go in embracing 'multi-cultural education', as it is often now called, given a society that is already culturally pluralistic.[14] Multi-cultural education may be interpreted in different ways. It may imply that children from all backgrounds should be introduced to the various cultures, systems of religious belief, etc., that are found in their society, with the aim of increasing mutual understanding and thereby tolerance. This seems a rather desirable goal, and may indeed indirectly help to foster a greater sense of unity between cultural groups. On the other hand, multi-cultural education may be taken to mean that the offspring of each culture should be instructed in that culture alone. Again that might seem unobjectionable, or even desirable if it referred only to matters that were essentially private (e.g. social mores or religious practices). It will be difficult, however, to keep these private questions separate from the broader issue of the group's relation to the wider society. How, in particular, will political education be handled? Will politics be looked at from the point of view of the cultural group, or will it be treated quite separately, from the standpoint of common citizenship? If the latter, how will the two visions of the

---

[14] The case for multi-cultural education is usefully presented in B. Parekh, 'The Concept of Multi-Cultural Education', in S. Modgil and G. Verma (eds.), *Multi-Cultural Education: The Interminable Debate* (London: Falmer Press, 1986).

child's place in the world—as Muslim, let us say, and as British—be harmonized?

It is interesting to see how this issue is skirted round in the recent Swann Report on the education of children from ethnic minority groups. Swann, it should be said at once, endorses the first of the two views of multi-cultural education sketched above.

In our view an education which seeks only to emphasize and enhance the ethnic group identity of a child, at the expense of developing both a national identity and indeed an international, global perspective, cannot be regarded as in any sense multicultural . . . We would instead wish to see schools encouraging the cultural development of all their pupils, both in terms of helping them to gain confidence in their own cultural identities while learning to respect the identities of other groups as equally valid in their own right.[15]

The question of political education is then raised, particularly in relation to the perceived alienation of young members of ethnic minorities from the political system. The problem is seen, however, as one of increasing their instrumental effectiveness as participants.

the political education offered to ethnic minority youngsters can play a major role in countering their sense of alienation, by informing them about the institutions and procedures available within the political framework for making their opinions known, and opening their minds to the possibility that existing practices may, and sometimes should, be altered or replaced. Effective political education can also provide ethnic minority youngsters with the skills necessary to participate in political activities, thus helping to channel their energies into positive rather than negative forms of expression.[16]

This is an impeccably liberal view. The state is a piece of machinery for producing policies favourable to this or that constituency, and here is a group who lack the information and skills to extract a fair deal from it; clearly, we must set about providing them. There is nothing wrong with this as far as it goes, but it makes no attempt to get to grips with the idea of citizenship and the beliefs that support it. Citizenship is not just a matter of

---

[15] *Education for All: The Report of the Committee of Inquiry into the Education of Children from Ethnic Minority Groups*, Cmnd. 9453 (London: HMSO, 1985), 322–3.
[16] Ibid. 339.

knowing how to be effective politically, but of identity and commitment. In order to see his fate as bound up with the fate of the rest of his people, a citizen must have some understanding of the collectivity to which loyalty is owed, which will normally include some understanding of its history. As I argued earlier, there cannot be a complete divorce between a person's public identity as a citizen and his private identity as a member of an ethnic group. Thus, whereas political education in the Swann view can be regarded as an extra element added on to a cultural education which tries to be neutral as between all cultures that happen to exist in a society, political education in this larger sense must try to shape cultural identities in the direction of common citizenship. It must try to present an interpretation of, let us say, Indian culture in Britain that makes it possible for members of the Indian community to feel at home in, and loyal to, the British state. In so far as there are elements in Indian culture that are at odds with such a reconciliation, the interpretation must be selective or, if you like, biased.

In case this should sound a conservative view, it may be worth reiterating the point that the sense of common identity which socialists wish to foster is not simply a historically given identity. Although historical continuity is normally to be welcomed rather than despised, since shared memories are a powerful force working for social unity, citizens will continually reshape their collective identity through democratic debate. The past is to be appropriated consciously rather than taken on board unconsciously. As new minority cultures appear, they may be expected to contribute to this reshaping. Thus the relationship between ethnic identity and national identity is not to be regarded as fixed; nor, therefore, should the content of political education.

Education does, in any case, pose in an acute form the issue of wider and narrower senses of toleration raised earlier in the chapter. In a narrow sense, educational toleration might simply mean that no pupil who held dissenting opinions was prevented from airing them in class; in a somewhat broader sense, that pupils were encouraged to respond critically to the views expressed in textbooks or by the teacher, rather than learning them by rote. Toleration in both these senses will contribute positively to democratic citizenship, since it will help to develop the intellectual and argumentative skills that future citizens will need in order to contribute effectively to political dialogue.[17] But we are still left with the question whether it is even possible, let alone desirable, to practise toleration in the widest sense in which it comes to mean neutrality between all the possible interpretations of the historical and political context in which the pupil finds himself. How, in subjects like politics and history, can we avoid slanting pupils' understandings in one direction or another, if only by the selection of what is taught?

Advocates of multi-cultural education seem to envisage a form of comparative study in which the history, culture, and politics of one's own nation are treated alongside those of many others, particularly of others with contrasting traditions.[18] The pupil is invited to identify with each in turn and to examine the remainder critically from that perspective. But it is very doubtful whether such proposals could be successfully implemented or, if they were, whether the outcome would genuinely be a neutral one. For the relationship between the (future) citizen and the history, etc., of his own country is not merely academic: an understanding of that history, etc., tells him (in part) who he is and how it is appropriate for him to behave. Were he really to achieve the detached perspective favoured by the multi-culturalist, he would *ipso facto* be alienated from the public culture of his own society—a free-floating, deracinated individual. This itself would be a politically charged outcome, albeit an improbable one.

The upshot is that in the case of educational subjects which have practical implications, such as politics and history, toleration in the strong sense in which it aspires to neutrality is impossible. The public culture and practices of the pupil's own society must occupy a privileged place in the syllabus. There is no question that he should be taught to study these things in a critical spirit. He should be made aware of different readings of the historical record and different interpretations of contemporary politics, and encouraged to form his own views. In this narrower sense, educational toleration is both possible and valuable. But socialists should not hesitate to abandon liberal aspirations to neutralist toleration, which appear very often to underlie proposals for

[17] See A. Gutmann, *Democratic Education* (Princeton: Princeton University Press, 1987), esp. chs. 2–3.
[18] See Parekh, 'The Concept of Multi-Cultural Education'.

multi-cultural education.[19] Recognizing that education in this area is unavoidably political, their aim should be to gear it to common citizenship—to producing citizens who have both the technical competence and the cultural understandings to participate as equals in political dialogue.

Let us return finally to our bewildered traveller and his experiences in Moscow and London. Which of these experiences represents the authentic face of socialism? Neither, according to the view I have been developing. There are no good grounds for socialists to follow the Eastern road, namely deliberate suppression of minority cultures within the boundaries of the state. Socialism, I have claimed, embodies no full-blown conception of the good life which might justify the imposition of one particular culture on all citizens. On the other hand, the view that socialist society should be no more than an arena in which many disparate forms of life co-exist is seriously flawed. It overlooks all the difficulties involved in creating and maintaining the kind of common identity that socialist principles require. This problem sets the parameters for the socialist view of toleration: there is no case for suppressing minority views and cultures, but at the same time the institutions of a socialist society should aim to foster a sense of common citizenship, which may in practice require some discrimination between cultures.[20] Whereas liberals attempt to formulate a policy of toleration which remains blind to the content of the beliefs and practices being tolerated, a socialist policy must take account of the interplay between public and private cultures. Citizen identity cannot be taken for granted, it may have to be protected against the encroachment of ethnic and other sectional loyalties.

[19] There is a splendid critique of liberal neutrality in education in Gutmann, *Democratic Education*, 33–41. Gutmann's book, which came into my hands just as my own was going to press, gives an excellent analysis of the kind of education that democratic citizenship requires.

[20] This conclusion also carries implications for the socialist movement. Although it may seem politically expedient to try to build a so-called rainbow coalition through a policy platform that appeals to the special interests of many diverse groups, it should be clear from what has been said in this chapter that a politics of this sort cannot provide the underpinning for a socialist state. The socialist movement must foreshadow in its own politics the ideal of citizenship that socialism itself demands.

THE SOCIALIST STATE

I

I have tried in the last three chapters to spell out the basic principles which ought to inform a socialist view of politics. In Chapter 9 I took up the socialist ideal of community and argued that the only feasible embodiment of overall community in the modern world was as citizenship in a nation state. In Chapter 10, I looked at alternative views of the political process, and argued that socialists ought to commit themselves to a conception of politics as a form of dialogue; I also began to explore the conditions under which political dialogue stood the greatest chance of success. In Chapter 11, I examined the implications of these principles for toleration, especially toleration of ethnic sub-cultures, and concluded that a socialist policy of toleration would depart from standard liberal practice in areas in which private culture might make a damaging impact on the public culture that sustains citizenship.

My aim now is to apply these principles to the socialist state—to ask, in short, what the functions of the state should be in the model of socialism I am outlining, and how the state should be constituted in order to discharge those functions. I shall not attempt to spell out in detail the institutional framework that would be required. This would be a fruitless exercise, because the outcome must depend on local circumstances—on the political traditions of particular countries, on economic conditions, and so forth. But it should none the less be possible to say something more concrete about the form and function of the socialist state, and in particular about its relationship to the economic market. We know that the state must play an extensive role if market socialist arrangements are to meet the ethical criteria reviewed in Part II. At the same time, markets cannot operate unless actors within them, whether individuals or collectives, are given extensive spheres of discretion and secure entitlements to resources. The problem then is: how can the state exercise enough control of markets to ensure that their outcomes are ethically acceptable without destroying the very mechanisms that enable them to work effectively?

It may be best to begin by thinking about the *functions* which the state is called on to perform in a market socialist society of the kind delineated here. I shall distinguish five such functions, though it is important to bear in mind that any particular piece of state activity (such as a piece of legislation) might discharge two or more simultaneously.

First, there is the protective function: that is, the function of safeguarding persons and the resources and benefits that accrue to them from encroachment by outsiders. What I have in mind here is simply this: given any allocation of freedoms, opportunities, material resources, and so on to individuals and to groups, we always face the problem of stabilizing that allocation. Some may be tempted to encroach upon others' shares by, for instance, theft, invasion of liberty, withholding of benefits owed, etc. We need some agency to deter potential encroachers and/or to make good the result of the encroachment. (Note that the encroachers may be private individuals, or groups, or state agencies, or foreign powers.) The value of the protective function should be plain enough. If we think that an allocation is justified in the first place, we are bound to value protecting it against involuntary disturbance. Beyond that, people generally benefit more from resources, freedoms, etc. if they know that their enjoyment of these things is protected. They feel secure, they can make long-term plans, and so on.

Notice that in describing and justifying the protective function, I have not made any reference to rights. A shorthand way of identifying this function might be to say that it consists in safeguarding established rights. In my view, however, the practice of rights is better regarded as *one* way in which the protective function can be discharged. Although I shall later argue in favour of rights under socialism, it is important to see that this requires a separate argument, which goes beyond the mundane considerations appealed to in the last paragraph to justify the protective function itself.

The second function is the distributive function: the function of allocating and re-allocating resources to meet standards of distributive justice. Broadly speaking, there are two aspects to this: one concerns justice in economic markets, where, as argued in Chapter 6, the relevant standard is one of desert. This function includes regulating access to capital, monitoring the development of particular markets to pre-empt exploitation, and applying appropriate tax policies to enterprises and/or individuals. The other concerns personal welfare, where the appropriate standard is distribution according to need. Included here are the various branches of the welfare state and income redistribution schemes. These two forms of distribution may in some cases complement one another and in other cases conflict. For instance, they are complementary when welfare services (say, free medicine) allow individuals to enter the market on a more equal footing; conflictual when the form of welfare provision creates a 'poverty trap'—when people entering or moving up in the labour market lose more in welfare benefits than they gain in income from their enterprise. It is obviously important that the distributive function should be discharged in a way that avoids such conflicts.

The third function is economic management: the function of regulating the economy so that it satisfies criteria of efficiency. This function covers a number of more specific tasks, of which the following may be taken as examples: controlling aggregate demand so that both labour and capital stocks are as far as possible fully employed; ensuring that particular industries remain competitive, through anti-trust legislation and through the creation (where appropriate) of new enterprises; managing industries in which the competitive solution is not, for technical reasons, a feasible option; directing investment so that new capital is put to its most productive use; disseminating information—both in the form of product information, to allow consumers to make more effective choices, and in the form of economic forecasts, to allow enterprises to plan their future activities with maximum chance of success; providing training programmes for people who want to switch into new lines of work or to update their existing skills.

We are reasonably familiar with most of these functions from our experience of existing capitalist economies. In what respects would a socialist state guided by the principles outlined here behave differently? It would unavoidably play a larger role in capital investment, in the absence of private holdings of capital. I shall look more closely below at different ways of carrying out this function. It would also, paradoxically at first sight, perhaps, have a more stringent policy for competition; this follows from its commitment to industrial democracy, which favours smaller enterprises, as well as its distributive concern with avoiding exploitation, which points to markets with many participants, and therefore less chance of one-sided dependency relationships. So although the headings under which economic management would be carried out are reasonably commonplace, the priorities are somewhat different. Allocative efficiency remains the broad aim, but an aim to be pursued within the constraints of other principles, particularly principles of distributive justice.

The fourth function is the provision of public goods. We know from the argument in Chapter 3 that markets are non-neutral where preferences for public goods are at stake, so the political supply of such goods is required not merely for utilitarian reasons but in order to respect people and their preferences equally. Now certain public goods are, so to speak, built into the market socialist framework itself—the good of co-operative work relationships, of citizenship, and so forth. But there are many others that are not: goods such as recreational facilities, public transport, and environmental protection. The state must record preferences for such goods and decide on the form and extent of provision. There is an ineliminable conflict between the different goods themselves (since each makes demands on scarce social resources) and between these goods and the private consumption of commodities. The aim here must be one of striking a fair balance between the various demands.

Finally, the state must perform the task of self-reproduction. This function is the easiest to overlook, but its importance should be clear in the light of the argument so far. In particular, if we want a society embodying a strong sense of citizenship, the state must ensure that present citizens are supported in that role, and future citizens prepared for it. At the most basic level, this means ensuring that the formal mechanisms for political participation are working properly; at a slightly higher level, that political information is freely available, that the communications media foster debate and discussion, and so forth; at the highest level, that the cultural prerequisites for citizenship are maintained, in ways discussed in the last chapter—the education system, for instance, working so as to produce adults with the capacities and the understandings to take part effectively in political dialogue. Beyond this, the state must protect is own integrity by, for instance, policing the border between its administrative apparatus and the various interest groups that may make demands upon it. It must regulate civil society as opposed to being captured by it.

II

If these are the key functions that we would require the state to discharge under market socialism, what form of state should we be looking for? This is a much more difficult question. The socialist tradition has usually answered it through a fairly straight-forward appeal to majoritarian democracy. As far as possible the state should be an apparatus whereby the popular will is translated into effective policy. If we start from this assumption, there are two main problems to solve. One is how to prevent permanent officials from thwarting the popular will and turning themselves into a new ruling élite—the problem of bureaucracy. The other is how, in a large, modern society, the popular will can be forged in the first place—the problem of scale. The preferred solution is usually some variant of what C. B. Macpherson calls the 'pyramidal system'.[1] Assemblies at local level elect delegates to convey their views to regional and national councils, so that higher level decisions are an aggregate of primary decisions arrived at through direct participation. Once again, the problem here is seen as one of ensuring adequate control of the delegates who are chosen.

In my view a state with such a rudimentary constitution would not be well suited for discharging the functions we have identified, even if one assumes that the problems of bureaucracy and of scale can be overcome. The objection to it is not so much that there are insuperable difficulties in implementing the popular will as that unqualified majoritarian democracy may not be the best basis for policy in the first place. I have already touched briefly on some reasons why the dialogue conception of politics advocated here may require that some limits be placed on the subject matter

[1] C. B. Macpherson, *The Life and Times of Liberal Democracy* (Oxford: Oxford University Press, 1977), ch. 5.

of political debate.[2] I want now to extend this discussion by examining the variety of reasons we might have for not wanting decisions made by simple majoritarianism.[3]

The first and most obvious reason is that certain matters should not be subject to collective decision in the first place. This may be because we hold that each person needs to have a protected sphere in which the state cannot legitimately intervene, or more prosaically because it simply seems absurd to treat certain issues as matters for political decision—say the particular sets of items that people choose to consume. Now it is true that the institutions of majoritarian democracy do not of themselves prevent the majority from staying its hand when issues of these kinds are at stake. We may, however, feel that this is too feeble a defence, and that it is better to remove such matters once and for all from the competence of the majority.

A second reason has to do with the definition of the relevant majority. Suppose we adopt something like the pyramid model envisaged by Macpherson. What if the majority decision in locality X on a matter chiefly of concern to the inhabitants of X is reversed by a majority at some higher   say, national—level? It is by no means self-evident that the higher level decision should prevail, if indeed the issue really is a local one. But if that is what we feel, then we need to be able to appeal to something beyond the majority principle itself to establish which majority is going to be sovereign in the case in question.

A third reason concerns decisions which involve specialist knowledge or expertise. Here a majority decision may produce a bad result even when taken by people who are perfectly well-intentioned. There is no need to assume that the knowledge

---

[2] See above, ch. 10, secs. iv, vi.

[3] I exclude here what has now become a common objection to majority rule, namely the problems posed for it by Arrow's theorem whenever three or more policy options are on the table. I exclude this because Arrow's theorem depends on regarding political choice as a matter of aggregating pre-existing policy preferences, whereas I have already (and partly for this reason—see above, p. 257) opted for the dialogue conception as an alternative. (I do not mean that Arrow-type problems could never arise when post-dialogue opinions have finally to be added up for purposes of decision, only that the process of dialogue itself will tend to reveal the *structure* of opinion in the discoursing body, and allow the participants—assuming good faith—to choose an appropriate formal method of resolution.) Of course, if one is sceptical about the chances of the dialogue model, and assumes that politics will continue to be predominantly a matter of interest-aggregation, then Arrow's theorem may provide additional reasons for limiting majority rule.

required to make a good decision is itself esoteric, or to invoke some Platonic view about a natural élite of decision-makers. The point may simply be that acquiring the knowledge to make certain decisions takes time, so it will be impossible for the same group of people to make a wide range of decisions competently without some division of labour. Here, sticking rigidly to the majority principle would guarantee incompetence.

Fourth, we may want to qualify the majority rule principle in cases which involve evident and deep conflicts of interest—say, where we have to choose between two economic policies each of which benefits a (different) plainly identifiable group at the expense of others. I rely here on the point made in Chapter 10 that impersonal dialogue may be impossible to sustain in cases where personal interests are so very directly at stake. One simple and familiar solution is to require the affected individuals or groups to withdraw from the assembly while the issue is decided—but more generally we may look for ways of hiving off such decisions to specially constituted bodies from which the interests in question are formally excluded.

Fifth, and last, we may be concerned about cases in which majorities make decisions that, taken singly, are perfectly rational, but taken together add up to a poor policy overall. I am not thinking here of decisions that are simply incoherent—say voting for various expenditure programmes and then a budget cut—but of decisions which have unanticipated side-effects that only become apparent when the decisions are considered together. A possible reason for this is that it takes time for people to adjust their behaviour properly to the requirements of a new political rule. A political body may enact rule X, then shortly afterwards enact rule Y because it seems that X isn't working, then shortly afterwards enact Z for the same reason, and so forth. Each decision may be quite rational on the evidence available at the time at which it is made, but over the whole period it would have been better for one rule—perhaps *any* of X, Y, and Z—to have been applied consistently. Here, then, we would look for a way of binding the majority to make long-term decisions, disabling itself from altering these decisions within a specified period.

These arguments taken together add up to a case for the constitutional state. What does this latter phrase imply? It means, to begin with, a state that is complex, in the sense that it is composed of different bodies each with its own prescribed function. There is no sovereign in the Hobbesian sense: no body with the final power to make decisions on issues of every kind. Instead, decision-making competence is parcelled out according to rules which thereby serve as constraints on each body taken separately. This further implies the need for a monitoring body to interpret the demarcation rules—say, whether a local authority is competent to decide what the children in its area are taught, or whether there should be a national curriculum. There needs, in fact, to be a Constitutional Court, a quasi-judicial body whose role is to settle the boundaries between spheres of authority in cases of dispute. And this in turn seems unavoidably to imply a written constitution which the court will refer to as the basis of its rulings.

The usual objection to an apparatus of this kind is that it is undemocratic. But I have suggested that if we want to have the optimum conditions for the functioning of democratic citizenship, we need just such a constitutional apparatus. For instance, a primary condition is democracy at local level, where each person can have an opportunity—perhaps on a rotating basis as suggested in Chapter 10—to become directly involved in making political decisions. But for this to be effective, we must mark out a sphere of protected authority for local assemblies—otherwise the decisions they make will simply be overturned by higher bodies, and the whole enterprise becomes pointless. Equally, if democratic decision-making is going to be feasible, it must avoid becoming involved in very specific issues which require specialist knowledge and/or directly involve the interests of some of the participants. We need to make room for specialist committees, and for administrators whose task is to apply general decisions to particular cases. Democratic participation works best when it is confined to establishing general ground rules and administrative priorities. Once again, a constitutional scheme is needed which demarcates the sphere of democratic citizenship from the spheres which are rightfully occupied by specialists and administrators.

One possible response to this line of argument is that if there are evident virtues in confining the operation of majority rule within certain boundaries, then we can trust the citizens them-

selves to observe these necessary limits. This response overlooks
the fact that it is far easier to endorse the general principle
involved in the abstract than in the heat of a concrete decision.
Most of us are familiar with committees which set up sub-
committees to produce detailed recommendations on some issue.
We can all endorse the principle that when the subcommittee's
proposals are brought back, the committee's task is not to reopen
discussion of detailed issues, but simply to accept or reject the
broad basis on which the recommendations are made. But we
know how hard it is in practice for committees to restrain
themselves in this way. So we evolve devices—for instance,
chairmen are given discretion to guide discussion, or we might
simply impose a guillotine and take a vote—which are properly
seen as disabling mechanisms. Our long-term selves are, as it
were, constraining our short-term selves. A constitution may
serve among other things as a formal way of providing such
mechanisms.

To do its job, a constitution needs to be relatively stable; it also
needs to be entrenched, in the sense that the means of amending
it cannot be a simple majority vote in any of the constituencies
whose behaviour it is meant to regulate—otherwise the constitution could simply be altered whenever it was necessary to do so to
accord with a particular decision. At the same time, constitutional
provisions cannot be regarded as God-given truths. Their function is to facilitate the workings of democratic citizenship, and
they should always be open to re-assessment from this vantage
point. So we need an amending procedure and a method by which
constitutional changes can finally be ratified. As to the latter, the,
only solution consistent with the general principles advanced in
this book appears to be a referendum of the entire political
community. As a general rule, the view of citizenship I have been
developing does not favour referendums, since it lays stress on
dialogue within assemblies that are small enough to allow each
participant to make a contribution. But the framework within
which these various political forums are set needs to be
authorized by the political community as a whole, which implies a
general vote.

So far I have laid stress mainly on the constitution's function as
public law, determining the competence of the various political
and administrative bodies that make up the state. From this

perspective, a constitutional question is a procedural question: is it within the powers of body X to take a decision of the kind that it proposes to take (or has taken)? But constitutions are often also thought to have a more substantive aim, namely that of limiting the scope of decision of *all* political bodies in the name of individual freedom. A popular version of this view is that constitutions are meant to protect fundamental rights—to render void any piece of legislation or other enactment that trespasses on the rights of citizens. Certainly this role corresponds to the first reason offered above for limiting the scope of majority rule—namely that some matters should be permanently exempted from political interference. However, there is resistance within the socialist tradition towards what is seen as the individualism of the idea of rights, so before concluding that the socialist constitution should embody fundamental rights as well as procedural provisions, we need to look more closely at the arguments for and against rights.

III

It is helpful here to begin by separating three questions that sometimes become confused in the debate about rights. The first concerns the general value of legality. Should the socialist state aim to embody the familiar liberal ideal of the rule of law? Second, granted that political bodies are constrained in their dealings with individual citizens by this broad requirement of legality, should the laws that are enacted be right-conferring laws—that is, should individual citizens be offered the special status that comes from having legal rights? Third, should certain of these rights be constitutionally entrenched so that altering their definition falls outside of the competence of ordinary legislative bodies? These three questions represent three successive stages away from simple majoritarianism in the direction of safeguarding individual persons.

The first step is perhaps the least controversial. Two sets of considerations converge on the view that the socialist state ought to embody the rule of law. By 'the rule of law' I mean the idea that the state should deal with its citizens by means of stable, general rules, openly announced in advance of the conduct to which they apply. Naturally this implies a distinction between legislative and judicial functions, with legislatures restricted to enunciating general laws and policy guidelines, and separate judicial bodies empowered to apply these provisions to particular cases, the aim of the latter bodies being consistency of treatment and fidelity to the intentions of the legislators. From the individual citizen's point of view the merit of the rule of law is that he knows where he stands and can make plans for the future with reasonable certainty about when and how the state will impinge upon his life. In particular, most citizens will be involved in economic decision-making in their enterprises, and it is well known that such decision-making becomes extremely difficult in the absence of a stable framework of rules governing the economy—rules specifying how enterprises may and may not behave, and rules specifying what treatment they may expect at the hands of government agencies. In short, the protective function of government is best discharged through conformity to the rule of law, which maximizes citizens' security and certainty about the future. From the point of view of the political community as a whole, the rule of law serves to bind legislatures in a way that we have already seen is desirable—preventing them from becoming directly entangled in individual cases and introducing a measure of stability into their decisions. Once democracy is seen not just as a matter of recording majority preferences but of creating the conditions under which dialogue can be carried on successfully, the apparent antagonism between democracy and the rule of law is seen to evaporate.

Resistance on the left to the rule of law can be attributed mainly to the belief that requirements of legality would hinder the state from carrying out necessary tasks such as economic management and welfare provision. This belief is the socialist equivalent of Hayek's view that the rule of law implies economic *laissez-faire*. In both cases the verdict is reached as a result of packing substantive political values into what is properly a procedural ideal.[4] There seems no reason why the kind of state activity that a socialist order requires should not be governed by general rules which are then applied to particular cases by authorized officials. Certainly this is true if we conceive the state's economic function as one of setting

---

[4] See J. Raz, 'The Rule of Law and its Virtue', in id., *The Authority of Law* (Oxford: Clarendon Press, 1979), for a good account of what is actually involved in the rule of law and a critique of inflated accounts.

the framework within which autonomous enterprises will make their production and trading decisions. The fact that the framework required will be rather different from the one that underpins the liberal economy does not mean that it must correspond worse (or better) to rule-of-law ideals.[5]

I shall have more to say later both about the economic functions of the state and about its welfare functions. Let me now proceed to the question whether the state's laws should generally aim to confer rights on individual citizens. Note that rights cannot be regarded as a direct corollary of the idea of law itself. Not all laws confer rights—for instance some serve to regulate the relations between public bodies, and others simply impose duties on officials, say to pursue a certain environmental policy. There is nothing incoherent in the suggestion that all laws should be treated in this way—as imposing duties on various bodies, which in some cases could include the requirement that individuals be treated in such-and-such a manner. What differentiates a legal system that confers rights from this? Where people have rights, they are seen as being entitled to demand what the law provides for them, and the practical expression of this is that there should be some independent tribunal to which they can take their case if they believe that they have been unfairly treated by an official agency, or of course by another private citizen.

At first sight it might seem that the case for rights is virtually self-evident. If we aim to secure a just distribution of resources, and if we assume that each person is likely to be best placed to know whether he has received his fair allocation, then it follows immediately that he should be provided with the means of redress in cases of unfairness. However, this argument overlooks something which has seemed important to some socialists, namely, that the practice of rights both expresses and fosters a certain understanding of the relationship between individual and community. In conferring rights, it is alleged, we represent individuals as self-contained atoms whose relationship to their fellow-citizens and to the state as a whole is essentially antagonistic. Each defends his little patch against the outside world, rather than looking on society as a co-operative enterprise in which common ends are

---

[5] The compatibility of the rule of law with state provision of welfare is defended in H. W. Jones, 'The Rule of Law and the Welfare State', *Columbia Law Review*, 58 (1958), 143–56.

pursued.[6] What is at stake here can perhaps best be brought out through some remarks of Feinberg's about why, from a liberal perspective, rights are valuable.

Even if there are conceivable circumstances in which one would admit rights diffidently, there is no doubt that their characteristic use and that for which they are distinctively well-suited, is to be claimed, demanded, affirmed, insisted upon. They are especially sturdy objects to 'stand upon', a most useful sort of moral furniture . . . Having rights enables us to 'stand up like men', to look others in the eye, and to feel in some fundamental way the equal of anyone.[7]

It is precisely the image of individual assertiveness captured here that explains the distaste many socialists feel for the idea of rights. Against this, however, I have argued that socialism must make room for individuality, in the sense of recognizing that people are distinct individuals with their own projects to pursue, as well as for community. Moreover it must do so practically as well as theoretically; a socialist society must contain institutions that actively encourage people to assert themselves as individuals, to make claims on their own behalf, besides contributing to common ends. If legally-conferred rights are such an institution, there is a strong positive case for having them under socialism.

Perhaps the resistance to this view stems from a confusion between the claim that rights are a necessary protection for individual autonomy and the claim that they are a necessary protection for individual self-interest. Rights can, of course, be used for narrowly selfish purposes; but that is not the only reason for claiming them. Some rights, for instance, serve to guarantee the conditions of citizenship—rights to education, free speech, and so forth. Other rights allow people to make direct social contributions—for instance to band together in voluntary associations to promote socially useful ends like environmental improvement. We need rights because our priorities may conflict,

---

[6] Campbell refers to this as 'the individualism of rights'. See T. Campbell, *The Left and Rights* (London: Routledge and Kegan Paul, 1983) ch. 5. For examples of socialist hostility to rights, see R. A. Putnam, 'Rights of Persons and the Liberal Tradition' in T. Honderich (ed.), *Social Ends and Political Means* (London: Routledge and Kegan Paul, 1976), and P. Q. Hirst, 'Law, Socialism and Rights', in *Law, Socialism and Democracy* (London: Allen and Unwin, 1986); the *locus classicus* is K. Marx, '*On the Jewish Question*', in T. B. Bottomore (ed.), *Karl Marx: Early Writings* (London: Watts, 1963).

[7] J. Feinberg, 'The Nature and Value of Rights', *Journal of Value Inquiry*, 4 (1970), 252.

so that I may have cause to protect my sphere of discretion against your claims, but the priorities at stake need not be egoistic.[8] They may, for instance, simply be different views about how best to promote social welfare. The practice of rights should be endorsed by all political outlooks that recognize the value of individual autonomy, although of course there will be sharply differing views as to what the *content* of these rights should be.

Finally in this section we come to the question whether certain rights should be constitutionally entrenched. Recall that we are asking this question on the premiss that democratic citizenship is in good working order, so that decisions are made by representative bodies after extensive, and often multi-tiered, debate.[9] The argument for entrenching rights would be that the requirements of legality so far described—viz. that legislatures should enact stable general rules, conferring enforcible rights on individuals where appropriate—are still not adequate to protect individuals or minorities from hostile majorities. Entrenching rights means, in practice, including a bill of rights among the provisions of the constitution and empowering a judicial body to invalidate legislation which is judged to infringe any of the protected rights.

Once again, there is a tradition of left-wing opposition to this idea, which takes the form of claiming either that constitutional entrenchment is inherently undemocratic, or that the judiciary is always a conservative force, or both. Both of these charges miss the point. We have seen already that there can be good, democratic reasons for qualifying the majority rule principle. As to the second charge, it is in one sense right and proper that the judiciary behaves conservatively, since the proper function of judicial bodies is the consistent application of established rules (including constitutional rules) to particular cases. A 'radical' judiciary would mean one that extended the law to encompass new social purposes, and this would genuinely be undemocratic since it would usurp the function of the legislative assemblies. The real question is whether a judicial body is an appropriate tool

[8] For fuller arguments in support of this claim, see Campbell, *The Left and Rights*, ch. 5; R. Keat, 'Liberal Rights and Socialism', in K. Graham (ed.), *Contemporary Political Philosophy* (Cambridge: Cambridge University Press, 1982); C. Sypnowich, 'Law as a Vehicle of Altruism', *Oxford Journal of Legal Studies*, 5 (1985): 276–84.

[9] I insert this reminder because it is quite possible to favour constitutional entrenchment under existing, very imperfect, democratic systems while opposing it in circumstances of the kind described.

for deciding whether legislation violates basic rights of the sort
that a constitutional bill would embody. For this is often much
more a substantive than a procedural question. The rights that
are entrenched must be defined fairly broadly, since the whole
point of the constitutional approach is to lay down basic rules
without knowledge of the specific cases to which they will apply.
So the bill of rights will refer to freedom of speech and association, the right to participate in government, and so forth. The
application of these rights to a proposed piece of legislation will
almost invariably involve policy questions. Does the right to
freedom of speech mean that legislation prohibiting incitement to
racial hatred is invalid, for instance? It is hard to maintain that this
is an essentially judicial issue, in the sense of an issue best
resolved by appeal to legislative intention, precedent and so forth.
Rather, it seems to involve a fairly straightforward trade-off
between two values, namely the freedom of individuals to speak
their minds and the protection of minority groups from harass-
ment and discrimination. The problem is compounded when we
consider that a socialist state will want to give an equally high
priority to various economic rights as to the traditional liberal
rights.[10] For instance, rights to welfare and rights to participation
in enterprises will be of paramount importance. But these are
rights whose content will inevitably vary according to economic
circumstances—for example, the level of welfare provision cannot be set without reference to the productive capacities of the
economy. Again it is not clear that judicial bodies are in the best
position to assess whether proposed legislation adequately recognizes such rights.

For these reasons, the question about constitutional entrenchment of rights is much more finely balanced than the question
about the rule of law and rights in general. It may be that the final
value of entrenchment is as much ethical as legal. By inscribing a
bill of rights in the constitution, the political community commits
itself to safeguarding individuals in certain ways, and this commitment can be appealed to in political debates on legislation.
Again, if a constitutional court turned down a piece of legislation
on what appeared to be substantive grounds, there would be
strong pressure—given our assumptions about a working
democracy—for the decision to be reversed through a constitu-

[10] e.g. Campbell, *The Left and Rights*, ch. 6.

tional amendment. But this in itself would underline the seriousness of the issue, would give time for additional discussion and so
forth. So we may want finally to come down in favour of
entrenchment without thinking of it as some kind of fail-safe
protection for individual interests.

IV

Turning now to the state's economic responsibilities, we find
ourselves faced with two contrary imperatives. On the one hand,
we know that a market economy can only be reconciled with
socialist values if the workings of such an economy are subject to
extensive political monitoring. On the other hand, we also know
that markets cannot operate effectively unless actors within them
are given adequate freedom to make their own decisions; we
know, too, that democratic assemblies should not be in the
business of making detailed economic decisions—say, about
the conduct of particular enterprises. The problem is to find the
institutional structure that best accommodates both of these
imperatives.

It seems clear that different kinds of economic decisions need
to be taken in different places. To return to our classification of
state functions, much that falls under the heading of economic
management is of a highly technical nature—control of interest
rates, the money supply, public borrowing, and so forth. The role
of the representative assembly here can only be to set down policy
guidelines within which administrative bodies will make day-to-
day decisions. Contrast with this the public goods function.
Although technical questions may arise concerning how best to
supply goods such as a pollution-free atmosphere, the more
fundamental issue of which goods to supply, and in what quantities, seems almost entirely a matter for democratic debate. The
problem is one of recording public demand for, say, areas of
natural beauty, or on the other hand improved road systems, and
then of striking a fair balance between these demands. This is
precisely the kind of issue where the idea of making policy
through democratic dialogue looks most persuasive, quite apart
from the intrinsic value of active citizenship.

I shall focus attention on one particular class of decisions,
decisions about capital investment. This is an issue of crucial

importance to market socialists. There is a clear case for treating investment as a public function, partly because socialists will oppose private returns from investment on grounds of justice, partly because investment decisions very often have social consequences reaching beyond the particular enterprises in question (for instance, they may alter the employment needs of different localities). Yet critics of market socialism often pick on this as a key weakness in the system: they allege that investment funds can only be allocated efficiently if there is a free market in capital itself, and also that personal freedom is seriously compromised if would-be producers have to rely on state agencies for their funding.[11]

There is a enough substance in the latter allegations to make us want the investment agencies to have a high degree of autonomy from central government. To be more specific, we should favour a plurality of investment agencies, with firms having the choice of which agency to approach for capital. One obvious possibility would be to have several national investment banks and many smaller banks based in different regions competing with each other to lend to enterprises. These banks would be constituted in such a way that they always remained at arm's length from the political centre. They would be given a formal mandate, but this would leave them substantially free to choose which particular investments to make. Although they would be funded by tax revenues, it seems desirable that they should be able to raise additional investment funds by attracting private savings.[12] In these ways the autonomy of the banks would be safeguarded, and this in turn would protect particular enterprises against direct political interference.

What remit would the investment banks be given? They would pay considerable attention to the expected profitability of enterprises that apply to them for funds; to that extent, their function is

---

[11] See J. N. Gray, 'Contractarian Method, Private Property and the Market Economy', paper presented to the American Society for Political and Legal Philosophy, Dec. 1986; J. A. Dorn, 'Markets, True and False: The Case of Yugoslavia', *Journal of Libertarian Studies*, 2 (1978), 243–68.

[12] I take it socialists have no objection to people receiving fixed rates of interest on money they choose to save, since this merely reflects a widely shared time discount (a pound today is worth considerably more to me than the promise of a pound in ten years time). They are likely to look less favourably on speculative investment (such as occurs in conventional stock markets) where luck, inside knowledge, and so forth may create large inequalities in people's assets.

to simulate a capital market by allocating capital among existing enterprises where its marginal returns are greatest. This aim would, however, be balanced against others. One important function of the banks would be enterprise creation, in response either to employment needs or to market opportunities.[13] We might envisage each bank having a department devoted specifically to this task, researching likely markets, bringing together potential enterprise members, and providing advice on the best structure for the proposed firm. Since co-operatives are known to be capital-hungry, the banks would have to earmark a proportion of their funds for this purpose, rather than allowing them to be swallowed up by the demands of established enterprises. Again, investment in each area should be sensitive to local needs—to the need to provide a balanced range of employment, to environmental needs, and so forth. These considerations preclude the banks from acting as simple profit-maximizers, which in turn has implications for their ownership structure. It is possible to envisage investment banks which were themselves (large) workers' co-operatives, paying their employees a profit-related income. Given the complexity of their task, however, it seems preferable to constitute the banks as public bodies staffed by salaried officials.[14] As I have stressed already, it is important that they should be given a clearly worded remit and then left to discharge it without interference. One might envisage an annual review of each bank's performance by the appropriate representative body, local or national. Performance would be judged by how successfully the bank had fulfilled its various objectives over a large number of decisions, not in particular cases. In this way the bank's employees would be protected against direct political lobbying on behalf of particular industries or firms.

Besides protecting the investment banks from undesirable political control (as opposed to the enforcement of general policy guidelines), we need also to protect individual enterprises from the lending agencies. Once co-operatives are established, they

[13] This function is stressed as essential to the efficient working of market socialism in J. Vanek, *The General Theory of Labor-Managed Market Economies* (Ithaca: Cornell University Press, 1970), esp. ch. 14.

[14] There may be other alternatives—for instance, banks constituted as private companies with equity shareholding, the shares owned by co-ops and the government in some proportion. For a fuller discussion, see S. Estrin, 'Workers' Co-operatives: Their Merits and Limitations', in J. Le Grand and S. Estrin (eds.), *Market Socialism* (Oxford: Clarendon Press 1989).

must have the right to manage their own affairs subject only to the financial conditions (concerning capital repayment, etc.) agreed with the bank. We might expect there to be a higher degree of *voluntary* co-operation between bank and enterprise than usually obtains now under a commercial banking system, since the bank would be in a position to provide services (such as market research) that the co-operative could not efficiently supply for itself.[15] It is important, however, that each co-operative should be formally constituted as a self-governing enterprise, and that the bank should not (for instance) be able to impose personnel on the co-operative or control its policy in other ways. A major safeguard here is the co-operative's right to transfer its borrowings from one bank to another. I believe these arrangements would adequately meet the fear sometimes expressed by libertarian critics of market socialism that public control of investment would allow the state to penalize dissidents by denying them access to funds. Employment in each co-operative is a matter for the members themselves, not for the funding agency, let alone the state. Even if an investment bank should want to pursue an anti-dissident policy (a supposition which is itself hard to make seem plausible) it has no real leverage against individual enterprises.

This brief discussion of capital investment extends my earlier contention that the socialist state must be a constitutional state. Rather than aiming at unitary democracy, with every decision potentially subject to the popular will, it should hive off major areas of decision to autonomous bodies—subject, of course, to guidelines of the kind discussed above in relation to investment. In this way it is possible to avoid each particular decision becoming directly political, which is desirable both from the point of view of making good and consistent decisions and from the point of view of not overloading the capacities of citizenship. It is implicit here that conscientious public servants can be found to staff the institutions in question—that is, people who are willing to act in the spirit of the constitutional provisions. This depends on the prevailing public and professional culture and cannot be taken for granted. In the absence of such a culture, the prospects for the kind of socialism I am outlining here are obviously poor.

[15] As I noted in ch. 3 n. 28, the Caja Laboral Popular in Mondragon provides a useful model of the role that we might expect investment banks to play in relation to co-operatives under market socialism. See the references cited there.

V

Finally in this chapter I shall consider the state's role in the provision of welfare—welfare in the restricted sense in which it covers goods and services required to meet basic needs. In chapter 4, I showed how, on liberal premises, it was possible to argue for the superiority of a state-funded welfare system to voluntary welfare provision through charities. As I indicated there, however, most socialists would prefer to approach the issue somewhat differently, seeing welfare provision as fundamentally a matter of justice rather than altruism (using the latter term to refer to people's compassionate concern for others in need, a feeling whose strength is likely to vary from one society to another). Welfare, that is to say, is not simply another public good whose supply should depend entirely on how much people actually want to see it provided; rather, welfare rights should take their place alongside other rights of citizenship, such as freedom of speech and political participation, in the constitution of the socialist state. If we decide to entrench certain basic rights formally, welfare rights should be included on the select list.

At the same time, it is important not to overstate the practical effect of such entrenchment, for reasons given earlier. Speaking generally, welfare rights are rights to have basic needs met—needs for medical care, housing, education, and so on. But the definition of 'basic need' here is inevitably a conventional one. The level of provision that is considered to be adequate must depend on prevailing social conditions. In modern Britain, 'adequate' housing is considered to include possessing a fixed bath, hot-water tap, and inside WC,[16] but in earlier societies and in other places the standard will have been set lower. The reason has partly to do with technical feasibility, but partly also to do with a social understanding of the level of deprivation which excludes a person from citizenship, in the wider sense outlined in Chapter 9. In London, someone who sleeps on the streets is a social outcast; in Bombay that is not necessarily the case.[17]

---

[16] See J. Parker, *Social Policy and Citizenship* (London: Macmillan, 1975), ch. 7.

[17] 'I was so happy in Bombay. I was respected, I had a certain position . . . I also had my friends. We met in the evenings on the pavement below the gallery of our chambers. Some of us, like the tailor's bearer and myself, were domestics who lived in the street. The others

This implies that the practical content of welfare rights must be determined by an ongoing political debate. Citizens must reach an agreement about how, for the time being, basic needs are to be understood, and formalize this in the appropriate legislation. The purpose of constitutional entrenchment cannot be to pre-empt this debate. It must rather be to protect citizens against the side-effects of other pieces of legislation or against the incompetence of administrators.[18] It does seem important that a person who is denied access to adequate medical care or whose child is excluded from the school system should have legal redress up to the highest level. This is one practical manifestation of regarding welfare as a matter of justice, rather than altruism, in other words as something which is owed to the citizen as of right.

So far I have been discussing in general terms how welfare rights may fit into the structure of the socialist state; I have not yet asked which kind of welfare system is to be preferred. Socialists have traditionally favoured a publicly administered welfare system, where goods and services are provided by salaried employees of the state. Recently there has been a tide of disillusion with such systems, bringing together libertarians and socialists in an unlikely alliance. The charges variously made are that state-administered systems are inefficient, inegalitarian, and subversive of the freedom and dignity of welfare recipients.[19] How should we respond to these claims?

We should be clear to begin with that the idea of rights to welfare does not prescribe any particular form of provision. Food, after all, is among the most basic of all needs, but we do not think it must be supplied by public soup-kitchens. Instead we usually suppose that so long as everyone has a guaranteed minimum income, they will meet this need by market purchases. There is

were people who came to that bit of pavement to sleep. Respectable people; we didn't encourage riff-raff'; V. S. Naipaul, *In a Free State* (Harmondsworth: Penguin, 1973), 21). This is a fictional account, but I assume one that is grounded in observation.

[18] It is important not to regard welfare rights as a panacea. Their value depends on the willingness and ability of citizens to make use of them. Since these qualities are not always present, we still need to devise good systems for administering welfare. For pessimism about the practical efficacy of welfare rights, see R. E. Goodin, 'Welfare, Rights and Discretion', *Oxford Journal of Legal Studies*, 6 (1986), 232–61.

[19] For a libertarian statement, see A. Seldon, *Charge* (London: Temple Smith, 1977); for a (more scholarly) socialist view, see J. Le Grand, *The Strategy of Equality* (London: Allen and Unwin, 1982).

nothing logically wrong with extending this approach to other forms of welfare, provided always that the state guarantees the wherewithal to make the necessary purchases, whether in the form of general income or in the form of vouchers tied to specific goods such as education and medicine.[20] The case for a public system must be made pragmatically, in terms of its expected consequences in comparison to proposed alternatives.

What, then, can be said in favour of such a system? The key argument, in my view, must be that a public system gets closer than any other to distributing the goods in question according to relative need. In other words, the system is the fairest possible *with respect to these particular goods*. I add the emphasis because this is not equivalent to saying that a public system necessarily creates fairness overall.[21] Some older defences of the welfare state do appear to have presented it as the centrepiece of a strategy for equality—the assumption being that a system that distributed certain key welfare goods according to need would lead to a significant equalization of people's life-prospects in general. This assumption has been exploded by more recent research, such as Le Grand's, which shows that market-derived differences in income are still a major factor determining people's life-chances—and indeed strongly affect the benefits that are derived from the public services themselves. As Le Grand puts it:

There is so much evidence from so many different areas that, almost regardless of the method of provision, the better off will always be able to make more effective use of even a freely provided service than the less well off. In that sense, the strategy of attempting to create equality through the provision of services that are free, or at a subsidized price to all, seems fundamentally misconceived.[22]

What this shows is that public welfare can contribute to egalitarian aims only in conjunction with a broader policy aimed at reducing inequalities in primary incomes; indeed, in the absence of such a policy, even the more limited aim of allocating

[20] It must also, of course, guarantee access to the various services, which may mean requiring suppliers to take on certain classes of client—for instance, high-risk patients in the case of medical care.
[21] This point is well made in M. O'Higgins, 'Welfare, Redistribution and Inequality: Disillusion, Illusion, and Reality', in P. Bean, J. Ferris and D. Whynes (eds.), *In Defence of Welfare* (London: Tavistock, 1985).
[22] Le Grand, *Strategy of Equality*, 137.

medical aid and so forth on the basis of need is compromised, since, as Le Grand's evidence shows, the needy rich are able to derive more real benefit from a public service than the equally needy poor. All that a public system can unquestionably achieve is horizontal redistribution within income strata between the less and the more needy (e.g. between the healthy and the sick).

When all this has been conceded, the relevant question is whether any alternative to a public system is likely to do better by the criterion of fairness we are employing. Consider medical care, and consider two possible alternatives: private insurance and a voucher scheme. Under the first, existing unfairness would almost certainly be amplified.[23] The rich would be able to afford superior insurance, and the chronically sick might have difficulty purchasing any insurance at all. Thus the better off would simply add higher purchasing power to the advantages they already enjoy in gaining access to medical treatment. A voucher scheme—e.g. one in which each person is given a voucher of equal value to enable them to purchase en bloc medical care from a supplier, for some fixed period, with no 'topping-up' allowed—would be less bad from this point of view, but it is difficult to see why it would represent an improvement on the public system.[24] Vouchers would mean that the users of medical services had the option of changing to another supplier, but why would this work in the direction of improving the share of resources going to the poorer groups?

If fairness is the key argument for a public welfare system, the arguments for a market-based alternative are the usual ones of productive efficiency and consumer sovereignty. The efficiency argument is hard to assess, in the case of public welfare systems, since we are dealing with outputs that are not priced; studies conducted in other areas have revealed little systematic dif-

---

[23] The precise outcome will depend on how the revenue saved by eliminating the public service is distributed. Defenders of private welfare claim that cash redistribution of the proceeds in favour of low income groups would increase overall equality. I am sceptical of this claim, partly because of the evidence, reviewed briefly in ch. 4 above, that people are more willing to support redistribution in the form of specific services than general income redistribution. Politically, therefore, it seems unlikely that people (even under the circumstances of socialism) would favour cash redistribution to the extent presupposed by the privatization argument.

[24] For further discussion, see A. Maynard, 'Welfare: Who pays?', in Bean, Ferris, and Whynes (eds.), *In Defence of Welfare*; J. Le Grand, 'Equality, Markets and Welfare', in J. Le Grand and S. Estrin (eds.) *Market Socialism*, (Oxford: Clarendon Press, 1989).

ference in efficiency between public and private organizations.[25] The consumer sovereignty argument is not seen at its most telling in the case of goods like medical care and education, where the recipients are unlikely to be well placed to make an informed judgement about the quality of the service they are given. Almost inevitably there will have to be external monitoring in these areas, and this reduces the practical contrast between 'public' and 'private' systems of welfare. There remains, however, the issue of personal choice: even if I am not particularly competent to pass judgement on the treatment I have received from my doctor, it may be important to me that I can switch to another practitioner if I feel dissatisfied. This freedom may also have some influence on the way in which dealings between doctor and patient are conducted; it may help to foster a more equal relationship.

Note, however, that this element of personal choice can be accommodated in a public system, as it is under the NHS to the extent that patients can choose their GPs. Perhaps the moral we should draw is that the difference between a sensitive public system, which opens up alternatives to users, and a private system operating under distributive constraints (say, a uniform voucher system) may turn out to be relatively slight. In general, the aim of this brief discussion of welfare has been to show that socialists should not be dogmatic about the form of welfare provision. They should hold on to the principle of welfare rights and distribution of welfare goods according to need, though without supposing that these are substitutes for a wider commitment to equality. The ineliminable role of the state is to ensure that these principles are realized, but whether this is done through a welfare state of the conventional sort or through a suitably regulated market is much more open to debate. My own view is that in the case of medicine and education (surely the key welfare goods), the balance of argument tips in favour of a public system incorporating a substantial element of consumer choice; in other cases—housing, for instance—it seems more appropriate to rely primarily on markets, with public authorities playing a subsidiary financial role where necessary.

[25] See J. Le Grand and R. Robinson, 'Privatisation and the Welfare State: An Introduction', in idd. (eds.) *Privatisation and the Welfare State* (London: Allen and Unwin, 1984).

VI

Before concluding this chapter there is one further issue that I want to address. I have tried to present a view of the relationship between the state and its individual citizens which sees the state not as some kind of godmother charged with the overall care of its members, but an institution with clearly defined functions and a structure to match; conversely, the citizens are to be seen as independent agents who on the one hand are actively involved in setting the goals of the state through political debate, and on the other are endowed with private rights which they are prepared to stand on in their dealings with one another and with government agencies. Welfare rights fit into this picture as a means of guaranteeing the other aspects of citizenship; their function is to safeguard independence and ensure that people are competent to take part in both economic and political life. It has sometimes been alleged, however, that an extensive welfare system produces not independence, but dependence on the agencies that provide the welfare; people see themselves not as citizens, but as claimants whose aim is to extract the maximum possible benefit from the services provided for them.

My first response to this charge is that, to the extent that we can observe such a culture of dependency in present-day societies, it is chiefly caused by a lack of job opportunities, together with the very restricted avenues of political participation open to ordinary people. People are thrust into dependency by the limited options that are available. However, although full employment and extended citizenship are key elements in the market socialist programme, it would be too bland to side-step the dependency issue entirely. If we think about it from the point of view of citizenship, it does seem undesirable for citizens to be involved in making a large number of means-tested claims from state agencies in order to ensure that their needs are properly met. Far better to ensure that everyone has a basic income more than adequate to meet routine needs (clothing, heating, transport) and then to provide universally for major needs where costs may vary considerably from person to person (health, education). Although most people would be expected to earn this income through employment, there would obviously have to be a safety-net for the disabled, the temporarily unemployed, those working in loss-making enterprises, and so forth. The safety-net might take the form of a negative income tax, or perhaps a social dividend—a fixed sum paid recurrently to each member of society regardless of all other earnings.[26] The point about these measures is that they are simple to implement and do not involve any elaborate investigation of the citizen's personal circum-stances.[27] So long as the baseline is a generous one, they seem more congruent with the principles I have been developing than a web of specific welfare benefits, which may encourage dependency and in addition create perverse incentives for people entering the labour market.

The socialist state, to sum up, must be a limited and constitu-tional state. It has radical tasks to perform, but many of those tasks are best achieved in a roundabout way. It needs to bind itself internally by specifying the functions of each constituent body (legislative, administrative, etc.) and appointing watch-dogs to guard the boundaries. Externally, its goals may best be achieved by, for instance, creating an appropriate incentive system and then allowing markets to operate; or by establishing semi-autonomous bodies acting under policy guidelines. It should not be the benevolent colossus of socialist myth; but nor, for the same reason, need it be the malevolent leviathan of libertarian nightmare.

---

[26] The social dividend is advocated in B. Jordan, *The State: Authority and Autonomy* (Oxford: Blackwell, 1985), ch. 13 and pt. iii; and in R. J. Van der Veen and P. Van Parijs, 'A Capitalist Road to Communism', *Theory and Society*, 15 (1986), 635–55. Its merits are that it is extremely simple to implement and that it has no possible disincentive effects. The problem is to make the dividend generous enough to meet basic needs adequately without imposing an unacceptable level of taxation on earnings; it therefore presupposes a society of considerable affluence.

[27] The social dividend requires no investigation at all; the negative income tax requires only the information already obtained for purposes of (positive) income tax.

CONCLUSION

The exposition and defence of the politico-economic system I call market socialism is now complete. Both the system and its justifying theory are radically pluralistic. Market socialism has a composite institutional structure whose various components are intended to counter-balance one another. Let us review these components briefly. The two main pillars are the market economy and the state. The market is relied on to produce most goods and services, but within a distributive framework established and enforced by the state. Moreover, government agencies are directly involved in provision in two areas at least: in the supply of public goods such as transport systems and environmental protection, and in guaranteeing rights to welfare (which in practice is sometimes likely to imply direct provision).

The market is also a composite structure. Individual freedom is enshrined in consumer choice, and in workers' rights to move in and out of enterprises. However, enterprise structure is constrained so as to promote other objectives: distributive justice and democratic control of the work environment. Hence as far as possible firms should be constituted as workers' co-operatives, with final control vested equally in all those who work in them. In striking this balance, we recognize that the market is not merely a device for co-ordinating production with consumer demand (though it certainly is that). It is also a major determinant of life-chances—since primary income earned through the market tends to outweigh all other receipts. Furthermore, producing for the market takes up a large part of (most people's) daily lives. This constraint cannot be lifted, but we can at least ensure that they have the greatest possible chance to shape the environment in which their time is spent.

In thinking about the constitution of the state, we are again concerned with balancing contrary imperatives. On the one hand, we look to citizenship as the means whereby people can collectively determine the future shape of their community. For this aspiration to be realized, we must envisage a radically participatory form of politics in which at some time each citizen has an opportunity to add his voice to the dialogue. Yet we must be concerned that the state should not spread its tentacles throughout social life. It is important that individuals should have a protected private sphere, and that the day-to-day working of the economy should be unhampered. We must therefore look to constitutional restraints on majoritarian democracy—these restraints being seen as a form of voluntary self-binding on the part of the whole citizen body. The socialist state has liberal features—division of powers, a constitutional court, etc.—but it allies them with a far more democratic way of formulating basic policy (primary assemblies, etc.) than we find in current liberal systems.

Suppose that the arguments I have been advancing for market socialism are accepted—suppose, that is, that the reader endorses the interpretation I have offered of values such as freedom, justice, and community, and agrees too that a social system of the kind described would embody the optimal mix of these values; there remains the question whether the ideal has any political relevance. Is it any more than an attractive-sounding pipe dream? This is the issue that I want to explore briefly in this conclusion.

An idea like market socialism might fail to be relevant for one of two reasons. On the one hand, it might hold out benefits in which no one was particularly interested. Suppose, to take an implausibly simple case, that the vast majority of people in our society were concerned only about maximizing their level of consumption. It then becomes irrelevant to develop and present a socialist theory stressing values such as worker control, distributive justice and citizenship. (The theory might not be irrelevant to every society, but it would certainly be irrelevant to this one.) On the other hand, the idea might link up with certain of people's aspirations, but in doing so make incompatible demands upon them. This would amount to an incoherence in the theory, though not one of a straightforward kind. Again, consider a very simple case. Suppose that a social theory included, along with others, the following two proposals: that families should be solely responsible for the care of their elderly members, and that children should be reared in collective nurseries. These proposals are neither logically nor empirically contradictory (we can describe a hypothetical world in which they are both realized). None the less they add up to an incoherent policy, in so far as the first proposal relies on intensifying family ties, whereas the second would have the effect of weakening or possibly even destroying such ties. One symptom of this incoherence is that the two proposals are likely to appeal to completely different audiences: the first, perhaps, to conservatives who see the family as a moralizing force; the second to radical feminists who see the family structure as an obstacle to women's freedom. The question, then, is whether market socialism might be incoherent in some rather similar (though perhaps less blatant) way, so that its various components would appeal, if at all, to mutually exclusive constituencies.

Let me canvass some reasons why market socialism might be considered irrelevant in either of the two senses noted above. One is that *no* form of socialism has any longer a mass appeal, in the developed West at least. Now this claim could be taken in a number of different ways. At one level, it might simply be making a point about the political impact of the term 'socialism'. If so, my guess is that we will find sharp variations from one country to the next, depending in particular on the configuration of the main political parties, and the vocabulary they use to describe themselves. At one extreme, nine out of ten Americans will declare themselves against replacing capitalism by any form of socialism;[1] at the other extreme we might take a case such as Sweden, where the hegemony of the Social Democratic Party has made socialism a familiar and unthreatening idea. But clearly we are dealing here with matters of surface rhetoric which may give little clue as to which more concrete objectives people are prepared to support. If the basic aims of market socialism turn out to be acceptable, we should not mind if part of the audience prefers to have the package labelled in some other way.

A more substantive criticism is that market socialism, although a radical departure from the socialist tradition in some respects, retains a fairly traditional view of the subject-matter of socialism. It sees socialism as a set of proposals for reforming the economy and the state. Now much recent socialist literature advocates incorporating new concerns into the canon: the position of women and ethnic minorities, environmental problems, the growing importance of leisure, international issues such as

---

[1] See H. McClosky and J. Zaller, *The American Ethos: Public Attitudes towards Capitalism and Democracy.* (Cambridge, Mass.: Harvard University Press, 1984) 135.

nuclear weapons. It is thought that these concerns are becoming more central to people's lives, and that unless socialists can address them directly, they risk becoming marginalized. Market socialism, then, is seen as too narrow a view upon which to base a popular political programme.

This criticism requires a response at two levels. At one level, we need to distinguish socialism itself from various other goals that socialists may adopt, and that may at some point become incorporated into the programme of a socialist party. The point is simply that these goals may be orthogonal to socialism: one can envisage a socialist society that achieves them and equally another that does not. In the case of environmental protection, for instance, people in a market socialist system might decide to impose strict anti-pollution legislation, to take large areas of the countryside into public ownership, and so on; on the other hand, they might opt for *laissez-faire*. Neither of these policies is in itself more 'socialist' than the other.[2] There may, I think, be affinities, stronger or weaker, between socialism and positions taken on the kind of issues mentioned above. It may, for instance, plausibly be argued that socialist institutions are in practice a precondition for an effective environmental policy.[3] But an affinity is only that; it does not amount to a conceptual connection.

At a second level, there is the question of the relative importance of traditional politico-economic concerns as against the newer issues. Here it is important not to transport ourselves by wishful thinking into a post-industrial utopia. In particular, the world of work remains of central importance to almost everyone except the rich leisured class.[4] It still takes up a substantial part of

---

[2] In the case of feminism we need to make some distinctions. Socialism is an egalitarian ideology: it insists that people should have equal opportunities in certain key areas of their lives, such as access to jobs, welfare services, and the arenas of politics. It goes without saying that this equality extends to women as well as to men. All of the arguments offered in this book, for instance, are intended to apply without distinction of sex (my use of male pronouns reflects only an attachment to traditional canons of English usage). However, feminism typically goes further than this and advances views about how domestic relations should be ordered, about the image of women conveyed by the prevailing culture, and so on. It is in this respect that socialism and feminism are orthogonal creeds. This is recognized by those who use designations such as socialist-feminist to signal commitment to both sets of ideals.

[3] There is a good sketch of an environmentally sensitive form of socialism in H. Stretton, *Capitalism, Socialism and the Environment* (Cambridge: Cambridge University Press, 1976).

[4] This is also true of the unemployed, for whom lack of work and the economic and

our waking lives; it is a key determinant of social identity; and the income it yields is the major determinant of life-chances generally. I believe, therefore, that a set of proposals which has at its core the restructuring of working relationships in a democratic and egalitarian direction must speak to the central interests of the overwhelming majority of people in the advanced societies. As to the political dimension of market socialism, it is clear that political reform is not presently *perceived* as a central interest by most people; equally, however, a more democratic political system seems a prerequisite for most of the other aims that people might want to pursue—the new issues I referred to above all throw up demands which can only be realized by action on the part of the state[5]—and in that sense the relevance of the political proposals is inescapable.

The intention of these remarks is not to derogate from the concerns of feminists, environmentalists, and others; I happen to sympathize with these concerns quite strongly. My point is that they cannot *substitute* for socialism conceived as a set of politico-economic ideas and proposals. We should aim to create a social order whose institutions are fair, freedom-maximizing, and so forth *and* we should aim to have non-exploitative personal relations, protect the natural environment, and so on. In that sense market socialism cannot be seen as a complete specification of everything that is worth striving for politically and by other means. But equally it proposes solutions to a set of problems that are of central importance to nearly all of us now, and that we can hardly imagine being displaced until many decades have passed.

From this rather general defence of market socialism as a political project, I pass to some more specific reasons why it might be thought practically irrelevant. I consider three charges to the effect that the benefits that it offers are unwanted, and two charges to the effect that it is made up of mutually incoherent elements (in the sense explained above).

---

social deprivation that goes with it are the central facts of life. It would be bizarre to see the unemployed as having slipped by a back door into the new society of leisure.

[5] I don't mean that these demands can be realized entirely through politics of the traditional sort: some feminist demands, for instance, require changes at a more personal level. But state action, whether in the form of legislation or of resource distribution, is certain to be an *element* in each of these packages. To try to by-pass the state entirely would inevitably be self-defeating.

1. *Market socialism implies that workers want to run their own firms, but there is no real evidence that they do.* To put this in perspective, let us note to begin with that market socialism does not require that industrial democracy should become the primary, overriding desire of those who engage in work. A recent cross-national study of attitudes to work drew a line between the values of material success and 'expressivism'—between those who saw work primarily as a means of increasing their standard of living and those who saw it as a means of self-fulfilment.[6] Although there has been a slow increase over time in the proportion of those displaying expressivist attitudes, a large majority still look at their work in instrumental terms. But this should not worry market socialists. Since the system relies primarily on material incentives, it is quite compatible with people's *predominant* attitudes to work, to choice of job, etc. being instrumentalist. All that does matter is that there should be *some* interest in self-management, so that the machinery of industrial democracy does not atrophy. And here the evidence is quite encouraging. When asked, large majorities of employees express themselves in favour of having more say over the way their firms are run.[7] They also state a preference for working in a firm owned and controlled by its employees rather than a company owned by outside investors.[8] Where industrial democracy is introduced, there is usually an increase in levels of satisfaction with work, indicating that the actual experience of self-management is valued.[9] This adds up to good evidence that democracy at work is

[6] D. Yankelovich *et al*; *Work and Human Values* (New York: Aspen Institute for Humanistic Studies, 1983). The study also uses a third category—'sustenance', work as a means of staying alive—which for present purposes can be considered along with 'material success' as a form of instrumentalism.

[7] Workers differ over the kind of control they would like to have, and there are significant variations between countries. For some recent British evidence, see C. Hanson and P. Rathkey, 'Industrial Democracy: A Post-Bullock Shopfloor View', *British Journal of Industrial Relations*, 22 (1984), 154–68. For a comparison between the US and Sweden, see A. Haas, 'Workers' Views on Self-Management: A Comparative Study of the United States and Sweden', in M. Zeitlin (ed.), *Classes, Class Conflict and the State* (Cambridge, Mass.: Winthrop, 1980).

[8] See the evidence cited in J. Rothschild and J. A. Whitt, *The Co-operative Workplace* (Cambridge: Cambridge University Press, 1986), ch. 8.

[9] For a useful survey see ibid. ch. 6. Even the more sceptical appraisal in E. S. Greenberg, *Workplace Democracy* (Ithaca: Cornell University Press, 1986), ch. 4 concludes that 'workplace democracy, in most places and at most times, will likely enhance worker control over the product and the formal decision-making process and will make workers more satisfied with their work situation' (p. 114).

positively valued, and would enhance the appeal of a market socialist programme.

A second point worth noting is that we must beware of making faulty inferences from the *behaviour* of workers under capitalism. There has recently been a mushrooming of experiments in industrial democracy, ranging from fully worker-managed firms to minor changes in management systems in privately owned firms. Nevertheless, the percentage of workers opting for the radical forms of industrial democracy remains quite small. For reasons given in Chapter 3, however, we should not infer from this that most workers do not want more control over their firms. If co-operatives are indeed placed at a disadvantage when competing with capitalist firms, and if economic security remains an overriding consideration, then we should expect the majority of workers to opt for the safety of the traditional capitalist firm even if they would ideally like more say over how their enterprise is run. The choice situation would then have the form of a Prisoner's Dilemma in which capitalist employment becomes the dominant strategy for each worker taken individually, but the collective preference is for an economy made up of labour-managed firms.[10] It would perhaps be too strong to ascribe this set of preferences to everybody. A more reasonable supposition is that there are a small minority of workers who value industrial democracy strongly enough to risk opting for it even in a predominantly capitalist environment, a small minority who barely value it at all, and a large group in the middle who would like to have more control over their work but for whom this value is outweighed in present circumstances by economic necessity. Market socialism, as a political programme for transforming the economy, would tap this latent demand not fully revealed in current behaviour.

2. *Market socialism requires a belief in greater equality, but again there is no evidence that people find equality an appealing idea.* In the realm of resource distribution, market socialism has two egalitarian elements: it attempts to reduce income differentials to some fraction of those that currently exist under capitalism, and it provides income supplements, in cash or in kind, to those in need. These are the elements we must match up against people's

---

[10] I have explored this idea more fully in D. Miller, 'Market Neutrality and the Failure of Co-operatives', *British Journal of Political Science*, 11 (1981), 309–29.

existing beliefs. It should immediately be clear that market socialism does not require an equal allocation of income, an idea that the vast majority of people find impractical and unfair.[11] What inhibits people from endorsing equality is a strongly held belief in desert: the incomes people earn ought to reflect their ability and effort, and since these latter qualities are unequally distributed, equality of result is ruled out.[12]

So far, popular attitudes mirror the case made in Chapter 6 above for the justice of income differentials under market socialism. The question is whether they go beyond this to legitimate all of the inequalities that arise under capitalism. If we probe more deeply, we uncover ambivalence. People have a strong faith in the market as an allocator of rewards, and tend to think that if a person earns something through engaging in market transactions, he deserves to keep it.[13] So, for instance, there is opposition to the idea of a politically imposed ceiling on incomes.[14] On the other hand, when looking at the overall distribution of rewards, people are less convinced that the prevailing inequalities are fair. They support increasing efforts 'to make everyone as equal as possible', and when asked to compare the receipts of businessmen and workers there is substantial (if not majority) support for the propositions that workers receive less, and businessmen more, than they deserve.[15] This suggests that the market socialist strategy of allowing primary incomes to be determined chiefly by the market, but framing the market in such a way that incomes will bear a closer relation to effort and ability—and hence fall within a narrower range—chimes well with existing attitudes.

[11] See R. E. Lane, 'The Fear of Equality', *American Political Science Review*, 53 (1959), 35–51.

[12] For a large opinion survey, see McClosky and Zaller, *American Ethos*, esp. 80–6. For a detailed exploration of individual attitudes see J. Hochschild, *What's Fair? American Beliefs about Distributive Justice* (Cambridge, Mass.: Harvard University Press, 1981), ch. 5. For a comparison between British and American attitudes, see W. Bell and R. V. Robinson, 'Equality, Success and Social Justice in England and the United States', *American Sociological Review*, 43 (1978), 125–43.

[13] See R. E. Lane, 'Market Justice, Political Justice', *American Political Science Review*, 80 (1986), 383–402.   [14] McClosky and Zaller, *American Ethos*, 120.

[15] Ibid. 180. See also the qualitative exploration of attitudes towards inequality in Hochschild, *What's Fair?*, ch. 5, and the British evidence cited in P. Taylor-Gooby, *Public Opinion, Ideology and State Welfare* (London: Routledge and Kegan Paul, 1985), ch. 2. Not surprisingly, those who are worse off themselves tend to be more critical of existing inequalities, although not by very much; see McClosky and Zaller, *American Ethos*, 153–6; Robinson and Bell, 'Equality, Success and Social Justice'.

The second element in the strategy is politically engineered distribution according to need. Here popular attitudes may be expected to reflect the historical development of the welfare state in different countries. In Britain, for example, there is general support for the institution of a welfare state, together with variations in attitude according to the nature of the provision in question.[16] Even in the US, however, where pro-welfare attitudes might be expected to be at their weakest, there is a high level of support for government provision for the poor, particularly for in-kind services such as medical care.[17] In both countries, there is concern that welfare should not go to the 'undeserving'—that is, people who are capable of earning a living in the market-place but choose not to do so.[18] This explains the preference for in-kind services, and also the fact that, whereas guaranteed-income programmes are regarded with suspicion, job-creation schemes are warmly welcomed. In particular, people look favourably on proposals that government should reimburse companies for some fraction of the cost of taking on unemployed people.[19] In this case, the market is being 'fixed', but the important point is that people are seen to be doing something to earn their income.

The market socialist programme does not sharply contradict these attitudes. It assumes that most people will earn their primary income through the labour market, and it places a strong emphasis on regulating investment so that enterprise creation matches the demand for work. Thus it can be regarded as a system which gives ordinary people the best chance to earn their fair rewards. At the same time, it treats welfare rights as a matter of distributive justice, and in this respect goes beyond prevailing attitudes, where welfare appears often to be seen as a form of collective charity.[20] Now, as I argued in Chapter 9 above, the practical condition for a shift to the socialist view seems to be a

[16] See Taylor-Gooby, *Public Opinion, Ideology and State Welfare*, ch. 2.

[17] See McClosky and Zaller, *American Ethos*, 266–77; N. Jaffe, 'Attitudes towards Public Welfare Programs and Recipients in the United States', Appendix to L. M. Salamon, *Welfare: The Elusive Consensus* (New York: Praeger, 1978).

[18] See Jaffe, 'Attitudes towards Public Welfare'; P. Golding and S. Middleton, *Images of Welfare* (Oxford: Martin Robertson, 1982), ch. 6.

[19] See McClosky and Zaller, *American Ethos*, 276.

[20] Questions about the provision of welfare do not make the fine distinction between providing it as a matter of justice and providing it as a matter of charity. However, claiming welfare benefits is widely regarded as personally degrading, and this must indicate a culture in which the idea of rights to welfare has not taken deep root.

strengthening of communal ties; in particular, the growth of an ethos of common citizenship in which welfare rights are seen as expressing the obligations we owe to one another as members of the same political community. At this point, then, the quest for equality becomes linked to the quest for citizenship which I shall examine shortly. But even if we remain with present-day attitudes, we have seen that there is no fundamental objection to welfare *provision* so long as it is not seen as feather-bedding the undeserving. The distance separating the market socialist from his audience consists less in the substance of welfare policy than in the understandings that inform it.[21]

3. *Market socialism requires that people participate actively in political decision-making but the vast majority prefer to leave this task to professional politicians.* I have already conceded that there is presently no overt demand for increased participation, and in that sense the market socialist is championing a cause that his potential constituency may not share. Yet we should recognize that there are long-term social changes which are likely to increase the salience of this issue over time. One of these is the rising level of general education: we know that currently people with more education tend to display a higher degree of political interest and activity.[22] So there is reason to expect this trend to produce increasing demands for opportunities to participate. A second factor, possibly correlated with the first, is the decline in authoritarian values: people are less inclined to defer to authority, more inclined to question established institutions, and so forth.[23] This should imply a diminished willingness to accept the higher wisdom of political leaders. Finally, increases in leisure time create spaces in which the participatory institutions outlined in Chapter 10 could emerge. The idea of the sabbatical is extending beyond the university to other types of work—albeit so far

[21] As I noted in ch. 12, market socialists will also want to find a welfare system that does not create perverse effects in the labour market—less perhaps for incentive reasons than for reasons of justice (the desert principle). We should recognize, though, that regarding welfare provision as a matter of justice makes a practical difference in at least one respect—namely that recipients should be given the legal power to enforce their rights. This is likely to be one area in which the market socialist programme is 'ahead' of public opinion.

[22] See S. Verba, N. H. Nie and J. O. Kim, *Participation and Political Equality* (Cambridge: Cambridge University Press, 1978), esp. ch. 4.

[23] See R. E. Lane, 'Waiting for Lefty: The Capitalist Genesis of Socialist Man', *Theory and Society*, 6 (1978), 1–28.

primarily to professional jobs. Sabbaticals for public service may soon become a realistic possibility. We may then be able to reverse Oscar Wilde's famous jibe that socialism takes up too many evenings by remarking that capitalism will shortly leave us with too many free afternoons.

I have so far pointed to some exogenous factors which may give rise to increasing demands for political participation, and thus to the more radical form of democracy that I see as integral to market socialism. There is also one endogenous factor of some significance. In so far as the running of industry is democratized, there is likely to be a spillover effect in the form of an increased desire for participation in wider political arenas. The correlation between democracy at work and an enhanced sense of political efficacy is now well established. There is also evidence, though less of it, that this translates into higher levels of political activity.[24] It would surely be surprising if such a spillover did not occur. Involvement in running your own firm teaches you political skills, and also increases your awareness of outside political decisions that may bear upon the firm's prospects. In this respect, the two elements in the socialist programme complement one another.

I do not want to underestimate the difficulties involved in the quest for a more active form of citizenship. As I noted in Chapter 9, the prevailing liberal culture constitutes a major obstacle. It is likely that the initial appeal of market socialism will lie in its economic programme; the political aims may take longer to achieve.

I turn now to possible reasons for thinking that market socialism is internally incoherent.

4. *Market socialism exposes workers more directly to the play of market forces; in so doing it will erode support for redistributive policies.* This assertion applies only to workers in the market sector of the economy. I assume, however, that these will form a substantial majority, so we must take the claim seriously. It amounts to saying that market socialism will produce 'bourgeois' workers whose experience of collective entrepreneurship will foster classical

---

[24] See J. M. Elden, 'Political Efficacy at Work: The Correlation between More Autonomous Forms of Workplace Organization and a More Participatory Politics', *American Political Science Review*, 75 (1981), 43–58; E. S. Greenberg, 'Industrial Democracy and the Democratic Citizen', *Journal of Politics*, 43 (1981), 964–81.

liberal attitudes: they will tend to think that people deserve to keep all that they earn in market transactions, oppose progressive income or profits taxes, see welfare provision as aiding the unworthy, and so forth. Behind this must lie the assumption that current support for redistribution comes from workers who are shielded from full exposure to the market by the traditional structure of the firm, and who enjoy solidaristic relations with one another (in particular, via trade unions) which encourage egalitarian attitudes generally.

E. S. Greenberg has produced some evidence which seems to bear out this fourth assertion. Comparing members of US plywood co-operatives with workers in conventional firms in the same industry, he found that the co-operative workers were more likely to explain poverty in terms of individuals' unwillingness to work, oppose measures to equalize incomes, and oppose public welfare provision.[25] Greenberg concedes, however, that these differences are to be explained very largely in terms of the attitudes already held by the workers who chose to join the co-operatives. Putting it simply, in capitalist societies co-operatives tend to attract 'bourgeois' workers. An examination of the effects of co-operative membership over time reveals no clear pattern: anti-egalitarian attitudes harden slightly, explanations of poverty in terms of laziness soften, attitudes to welfare provision remain the same.

Greenberg's evidence does not show that self-management in a market context makes workers more 'bourgeois' than they already were. What it does show is that self-management alone does not create egalitarian attitudes. The solidarity and equality enjoyed inside the co-operatives does not necessarily extend to a vision of society in which these relationships are universalised. The crucial factor is the general political setting in which the co-operatives exist.[26] In direct contrast to the individualistic plywood co-operatives, for instance, the Mondragon co-operatives regard themselves as belonging to a broader movement whose aims include expanding employment in the region, providing public goods, and preserving social equality.[27]

[25] Greenberg, *Workplace Democracy*, ch. 6.
[26] This is Greenberg's own conclusion; ibid. , ch. 7.
[27] See H. Thomas and C. Logan, *Mondragon: An Economic Analysis* (London: Allen and Unwin, 1982).

The account offered here of market socialism already accommodates this point. I insisted in Chapter 9 on the importance of overall community, arguing that a society composed of small solidaristic communities would not necessarily support a general scheme of redistribution. It is important that, alongside their role as enterprise members, workers should have an active role as citizens, a vantage point from which they have to confront such issues as poverty and welfare provision directly. I argued above that these roles are complementary, especially in the sense that an active role in enterprise self-government prepares people for citizenship. But they are not substitutes: market socialism is unlikely to remain stable if people's only active involvement is in the running of their own enterprises.

Finally, it is important not to exaggerate the egalitarianism of workers in present-day capitalist societies. As noted above, people on low incomes are slightly more prepared to be critical of existing differentials, but in respect of general attitudes towards the welfare state and so forth, the picture is overwhelmingly one of inter-class consensus.[28] From an egalitarian point of view, workers are already alarmingly 'bourgeois' in outlook. There is little reason to think that the economic programme of market socialism will make things worse.

5. *Market socialism attempts to combine economic markets, political regulation and radical democracy; but in practice workers will simply use their new-found power to subvert the market.* This charge is really an updated version of the common nineteenth-century belief that capitalism and democracy were incompatible. The fear of men like Mill and the hope of men like Marx was that the working class would use the power of suffrage to overthrow the capitalist system. The recent version is more subtle: democracy brings about a situation in which organized groups of workers are able, not to abolish the market outright, but to manipulate it in their sectional interests—through regulation, subsidies, and so forth.[29]

[28] See Taylor-Gooby, *Public Opinion, Ideology and State Welfare*, ch. 2; P. Whiteley, 'Public Opinion and the Demand for Social Welfare in Britain', *Journal of Social Policy*, 10 (1981), 453–76.
[29] See e.g. S. Brittan, 'The Economic Contradictions of Democracy', *British Journal of Political Science*, 5 (1975), 129–59, repr. as 'The Politics of Excessive Expectations', in S. Brittan, *The Economic Consequences of Democracy* (London: Temple Smith, 1977). Brittan's paper was a response to the apparent power of organized labour in the early 1970s, leading to claims that the advanced capitalist democracies were becoming 'ungovernable'. Although this extreme claim no longer seems realistic, a more moderate version of the

The case is usually made out in relation to capitalism, but it might appear to extend naturally to market socialism. Sam Brittan has put the argument eloquently. Under market socialism,

There is, however, no reason to suppose that industry-wide monopolistic behaviour by organized workers would stop. It would, of course, take the form of raising prices rather than wages, but the distinction would be one of form. Indeed, workers' co-ops could more easily combine directly with each other to raise return by limiting output if they did not have to go through the inconveniences of threatened or actual strike behaviour first. Nor is there any reason to suppose that the tensions produced by an unstable balance of power between different groups of workers, and the resulting threat to employment and temptation to inflationary policies, would be any less than they are today . . . So long as there is a state sector with custom to bestow; so long as there is a possibility of state subsidies, tariffs, import controls or official restraints on domestic competitors, workers in different industries will have demands for changes in public policy. I can see no more reason why they should abjure the threat to withdraw all output completely as a means of pressure on the authorities under the new regime than they would today.[30]

The upshot of this line of thought is that the market side of market socialism can only be achieved at the expense of its democratic side—i.e. by having market discipline imposed by a state that is not responsive to public demands for intervention.

There are, however, three factors which make market socialism potentially less vulnerable to political degeneration than contemporary capitalism. The first is its industrial structure. Under market socialism, large conglomerates are likely to be broken down into smaller units, and in general we should expect that in any given industry there will be a larger number of smaller firms and less tendency to monopoly or oligopoly.[31] This will tend to discourage the formation of cartels, either to exert pressure on the state indirectly by economic action, or to engage in political lobbying. (It comes as no surprise that big business is currently

thesis, focusing on the degeneration of the market under democracy, still deserves consideration.

[30] Id. 'Property Rights for Workers' in his *The Economic Consequences of Democracy*, 203–4.

[31] See J. Vanek, *The General Theory of Labor-Managed Market Economies* (Ithaca: Cornell University Press, 1970), 272–4.

more effective than small business in bringing pressure to bear on government.) Thus, even supposing that workers are inclined to use political means to pursue their special economic interests, the structure of the economy will tend to make it more difficult to do so.

Secondly, if the arguments about distribution so far advanced are correct, the outcomes of a socialist market economy will be widely perceived as fair and legitimate, and this will dampen down attempts to alter them politically. There is a sense in which objection 4 and objection 5 rest on opposing assumptions: objection 4 says that market socialism will inculcate bourgeois norms of distribution in workers; objection 5 that each group of workers will none the less try to grab a larger slice of the cake for itself by political means. We know from our experience of capitalism, alas, that there is no strict incompatibility here: businessmen now proclaim their faith in the justice of market rewards, while at the same time trying to rig the market in favour of their particular firm or industry. My point, none the less, is that a market economy whose ground rules are seen to be fair according to widely held standards of justice is less vulnerable to manipulation than one which does not command such a consensus.

Thirdly, the political institutions of market socialism are explicitly designed to encourage (authentic) citizenship and to discourage the political pursuit of private or sectional interests. Let me recall here two key features of the socialist state as described in Part III. One is the attempt to create legislative institutions in which dialogue on matters of common concern rather than interest-aggregation is the normal mode of politics. The other is the constitutional structure which hives off specific decisions (for instance concerning capital investment) to semi-autonomous bodies. The aim of both these features is to create a setting in which people are encouraged to become involved in politics as citizens, rather than for narrowly instrumental reasons. As I indicated at the end of Chapter 10, there is no cast-iron guarantee that this aim will succeed. In so far as it does, however, the state's decisions will carry far greater authority than they often now do. A sectional group which decides to challenge such a decision cannot fail to be aware that it is standing in the face of considered majority opinion.

In the last resort, someone who believes that democracy and markets are incompatible must hold either that the ethical case for markets can never gain popular support, or that democracy must inevitably degenerate to the extent that its outcomes reflect, not the genuine wishes of the majority, but the play of sectional interests. Neither of these beliefs seems to me to be adequately supported by the evidence.

If all that I have said is true, the relevance of market socialism is established: it speaks to people's real aspirations, and it does not make incompatible demands on them. There is still the question whether it is likely to arrive, whether people have an *adequate* incentive to act so as to change their institutions in a socialist direction. Although an economic case for market socialism can be made to most people (apart from the owners of private firms and the top managers of industry—these groups would almost certainly lose out relative to their present position under the system envisaged), I am doubtful whether economic motives alone would be a sufficient propellant. One reason is that the transitional costs may be high enough to act as a deterrent, at least so long as capitalism continues to offer a steadily rising standard of living to most employed people.[32] We have to assume that other demands acquire increasing importance: the demand for self-direction at work, the demand for an increasing say in government, the demand to live in a fairer society. Since these demands are incremental, we need to think of ways in which they can be met incrementally; we should not envisage the transition to socialism as a sudden, once-and-for-all affair. For instance, we shall want to think of ways of sponsoring a co-operative sector within the capitalist economy, to provide for those who are already strongly committed to self-management, and to act as a beacon to others who are held back by the belief that workers are incompetent to control their own firms. We should look for political reforms that draw ordinary people into the making of decisions, without at first dismantling the prevailing machinery of representative democracy.

It is not my intention here to start drawing up manifestos for market socialists, which in any case will vary according to the political situation in each country. My aim in general has been to

---

[32] This possibility is explored in some detail in A. Przeworski, *Capitalism and Social Democracy* (Cambridge: Cambridge University Press, 1985), ch. 5.

show that market socialism embodies in a coherent way a range of values that stand up to theoretical scrutiny. Theoretical validity and practical popularity do not always go hand-in-hand. It would be rash to expect anything approaching a full-blown transition to market socialism in the near future. Nevertheless I hope it has proved useful to spell out with some theoretical precision an alternative to the present system and the libertarian philosophy that increasingly dominates it. There are many who seek to alter that system, but who also understand that traditional socialist prescriptions are outmoded. I have tried to fortify them by showing that there is indeed a third alternative, drawing elements from both libertarianism and socialism, but combining them in a new and radical synthesis.

Bibliography

ACKERMAN, B., *Social Justice in the Liberal State* (New Haven and London: Yale University Press, 1980).

ADKINS, A. W. H., *Merit and Responsibility* (Oxford: Clarendon Press, 1960).

ARENDT, H., *The Human Condition* (Chicago: University of Chicago Press, 1958).

—— 'Truth and Politics', in P. Laslett and W. G. Runciman (eds.), *Philosophy, Politics and Society*, 3rd ser. (Oxford: Blackwell, 1967).

—— *On Revolution* (Harmondsworth: Penguin, 1973).

ARISTOTLE, *Nicomachean Ethics*, trans. J. A. K. Thomson (London: Allen and Unwin, 1953).

ARROW, K., *Social Choice and Individual Values* (New Haven: Yale University Press, 1963).

ATKINSON, A. B., *The Economics of Inequality*, 2nd edn. (Oxford: Clarendon Press, 1983).

AVINERI, S., 'Marx's Vision of Future Society', *Dissent*, 20 (1973), 323–31.

BARBER, B., *Strong Democracy* (Berkeley: University of California Press, 1984).

BARRY, B., *Political Argument* (London: Routledge and Kegan Paul, 1965).

—— *The Liberal Theory of Justice* (Oxford: Clarendon Press, 1973)

—— 'Political Accommodation and Consociational Democracy', *British Journal of Political Science*, 5 (1975), 477–505.

—— 'Self-Government Revisited', in D. Miller and L. Siedentop (eds.), *The Nature of Political Theory* (Oxford: Clarendon Press, 1983).

BARRY, N. P., 'Hayek on Liberty', in Z. Pelczynski and J. Gray (eds.), *Conceptions of Liberty in Political Philosophy* (London: Athlone Press, 1984).

—— *On Classical Liberalism and Libertarianism* (London: Macmillan, 1986).

BECKER, L., *Property Rights: Philosophical Foundations* (London: Routledge and Kegan Paul, 1977).

BEINER, R., *Political Judgement* (London: Methuen, 1983).

BELL, W., and ROBINSON R. V., 'Equality, Success and Social Justice in

England and the United States', *American Sociological Review*, 43 (1978), 125–43.

BENN, S. I., and WEINSTEIN, W. L., 'Being Free to Act and Being a Free Man', *Mind*, 80 (1971), 194–211.

BENNETT J., 'Morality and Consequences' in *The Tanner Lectures on Human Values*, ed. S. M. McMurrin, vol. ii (Salt Lake City: University of Utah Press, 1981).

BERKI, R. N., *Insight and Vision: The Problem of Communism in Marx's Thought* (London: Dent, 1983).

BERLIN, I., 'Two Concepts of Liberty', in id., *Four Essays on Liberty* (Oxford: Oxford University Press, 1969).

BERRY, C., 'Idiotic Politics', *Political Studies*, 27 (1979), 550–63.

BRAYBROOKE, D., *Meeting Needs* (Princeton: Princeton University Press, 1987).

BRITTAN, S., 'The Economic Contradictions of Democracy', *British Journal of Political Science*, 5 (1975), 129–59, repr. as 'The Politics of Excessive Expectations', in id., *The Economic Consequences of Democracy* (London: Temple Smith, 1977).

—— 'Property Rights for Workers', in id., *The Economic Consequences of Democracy* (London: Temple Smith, 1977).

BUCHANAN, A., *Ethics, Efficiency, and the Market* (Oxford: Clarendon Press, 1985).

BURKE, E., *Reflections on the Revolution in France* (London: Dent, 1967).

—— *Thoughts on the Present Discontents*, in *The Writings and Speeches of Edmund Burke*, vol. ii, ed. P. Langford (Oxford: Clarendon Press, 1981).

BURNHEIM, J., *Is Democracy Possible?* (Oxford: Polity Press, 1985).

CAMPBELL, T. D., *The Left and Rights* (London: Routledge and Kegan Paul, 1983).

CANOVAN, M., 'A Case of Distorted Communication: A Note on Habermas and Arendt', *Political Theory*, 11 (1983), 105–16.

—— 'Politics and Culture: Hannah Arendt and the Public Realm', *History of Political Thought*, 6 (1985), 617–42.

CARENS, J., *Equality, Moral Incentives and the Market: An Essay in Utopian Politico-Economic Theory* (Chicago: University of Chicago Press, 1981).

CLAYRE, A. (ed.), *The Political Economy of Co-operation and Participation* (Oxford: Oxford University Press, 1980).

COHEN, G. A., 'Marx's Dialectic of Labour', *Philosophy and Public Affairs*, 3 (1973–4), 235–61.

COHEN, G. A., *Karl Marx's Theory of History* (Oxford: Clarendon Press, 1978).

—— 'The Labour Theory of value and the Concept of Exploitation', *Philosophy and Public Affairs*, 8 (1978–9), 338–60.

——'Capitalism, Freedom and the Proletariat', in A. Ryan (ed.), *The Idea of Freedom* (Oxford: Oxford University Press, 1979).

—— 'The Structure of Proletarian Unfreedom', *Philosophy and Public Affairs*, 12 (1983), 3–33.

COHEN, J. and ROGERS, J., *On Democracy* (New York: Penguin, 1983).

COLE, G. D. H., *A Century of Co-operation* (Manchester: Co-operative Union, 1945).

COLLARD, D., *Altruism and Economy: A Study in Non-Selfish Economics* (Oxford: Martin Robertson, 1978).

CONNOLLY, W., 'The Public Interest and the Common Good', in *Appearance and Reality in Politics* (Cambridge: Cambridge University Press, 1981).

COTTINGHAM, J., 'Partiality, Favouritism and Morality', *Philosophical Quarterly*, 36 (1986), 357–73.

CROSLAND, C. A. R., *The Future of Socialism* (London: Cape, 1956).

DAHL, R. A., *Dilemmas of Pluralist Democracy* (New Haven and London: Yale University Press, 1982).

DARLEY, J. M. and LATANE B., 'Bystander Intervention in Emergencies: Diffusion of Responsibility', *Journal of Personality and Social Psychology*, 8 (1968), 377–83.

DAWKINS, R., *The Selfish Gene* (Oxford: Oxford University Press 1976).

DIAMOND, A. S., *Primitive Law Past and Present* (London: Methuen, 1971).

DIQUATTRO, A., 'Alienation and Justice in the Market', *American Political Science Review*, 72 (1978), 871–87.

DORN, J. A., 'Markets, True and False: The Case of Yugoslavia', *Journal of Libertarian Studies*, 2 (1978), 243–68.

DOUGLAS, M. and ISHERWOOD, B., *The World of Goods* (New York: Basic Books, 1979).

DRÈZE, J. H., 'Some Theory of Labour Management and Participation', *Econometrica*, 44 (1976), 1125–39.

DRURY, S. B., 'Locke and Nozick on Property', *Political Studies*, 30 (1982), 28–41.

DUNCAN, G. and STREET, J., 'Marxism and Tolerance', in S. Mendus (ed.), *Justifying Toleration* (Cambridge: Cambridge University Press, 1988).

DWORKIN, R., 'Liberalism' in S. Hampshire (ed.), *Public and Private Morality* (Cambridge: Cambridge University Press, 1978).

—— 'Equality of Resources', *Philosophy and Public Affairs*, 10 (1981), 283–345.

Education for All: The Report of the Committee of Inquiry into the Education of Children from Ethnic Minority Groups, Cmnd. 9453 (London: HMSO, 1985).

ELDEN, J. M., 'Political Efficacy at Work: The Correlation between More Autonomous Forms of Workplace Organization and a More Participatory Politics', *American Political Science Review*, 75 (1981), 43–58.

ELLIOTT, J. H., 'Marx and Contemporary Models of Socialist Economy', *History of Political Economy*, 8 (1976), 151–84.

—— 'Continuity and Change in the Evolution of Marx's Theory of Alienation: From the *Manuscripts* through the *Grundrisse* to *Capital*', *History of Political Economy*, 11 (1979), 317–62.

ELSTER, J., *Ulysses and the Sirens* (Cambridge: Cambridge University Press, 1979).

—— *Sour Grapes: Studies in the Subversion of Rationality* (Cambridge: Cambridge University Press, 1983).

—— 'Exploitation, Freedom and Justice', in J. R. Pennock and J. W. Chapman (eds.), *Nomos XXVI: Marxism* (New York: New York University Press, 1983).

—— *Making Sense of Marx* (Cambridge: Cambridge University Press, 1985).

—— 'The Market and the Forum', in J. Elster and A. Hylland (eds.), *Foundations of Social Choice Theory* (Cambridge: Cambridge University Press, 1986).

—— 'From Here to There, Or: If Co-operative Ownership Is So Desirable, Why Are There So Few Co-operatives?' *Social Philosophy and Policy* (forthcoming).

ENGELS, F., 'On Authority', in K. Marx, F. Engels, V. Lenin, *Anarchism and Anarcho-Syndicalism* (Moscow: Progress Publishers, 1972).

ESTRIN, S., *Self-Management: Economic Theory and Yugoslav Practice* (Cambridge: Cambridge University Press, 1983).

—— 'Workers Co-operatives: Their Merits and Limitations' in J. Le Grand and S. Estrin (eds.), *Market Socialism* (Oxford: Clarendon Press, 1989).

FEINBERG, J., 'Justice and Personal Desert', in *Doing and Deserving* (Princeton: Princeton University Press, 1970).

FEINBERG, J., 'The Nature and Value of Rights', *Journal of Value Inquiry*, 4 (1970), 243–57.

—— 'Noncomparative Justice', *Philosophical Review*, 83 (1974), 297–338

FRIEDMAN, M., *Capitalism and Freedom* (Chicago: University of Chicago Press, 1962).

FROHLICH, N., and OPPENHEIMER, J., 'Beyond Economic Man: Altruism, Egalitarianism and Difference Maximizing', *Journal of Conflict Resolution*, 28 (1984), 3–24.

FÜRER-HAIMENDORF, C. VON, *Morals and Merit* (London: Weidenfeld and Nicolson, 1967).

FURUBOTN, E. G., 'The Long Run Analysis of the Labor Managed Firm: An Alternative Interpretation', *American Economic Review*, 66 (1976), 104–23.

FURUBOTN, E. G., and PEJOVICH, S., *The Economics of Property Rights* (Cambridge, Mass.: Ballinger, 1974).

GALBRAITH, J. K., *The Affluent Society* (Harmondsworth: Penguin, 1962).

GELLNER, E., *Nations and Nationalism* (Oxford: Blackwell, 1983).

GERAS, N., *Marx and Human Nature: Refutation of a Legend* (London: Verso, 1983).

GLUCKMAN, M., *The Ideas in Barotse Jurisprudence* (Manchester: Manchester University Press, 1972).

GOLDING, P., and MIDDLETON, S., *Images of Welfare* (Oxford: Martin Robertson, 1982).

GOODIN, R., 'No Moral Nukes', *Ethics*, 90 (1979–80), 417–49.

—— 'Making Moral Incentives Pay', *Policy Sciences*, 12 (1980), 131–45.

—— 'Welfare, Rights and Discretion', *Oxford Journal of Legal Studies*, 6 (1986), 232–61.

—— 'Laundering Preferences', in J. Elster and A. Hylland (eds.), *Foundations of Social Choice Theory* (Cambridge: Cambridge University Press, 1986).

—— 'Exploiting a Situation and Exploiting a Person', in A. Reeve (ed.), *Modern Theories of Exploitation* (London: Sage, 1987).

GOODIN, R., and LE GRAND, J., *Not Only the Poor: The Middle Classes and the Welfare State* (London: Allen and Unwin, 1987).

GORDON, D., 'Miller on Market Neutrality, Co-operatives and Libertarianism', *British Journal of Political Science*, 13 (1983), 125–8.

GRAY, J., 'On Negative and Positive Liberty', *Political Studies*, 28 (1980),

507–26, repr. in Z. Pelczynski and J. Gray (eds.), *Conceptions of Liberty in Political Philosophy* (London: Athlone Press, 1984).

—— 'Hayek on Liberty, Rights and Justice', *Ethics*, 92 (1981–2), 73–84.

—— 'Contractarian Method, Private Property and the Market Economy', paper presented to the American Society for Political and Legal Philosophy, Dec. 1986.

GREEN, P., *Retrieving Democracy* (London: Methuen, 1985).

GREENBERG, E. S., 'Industrial Democracy and the Democratic Citizen', *Journal of Politics*, 43 (1981), 964–81.

—— *Workplace Democracy* (Ithaca: Cornell University Press, 1986).

HAAS, A., 'Workers' Views on Self-Management: A Comparative Study of the United States and Sweden', in M. Zeitlin (ed.), *Classes, Class Conflict and the State* (Cambridge, Mass.: Winthrop, 1980).

HABERMAS, J., *Legitimation Crisis* (London: Heinemann, 1976).

—— 'Hannah Arendt's Communications Concept of Power', *Social Research*, 44 (1977), 3–24.

—— 'A Reply to my Critics', in J. B. Thompson and D. Held (eds.), *Habermas: Critical Debates* (London: Macmillan, 1982).

—— *Autonomy and Solidarity*, ed. P. Dews (London: Verso, 1986).

HADLEY, R., and HATCH, S., *Social Welfare and the Failure of the State* (London: Allen and Unwin, 1981).

HAMOWY, R., 'Freedom and the Rule of Law in F. A. Hayek', *Il Politico*, 36 (1971), 349–77.

HANSON, C., and RATHKEY, P., 'Industrial Democracy: A Post-Bullock Shopfloor View', *British Journal of Industrial Relations*, 22 (1984), 154–68.

HARRIS, D., *Justifying State Welfare* (Oxford: Blackwell, 1987).

HAYEK, F. A., *Individualism and Economic Order* (London: Routledge and Kegan Paul, 1949).

—— *The Constitution of Liberty* (London: Routledge and Kegan Paul, 1960).

—— *Studies in Philosophy, Politics and Economics* (London: Routledge and Kegan Paul, 1967).

—— *Law, Legislation and Liberty, i. Rules and Order* (London: Routledge and Kegan Paul, 1973).

—— *Law, Legislation and Liberty, ii. The Mirage of Social Justice* (London: Routledge and Kegan Paul, 1976).

—— *Law, Legislation and Liberty, iii. The Political Order of a Free People* (London: Routledge and Kegan Paul, 1979).

HELD, V., 'John Locke on Robert Nozick', *Social Research*, 43 (1976), 169–95.

HIRSCH, F., *Social Limits to Growth* (London: Routledge and Kegan Paul, 1977).

HIRST, P. Q., 'Law, Socialism and Rights', in *Law, Socialism and Democracy* (London: Allen and Unwin, 1986).

HOCHMAN, H. M., and ROGERS, J. D., 'Pareto Optimal Redistribution', *American Economic Review*, 59 (1969), 542–57.

HOCHSCHILD, J., *What's Fair? American Beliefs about Distributive Justice* (Cambridge: Mass.: Harvard University Press, 1981).

HOLLANDER, S., *The Economics of John Stuart Mill* (Oxford: Blackwell, 1985).

HOLLIS, M., *Models of Man* (Cambridge: Cambridge University Press, 1977).

HONORÉ, A. M., 'Ownership' in A. G. Guest (ed.), *Oxford Essays in Jurisprudence*, 1st ser. (Oxford: Oxford University Press, 1961).

—— 'Property, Title and Redistribution', *Archiv fur Rechts und Sozialphilosophie*, 10 (1977), 107–15.

HOROWITZ, D. L., 'Ethnic Identity', in N. Glazer and D. P. Moynihan (eds.), *Ethnicity: Theory and Experience* (Cambridge and London: Harvard University Press, 1975).

HORVAT, B., *The Political Economy of Socialism* (New York: Sharpe, 1982).

HUME, D., *An Enquiry Concerning the Principles of Morals*, in *Enquiries Concerning Human Understanding and Concerning the Principles of Morals*, ed. L. A. Selby-Bigge (Oxford: Clarendon Press, 1975).

JAFFE, N., 'Attitudes towards Public Welfare Programs and Recipients in the United States', Appendix to L. M. Salamon, *Welfare: The Elusive Consensus* (New York: Praeger, 1978).

JANIS, I., *Groupthink*, 2nd edn. (Boston: Houghton Mifflin, 1982).

JONES, A. H. M., *Athenian Democracy* (Oxford: Blackwell, 1964).

JONES, D. C., 'The Economic and Industrial Relations of American Producer Co-operatives, 1791–1939', *Economic Analysis and Workers' Management*, 11 (1977), 295–317.

JONES, H. W., 'The Rule of Law and the Welfare State', *Columbia Law Review*, 58 (1958), 143–56.

JORDAN, B., *The State: Authority and Autonomy* (Oxford: Blackwell, 1985).

JOWELL, R., and WITHERSPOON, S. (eds.), *British Social Attitudes: The 1985 Report* (Aldershot: Gower, 1985).

KEAT, R., 'Liberal Rights and Socialism' in K. Graham (ed.), *Contemporary Political Philosophy* (Cambridge: Cambridge University Press, 1982).

KING, D. S., and WALDRON, J., 'Citizenship, Social Citizenship and the Defence of Welfare Provision', *British Journal of Political Science*, 18 (1988), 415–43.

KLASS, G. M., 'Explaining America and the Welfare State: An Alternative Theory', *British Journal of Political Science*, 15 (1985), 427–50.

KNIGHT, F. H., 'The Ethics of Competition', *Quarterly Journal of Economics*, 37 (1922–3), 579–624.

KOLM, S-C., 'Altruism and Efficiency', *Ethics*, 94 (1983–4), 18–65.

KRISTOL, I., '"When Virtue Loses All Her Loveliness": Some Reflections on Capitalism and "The Free Society"', *Public Interest*, 21 (Fall, 1970), 3–15.

KROPOTKIN, P., *The Conquest of Bread* (New York: Vanguard Press, 1926).

KROUSE, R., and McPHERSON, M., 'A "Mixed"-Property Regime: Equality and Liberty in a Market Economy', *Ethics*, 97 (1986–7), 119–38.

KUKATHAS, C., *Hayek and Modern Liberalism* (Oxford: Clarendon Press, 1989).

LANE, R. E., 'The Fear of Equality', *American Political Science Review*, 53 (1959), 35–51.

—— 'Markets and the Satisfaction of Human Wants', *Journal of Economic Issues*, 12 (1978), 799–827.

—— 'Waiting for Lefty: The Capitalist Genesis of Socialist Man', *Theory and Society*, 6 (1978), 1–28.

—— 'Government and Self-Esteem', *Political Theory*, 10 (1982), 5–31.

—— 'From Political to Industrial Democracy?', *Polity*, 17 (1985), 623–48.

—— 'Market Justice, Political Justice', *American Political Science Review*, 80 (1986), 383–402.

—— 'Procedural Justice: How One Is Treated vs. What One Gets' (unpublished).

LANGE, O., and TAYLOR, F., *On the Economic Theory of Socialism* (Minneapolis: University of Minnesota Press, 1938).

LASLETT, P., 'The Face to Face Society', in P. Laslett (ed.), *Philosophy, Politics and Society* (Oxford: Blackwell, 1956).

LE GRAND J., *The Strategy of Equality: Redistribution and the Social Services* (London: Allen and Unwin, 1982).

LE GRAND, J., 'Equality, Markets and Welfare', in J. Le Grand and S. Estrin (eds.), *Market Socialism* (Oxford: Clarendon Press, 1989).

LE GRAND, J., and ROBINSON, R., 'Privatisation and the Welfare State: An Introduction', in J. Le Grand and R. Robinson (eds.), *Privatisation and the Welfare State* (London: Allen and Unwin, 1984).

LERNER, M. J., 'The Justice Motive: "Equity" and "Parity" among Children', *Journal of Personality and Social Psychology*, 29 (1974), 539–50.

LIJPHART, A., *Democracy in Plural Societies* (New Haven and London: Yale University Press, 1977).

LINDBLOM, C., *Politics and Markets* (New York: Basic Books, 1977).

LOCKE, J., *Two Treatises of Government*, ed. P. Laslett (New York: Mentor, 1965).

LUKES, S., 'Of Gods and Demons: Habermas and Practical Reason', in J. B. Thompson and D. Held (eds.), *Habermas: Critical Debates* (London: Macmillan, 1982).

—— *Marxism and Morality* (Oxford: Clarendon Press, 1985).

LYDALL, H., *Yugoslav Socialism: Theory and Practice* (Oxford: Clarendon Press, 1984).

McCLOSKY, H., and ZALLER, J., *The American Ethos: Public Attitudes towards Capitalism and Democracy* (Cambridge, Mass., and London: Harvard University Press, 1984).

McCULLOCH, C., 'The Problem of Fellowship in Communitarian Theory: William Morris and Peter Kropotkin', *Political Studies*, 32 (1984), 437–50

MACINTYRE, A., *Is Patriotism a Virtue?* Lindley Lecture (University of Kansas, 1984).

McLEAN, I., 'The Social Contract in Leviathan and the Prisoner's Dilemma Supergame', *Political Studies*, 29 (1981), 339–51

MACPHERSON, C. B., *The Life and Times of Liberal Democracy* (Oxford: Oxford University Press, 1977).

MANIN, B., 'On Legitimacy and Political Deliberation', *Political Theory*, 15 (1987), 338–68.

MANSBRIDGE, J. J., *Beyond Adversary Democracy* (Chicago and London: University of Chicago Press, 1983).

MARGOLIS, H., *Selfishness, Altruism and Rationality* (Chicago: University of Chicago Press, 1982).

MARSHALL, T. H., 'Citizenship and Social Class', in *Sociology at the Crossroads and Other Essays* (London: Heinemann, 1963).

MARWELL, G., and AMES, R., 'Experiments on the Provision of Public Goods: I', *American Journal of Sociology*, 84 (1979), 1335–60.
—— 'Experiments on the Provision of Public Goods: II', *American Journal of Sociology*, 85 (1980), 926–37.
MARX, K., *Capital* (London: Glaisher, 1909).
—— *Karl Marx: Early Writings*, ed. T. B. Bottomore (London: Watts, 1963).
—— *Writings of the Young Marx on Philosophy and Society*, eds. L. D. Easton and K. H. Guddat (Garden City, NY: Anchor, 1967).
—— *Grundrisse* (Harmondsworth: Penguin, 1973).
MARX, K., and ENGELS, F., *The Communist Manifesto*, in *Selected Works*, vol. i (Moscow: Foreign Languages Publishing House, 1962).
MAYNARD, A., 'Welfare: Who Pays?' in P. Bean, J. Ferris, and D. Whynes (eds.), *In Defence of Welfare* (London: Tavistock, 1985).
MEADE, J. E., 'The Theory of Labour-Managed Firms and Profit Sharing', *Economic Journal*, 82 (1972), 402–28.
MILENKOVITCH, D. D., *Plan and Market in Yugoslav Economic Thought* (New Haven: Yale University Press, 1971).
—— 'Is Market Socialism Efficient?', in A. Zimbalist (ed.), *Comparative Economic Systems* (Boston: Kluwer-Nijhoff, 1984).
MILL, J. S., *On Liberty*, in *Utilitarianism; On Liberty; Representative Government*, ed. A. D. Lindsay (London: Dent, 1964).
—— *Principles of Political Economy*, in *Collected Works of John Stuart Mill*, vols. ii–iii (Toronto: University of Toronto Press, 1965).
MILLER, D., *Social Justice* (Oxford: Clarendon Press, 1976).
—— 'Democracy and Social Justice', *British Journal of Political Science*, 8 (1978), 1–19, repr. P. Birnbaum, J. Lively and G. Parry (eds.), *Democracy, Consensus and Social Contract* (London: Sage, 1978).
—— 'Social Justice and the Principle of Need', in M. Freeman and D. Robertson (eds.), *The Frontiers of Political Theory* (Brighton: Harvester, 1980).
—— *Philosophy and Ideology in Hume's Political Thought* (Oxford: Clarendon Press, 1981).
—— 'Market Neutrality and the Failure of Co-operatives', *British Journal of Political Science*, 11 (1981), 309–29.
—— 'The Competitive Model of Democracy', in G. Duncan (ed.), *Democratic Theory and Practice* (Cambridge: Cambridge University Press, 1983).
—— *Anarchism* (London: Dent, 1984).

MILLER, D., 'Exploitation in the Market', in A. Reeve (ed.), *Modern Theories of Exploitation* (London: Sage, 1987).

—— 'The Ethical Significance of Nationality', *Ethics*, 98 (1987–8), 647–62.

—— 'Why Markets?', in J. Le Grand, and S. Estrin (eds.), *Market Socialism* (Oxford: Clarendon Press, 1989).

—— 'In What Sense Must Socialism be Communitarian?', *Social Philosophy and Policy* (forthcoming).

MILLER, D., and ESTRIN, S., 'Market Socialism: A Policy for Socialists' in I. Forbes (ed.), *Market Socialism: Whose Choice?*, Fabian Pamphlet No. 516 (London: Fabian Society, 1986).

MILSOM, S. F. C., *The Legal Framework of English Feudalism* (Cambridge: Cambridge University Press, 1976).

MOORE, S., *Marx on the Choice Between Socialism and Communism* (Cambridge, Mass., and London: Harvard University Press, 1980).

MORRIS, W., *News from Nowhere* (London: Longmans Green, 1918).

NAIPAUL, V. S., *In a Free State* (Harmondsworth: Penguin, 1973).

NISBET, R., *The Quest for Community* (New York: Oxford University Press, 1953).

NOVE, A., *The Economics of Feasible Socialism* (London: Allen and Unwin, 1983).

NOZICK, R., 'Coercion', in P. Laslett, W. G. Runciman and Q. Skinner (eds.), *Philosophy, Politics and Society*, 4th ser. (Oxford: Blackwell, 1972).

—— *Anarchy, State and Utopia* (Oxford: Blackwell, 1974).

OAKESHOTT, M., *On Human Conduct* (Oxford: Clarendon Press, 1975).

OAKESHOTT, R., *The Case for Workers' Co-ops* (London: Routledge and Kegan Paul, 1978).

OBLER, J., 'Private Giving in the Welfare State', *British Journal of Political Science*, 11 (1981), 17–48.

O'HIGGINS, M. , 'Welfare, Redistribution and Inequality: Disillusion, Illusion, and Reality' in P. Bean, J. Ferris, and D. Whynes (eds.), *In Defence of Welfare* (London: Tavistock, 1985).

OLDENQUIST, A., 'Loyalties', *Journal of Philosophy*, 74 (1982), 173–93.

OLIVECRONA, K., 'Locke's Theory of Appropriation', *Philosophical Quarterly*, 24 (1974), 220–34.

OLLMAN, B., 'Marx's Vision of Communism: A Reconstruction', *Critique*, 8 (1977), 4–41.

PAREKH, B., 'The Concept of Multi-Cultural Education', in S. Modgil and G. Verma (eds.), *Multi-Cultural Education: The Interminable Debate* (London: Falmer Press, 1986).

PARIJS, P. VAN, 'Some Problems with the Labour Theory of Exploitation', Working Paper No. 8212, Institut des Sciences Économiques, Université Catholique de Louvain, 1982.

—— 'Thin Theories of Exploitation', Working Paper No. 8213, Institut des Sciences Économiques, Université Catholique de Louvain, 1982.

PARKER, J., *Social Policy and Citizenship* (London: Macmillan, 1975).

PARRY, G., 'Tradition, Community and Self-Determination', *British Journal of Political Science*, 12 (1982), 399–419.

PENZ, G. P., *Consumer Sovereignty and Human Interests* (Cambridge: Cambridge University Press, 1986).

PETTIT, P., 'Social Holism and Moral Theory', *Proceedings of the Aristotelean Society*, 86 (1985–6), 173–97.

PLANT, R., *Community and Ideology* (London: Routledge and Kegan Paul, 1974).

—— 'Community: Concept, Conception and Ideology', *Politics and Society*, 8 (1978), 79–107.

PLANT, R., LESSER, H., and TAYLOR GOODY, P., *Political Philosophy and Social Welfare* (London: Routledge and Kegan Paul, 1980).

PRZEWORSKI, A., *Capitalism and Social Democracy* (Cambridge: Cambridge University Press, 1985).

PUTNAM, R. A., 'Rights of Persons and the Liberal Tradition', in T. Honderich (ed.), *Social Ends and Political Means* (London: Routledge and Kegan Paul, 1976).

RAWLS, J., *A Theory of Justice* (Cambridge, Mass.: Harvard University Press, 1971).

—— 'Fairness to Goodness', *Philosophical Review*, 84 (1975), 536–54.

RAZ, J., 'The Rule of Law and its Virtue', in id., *The Authority of Law* (Oxford: Clarendon Press, 1979).

—— *The Morality of Freedom* (Oxford: Clarendon Press, 1986).

REEVE, A., *Property* (London: Macmillan, 1986).

REEVE, A., and WARE, A., 'Interests in Political Theory', *British Journal of Political Science*, 13 (1983), 379–400.

REITH, J., *Broadcast Over Britain* (London: Hodder and Stoughton, 1924).

RIKER, W., *Liberalism against Populism* (San Francisco: Freeman, 1982).

ROEMER, J., *A General Theory of Exploitation and Class* (Cambridge and London: Harvard University Press, 1982).

350 BIBLIOGRAPHY

ROEMER, J., 'Property Relations vs. Surplus Value in Marxian Exploitation', *Philosophy and Public Affairs*, 11 (1982), 281–313.

—— 'New Directions in the Marxian Theory of Exploitation and Class', *Politics and Society*, 11 (1982), 253–87.

—— 'Should Marxists be Interested in Exploitation?', *Philosophy and Public Affairs*, 14 (1985), 30–65.

—— 'Equality of Talent', *Economics and Philosophy*, 1 (1985), 151–87.

ROTHBARD, M., 'Justice and Property Rights' in S. Blumenfeld (ed.), *Property in a Humane Economy* (La Salle, Ill.: Open Court, 1976).

—— *The Ethics of Liberty* (Atlantic Highlands, NJ: Humanities Press, 1982).

ROTHSCHILD, J., and WHITT, J. A., *The Co-operative Workplace* (Cambridge: Cambridge University Press, 1986).

ROUSSEAU, J-J., *The Social Contract*, trans. M. Cranston (Harmondsworth: Penguin, 1968).

SAHLINS, M., *Stone Age Economics* (London: Tavistock, 1974).

SANDEL, M., *Liberalism and the Limits of Justice* (Cambridge: Cambridge University Press, 1982).

SCHUMPETER, J. A., *Capitalism, Socialism and Democracy*, 5th edn. (London: Allen and Unwin, 1976).

SCHWARTZ, A., 'Moral Neutrality and Primary Goods', *Ethics*, 83 (1972–3), 294–307.

SELDON, A., *Charge* (London: Temple Smith, 1977).

SELUCKY, R., *Marxism, Socialism, Freedom* (London: Macmillan, 1979).

SEN, A., 'Rational Fools: A Critique of the Behavioural Foundations of Economic Theory', *Philosophy and Public Affairs*, 6 (1977), 317–44, repr. in id., *Choice, Welfare, and Measurement* (Oxford: Blackwell, 1982).

—— 'Equality of What?', in id., *Choice, Welfare and Measurement* (Oxford: Blackwell, 1982).

SHAPIRO, E. C., 'Effect of Expectations of Future Interaction on Reward Allocation in Dyads: Equity or Equality', *Journal of Personality and Social Psychology*, 31 (1975), 873–80.

SHER, G., 'Effort, Ability and Personal Desert', *Philosophy and Public Affairs*, 8 (1978–9), 361–76.

SIDGWICK, H., *The Methods of Ethics* (London: Macmillan, 1907).

SMITH, A. D., *The Ethnic Origins of Nations* (Oxford: Blackwell, 1986).

STARK, T., *A New A–Z of Income and Wealth* (London: Fabian Society, 1988).

STEINER, H., 'Individual Liberty', *Proceedings of the Aristotelian Society*, 65 (1974–5), 33–50.

—— 'Liberty and Equality', *Political Studies*, 29 (1981), 555–69.

—— 'How Free? Computing Personal Liberty', in A. Phillips-Griffiths (ed.), *Of Liberty* (Cambridge: Cambridge University Press, 1983).

—— 'A Liberal Theory of Exploitation', *Ethics*, 94 (1983–4), 225–41.

—— 'Exploitation: A Liberal Theory Amended, Defended and Extended' in A. Reeve (ed.), *Modern Theories of Exploitation* (London: Sage, 1987).

STEINHERR, A., 'The Labour-Managed Economy: A Survey of the Economics Literature', *Annals of Public and Co-operative Economy*, 40 (1978), 129–48.

STRETTON, H., *Capitalism, Socialism and the Environment* (Cambridge: Cambridge University Press, 1976).

SUGDEN, R., 'On the Economics of Philanthropy', *Economic Journal*, 92 (1982), 341–50.

—— 'Reciprocity: The Supply of Public Goods through Voluntary Contributions', *Economic Journal*, 94 (1984), 772–87.

SYPNOWICH, C., 'Law as a Vehicle of Altruism', *Oxford Journal of Legal Studies*, 5 (1985), 276–84.

TAYLOR, C., *Hegel* (Cambridge: Cambridge University Press, 1975).

—— 'What's Wrong with Negative Liberty', in A. Ryan (ed.), *The Idea of Freedom* (Oxford: Oxford University Press, 1979).

TAYLOR, M., *Community, Anarchy and Liberty* (Cambridge: Cambridge University Press, 1982).

—— *The Possibility of Co-operation* (Cambridge: Cambridge University Press, 1987).

TAYLOR, M., and WARD, H., 'Chickens, Whales and Lumpy Goods', *Political Studies*, 30 (1982), 350–70.

TAYLOR-GOOBY, P., *Public Opinion, Ideology and State Welfare* (London: Routledge and Kegan Paul, 1985).

TEITELMAN, M., 'The Limits of Individualism', *Journal of Philosophy*, 69 (1972), 545–56.

THOMAS, H., and LOGAN, C., *Mondragon: An Economic Analysis* (London: Allen & Unwin, 1982).

TITMUSS, R. M., *The Gift Relationship* (London: Allen & Unwin, 1970).

TÖNNIES, F., *Gemeinschaft und Gesellschaft*, trans. as *Community and Association* (London: Routledge and Kegan Paul, 1955).

VAN DER VEEN, R. J., and VAN PARIJS, P., 'A Capitalist Road to Communism', *Theory and Society*, 15 (1986), 635–55.

VANBERG V. , 'Spontaneous Market Order and Social Rules: A Critical Examination of F. A. Hayek's Theory of Cultural Evolution', *Economics and Philosophy*, 2 (1986), 75–100.

VANEK, J., *The General Theory of Labor-Managed Market Economies* (Ithaca: Cornell University Press, 1970).

—— 'The Basic Theory of Financing of Participatory Firms', in id. (ed.), *Self-Management: Economic Liberation of Man* (Harmondsworth: Penguin, 1975).

—— 'The Yugoslav Economy Viewed Through the Theory of Labor Management', in *The Labor-Managed Economy* (Ithaca: Cornell University Press, 1977).

VERBA, S., NIE, N. H., and KIM, J. O., *Participation and Political Equality* (Cambridge: Cambridge University Press, 1978).

WALDRON, J., 'Two Worries about Mixing One's Labour', *Philosophical Quarterly*, 33 (1983), 37–44.

WALT, S., 'Comment on Steiner's Liberal Theory of Exploitation', *Ethics*, 94 (1983–4), 242–7.

WALZER, M., 'A Day in the Life of a Socialist Citizen', in *Obligations* (Cambridge, Mass.: Harvard University Press, 1970).

—— *Spheres of Justice* (Oxford: Martin Robertson, 1983).

—— 'Interpretation and Social Criticism' in *The Tanner Lectures on Human Values*, ed. S. M. McMurrin, vol. viii (Salt Lake City: University of Utah Press; Cambridge: Cambridge University Press, 1988).

WARD, B., 'The Firm in Illyria: Market Syndicalism', *American Economic Review*, 48 (1958), 566–89.

WATKINS, J. W. N., 'Philosophy' in A. Seldon (ed.), *Agenda for a Free Society: Essays on Hayek's The Constitution of Liberty* (London: Institute of Economic Affairs, 1961).

WEALE, A., *Equality and Social Policy* (London: Routledge and Kegan Paul, 1979).

—— 'Procedural Fairness and Rationing the Social Services', in N. Timms (ed.), *Social Welfare: Why and How?* (London: Routledge and Kegan Paul, 1980).

—— *Political Theory and Social Policy* (London: Macmillan, 1983).

—— 'Toleration, Individual Differences and Respect for Persons' in J. Horton and S. Mendus (eds.), *Aspects of Toleration* (London: Methuen, 1985).

WEIZSACKER, C. VON, 'Notes on Endogenous Change of Tastes', *Journal of Economic Theory*, 3 (1971), 345–72.

WHITE, S. K., *The Recent Work of Jurgen Habermas* (Cambridge: Cambridge University Press, 1988).

WHITELEY, P., 'Public Opinion and the Demand for Social Welfare in Britain', *Journal of Social Policy*, 10 (1981), 453–76.

WICKSTEED, P. H., *The Common Sense of Political Economy*, ed. L. Robbins (London: Routledge, 1933).

WILES, P., *Economic Institutions Compared* (Oxford: Blackwell, 1977).

YANKELOVICH, D., *et al.*, *Work and Human Values* (New York: Aspen Institute for Humanistic Studies, 1983).

ZAITCHIK, A., 'On Deserving to Deserve', *Philosophy and Public Affairs*, 6 (1976–7), 371–88.

Index